VOCAL TECHNIQUE

Second Edition

VOCAL TECHNIQUE

A Guide to Classical and Contemporary
Styles for Conductors, Teachers, and Singers

Second Edition

Julia Davids, D.M.A.

Stephen LaTour, Ph.D.

Long Grove, Illinois

For information about this book, contact:
Waveland Press, Inc.
4180 IL Route 83, Suite 101
Long Grove, Illinois 60047-9580
(847) 634-0081
info@waveland.com
www.waveland.com

Illustrations and cover design by Evelyn LaTour

Copyright © 2021 by Stephen LaTour and Julia Davids

10-digit ISBN 1-4786-4022-7
13-digit ISBN 978-1-4786-4022-6

All rights reserved. No part of this book may be reproduced, stored in a retrieval system, or transmitted in any form or by any means without permission in writing from the publisher.

Printed in the United States of America

Second Edition

7 6 5 4 3 2 1

Table of Contents

Second Edition Acknowledgements xi

Introduction: A guide to stylistically flexible vocal technique 1
Contemporary styles encompass CCM and musical theatre 1
Second edition coverage 2
Benefits of improved vocal technique 3
Intentional use of exercises is essential to vocal development 4
Importance of attention to vocal technique in the choral setting 5
Improving communication among singers of different styles
 and between voice teachers and conductors 6
A note about symbols used in this book 7
A word about terminology 8

Chapter 1: Posture/Alignment 9
Essentials of proper posture/body alignment 9
Important aspects of body alignment 12
Common alignment problems 14
Avoid extraneous body movement 14
Sitting posture and seat types 16
Exercises for body alignment 17

Chapter 2: Breath Control 19
Phases of the breathing cycle 19
Inhalation 19
Very brief suspension 24
Exhalation 25
Additional points about exhalation 29
Recovery 30
Timing of breathing 31
Breathing in contemporary styles—limitations imposed by dancing 31
Respiratory muscle training 32
Breathing exercises 32

Chapter 3: Initiation, Creation, and Release of Sound 37
How sound is initiated and created 37
Good hydration is critical for proper vocal fold vibration 38
Components of the singer's instrument 39
Muscles affecting pitch 41
Sound level and timbre affected by firmness of vocal fold closure 45

Method of initiating sound affects glottal tension 49
Coordinated onset should be used for most singing 49
Some glottal onsets are useful 50
Is belting less healthy than classical/legit vocal production? 51
Breathy onset is generally undesirable 53
Onset and younger singers 53
Release of sound 54
Semi-occluded vocal tract (SOVT) exercises assist vocal fold vibration 54
Onset and release exercises 60

Chapter 4: Resonance --- 63

Superior resonance improves tonal quality and vocal efficiency 63
Fundamental frequency and higher harmonics 64
Structure of the vocal tract 65
Resonance and formants 67
Adjusting the larynx 78
Adjusting the oral pharynx 79
Adjusting the mouth 81
Classical versus contemporary resonance and vocal tract shape 83
Good resonance helps intonation 85
Resonance and the concepts of "chest voice" and "head voice" 85
Resonance and "placement" 86
Exercises for enhancing resonance 89

Chapter 5: Vowels --- 93

Tip of the tongue should rest at the base of the lower front teeth 93
Basic vowel production for classical/legit styles 94
Perceptions of vowels as "bright" versus "dark" 100
Vowels in contemporary styles 101
Vowel consistency for intonation and ensemble blending 102
Problematic vowels 102
Modification of vowels for higher pitches 107
Diphthongs, triphthongs, and glides 114
Altering the tonal color of vowels 116
A summary philosophy of vowel formation 118
Vowel exercises 119

Chapter 6: Consonants -- 123

The articulators 123
Quick, efficient consonant formation in classical singing 123
Consonant length is often extended in contemporary styles 124
Classical/legit singers should be judicious about exaggeration 124
Consonants requiring special consideration 125
Jaw position when singing l, k, g, t, d, m, n, ng 126

Think of [w] and "y" in terms of the vowels [u] and [i] 127
Voiced versus unvoiced consonants 127
Final consonants 131
Adding "uh" or "ah" to final consonants versus elision 131
Sometimes consonants should precede the beat 132
Consonant exercises 133

Chapter 7: Vibrato — 135

Vibrato is a natural phenomenon 135
Desirable vibrato rate and extent 136
Style implications for vibrato 139
Solving vibrato problems 140
Modifying vibrato 145
Vibrato in choral singing 147
Vibrato in early music 150
Vibrato exercises 154

Chapter 8: Negotiation of the Vocal Registers — 157

What are vocal registers? 157
Two main (modal) registers 158
Middle register (mixed voice) 160
Children's registers 161
Differences in chest and head voice use in classical and
    contemporary styles 162
Modern singers most likely to struggle with the upper register 164
Transitions between registers (passaggi) 164
Negotiating the register transitions 167
Special registers 170
Register exercises 173

Chapter 9: Voice Classification and Improving Range — 177

Distribution and classification of voice types 177
Tessitura versus range 180
Classification of voices in contemporary styles 181
Singing higher pitches 182
Accessing lower pitches for female singers 184
Handling leaps in pitch 185
Exercises to increase range 186

Chapter 10: Improving Intonation — 189

Causes of poor intonation 189
Repertoire-specific intonation issues 192
Extraneous factors affecting intonation 194
Concluding thoughts about intonation 196
Exercises to improve intonation 196

Chapter 11: Legato, Staccato, Accents, Melismas/Riffs, Dynamic Control, and Special Vocal Effects --- 199
Legato involves vowel-to-vowel continuity ... 199
Staccato ... 202
Accents ... 203
Vocal ornaments and embellishments ... 203
Dynamic control ... 206
Special vocal effects ... 208
Exercises for legato, staccato, accents, melismas, and dynamics ... 209

Chapter 12: Improving Choral Blend --- 213
Blend philosophies ... 213
Choral sound ... 214
Keys to a blended sound ... 214
The role of timbre in blending ... 218
Voice positioning ... 219
Concluding thoughts on blend ... 222

Chapter 13: Changing Voices --- 223
Overview of voice change during childhood and puberty ... 223
Voices are changing at younger ages ... 224
Vocal development in adolescent males ... 227
Vocal development in adolescent females ... 229
Part assignment during vocal change ... 232
Vocal technique issues in child and adolescent voices ... 233
Vocal exercise issues specific to adolescents ... 237
Transgender singers ... 238
Aging voices ... 241

Chapter 14: Reducing Tension --- 245
Larynx and neck/pharynx tension ... 245
Jaw tension ... 247
Tongue tension ... 249
Tongue groove—is it a sign of tension? ... 251
Lip tension ... 252
Shoulders ... 252
Legs ... 253
Concluding thoughts on tension ... 253
Exercises to reduce tension ... 254

Chapter 15: Guarding Singers' Vocal Health --- 257
Hydration ... 258
Vocal stamina and fatigue ... 260
Stress, anxiety, and vocal health ... 261

Meal consumption prior to singing..262
Mucus 262
Gastric reflux 263
Singing and the common cold 264
Medications with the potential to cause vocal fold bleeding.....................267
Hormonal factors affecting the voice 268
Additional medication considerations 271
If surgery is contemplated...271
Vocal health concerns of professional singers 274
Vocal health of amateur singers...275
Choral conductor's role in maintaining vocal health 276

Chapter 16: A Productive Warm-Up ---------------------------------- 281
Why are warm-ups important?..281
Specific benefits of a thoughtful warm-up sequence...................282
Warm-up sequence..283
Sample warm-up sequences...286
Vocal cool-down 287
Compendium of suggested exercises for warm-up 288

Appendix: IPA Symbols for Important Vowels and Consonants ------ 297

References --- 299

Index -- 323

Second Edition Acknowledgements

In addition to the many people who contributed their advice about the first edition, we want to acknowledge those who made important contributions to the second edition.

The following served as reviewers and made particularly detailed comments on the entire manuscript:

- Professor Karen Brunssen, Co-chair of Music Performance at Northwestern University and President of the National Association of Teachers of Singing. She is also author of *The Evolving Singing Voice: Changes Across the Lifespan.*
- Dr. Rollo A. Dilworth, Vice-Dean and Professor of Choral Music Education, Temple University. More than 150 of his choral compositions and arrangements have been published. He is also the author of three books of choral exercises, entitled *Choir Builders.*
- Dr. Matthew Edwards, Coordinator of Musical Theatre Voice and Associate Professor of Voice and Voice Pedagogy at the Shenandoah Conservatory. He is also Artistic Director of the CCM Vocal Pedagogy Institute at Shenandoah University and author of, *So You Want to Sing Rock 'n' Roll: A Guide for Professionals.*

Evelyn LaTour designed a wonderful new cover for the second edition and updated several of the illustrations that she created for the first edition. She also sketched an additional illustration for this edition.

Sarah Ponder, mezzo-soprano extraordinaire, continues as our model for illustrations of posture/alignment, vowel production, and tension.

Dr. Pauline Houlden performed comprehensive editing of the manuscript, substantially improving its organization and readability. Any remaining errors are ours!

Dr. Larry Abernathy, Director of Music & Arts at the Kirk of Kildare Presbyterian Church has been an enthusiastic supporter of this second edition. Steve spent many hours in discussion with him and the following choir members who provided excellent advice for improvements to the first edition: Dr. Moon Choi, Allison Connors, Sue Durham, Emyr Edwards, Keith Gausman, Linda Harrison, Blair Hatcher, Madison Lamphear, Barbara Moore, Kat Russell, DJ Sellers, Dr. Robert Starbuck, and Nan Warren.

We are also grateful to the following individuals for particularly detailed comments and discussion of specific vocal technique issues: Elizabeth Jackson Hearns, Dr. Sue Kim, Kyle Sackett, Lorian Schwaber, Dr. Danielle Sirek, Lauren Sklar, Dr. Joel Tranquilla, and Elizabeth Weismehl.

The following provided helpful comments: Matthew Blanks, Chris Bowman, Cristina Bueno Brown, Deborah Buck, John Darrow, Klaus Georg, Sandra Jasper, Dr. Sarah Morrison, Kateri Gormley Sackett, Angela Young Smucker, and Amy Weller.

Julia wishes to thank the many workshop participants, voice students, and choristers who have motivated me to learn and share more! Special thanks to the North Shore Choral Society, North Park University choirs, Trinity United Methodist Church Chancel Choir, and members of the Canadian Chamber Choir (who have participated avidly in over 100 workshops!). In addition, thank you to my family and especially my awesome husband Martin and our kids (who regularly sing through straws with me!). You inspire me to keep learning and you keep me laughing! Thanks to dear friend Emily for being there when the going got tough and to Pauline, Steve's wife, who has not only supported Steve through this 2nd edition, but also took care of my children while were writing in North Carolina! And, of course, to Steve. Your work ethic and curiosity are simply boundless, perhaps only eclipsed by your kindness and patience! Thank you for jumping in again with me on this! Finally, I dedicate this book to Antonia Syson, a dear friend and passionate student of voice who was very proud of the first edition and would have whole-heartedly supported this one. You are missed and remembered.

Steve thanks Dr. Larry Abernathy and members of the Chancel Choir of Kirk of Kildare Presbyterian Church for their warm welcome when he moved to North Carolina. While working on the second edition, I had the opportunity to participate in the CCM Vocal Pedagogy Institute at Shenandoah University. This was a delightful experience that helped to confirm our approach to incorporating contemporary styles in this edition. My wonderful wife, Pauline, has been extraordinarily supportive of this effort, as she was with the first edition. Our adult children, Paul and Evelyn, have provided us with interludes of laughter throughout the process. Evelyn, whose art adorns our home, created a marvelous new cover design which is at once modern and evocative of our first edition. Julia, as always it is a pleasure to work with you, whether writing or singing. You are the consummate professional!

Introduction: A guide to stylistically flexible vocal technique

The better conductors, teachers, and singers understand effective vocal technique and the science underlying it, the more readily they can apply these concepts to both individual and ensemble singing. While there are excellent resources that concentrate on one of three areas: vocal science, vocal pedagogy, or choral rehearsal technique, this book integrates the three.

In our first edition we presented an approach to classical vocal technique grounded in authoritative pedagogical sources and vocal science research. There is an increasing demand for contemporary voice training. We are now at a point where substantial research in contemporary styles and significant contemporary-style vocal pedagogy resources allow us to address vocal technique across styles in the same comprehensive format as the first edition.

Our perspective is that variations in the elements of vocal technique are the tools that singers can use to sing in virtually any style. And, we believe that all singers would be well served by the ability to be flexible in how they create sound. This is particularly true for developing singers who are searching for the style or styles for which they are most suited, and which are of greatest interest to them. For experienced singers, training in other styles adds flexibility and marketability.

Contemporary styles encompass CCM and musical theatre

Contemporary Commercial Music (CCM) is an umbrella term for a large variety of non-classical styles. LoVetri (2008) says, "Contemporary commercial music (CCM) is the new term for what we used to call non-classical music. This is a generic term created to cover everything including music theater, pop, rock, gospel, R&B, soul, hip hop, rap, country, folk, experimental music, and all other styles that are not considered classical" (p. 260).

Nonetheless, this term has evolved in recent years. Musical theatre is now viewed by many as a separate category (Edwards & Hoch, 2018). It requires an ability to sing a variety of CCM styles as well as a variation on classical style (legit). For this reason, we use the term "contemporary styles" to encompass both CCM and musical theatre.

- ❖ There is some controversy about "music" versus "musical" and "theater" versus "theatre." These terms are generally interchangeable with each other, but we have chosen to use "musical" because that is the short descriptor of this art form, and it is in the title of the National Alliance for Musical Theatre, and the Musical Theatre Educator's Alliance. While "theater" has become more widely used than "theatre" in general writing in the United States, we have chosen to use "theatre" in part because of the use of this spelling in the names of these and other organizations (e.g., Educational Theatre Alliance) and its widespread use outside of the U.S.

This book does not address the intricacies of interpretive nuances and performance practices of any given style. Rather, our approach is to present commonalities and differences concerning the elements of vocal technique. For information about detailed performance practices of contemporary styles, we recommend the *So You Want to Sing* series of books sponsored by the National Association of Teachers of Singing. We reference several of these volumes in this book.

Second edition coverage

The major technique issues comprehensively covered in the first edition are included in this edition:

Fundamentals of vocal technique: Posture/body alignment; breath control; initiation, creation, and release of sound; resonance; vowels; consonants. These are covered in Chapters 1–6.

Enhancements of vocal technique: Vibrato; negotiation of the vocal registers; voice classification considerations and improving range; improving intonation; legato, staccato, accents, melismas, and dynamic control. See Chapters 7–11.

Important special topics: Improving ensemble blend; changing voices; reducing tension; guarding singers' vocal health, and a productive warm-up. These are covered in Chapters 12–16.

In addition, material from more than 160 additional references provides a wealth of new information. These both update the first edition and provide information about stylistic differences and similarities in technique. Here are some examples of new material:

- ❖ A more nuanced approach to posture, based on modern conceptions of

body alignment and flexibility.
- Additional information about the onset of sound, including the use of a relaxed vocal fry onset.
- A new 7-point scale to illustrate firmness of vocal fold closure (glottal closure) in various styles.
- Greatly expanded treatment of Semi-Occluded Vocal Tract (SOVT) exercises, including the science behind their effectiveness.
- Extensive discussion of belting in many chapters, based on recent research and vocal pedagogy practices of expert musical theatre teachers.
- Resonance strategies for classical and contemporary styles including differences in vocal tract length and shape.
- A brief primer on electronic amplification and sound processing, including microphones, equalization, and reverberation.
- Approaches to vowel modification for classical and contemporary styles.
- Expanded treatment of vibrato including approaches to varying vibrato extent and rate.
- Chart of vibrato practices according to style.
- Expanded treatment of vocal registers and strategies for register transitions and register use in various styles.
- More detailed explanations of strategies for singing in special registers such as the whistle register for females and reinforced falsetto for males.
- Discussion of special techniques such as speech-like singing, riffs, growls, and squalls.
- Information on changing voices now includes transgender voice change with a discussion of methods to accomplish voice change and the likely results of those methods.
- Expanded vocal health chapter with updated research implications (e.g., for hormone replacement therapy, tonsillectomy for those with chronic tonsillitis, non-surgical treatment of vocal fold nodules and polyps), and special consideration of the vocal health concerns of professional singers.
- Additional vocal exercises in most chapters. Many exercises help singers learn to adjust the vocal tract in various ways to create both classical and contemporary sounds (e.g., firmness of glottal closure, larynx position, tongue position, soft palate position, jaw position, lip shape).

Benefits of improved vocal technique

There are many ways that singing can be improved by utilizing excellent vocal technique. A few examples are listed below.

- Singing with greater ease and efficiency, including the elimination of extraneous tensions that tire singers and result in reduced sound quality.

- Better control over resonance and timbre, key aspects of stylistic differences.
- Improved control over vowel formation and consonant enunciation, resulting in both enhanced sound quality and greater intelligibility.
- Improved register transitions and flexibility to change register use according to style.
- Singing in-tune.
- Enhanced choral blend.
- Expressive flexibility, including control over sound intensity, variation in the amount of vibrato, and articulatory variation.
- Improved vocal health.
- The potential to sing well throughout the life span.

A guiding principle for this book is that singers should understand how their voices produce sound and how they can vary that sound in a healthy manner. Throughout this book we endeavor to use the findings of voice science research to explain why a specific strategy should be applied. We encourage teachers and conductors to share this information with their singers. Too often singers are expected to accept a technique or related exercise on faith, yet, if conductors and teachers communicated the reason for their recommendation, singers would implement it more effectively and enthusiastically.

We agree with Edwards (2014) that vocal pedagogy should not be based excessively on imagery. We cite examples of commonly used misleading images that can produce inconsistent results and have unwanted side effects. Nonetheless, some images do have value, and we recommend them in certain exercises.

To summarize, we have focused on creating a guide to singing well that is at once practical and grounded in vocal science. Read from cover to cover it will provide a comprehensive yet concise overview of vocal technique, with a continual focus on linking technique to the musical product. This book can also be used as a reference for a specific topic or concern, providing quick access to the best research-based advice available.

Intentional use of exercises is essential to vocal development

Thoughtful use of exercises is necessary to help singers develop their voices and improve their function. Virtually all the chapters in this book contain exercises targeted to the specific concerns of that chapter.

- Careful selection of exercises also makes the warm-up period prior to rehearsal more useful. While some exercises are largely for the purpose of warming the voice, others can be chosen to work on aspects of vocal technique needing improvement and/or to address issues of importance to the repertoire that will be rehearsed.

Research on and our use of SOVT exercises have shown that they are practical and useful for all styles and stages of vocal development. As outlined in Chapter 3, we strongly suggest using at least two or three of these exercises before every rehearsal (individual or ensemble). Singing through straws is particularly beneficial. Singing through straws is not a gimmick—it has incredible benefits for singing and everyday voice use.

The final chapter includes sequences of suggested general exercises for both warm-up and vocal development. We also include suggestions for vocal cool-down.

Our philosophy about exercises

Our suggested exercises are intentionally simple—our governing philosophy is that the focus of singers should be on the technical process and goals rather than the execution of a complicated sequence. For this reason, it is important to explain the purpose of an exercise to singers. Explanations need not be technical, but singers should understand what they are trying to accomplish.

Included in most chapters are some exercises designed for children, but which adults may appreciate as well. Starting pitches for exercises are merely suggestions. In some cases, we show exercises starting on middle-C (C_4) for simplicity, but the starting pitch and key should be varied as needed and desired. We suggest vowels for exercises, but other vowels may often be employed.

Singers benefit from repetition of exercises over time. Repetition helps to develop the muscle memory that allows proper vocal technique to become automatic. Both massed practice (multiple repetitions within a given warm-up/rehearsal) and spaced practice (repetition over time) are essential for learning and retention of good technique.

Importance of attention to vocal technique in the choral setting

For many amateur singers, such as those in school and community choirs, conductors may be their only source of information about vocal technique. Even singers who regularly study with a voice teacher may spend more time singing with their choral conductor. The conductor thus has a valuable opportunity and, indeed, a responsibility to teach great vocal technique and support vocal health. Attention to vocal technique is indispensable for untrained singers. It is valuable as well for developing and trained singers, who will benefit from the opportunity to apply appropriate technique in a choral setting.

Addressing vocal technique during warm-up and rehearsal helps singers become responsive to the artistic goals of the conductor. In the choral context, trained and untrained singers can then speak the same language and can be active participants in improving choral singing.

Some ensembles sing particular styles and periods of music (e.g., early music ensemble, gospel choir) while others endeavor to sing a wide variety of styles. Knowledge of stylistically flexible vocal technique will allow all ensembles to better achieve tonal and stylistic goals in a healthy, informed manner.

Improving communication among singers of different styles and between voice teachers and conductors

Enhancing understanding of other styles

Some voice teachers and singers of classical styles may think that singers of contemporary styles use poor technique and thus can damage their voices. At the same time, singers of contemporary styles may avoid voice lessons that could improve their technique because they are afraid of being transformed into opera singers (Edwards, 2014) and ruining the unique artistry which they have cultivated.

Lack of knowledge and information about other styles leads to distrust, miscommunication, and avoidance of exploration of techniques that could expand a singer's capabilities. Moreover, how to produce sound in various styles often seems to be a mystery. We hope this book helps to dispel some of that mistrust and mystery by addressing how the elements of vocal production vary by style and how all styles can be sung in a healthy manner.

Enhancing communication between conductors and voice teachers

Voice teachers are often concerned that singers must sacrifice healthy vocal production to fit in with a chorus. This view may be based on their experiences working with conductors who know little about the voice, or conductors who ask their singers to use inappropriate vocal techniques.

We believe that when conductors are cognizant of good vocal technique, each member of a choral group can sing in a healthy manner. In such an environment, choral singing can offer the benefits of musicianship training, ensemble skills, and knowledge of repertoire, while providing support and encouragement for progress with singing technique.

As mentioned above, choral conductors often spend more time with singers than do voice teachers and can have a profound impact on singers' vocal production. The opportunity is enormous, therefore, for choral conductors to reap the rewards of applying vocal technique in the choral context and supporting the work of their voice-teacher colleagues. This book thus attempts to bridge and merge the disciplines of solo and choral singing. Moreover, we want to continue to open opportunities for dialogue and cooperation between voice teachers and conductors.

A note about symbols used in this book

To indicate a given pitch, we use the standard Acoustical Society of America designation of C_4 for middle-C and A_4 for a concert-A. A note which is an octave above middle-C is thus C_5, and the note a full step above C_5 is D_5. C is always the first note in a transition to a higher numbered set of pitches.

Figure I.1 Illustration of pitch notation

Specific vowels and consonants are shown between square brackets. For example, the vowel sound in "ghost" is [o]. We use the International Phonetic Alphabet (IPA) to illustrate vowel sounds. (Because IPA symbols for some consonants and even some vowels are not intuitive, IPA symbols for common vowels and some consonants in English, German, French, and Italian are contained in the Appendix.) Table I.1 lists the symbols for what are often called the five basic "cardinal" vowels. Chapter 5 on vowels expands this chart. (Note that vowel symbols in IPA largely reflect the vowel sounds of the Romance languages, such as Spanish and Italian.)

Vowel	Example
[i]	Need
[e]	Gate
[ɑ]	Father
[o]	Go
[u]	Choose

Table I.1 IPA symbols for cardinal vowels

A word about terminology

Some authors use the term "tone" to refer to the note being sung. Tone, however, can be confused with the concept of the color or timbre of the sound. We think "pitch" is a better choice, even though from a technical standpoint, pitch refers to what we *perceive* the note to be (the heard fundamental frequency). This can differ from what the singer intends, as outlined in Chapter 4 on resonance. Nonetheless, for simplicity, we will use "pitch" to refer to the sung note.

As noted above, legit is a form of classical style used in musical theatre. Legit has evolved, however, so that its timbre has become brighter today and involves some differences in use of vibrato. We address these issues in more detail in later chapters, particularly Chapter 3 on resonance and Chapter 7 on vibrato. We want to emphasize, however that we do not use legit to encompass more broadly some contemporary styles of singing such as pop, even though modern musical theatre legit has some pop influences. Moreover, though pop may have elements of classical and legit singing, it is generally a distinctive style.

Chapter 1: Posture/Alignment

Appropriate body posture or alignment has three major benefits for singers (Bunch, 1995):

- ❖ Breathing is easier
- ❖ Tension is reduced
- ❖ Singing is less tiring

Correct body alignment elevates the ribs, allowing greater lung expansion and finer control over breathing. Without proper alignment, muscles that can affect vocal production must compensate to maintain body position.

> ➢ Whether a singer is moving, standing, or sitting, good body alignment facilitates the shifting of tension among different muscles, aiding vocal production (Cardoso, Lumini-Oliveira, & Meneses, 2017).

Excess or misplaced muscle tension limits freedom in the breathing mechanisms, degrades sound quality, and makes it challenging to sing higher pitches. Indeed, singing with poor posture is associated with greater vocal effort (Gilman & Johns, 2017). Singers with poor posture tire easily because they spend too much energy maintaining balance. Even singers who know posture is important need reminders from time to time.

Essentials of proper posture/body alignment

For some, the term "posture" has negative connotations, conjuring images of body tension and militaristic, muscular rigidity. Perhaps as a consequence, many have begun to use the term "body alignment" to refer to an individual's ideal postural position for singing (or for life!). It is important to remember that all bodies are slightly different, and that the dynamic nature of singing requires flexibility rather than rigidity. While singing, we will not all look alike, but we should all be working towards a posture that supports what the body is required to do.

> ➢ "Our vocal instruments require spines free of postural distortions, dynamically stabilized rather than rigidly held" (Friedlander, 2018, p. 1).
>
> ➢ "The posturing of the body contributes not only to controlled respiration, but to all aspects of sound production, through the relationships established between the respiratory system, the

phonatory mechanism, and the resonators, and through feedback of the muscles to the nervous system" (Callaghan, 2014, p. 22).
➢ "Balance around our ... spines and legs is the best postural condition for singing. The enemies of balance are 'standing up straight' and slouching. 'Standing up straight' is rigid, pulled up and back ... slouching is pulled down and in ..." (Conable, 2000, p. 15).

For many people, proper body alignment does not feel natural and requires expert guidance. Most of us adapt our posture over time during work and everyday activities, creating postural distortions that become habitual. Alexander Technique and the Feldenkrais Method are particularly helpful for performers who desire optimal body alignment, efficiency, and freedom. (See, for example, alexandertechnique.com and feldenkrais.com.)

Achieving good posture/body alignment

To help achieve good posture, align your body so that an imaginary straight line passes through the back of the ear, the center of the shoulder, the highest point of the hip bone, the knee joint, and just in front of the ankle. Place your feet directly beneath the shoulders (i.e., a shoulder's width apart) to help maintain balance. Keep one foot *slightly* in front of the other to counteract any tendency to rock from side to side. Weight should be evenly distributed over the feet—avoid placing too much weight either on the heels or on the balls of the feet. Note that because of differences in physiology, each singer must find their optimal singing posture (Conable, 2000).

Figure 1.1 illustrates a good standing posture for one particular singer, showing both frontal and side views.

The sternum (breastbone) should not be artificially high such that the back is over-arched. Nor should it be artificially low due to a hunched posture. It should be reasonably high to lift the ribs to create space for breathing. An elevated sternum increases lung capacity (Bunch, 1995). Avoid holding the sternum artificially high in a military posture. Strive for a sense of buoyancy.

Try this exercise to find a comfortable position for the sternum: *Roll the shoulders forward, curl the sternum towards the belly button and pull the chin down. Then reverse, expand outwards, elevating the breastbone (sternum) toward the ceiling, pulling the shoulders back, and arching the lower back. Then allow the body to come to a balanced, neutral position as described above.*

Posture/Alignment 11

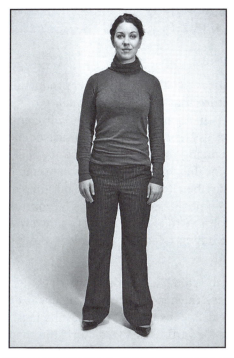

Figure 1.1 Illustrations of good standing posture

Important aspects of body alignment

Head and chin position

Head position is critical for excellent sound production; it can also affect other aspects of posture that influence the quality of singing. If the head is aligned improperly, other parts of the body will compensate to maintain balance, leading to excess tension and expenditure of energy (Dayme, 2009). For many styles of singing the chin should be parallel with the ground to allow the larynx some flexibility. For some contemporary styles such as belting, the larynx may be allowed to rise to aid in creating a bright sound. Raising the chin accommodates the rise of the larynx. For classical singing, a slight tilt down is desirable to allow the larynx a lower, stable position. If the chin is tilted too far down, releasing the jaw at the back and opening the mouth will be difficult.

Refrain from pulling the chin back, as this constricts the throat. X-ray studies reveal that pulling back the head depresses the larynx excessively (Vennard, 1967). This creates extraneous tension and results in a "woofy" sound. Also, avoid jutting the chin forward. This, too, distorts the shape of the vocal tract.

The way head position affects your sound illustrates how you are your instrument. You wouldn't bend a trumpet and expect it to play well, nor should you bend your vocal tract. *To demonstrate the effect of doing this on the quality of sound, sing* [ɑ] *or* [ae]. ([ae] *is the vowel sound in "cat.") Move your head back and then forward, jutting out the chin. Note how the sound changes. Now try singing* [ɑ] *or* [ae] *and move your chin position up and down to see how that changes the tone.*

Head and chin position in children and adolescents

Children and adolescents commonly exhibit an unconsciously raised chin/tilted head, especially as their voices ascend. While a somewhat raised chin may be appropriate for some contemporary styles, it should not be a default position for all singing. Conductors and voice teachers need to help their young singers to develop an awareness of head and chin position.

Head-turning to see the conductor

In some choral settings singers may need to turn their heads slightly to the left or right to see the conductor. Ideally, singers should turn their bodies to face the conductor so that the head faces straight forward. A *slight* turn of the head toward the conductor, however, should not pose serious problems. If singers turn their heads excessively, the neck muscles will tense, consuming energy, and compromising sound.

Singers must also have adequate space to be able to see the conductor easily—those who cannot may resort to contorting themselves, leading to undesirable tension. Appropriate spacing is also necessary for singers to hear both themselves and others, a significant factor affecting the ability to sing in-tune. (See Chapter 10, which treats intonation in more detail.)

Holding music and seeing the conductor

Singers often experience head posture problems when holding music. Singers holding their music in a low position will tilt the chin down when reading music and, if singing in an ensemble, raise the chin when looking at a conductor. Singers holding their music relatively high need to move only their eyes up and down to see music and look at the conductor or audience. Figures 1.1 and 1.3 illustrate proper ways to hold a music folder in both standing and seated positions. Note how the folder is cradled in the singer's hands and wrists. The position of the folder facilitates viewing the conductor or audience without interfering with the path of sound. Such interference attenuates critical higher harmonic frequencies, discussed further in Chapter 4 on resonance (Galante, 2011).

When holding a folder, be mindful that this will tend to shift your balance forward, creating back and shoulder problems. Alleviate this by moving some of the weight to your heels without leaning back.

Relaxed shoulders

Shoulder position affects the amount of tension in the body. The shoulders should be relaxed in their sockets. They should not be rigid or locked. Shoulder blades and arms should also be relaxed.

Arms, hands, and feet

The arms and hands should hang at the side (if singing from memory), and singers should avoid clenching the hands (McKinney, 2005). Some singers hold their hands together in front or back. We do not recommend this practice, for it creates unproductive tension in the arms and shoulders.

When singing with music, think carefully about the weight of music folders. Consider investing in a lightweight, easy-to-hold folder. A hefty folder increases the likelihood of tension in the arms and shoulders, not to mention anxiety about dropping the folder.

Clenching the feet should be avoided as well. This is a surprisingly common problem, for as singers release extraneous tension in one group of muscles, they often make the mistake of transferring it to another.

Knees

It is imperative to avoid locking the knees. Locked knees are often associated with tensed quadriceps (front thigh muscles), tensed lower back muscles, and an undesirable swayback posture. Singers who frequently have locked knees should try the quadriceps stretching exercise outlined in Chapter 14 on reducing tension. Even if your knees are not locked, tight quads can cause the pelvis to tilt forward, affecting body alignment unfavorably.

Shoe heel height

High heels have a variety of effects on posture, including a backward tilt of the pelvis and backward displacement of the thoracic spine and head (Opila, Wagner, Schiowitz, & Chen, 1988). This can add to tension and create subtle, but poorly understood effects on timbre (perceived tonal quality), and resonance (Rollings, 2018). Heels also create a lowered head position, which Rollings suggests may help to keep the larynx low. A lowered head position may be desirable, as we will see later, for classical styles, but be undesirable for contemporary styles. Consider heel height when choosing performance shoes and practice in those shoes before a performance.

Common alignment problems

Choral directors and teachers may observe the following common alignment problems that tire singers, disrupt breath control, and create tension (Dayme, 2009):

- Rounded or hunched shoulders (particularly when sitting)
- Collapsed chest
- Excessively arched lower back
- Excessively raised or lowered chin

A related issue is the "overeager" posture. This includes holding the music too high, leaning forward and lifting the chin.

Figure 1.2 illustrates both hunched and overeager postures. Notice how these postures result in body misalignment.

Avoid extraneous body movement

Many people engage in a variety of superfluous body movements while singing. Such actions interfere with good vocal production because they expend energy unproductively and introduce extraneous tensions affecting the breathing mechanisms and vocal tract. These create strain and, thus, poor tone. (We are not speaking of natural movements required when acting, or choreographed moves.)

Body movement and other indicators of inappropriate tension such as strained neck and facial muscles often fall outside of a singer's awareness. Singing in front of a mirror is a helpful way to create awareness of them.

In the choral setting, conductors should spend a few minutes during the warm-up on body awareness and provide feedback to singers. Further postural reminders can be given from time to time in rehearsals.

Figure 1.2 Examples of hunched and "overeager" postures

Movement is often a response to nervousness and tension, stemming from a lack of confidence in one's vocal technique. Or, movement may be used to compensate for a missing element of technique such as breath support. To counteract this, singers can focus on positive actions that promote good vocal technique. For example, concentrating on maintaining breath support may be more constructive than focusing on not tightening the arms or swaying. Focus less on the negative and more on what should be done. Singers should occasionally monitor themselves for signs of progress.

Sitting posture and seat types

Choral groups spend much of their rehearsal time seated. While most aspects of standing posture also apply to a sitting position, the legs and feet are less relevant—they are no longer supporting your weight. From the hips up, though, you should feel as though you are standing (Henderson, 1979).

Unfortunately, when sitting, we tend to collapse or slump our chests. While seated, singers should maintain a comfortably elevated sternum; otherwise breath control will suffer (as outlined in Chapter 3 on breathing).

Figure 1.3 Illustrations of good seated posture

Some singers sit near the front edge of their seats to maintain a standing posture from the hips up, but McKinney (2005) suggests sitting well back in the seat. We think that either method can work, as long as a good alignment is maintained. People with shorter legs may need to sit near the edge of the seat. The key is to avoid slumping!

Optimal seats are fairly flat and without arms. Raised fronts (e.g., church pews) fold the body inward, and chairs with arms lead to raising of shoulders. Lacking an ideal chair, singers will need to find the best solution for good posture (e.g., sitting near the front of the seat).

Choral conductors should remind singers about body alignment and should monitor their own alignment as well. Ask singers to switch occasionally from sitting to standing positions during rehearsal. This will reduce the tension that accumulates from remaining in one position for too long.

Figure 1.3 illustrates a good seated posture. The alignment of the upper body resembles proper standing posture, as demonstrated in Figure 1.1.

Exercises for body alignment

Before singing, a few physical exercises can help to align the body and give singers better awareness of the positioning of their head, shoulders, torso, and knees. (As with all exercises in this book, singers should not attempt them if physical or health limitations would put them at risk.)

Tension release and body alignment

Stand with the feet a shoulder's width apart, one foot very slightly in front of the other. Bend the knees slightly to make sure they are unlocked. If you experience leg or foot tension, shake each leg and foot. If you experience arm or hand tension, shake each arm and hand.

Raise the arms over the head. Move the torso and head from side to side. Next, with the arms down, turn the head from left side to right side and back. Then tip the head forward and move it slowly in a half circle, tip it back and repeat. This will help to release neck tension. Finally, roll the shoulders in a circle to the back and then to the front, letting them relax into their sockets.

See Chapter 14 on reducing extraneous tension for information about decreasing pharyngeal/laryngeal, jaw, tongue, shoulder, and leg tension.

"Rag doll"

"Rag doll" is an excellent exercise to help with both posture and relaxation.

While standing, drop the body forward at the waist with the head and arms hanging limp. If there is tension in the shoulders or neck, first move the head from side to side and roll the shoulders as described above. Avoid locking the knees. Then slowly roll the torso up to a standing position with the sternum comfortably high and the shoulders falling into their sockets. Inhale fully (but not excessively) and sing a prolonged [ɑ] ("ah") vowel or exhale on [s].

This exercise can also be applied to a sitting posture:

Put the knees together and drop the torso forward so that the shoulders rest on the knees (or as low as comfortable). Then follow the standing version.

Head position

Sing [ɑ]. Move your head back and then forward, jutting out the chin. Note how the sound changes. Now try singing [ɑ] and move your chin up and down to see how that changes the sound. Try this in front of a mirror.

For kids and everyone! Neck relaxation and chin position

Yes, and No—raise and lower the head for yes, rotate head back and forth for no. Ask questions about the singers' weekend or day that have yes or no answers. (Adapted from Phillips, 1996)

For kids and everyone! Brain/body coordination

Try a variety of motions and have the singers follow you, either changing together with you or in a delayed sequence, for example, as in "Simon Says." (Adapted from Cooksey, 1999)

For kids and everyone! Body awareness and physical warm-up

Disco Dance—use funny "disco" motions such as "the sprinkler" and "starting the lawnmower." Invent your own moves.

For kids and everyone! Porcupine and sea star for alignment

Curl your body into a small, tight ball like a porcupine in defensive mode. Then stand and expand like a big, wide sea star (starfish). Next, gradually relax your body towards the center. The arms float down to the sides, shoulders become comfortably level, the legs move in, to about a foot apart, and the head comes to a level, comfortable position. Take some relaxed, low breaths and imagine your limbs and ribcage circling your spine.

Body alignment while moving

Maintain an optimal, yet flexible alignment for singing while walking around your practice room. Move side to side and back to front. Sit down and stand up. Raise and lower your arms. Then try singing a song while engaging in these movements. Avoid postural rigidity when doing this—body alignment should be adaptive and dynamic. Maintain breath support as well (Chapter 2).

Chapter 2: Breath Control

Breathing is *the* foundation of singing. As Tetrazzini says, "... uncontrolled breath is like a rickety foundation on which nothing can be built, and until that foundation has been developed and strengthened, the would-be singer need expect no satisfactory results" (Caruso & Tetrazzini, 1975, p. 10).

Why is proper breathing so critical? Why is the term "breath support" so prevalent in the vocabulary of voice teachers, conductors, and singers? The reasons are numerous—a singer with proper breathing technique will:

- Create the breath pressure necessary to sing throughout the range
- Control exhalation to handle long phrases
- Modulate breath pressure to control dynamic level better
- Have more control over tone quality
- Relax the breathing muscles between phrases, easing tension and producing a freer sound
- Have a more controlled vibrato

Vennard (1967) sums up these advantages rather nicely, saying that no matter how well people sing, their singing will be further enhanced with improvement in breathing technique. We would add that improved breath control will benefit singers of all styles.

Phases of the breathing cycle

The four primary phases of the breathing cycle in singing are:

- Inhalation
- A very brief suspension of airflow
- Exhalation
- Recovery (brief release of tension in breathing muscles)

Inhalation

How to achieve proper inhalation

The diaphragm and the external intercostals (outer rib muscles) are the two major muscles contracted during inhalation for singing (Sundberg, 1993).

The diaphragm is one of the most discussed muscles in singing. It is a dome-shaped muscle underlying the lungs, separating them from the abdominal contents. When the diaphragm contracts, it descends, creating a vacuum within the lungs (see Figure 2.1). Air then flows in and fills the lungs. As the diaphragm descends it displaces the contents of the abdominal cavity.

Based on the advice to "sing from the diaphragm," singers often mistakenly assume that the diaphragm lies in the abdominal area. As Figure 2.1 shows, however, the top of the diaphragm is surprisingly high. The advice should be to focus on the abdominal and intercostal muscles, as outlined below.

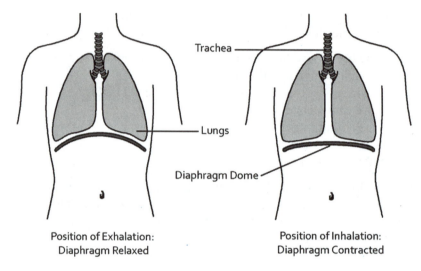

Figure 2.1 Simplified illustration of the diaphragm

The diaphragm will descend fully, and maximum air will be inhaled only when the abdominals are relaxed. Think of this as creating vertical space for the lungs. At the same time, think of creating horizontal space by moving the ribs outward.

> ➤ Tetrazzini suggests imagining the lungs as empty sacks that are filled with air from the bottom up (Caruso & Tetrazzini, 1975). Or think of them as an expanding balloon.
> ➤ Fleming (2005) advises release of the abdominal wall outward—without pushing—so that the diaphragm can descend, allowing the lungs to fill to their highest capacity. The chest should also expand slightly, but this is only in the final stage of inhalation when air fills the lungs completely.

When we speak of releasing the abdominals, we are not including the lower abdomen (the area below the navel). Expanding this portion of the abdomen simply pushes out the intestines and internal organs; it does not create additional room for the diaphragm to descend. Singers who push out the lower abdomen may cave in the ribs, resulting in less room for the lungs to expand (R. Miller, 1993).

Note that the expansion of the ribs and abdomen should be visible and is a good sign that a singer is inhaling correctly.

Back expansion

The back will expand slightly as a natural consequence of the ribs moving outward, but some singers find it helpful to focus a bit more on back expansion as a method of increasing room for the lungs to expand. Fleming (2005), for example, argues that singers should imagine their torsos as a barrel and that expansion should include the back muscles.

We think that singers who desire additional lung capacity can benefit from monitoring back expansion in addition to side and frontal expansion. Nonetheless, a caution is in order:

- Singers should not concentrate so much on back expansion that frontal expansion suffers (McKinney, 2005). Abdominal expansion is essential for proper inhalation. As outlined below, it is also crucial for enhanced control over exhalation.

Keep the sternum/chest comfortably high

Chapter 1 explains why good alignment for singing includes maintaining the sternum in a comfortably high position. We want to re-emphasize this point: a reasonably high sternum is crucial for creating room for the diaphragm to descend and for the lungs to expand. (See Figure 2.2, which illustrates the location of the sternum.) With the sternum in the proper position, greater vertical space is created, and it is easier to expand the ribs.

Inhalation should be silent

Breath intake should be noiseless. Noise indicates throat constriction (R. Miller, 1996), which inhibits tone quality.

Typical causes of constriction include one or more of the following:

- Soft palate (velum) too relaxed (See Figure 4.2 in Chapter 4 on resonance.)
- Jaw lowered insufficiently
- Tongue contracted too far back in the throat

❖ Tense muscles surrounding the vocal tract

Singers who inhale with the space between the vocal folds partially closed will also be noisy. This may occur when singers begin to sing without proper preparation. (The vocal folds vibrate to produce sound; they are also commonly called vocal cords.) Try this exercise for noiseless inhalation:

Open the mouth, lower the jaw, open the space between the vocal folds (technically referred to as the glottis), release the abdominal muscles, and allow the lungs to fill with air.

Inhale with the tongue, mouth, and jaw in the position of the vowel that is to be sung. This is highly efficient and has the added benefit of avoiding an unwanted and unpleasant changing vowel sound as singing is initiated.

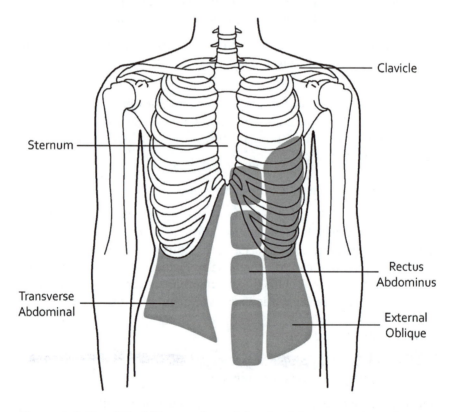

Figure 2.2 Simplified illustration of the clavicles, sternum, rib cage, and abdominal muscles—all muscles are on both sides of the body

Avoid clavicular breathing (upper chest breathing)

Singers may use clavicular (collar bone) breathing in the mistaken belief that they must expand the chest as much as possible to fill the lungs completely. Clavicular breathing is commonly known as upper chest breathing because moving the collar bones expands the upper chest. Figure 2.2 includes an illustration of the clavicles.

Clavicular breathing results in several problems:

❖ Insufficient air for extended phrases. The volume of the upper area of the lungs is less than the capacity of the lower area. (See an illustration of the lungs in Figure 2.1.)
❖ Lack of fine control over exhalation. The abdominal muscles must be relaxed during inhalation to allow the full range of contraction required to create and modulate the breath pressure necessary for singing.

Other causes of clavicular breathing include:

❖ Singers holding in the abdomen to keep the stomach flat for the sake of appearances. (If the abdomen is held in, upper chest breathing is about the only option available.)
❖ Inappropriate carryover from other activities. Singers who engage in strenuous exercise (e.g., running) may unconsciously adopt clavicular breathing because this is how people often respond to being out of breath while exercising. (The solution is to learn to use abdominal and rib muscle breathing technique in those other activities. While exercising, for example, focus on inhaling by releasing the abdominal muscles and expanding the ribs.)
❖ Because dancing requires high levels of exertion and places demands on the core muscles, clavicular breathing is common among dancers. As outlined below, this requires a shift in muscle use for singing longer passages.

Upper chest breathing and shoulder movement

Shoulder movement may accompany upper chest breathing (Vennard, 1967). Such movement occurs unconsciously because shoulder movement helps to compensate for the shallowness of inhalation achieved by upper chest breathing. Various muscles connect the shoulders and the ribs. Raising the shoulders can lever the ribs, exerting a bellows-like effect that draws air into the lungs. Shoulder movement will, however, result in neck tension because of the muscle groups involved in shoulder raising. These are the sternocleidomastoids and scalenes, which extend from behind the ears down to the clavicle and sternum (Fisher, 1966; Vennard 1967). Singers should be mindful of shoulder movement—even if it is not always a sign of upper chest breathing, it is a sure sign of unproductive tension.

Take a full breath, but avoid excessive inhalation

Singers should take full breaths to have sufficient capacity for long passages. It is essential, however, to avoid the temptation to take as deep a breath as possible.

 Richard Miller (1996) argues that "... the lungs should never feel crowded—only satisfied" (p. 26).

There are two main reasons to avoid overfilling the lungs:

- It increases the rate of exhalation (R. Miller, 1996), defeating the purpose of taking such a large breath. Also, overblown exhalation produces a breathy, grainy-sounding, or "unfocused" tone.
- It may lead to excess tension in the chest/neck/larynx.

Open the glottis and try filling the lungs slowly. Breathe through the mouth, not the nose. Notice the point at which you feel that the lungs are overfilled. Tension in the chest/neck is a clear indication you have reached that point. Exhale. Next, take a relaxed, slow breath and stop before the point where you experience tension. Finally, inhale normally, again stopping before you feel tension. This exercise will give you a sense of the amount of air you should inhale for singing.

Very brief suspension

A very short suspension prior to exhalation allows a transition from using muscles for inhalation to using muscles for exhalation. In everyday breathing there is often no real suspension, but rather an immediate shift from inspiration to exhalation. But this brief pause is necessary for singing in order to set the stage for excellent breath support.

After inhalation, the glottis naturally closes in a relaxed fashion. Several authorities recommend specific exercises for suspension. If less-experienced singers engage in drawn-out suspension exercises, however, they tend to tense laryngeal and neck muscles and close the glottis too tightly. This may inadvertently encourage a hard onset (glottal attack—see Chapter 3).

Nonetheless, suspension exercises are helpful for learning to maintain the inhalation position of the abdomen and ribs, paving the way for proper exhalation (see below). Conductors and teachers should encourage singers to keep the glottal closure relaxed and to avoid tensing laryngeal and neck muscles during such exercises.

Exhalation

After inhalation and brief suspension, the ribs and abdomen are expanded slightly outward and we are poised and ready to sing. At this point, many singers have heard that they need "breath support" to exhale and sing properly. But what does this truly mean?

Achieving breath support

Breath support means delivering the right level of breath pressure to the vocal folds. Two main muscles contract during exhalation:

- Internal rib muscles (internal intercostals)
- Abdominals

The contraction of these muscles will move the abdominal contents upward, in turn raising the diaphragm and pushing air out of the lungs (Sundberg, 1993). Some authors emphasize the role of the internal rib muscles in the modulation of breath pressure (e.g., Emmons & Chase, 2006). But both rib and abdominal muscles are important. If anything, the abdominal muscles may be more significant:

> In a study of perceived singing quality, Robison, Bounous, and Bailey (1994) found that those singers judged to have the best tone and most consistent vibrato used the abdominal muscles more than the intercostals.

An important key to using these exhalation muscles for fine control of breath pressure is to *resist collapsing the abdominal musculature and the ribs as much as possible until the very end of a phrase* (Vennard, 1967). The inhalation and exhalation muscles must be in balance to accomplish this. For example, the external intercostal muscles have to oppose slightly the internal intercostals as breath is exhaled. (This is an oversimplification of the role of these and other rib muscles, but the concept of muscular opposition is nonetheless correct—see Dayme [2009] and Vennard [1967].)

> McKinney (2005) says that breath support entails the delivery of sufficient air pressure to the vocal folds through dynamic tension between the muscles of inhalation and exhalation. This dynamic tension was termed by the great Italian singing teacher Lamperti as "appoggio," which comes from "appoggiare," meaning "to lean upon," or more freely translated, "to support" (Lamperti, 1877).

Richard Miller (1996) discussed the need to initiate appoggio consciously. That is, there must be a gentle activation of the abdominal muscles, which the singer will feel as a slight pushing out of the abdomen but with little or no muscle wall excursion. If you place your fingers on the abdomen between the sternum and the navel, you should feel an engaged muscle that nonetheless has some give, like a firm mattress (S. Beatty, personal communication, April 12, 2010).

The appoggio technique also reduces tension in the vocal tract

Great artists have noted the benefits of the appoggio technique for reducing extraneous muscle tension and consequent strain in the vocal tract. Tetrazzini (Caruso & Tetrazzini, 1975) explicitly warns that without proper support, breath pressure must be created in the throat; this will stress the vocal folds. Similarly, Fleming (2005) states that appropriate breath support relieves throat strain. (The nebulous concept of "throat" may be thought of as the portion of the vocal tract from the larynx up through the back of the mouth.)

Many singers and speakers move air through the vocal tract in part by constricting the muscles that surround the tract, particularly at the end of phrases. This is a compensatory response to inadequate breath pressure resulting from suboptimal methods of breathing. It is better to use the abdominals and rib muscles to provide the breath needed at the end of a phrase. Problems associated with constricting the muscles surrounding the vocal tract include:

- Harmful tension, which can result in a strained sound and a tired singer
- Difficulty developing a resonant tone (See Chapter 4 on resonance.)
- Difficulty singing high pitches because of insufficient breath pressure; for the same reason, it is hard to sing loudly (see below)
- Difficulty sustaining long notes

Upper chest breathing results in poor control over exhalation

Earlier we outlined the problems associated with upper chest breathing during inhalation. Upper chest breathing also makes it more challenging to control exhalation. Exhalation in this mode is assisted mostly by elastic recoil of the lungs and upper ribs and receives limited to no assistance from the abdominal muscles. Nor are the intercostal muscles activated.

> In Vennard's words, "Since phonation [creation of sound with the vocal folds] is expiratory, and singing especially demands fine control, we see here the prime reason why this kind of breathing [upper chest

breathing] is inefficient for singers" (1967, p. 27). Vennard thus advocates using the abdominal and intercostal muscles to control exhalation.

Recall that singers who use upper chest breathing often hold in their abdomens. This compromises control over exhalation because it limits the range of potential muscle contraction (Hixon & Hoffman, 1978).

Specific abdominal muscles involved in exhalation

The contraction of the abdominal muscles moves the abdominal contents upward, in turn raising the diaphragm and exhaling air from the lungs (Sundberg, 1993). An understanding of the abdominal muscles involved is thus helpful.

Recall that Figure 2.2 illustrates the three main abdominal muscle groups. (The illustration shows each muscle group on only one side of the body to allow an illustration of all the muscles in one drawing. Each muscle group exists on both sides of the body.)

The vertical sets of abdominal muscles on either side of the center of the abdomen are the rectus abdominus muscles. The abdominal muscles on the side of the abdomen are the internal and external obliques. The internal obliques are not shown in Figure 2.2 because they underlie the external obliques. Although both the rectus abdominus and obliques play a role in breath support, the internal obliques are particularly important (Sears, 1977). The transverse muscles are the most interior abdominal muscles. They wrap around the abdomen and extend back to the spine. Relaxing the transverse abdominals is crucial to allow the diaphragm to descend appropriately into the abdominal cavity during inspiration; contraction of this muscle also plays an important role in the control of exhalation (Vennard, 1967; Dayme, 2009). The transverse abdominals additionally provide core support for the torso, which is essential for maintaining good posture when singing for long periods.

Strengthening the abdominal muscles through exercises is an excellent way to improve breath support (Vennard, 1967). Abdominal crunches are one obvious option for exercising the abdominals, but straight crunches are not sufficient as these primarily focus on the rectus abdominus. Try this exercise for the obliques:

Lie on your back with knees drawn up. With your hands lightly cradling your head, contract the abdominal muscles to raise the shoulders and head off the floor—first toward one knee and then toward the other. It is not necessary to lift more than the shoulders off the floor (i.e., abdominal crunches are sufficient). Be careful not to use your neck and upper back muscles to raise the head and shoulders; use only the abdominal muscles.

To strengthen the transverse abdominal muscle, try this: *In a sitting or kneeling position exhale and attempt to suck in the area around the navel, compressing the waist. A more effective exercise is the pelvic tilt: lie on your back with knees drawn up and a towel under the small of the back. Attempt to tilt the pelvis up using only your abdominal muscles.*

The plank is another useful exercise to stabilize and strengthen the core. *Kneel on a mat and then stretch forward to support your body with only your forearms and feet. Keep your head down, your back flat. Keep breathing naturally and hold this position for 15–30 seconds.*

The "Superman" exercise is also good for the core. *Lie on your stomach, extend your arms out in front of you, palms down. Lift your upper body and legs as high off the floor as you can. Keep your head facing down.*

> ➤ Fleming (2005) recommends Pilates to exercise the entire core. Yoga can also be helpful. As singers age they often fail to maintain core strength, which can result in poor breath support and a wavering vibrato.

The diaphragm plays no role in the control of exhalation

Singers control exhalation with abdominal and rib muscles rather than direct control of the diaphragm. Singers should not be advised to "sing from the diaphragm" or "bounce the diaphragm" for staccato passages or those involving melismas. (See Chapter 11 for more accurate and helpful ways to talk with singers about how to achieve these special techniques.)

There are, however, significant advantages to delaying the ascent of the diaphragm during exhalation. Sundberg (1993) found that trained singers appear to do this and that it yields two benefits: finer control over breath pressure and creation of a pull on the trachea (see Figure 2.1 for an illustration of the diaphragm, lungs, and trachea). The pull on the trachea lowers the larynx, which enhances a particular type of resonance discussed in Chapter 4. It also reduces excessive pressing together of the vocal folds at high pitches, avoiding a strained sound.

But how to delay the ascent of the diaphragm? A suggestion appears in Henderson's (1979) fluoroscopic observations of one of her students. When the singer did not keep the abdominal and intercostal muscles engaged during exhalation, Henderson observed that the diaphragm ascended more quickly. Thus, resistance to the collapse of the abdominal and intercostal muscles may play an essential role in preventing premature ascension of the diaphragm.

Additional points about exhalation

Breath metering

"Breath metering" refers to conserving air during singing to complete musical phrases with sufficient breath energy. As outlined above, breath pressure must be modulated as well through "breath support." Both breath metering and breath support are essential components of "breath control."

Efficient metering of air requires exhaling no more and no less than what is necessary to produce the desired tone. Fleming (2005) states that the key to efficient metering of air is to resist collapse of the abdomen and the ribs. Fleming further argues that a singer must not collapse the chest. In short, the appoggio technique essential for proper breath support is also necessary for breath metering.

The ability to achieve breath metering can also be affected by how firmly a singer closes the vocal folds. This is covered in more detail in the next chapter, as is a more comprehensive conception of support.

Higher pitches and dynamic levels require higher breath pressure

With experience, singers learn the amount of breath pressure necessary for a given pitch and dynamic level. Loud singing requires high levels of breath pressure (technically known as subglottal [below the glottis] pressure). Doubling breath pressure generally doubles the sound level (Sundberg, 1987). However, trained singers may achieve more than a doubling of sound level—e.g., 15 dB for musical theatre, 12 dB for opera (Björkner, 2008). (6 dB is a doubling of perceived sound level as discussed below.) This may be due to the superior resonance of trained singers.

Higher pitches also require more breath pressure—for example, a tenor moving from A_3 to E_4 at moderate loudness will need to increase breath pressure by about 150% (Sundberg, 1987). Since the vocal folds are under greater tension at higher pitches, more force is required to open them (Titze, 1989). This explains why more breath support is necessary for higher pitches.

High pitches do not, however, require more airflow (Sundberg, 1987; Rubin, Lecover, & Vennard, 1967). If singers push too much air through the vocal folds at high pitches, it can result in both undesirable sound quality and poor intonation.

Additional breath support is critical for leaps in pitch

Additional breath support is critical in changing from a low to a high pitch. This support must be engaged *before* the move is made from the low note to the high note. Many singers mistakenly add support only as they sing the higher note. This can lead to singing under the desired higher pitch or "scooping" up to the correct pitch.

Breathiness of younger voices

Choral directors and teachers should be particularly patient with young voices, which often have a breathy quality (particularly, girls' voices). Such breathiness is associated with developmental changes during adolescence, specifically the inability of certain laryngeal muscles (the interarytenoids) to close the back third of the space between the vocal folds. In some cases, breathiness is also due to the imitation of other singers. A clearer tone will emerge with training, experience, and physical maturity.

Vocal exercises can help. In our experience this is particularly useful for middle and high school choral groups in which the sound balance between girls and boys can pose difficulties due to overly breathy singing by the girls (and heavy chest voice production by some boys). Chapter 3 on initiation and creation of sound contains some exercises to help reduce breathiness where it is not a stylistic choice. We also highly recommend the use of semi-occluded vocal tract exercises, especially singing through a straw. See Chapter 3 for more details.

Recovery

Recovery should be a conscious part of the breathing cycle. Muscles need to relax after singing each phrase so that they can recover and perform efficiently for the next. As McKinney (2005) notes, this includes the laryngeal muscles, the muscles involved in creating resonance (such as those of the pharynx and mouth), and the muscles involved in articulation of vowels and consonants (such as the tongue, lips, and jaw). Without a rest period (brief as it may be in singing), tension will build.

In cases where phrases are long (without rests) and, in particular, where there is also a high tessitura (high average pitch), it may be judicious to add an eighth or quarter rest at some points of punctuation. This provides needed rest and recovery, brief as it may be. In the choral setting, singers should be encouraged to take adequate time for recovery when stagger breathing.

Timing of breathing

In classical/legit singing, breaks for breathing are generally dictated by punctuation, explicit breath marks, and the melodic line. In contemporary styles, breath cycles usually are shorter and often dictated by the text and artistic considerations.

Very long phrases are common in the choral literature. Choral singers may stagger breaths within sections to achieve long phrases. Here are some tips for staggered breathing:

- Some singers should breathe early and others late in a phrase
- Choose a subtle place to breathe, for example, in the middle of a sustained note
- After taking a staggered breath, come back in at a lower sound level, though be careful about intonation when doing this
- Omit consonants when taking a staggered breath

Breathing in contemporary styles—limitations imposed by dancing

The general approach to breathing should be similar for all styles of singing as it gives singers the highest level of control over breath support and breath metering. Indeed, interviews with expert musical theatre voice teachers from around the world support this idea (Bourne & Kenny, 2016).

Increasingly, singers are also required to dance in musical theatre productions and pop performances. Breathing while dancing is quite different than while singing with no or only modest body movement. As noted above, it may also involve more clavicular breathing as the core muscles are already in use for the dance movements (LeBorgne & Rosenberg, 2019). Furthermore, as noted by Sliiden, Beck, and MacDonald, (2017), dancing requires:

- Spontaneous breathing with high volumes and airflows
- A fully open glottis during exhalation

Singers must switch consciously from open-glottis exhalation during dancing to closed-glottis exhalation when singing, and they must switch to abdominal/rib muscle control over exhalation. This requires substantial practice.

The major consequence of cardiovascular exertion during dancing is a decrease in maximum phonation time (MTP)—from an average of roughly 20 seconds to 7 seconds (Sliiden et al., 2017). Thus, long phrases and very long-held notes will require a reduction in dance intensity.

Respiratory muscle training

Devices that provide resistance to inhalation and exhalation are readily available to help strengthen respiratory muscles. (Singers can also use narrow straws, but specialized devices allow better control over airflow resistance and are reasonably inexpensive.) A variety of studies in the speech rehabilitation literature demonstrate the improvement in breathing obtained by this type of muscle training.

> ➤ Ray, Trudeau, and McCoy (2018) replicated these improvements in breathing in a study of singers. They demonstrated substantial increases in maximum inspiratory and expiratory pressures. The use of these devices should enable singers to inhale more efficiently and develop greater control over breath pressure.

Breathing exercises

Proper breathing is not difficult to learn. It is, however, difficult for singers to apply knowledge of correct breathing technique every time that they sing. It takes much practice and repetition over time (measured in years!) before excellent breathing technique becomes second nature. Conductors and teachers need to remind their singers to work on this individually, as well as during rehearsals and lessons.

Breathing while lying on the back

The following is a simple method for experiencing proper breathing technique that singers can try at home. (For choral conductors, if you have enough room in the rehearsal space, it could also be done there.) It encourages the use of the intercostal and abdominal muscles and naturally limits upper chest and shoulder breathing.

Lie flat on the back with a book under the head to create better body alignment.

Think about how babies breathe when they are asleep on their backs. Their bellies rise as they take in air. Release the abdominal and rib muscles and let the belly rise and ribs expand during inhalation. The chest may expand slightly as well, but it should expand only after the abdomen has risen (good evidence that the lungs are filling properly).

To better monitor the pattern of abdominal expansion and contraction, place a lightweight book on the abdomen. As you breathe, observe when the book moves. (We do not recommend a heavy book or stack of books to exercise abdominal muscles!)

After spending several minutes watching and adjusting your breathing on the floor, move to a standing position and repeat, again observing the abdomen and lower ribs moving outward during inhalation.

Silent inhalation

Try noisy inhalation. Notice what seems to be causing this for you (e.g., relaxed soft palate, insufficiently lowered jaw, tongue too far back in the throat, neck muscle tension, and/or partially closed space between the vocal folds). Follow this with a silent inhalation. Notice the sensations associated with each intake of breath.

The sibilant exercise to improve control over exhalation

One of the most commonly recommended exercises to increase control over exhalation is the sibilant exercise, so named because it involves saying [s] over an extended period (i.e., hissing through the teeth). This restricts airflow and allows concentration on metering the breath. Richard Miller (1996) suggests the following to improve control over the muscles involved in metering:

Place one hand over the center of the abdomen, with the lower portion just covering the navel.

Place the other hand on the side, just below the rib cage.

Hiss and concentrate on not allowing the abdominal wall or the ribs to collapse until the very end. Having the hands in the above positions helps to monitor the expansion of the abdominal area and the ribs and to provide feedback that will increase control over this process.

For an extension of this exercise, try the voiced consonant [v]. This is more like singing and requires further engagement of the support muscles (K. Brunssen, personal communication, November 28, 2011).

Another approach to monitoring the abdominal area during the sibilant or [v] exercise is to place both hands on the upper abdomen, thumbs touching lower ribs, little fingers near the waist, and middle fingers just touching (McKinney, 2005). Then:

Release the abdominal muscles and expand the ribs to fill the lungs. The middle fingers should part slightly. This is a good sign that abdominal muscles are allowing the diaphragm to descend correctly. If you feel some rib expansion, this is a further good sign that the intercostal muscles are engaged. Press the abdomen gently with your fingertips. You should feel firm muscle with a small bit of give—like a firm mattress.

Hold this expanded position briefly and observe how it feels. Remember, the goal is to maintain this expanded position (within reason) while saying [s] or [v] and, ultimately, while singing.

Be sure that the vocal folds remain open while engaging in the sibilant exercise (they will need to close if using [v]). Closing the folds to prevent the escape of breath may negatively affect the onset of tone when singing. Keep the vocal folds open and prevent excessive escape of air during this exercise through control of the abdominal muscles and intercostals.

Make the [s] or [v] sound with a metered flow rate, all the while trying to keep the abdominal and rib area expanded (i.e., holding fingers on your abdomen apart), allowing collapse only at the very end. Maintaining full expansion should be considered a goal, but this should not lead to strain. There will naturally be some contraction, but the idea is to prevent ascent of the diaphragm as much as possible.

Snap (quick) breath

Henderson (1979) introduces a useful variation on the sibilant exercise that may be helpful when preparing to sing passages with limited time for breathing.

Take a "snap-like" or quick breath, letting the abdomen spring out naturally for the intake of air and then meter the air on exhalation as in the sibilant exercise. Be sure to breathe in silently when doing this exercise, as quick breaths are often associated with constriction in the vocal tract.

Practice breathing in front of a mirror at home

At home, singers should practice their breathing exercises while singing in front of a mirror, when possible. Conductors and teachers can function as a mirror during rehearsal and lessons.

Conductors and teachers should give helpful feedback to singers about their breathing. Look carefully for visual clues that indicate tension. Head movement is especially chronic in choral singers who feel the need to "cue" the beginnings of phrases with the chin or neck. Some also sway on inhalation.

Shoulder movement may indicate upper chest breathing. Encourage good posture and inhalation that not only sounds silent but "looks quiet" too.

Singers can experiment with the effect of movement by nodding the head with every intake of breath and then keeping the head still for each inhalation.

Breath support

Practice exercises with a variety of melodic patterns (e.g., slides of a fifth, arpeggiated triads) that indicate whether support muscles (abdominals and rib muscles) are engaged. A lapse in support will be revealed by variation in tone quality and, in some cases, by breaks in phonation.

Tongue/lip trills will also indicate if support lapses—the trill will be interrupted, or tone quality will be variable when this occurs. Trills are particularly useful for the development of breathing skills because they create high resistance to airflow and thus require excellent technique to maintain consistent breath pressure.

Experiencing important breath support muscles

To experience support muscles, try this exercise. *While seated, lean forward to a 45-degree angle and allow the arms to dangle at your sides. Take a relaxed, low breath as for singing. The core of the body should raise the torso. (Adapted from K. Brunssen, personal communication, February 18, 2020)*

For kids and everyone! Maintaining breath support

Staccato Boo-Boo-Boo—*release each pitch marked staccato (see Chapter 11 for more on staccato production) and slur the remaining notes. Repeat, moving by half steps. Sing Bey-Bey-Bey to access a brighter, contemporary sound. (Adapted from Phillips, 1996)*

Boo Boo Boo Boo Boo --
Bey Bey Bey Bey Bey --

For kids and everyone! Big dog

Ask singers to "woof" like a big dog; listen to make sure the pitch is neither too low nor too high. Woofing encourages a feeling of openness in the vocal tract as well as abdominal support. (Adapted from Phillips, 1996)

For kids and everyone! Hoberman Sphere

A Hoberman Sphere is a flexible sphere that singers can use as an interactive device to help with the expansion necessary for good inhalation. *Conductors and teachers can encourage their singers to open their mouths and throats (glottis) and feel their lungs gradually expand as they open the sphere. Reverse the process for gradual exhalation. We suggest using the Mini Sphere.* See hoberman.com/fold/Sphere/minisphere.htm

Don't drop breathing exercises from your warm-ups too quickly!

Breathing exercises are often the first to be dropped from both individual and choral warm-ups. Perhaps this is because we think of breathing as something we do every day, and thus easily modified to accommodate the demands of singing. We may also assume that once we have done some breathing exercises, we will employ what we have learned. Nothing could be further from the truth. Developing excellent control over all the muscles involved in breath support and control takes months, or even years, to become fully automatic. Breathing practice is needed until the proper movements become automatic and reflexive (Bunch, 1995).

Chapter 3: Initiation, Creation, and Release of Sound

How we initiate a pitch at the beginning of a musical phrase has a substantial effect on the sound of the phrase. If a phrase *begins* with the appropriate technique for the desired style, it is more likely to be maintained. Conversely, if a singer uses poor technique to start a phrase, it is very difficult to make an adjustment mid-phrase. More generally, singers who understand the vocal mechanism are likely to appreciate better the issues involved in the initiation, creation, and release of sound.

Among the many benefits of proper initiation, creation, and release of sound are:

- Control over timbre
- Efficient sound production
- Effective breath control
- Better vocal health
- Controlled phrase endings

How sound is initiated and created

Vocal science textbooks and some vocal pedagogy texts examine laryngeal anatomy and physiology in detail. This chapter covers only those essentials necessary to understand how the vocal folds create sound, how pitch is controlled, and how various approaches to the onset of sound are related to the degree of closure of the vocal folds.

Our voices are essentially wind instruments. All wind instruments produce sound by sending pressurized air through a vibrator, which creates sound waves that are then acoustically enhanced in one or more resonators. For example, a clarinet's sound is the result of air pressure vibrating a reed. The vibrations of the reed are selectively amplified in the body of the clarinet.

Singers use their abdominal and intercostal muscles to create the necessary lung pressure to activate the singer's vibrator, known as the "vocal folds." The folds are also commonly called "vocal cords." Still, modern scientific study has shown that they are not merely ligaments, but rather a complex structure composed of multiple layers of tissue. As a result, "vocal folds" has become the more widely used term.

Sound initiates when a singer closes the space between the two vocal folds (recall that the space is known as the glottis; see Figure 3.2), and sufficient air pressure is created beneath the folds to open them. This opening lasts only a split second, because the quick passage of air through this narrowed area of the vocal tract creates a zone of low pressure, drawing them shut. (The passage of air through the narrowed area that forms the lower pressure is technically known as a Bernoulli Effect.) Think of this lower pressure like a vacuum that sucks the folds closed.

Elastic reversion of the tissues also aids the closing of the folds (van den Berg, 1958). An example of elastic reversion is a rubber band returning to its original form after being stretched.

> ➤ Titze (2000) has shown that the "myoelastic-aerodynamic theory" ("myoelastic" for the elastic reversion of the vocal folds and "aerodynamic" for the Bernoulli effect) is too simple to account fully for continuous vocal fold vibration. He and his colleagues have demonstrated that additional factors likely contribute to sustained vibration, among them a wave-like motion in the vocal folds and a zone of low pressure that develops momentarily above the glottis, aiding their closure.

The rapid closing and opening of the vocal folds is called vocal fold vibration. The number of openings and closings per second determines the fundamental frequency of the sung pitch. For example, singing A_4 causes the vocal folds to open and close 440 times per second.

Vocal fold vibration creates puffs of air. The alternating compression and rarefaction (increasing and decreasing density of the air above the glottis) create sound waves. Structures of the vocal tract above the vocal folds modify these sound waves. Chapter 4 on resonance explores how this occurs and how singers can control sound modification.

Good hydration is critical for proper vocal fold vibration

When our bodies are not adequately hydrated, the mucus coating of the vocal folds becomes more viscous, making it more difficult for the folds to vibrate. Several studies have shown that higher breath pressure and increased phonatory effort are necessary to achieve vocal fold vibration when a singer is dehydrated (e.g., Verdolini-Marston, Titze, & Druker, 1990; Verdolini, Titze, & Fennell, 1994). Higher pitches become particularly challenging to sing. Chapter 15 on vocal health addresses hydration in more detail.

Initiation, Creation, and Release of Sound 39

Components of the singer's instrument

Figure 3.1 is a simplified illustration of the components of the singer's instrument. (The singer's head is turned sideways for illustrative purposes. One would never want to sing in this position.) Breath energy produced by the action of the abdominals and intercostals on the lungs is converted to sound energy by the vocal folds. The sound energy is further modified (filtered/resonated) by the vocal tract. Although sound production might seem to be a linear process, research has shown that feedback of energy from the vocal tract to the vocal folds can occur, illustrated by the return arrow in Figure 3.1. If the vocal tract is configured correctly, this can assist vocal fold vibration. If misconfigured, it can destabilize vibration. Chapter 4 on resonance and Chapter 5 on vowels discuss methods of producing helpful energy feedback and avoiding destructive feedback.

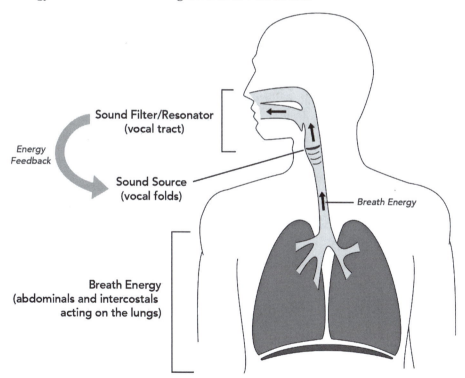

Figure 3.1 Simplified illustration of the singer's instrument

Figure 3.2 provides a cross-sectional view of the larynx, illustrating the flow of air through the glottis. Figure 3.3 presents a side view of the larynx. Notice that the larynx is suspended from the hyoid bone by the thyrohyoid membrane, which connects it to the major cartilage of the larynx, the thyroid cartilage. The vocal folds and some of the important muscles controlling them are within this cartilage. The thyroid cartilage is connected to the cricoid cartilage (the cartilage at the top of the trachea) by the cricothyroid muscles, which play a significant role in pitch control.

The hyoid bone is particularly important because it also connects to the tongue. Tongue position and tension can thus affect the larynx, a point of significance for later chapters on tongue position, vowel formation (Chapter 5 on vowels), and tension (Chapter 14 on reducing tension).

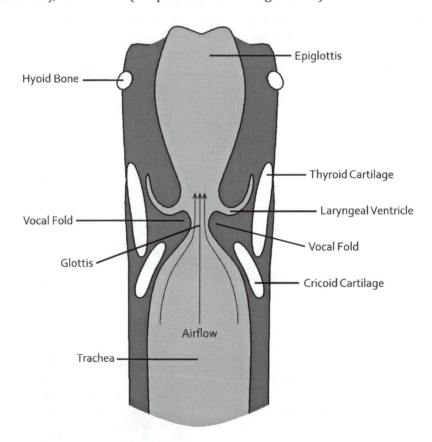

Figure 3.2 Illustration of the larynx (cross-section, posterior view)

Figure 3.4 illustrates an open glottis during normal inhalation/exhalation, a closed glottis, and the opening of the glottis during a vibratory cycle. The view is looking down from the area of the throat at the back of the mouth, with the front of the larynx at the top of the illustration. (The opening of the glottis during the vibratory cycle is so fast that it cannot be seen with the naked eye. This is a simplified illustration of what might be seen with stroboscopic video.)

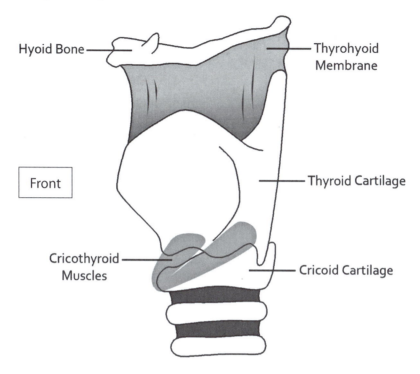

Figure 3.3 Side view of the larynx

The two vocal folds are surprisingly small. An X-ray study found that vocal folds average 14.9 mm for sopranos, 16.6 mm for contraltos, 18.4 mm for tenors, and 20.9 mm for basses (a range of 9/16 in. to 13/16 in.; Roers, Mürbe, & Sundberg, 2009). This small mechanism can, together with vocal tract resonance, produce amazing sound.

Muscles affecting pitch

Some of the muscles that control the vocal folds have a direct effect upon pitch and tonal quality. Muscles affect the frequency at which the folds vibrate by:

❖ Altering the thickness of the folds. A thick fold generally vibrates more slowly (i.e., at a lower pitch) because of its greater mass per inch.
❖ Altering the tension of the folds. A slack fold vibrates more slowly than a tense fold.

42 Vocal Technique: A Guide to Classical and Contemporary Styles

Two major sets of muscles affect pitch: the cricothyroid (CT) muscles and thyroarytenoid (TA, also known as vocalis) muscles. Singers do not have direct, conscious control over muscles affecting pitch. Rather they are controlled through mental imagery (as outlined in the following section) and by biofeedback. (See the text box on this subject.)

The role of the cricothyroid muscles is clear: contracting these muscles stretches and thins the vocal folds by pulling down on the thyroid cartilage (hinged at the back), tilting it forward (see Figure 3.5). This tilting raises the pitch (fundamental frequency). Think of the violin, for which the thinnest strings create the highest pitches because the strings with the lowest mass per inch vibrate most quickly.

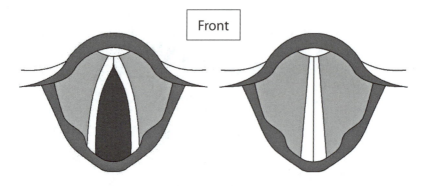

Glottis Open During Normal Inhalation/Exhalation; Glottis Closed

Glottis Open During a Vibratory Cycle

Figure 3.4 Illustrations of the glottis as viewed from above. Front of larynx is at the top of each illustration.

➢ Hammer, Windisch, Prodinger, Anderhuber, and Friedrich (2010) provide evidence that the amount of potential movement in the thyroid cartilage differs among singers. Roughly 55% of females and 66% of males have an anatomical structure that allows less movement. This likely makes it more difficult for these individuals to sing higher pitches.

The role of the thyroarytenoid muscle, the innermost layer of the vocal folds, is more complex and less well understood (see Figure 3.6, an illustration of a cross-section of the vocal fold area of the larynx). Contraction of this muscle in lower portions of a singer's range can lower the pitch by thickening the vocal folds. However, in other circumstances, such as with ascending pitch, contraction of this muscle can stiffen the vocal folds, causing them to vibrate more rapidly.

> An imaging study involving professional sopranos supports the idea of some TA involvement at high pitches. Thyroaretenoids stabilize the vocal folds so that they are not separated excessively by the high breath pressure required for these pitches (Unteregger et al., in press).

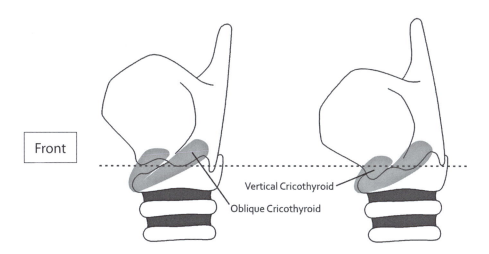

Figure 3.5 Illustration of tilting of the thyroid cartilage by the cricothyroid muscles (side view)

Although both TA and CT muscle groups tend to be involved to some extent at all pitch levels, greater involvement of the cricothyroids is crucial for singing high pitches easily and efficiently. While conscious control of the relative participation of the cricothyroids is impossible, indirect control is feasible through methods described in Chapter 4 on resonance and the portion of Chapter 9 addressing range extension.

Controlling pitch and tone through mental images

How do singers control pitch without conscious control over the muscles affecting the tensioning and thinning of the vocal folds? Surprisingly, control over pitch and even tone quality are achieved by thinking about the sound we want to produce and then making that sound. Psychologists call this a "mental representation," and view it as critical to the development of musical ability (Lehmann, Sloboda, & Woody, 2007).

> ➢ McKinney (2005) says, "Beautiful sounds start in the mind of the singer. If you cannot think of a beautiful sound, it is an accident if you make one. You must learn to 'picture' the sound in your mind's eye and 'hear' it in your mind's ear before it can become a consistent reality" (p. 78). To this end, he argues that it is best to think about the kind of sound one wants to produce and *the sensations associated with good sound* (emphasis ours) rather than about the larynx and the vocal folds.
>
> ➢ It is critical to have a clear mental image of the desired sound before singing (e.g., Dayme, 2009). This image should include thought about the desired firmness of vocal fold closure, the pitch, and the dynamic level. The vocal system should be pre-tuned in response to this mental concept just before singing. Without advance thought, the singer may enter under the pitch or "scoop up" to the correct pitch.

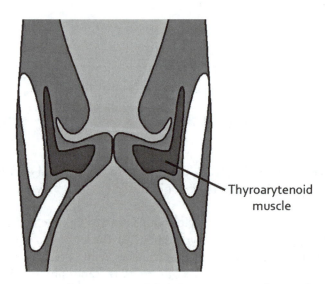

Figure 3.6 Illustration of the thyroarytenoid muscles (cross-sectional view)

Sound level and timbre affected by firmness of vocal fold closure

The only internal (intrinsic) muscles of the larynx over which we have conscious control are those that open and close the glottis, the space between the vocal folds. The posterior cricoarytenoid opens the vocal folds. The lateral cricoarytenoids and the interarytenoids are two muscles involved in closure. The lateral cricoarytenoids bring the vocal folds together, but action of the interarytenoids is necessary to close the posterior (back) portion of the glottis (Ware, 1998).

How firmly the glottis (the space between the vocal folds) is closed has a direct impact on the nature of the sound created. For example:

❖ If the glottis is firmly closed, the sound level will be higher with numerous overtones (harmonics); done excessively, in an untutored fashion, this can create a strained, pressed quality in the sound.
❖ If the folds are held together lightly or slightly apart, the sound will have an airy or breathy quality as air escapes through the folds. There will be few overtones.

Different styles of music require different degrees of glottal closure to create the desired quality of sound. Anchor points are:

❖ Very relaxed—in which the folds are held together lightly or slightly apart to create a breathy sound.
❖ Very firm—in which the folds are tightly compressed together to create a heavy belt sound.
❖ Moderate—associated with a classical/legit sound. This degree of closure produces what Sundberg (1987) refers to as flow phonation.

Table 3.1 illustrates the relationship between firmness of glottal closure on a scale from one to seven and associated sound.

Firmness of Glottal Closure

1 Very Relaxed	2	3	4	5	6	7 Very Firm
Breathy			Classical/Legit			Heavy Belt

Table 3.1. Firmness of glottal closure scale and associated sound

Variations in the firmness of glottal closure according to style

Degree of glottal closure does not fully define a style: numerous other aspects of technique contribute to differences among styles. Furthermore, some styles, particularly pop, use a range of closures. Nonetheless, the following generalizations are possible:

- Traditional musical theatre involving heavier belting styles often requires level 6 or 7 vocal fold closure. Modern musical theatre is more likely to use level 5, or possibly 6, and mix belt. Nonetheless, as musical theatre is continually changing and incorporates many different styles depending upon the type of show, it may involve any of the degrees of vocal glottal closure. Musical theatre singers need to be able to sing comfortably over the entire continuum.
- Pop tends to involve level 3 ("airy") through level 5 ("mix belt") levels of vocal fold closure. Within a given song the degree of glottal closure may vary according to the desired sound. For example, Taylor Swift may switch between an airy and a mix belt sound within a song. Additionally, a pop singer may at times choose to sound breathy (level 1, or perhaps 2) or elect a level 6 belt. The sound the singer is trying to achieve, and the type of song dictate the choice(s).
- Rock is typically produced in the belting end of the compression levels of the table, though moderate glottal closure might be employed for rock ballads. Even airy production might be used occasionally.
- Jazz is typically a more relaxed style, ranging from level 3 (airy) to level 4 (moderate), depending upon the desired sound. Of course, there can always be exceptions for artistic reasons.
- Gospel and soul styles cover the range of glottal closure levels.
- Classical/legit production generally involves moderate glottal closure (level 4).

An exercise to experiment with glottal closure is provided at the end of this chapter.

Firmness of glottal closure and a broader conception of breath support

Recall that as pitch and loudness increase, increased breath pressure is necessary. Firmer glottal closure is necessary to achieve higher breath pressure. Cottrell (2010) thus argues that glottal resistance is an integral aspect of breath support. Without sufficient resistance even a singer with the best appoggio technique cannot correctly control breath pressure (subglottal pressure), resulting in a breathy sound or breaks in the voice.

Breath pressure for chest belting is particularly high due to the very firm glottal closure of this style.

> ➢ Sundberg, Thalen, and Popeil (2012) conclude that various types of belting require different degrees of glottal closure and, therefore, different breath pressures. Breath pressure is roughly 50% higher in chest (heavy) belt compared to classical production. Brassy, ringy, and speech-like belting require breath pressures slightly above the classical style.
>
> ➢ Schutte, and Miller (1993) find that breath pressure is moderate for females singing pop, legit, and classical in chest voice but high for belt.

Herbst (2017) further expands the definition of support to include a variety of elements, all of which interact and cannot be considered in isolation:

- ❖ Respiratory system
- ❖ Glottal resistance
- ❖ Resonance which supports vocal fold vibration, including a narrow epilarynx tube (see Chapter 4) and vocal tract adjustments above this tube.

The respiratory system influences resonance through the phenomenon of tracheal pull, which occurs upon inhalation. Tracheal pull lowers the larynx and narrows the epilarynx tube, increasing resonance and feeding back energy to support vocal fold vibration. Even in contemporary styles there is a likely benefit to not allowing the larynx to rise excessively so that some narrowing can be maintained. Indeed, there is evidence for a singer's formant (a high-frequency vocal tract resonance) or an even higher-frequency speaker's formant (e.g., LeBorgne, 2001) in elite musical theatre and rock singers. See Chapter 4 for more information about this topic.

Firmness of glottal closure and the "closed quotient"

A measure correlated with the firmness of vocal fold closure is the percentage of time the vocal folds are closed during each vibratory cycle. Voice scientists refer to this as the "closed quotient." If the folds stay closed for a high percentage of the time, resonance is generally enhanced because the vocal tract resonates best during the closed phase of the vibratory cycle (Rothenberg, 1981; D. Miller, 2008). During the open phase there is a loss of higher frequency harmonics. Furthermore, when the glottis is open, some sound energy is sent down into the trachea and absorbed (Sundberg, 1995). A higher closed quotient would generally be expected to be associated with a sound having a higher dynamic level and more overtones.

A closed quotient can be too high, however. Excessive glottal tension can result in a pressed or strained sound.

> ### Biofeedback improves singers' control
>
> While conscious control over most laryngeal muscles is impossible, psychological research has shown that people can use biofeedback to gain control over unconscious physiological processes. For example, one can gain some control over blood pressure through biofeedback, even though direct conscious control is not possible (Nakao, Yano, Nomura, & Kuboki, 2003). Physical sensations (kinesthetic feedback) associated with given pitches and beautiful tones are examples of biofeedback for singers.
>
> Auditory feedback is important as well, particularly for pitch control. Nonetheless, auditory feedback has limitations—because bone conductance emphasizes lower frequencies, singers do not hear the spectral qualities of their own sound accurately (Ware, 1998). Also, some of the sound they hear is reflected sound. Because of this, singers need feedback from teachers and conductors and must learn to correlate that with how "good singing" feels. With training and experience, dependence on auditory feedback is reduced somewhat, but not eliminated (Mürbe, Pabst, Hofmann, & Sundberg, 2002). The ability to rely more heavily on kinesthetic feedback and muscle memory can be particularly crucial in choral settings. Here the presence of other singers, differences between performance venue and rehearsal space acoustics, and accompanying instruments can mask singers' ability to hear their own voices.
>
> A further example involves development of the singer's formant, as outlined in Chapter 4 on resonance. (The singer's formant is an enhanced set of high frequency overtones.) With proper technique, as described in Chapter 4, singers will start to produce this formant occasionally and will recognize it by hearing a "ring" in the voice. Over time, a singer will subconsciously adjust vocal production and create this formant more consistently by listening for the ring. Learning to produce the singer's formant can be accelerated with visual feedback such as that provided by computer programs such as *VoceVista* (D. Miller, 2008), which display the amplitudes of the various harmonic frequencies produced by a singer.

Howard (1995) has demonstrated that training increases the closed quotient of singers with some breathiness in their voices who wish to achieve a clearer tone. Teachers and conductors can use the onset exercises delineated at the end of this chapter to train their singers. These are particularly helpful for developing the desired degree of glottal closure. The semi-occluded vocal tract exercises discussed later in this chapter are also beneficial.

Method of initiating sound affects glottal tension

How we initiate sound strongly influences how firmly the folds are held together during the subsequent phrase. There are three basic approaches to sound initiation, plus one special method, the "vocal fry onset." These include the following:

- **Coordinated Onset** involves inhaling, then closing the glottis at the same time as exhalation of air. This onset method usually is preferred.
- **Glottal Onset**, involves inhaling, closing the glottis, and then beginning to sing. Glottal tension is eased just enough to cause the vocal folds to vibrate and produce sound.
- **Breathy Onset** occurs when singers inhale and then start to exhale while leaving the glottis open or partially open.
- **Vocal Fry Onset (Growl Onset)** typically involves very relaxed vocal fold closure and high airflow. It is a unique technique used for growls and similar sounds in rock, gospel, and jazz styles and may resolve into a clearer tone with firmer vocal fold closure. Vocal fry is considered in more detail in Chapter 8 on vocal registers.

Coordinated onset should be used for most singing

In most cases a coordinated onset should be used to initiate sound. As noted above, this involves controlling the timing of breath exhalation and closure of the glottis so that they occur simultaneously. The abdominal and intercostal muscles must be engaged just before singing to provide sufficient breath support for the coordinated onset of sound.

Even when somewhat firm vocal fold closure is desired (e.g., for mix belting), a coordinated onset is appropriate. The same holds when a singer desires a lighter vocal fold closure to create an airy sound.

Unconscious physical movement makes consistent onset difficult

Unconscious movement is a common roadblock for singers learning consistent, coordinated onset. For example, some amateur singers may unconsciously move their heads or upper bodies when inhaling and beginning sound. Such movement creates tension (or may be a sign of tension) and distracts from attention to proper technique. These movements can cause singers to revert to what is often a habitual, glottal onset. (We are not speaking here of intentional movement in musical theatre or opera, or *conscious* use of arm/hand gestures to assist learning to use coordinated onset.)

Steps to achieve a coordinated onset

To encourage a coordinated onset, singers should observe the following sequence:

- Imagine both the pitch and vowel to be sung
- Create the space necessary for both the pitch and vowel (Chapter 4 on resonance and Chapter 5 on vowels)
- Fully open the glottis
- Inhale silently without extraneous movement
- Engage the breath support muscles
- Exhale and close the glottis at the same time with the desired firmness of vocal fold closure

As mastery of this process occurs, the detailed steps should not require conscious attention. Singers can then simply think to themselves: "Imagine, Inhale, and Sing" (D. Edwards, personal communication, November 30, 2011).

Some glottal onsets are useful

A glottal onset will improve clarity of diction in all singing styles. For example, when singing "her eyes," it is helpful to use an intentional, soft glottal when singing "eyes" to make the two words distinct. (A soft glottal involves less firm glottal closure than a hard glottal.) A soft-glottal onset can also be helpful for choral groups to ensure rhythmic precision.

- In German, a soft glottal should be employed for words beginning with a vowel within a phrase. If a phrase starts with a vowel, a coordinated onset is more appropriate.

Problems with hard-glottal onsets

There are several problems associated with a hard-glottal onset:

- A hard-glottal onset bursts open the vocal folds, which may create pitch distortions or noise before the sound of the desired note.
- A hard-glottal onset may lead to a harsh sound during the rest of a musical phrase. This is undesirable in most styles. Even when belting, a hard-glottal onset is not appropriate (Gagné, 2015). Rock singers are

often tempted to use this to create a rough sound, but singers may create this effect in a healthier way by using vocal fry (Gagné, 2015). See Chapter 8 on registers for more discussion of vocal fry.
- ❖ When singers use a hard-glottal onset, the amplitude (loudness) of the fundamental frequency is substantially less than with coordinated onset using moderate vocal fold closure. Understanding this issue is particularly crucial for classical sopranos, who depend upon a robust fundamental frequency to create high sound levels at high pitches. (See Chapter 4 on resonance.) Sound intensity above roughly D_5 is determined mostly by the intensity of the fundamental frequency unless the singer also exhibits the singer's formant (Titze, 1992). (Chapter 4 on resonance discusses the singer's formant.)
- ❖ Excessive use of hard-glottal onsets can damage the vocal folds over time due to the high collision forces. A hard-glottal onset creates tremendous friction between the vocal folds, similar to coughing or clearing the throat (Bunch, 1995). In some cases, nodes or polyps on the vocal folds may develop. While some singers can use hard attacks for many years without apparent problems, ultimately there is a price to be paid. Many contemporary pop and rock singers have had to undergo surgery or long periods of being unable to perform (or both). See Chapter 15 on vocal health for more about the relationship between hard-glottal onsets and vocal fold pathology.

Singing with a glottal onset can be an unconscious habit most likely to occur with passages beginning on a vowel. It often occurs when singers do not think about coordinating breath with vocal fold closure. When asked to sing a passage, singers with this habit merely close the folds and then engage the breathing muscles to sing.

Encouraging singers to be aware of their use of a glottal onset and using the exercises outlined at the end of this chapter will go a long way toward eliminating this problem.

Is belting less healthy than classical/legit vocal production?

We raise this topic in this chapter because belting involves firm vocal fold closure, and in the case of chest belting, very firm vocal fold closure along with substantially higher breath pressure. "Raw belting" involves very firm closure and continued exclusive use of the thyroarytenoid muscles as pitch ascends—with very little/no use of the stretching/thinning muscles (cricothyroids). This is what is meant by carrying "chest voice" very high. It is characteristic of early Broadway belters such as Ethel Merman and many modern rock singers.

Wells (2006) describes a more refined, healthier approach to belting used by virtually all modern Broadway belters. It is commonly referred to as mix belt (or simply "mix" in Broadway terminology). It is called mix because it involves mixed-use of thyroarytenoid and cricothyroid control—i.e., mixed voice but with more emphasis on thyroarytenoid control than in classical/legit styles. By using a mixed voice approach, modern female belters can extend their range up to G_5 (Wells, 2006). See Chapter 8 on registers for a more detailed discussion of mixed voice.

❖ Significant health advantages of mix belting are vocal fold compression levels only modestly higher than in classical singing and breath pressure levels that are on par with or only slightly above classical/legit production. In comparison, chest belting involves substantially firmer vocal fold closure and considerably higher breath pressure, the combination of which creates sizeable collision forces between the vocal folds, risking damage in the form of polyps, nodules, and granulomas (Bunch, 1995; Reid, 1983).

Any style of singing can pose vocal health problems

There has been substantial controversy about the effects of belting on vocal health, with some classical voice teachers believing that belting risks vocal fold damage. At the same time, teachers of contemporary styles argue that singers can belt in a healthy manner, as we have described above. Moreover, those involved with contemporary styles often contend that classical singers can develop many of the same problems with vocal fold abnormalities (e.g., cysts, nodules, inflammation). For example, Phyland, Oates, and Greenwood (1999) observed that individuals singing opera, musical theatre, and contemporary commercial styles have a similar prevalence of vocal fold injury.

There may be a greater risk of these problems with belting (particularly chest belting), but this is likely due to insufficient training which would allow singers to avoid the above issues. Indeed, untrained belters (mostly heavy/chest belters) often have little understanding of their vocal production (Schutte and Miller, 1993).

➢ Lawrence (1979) found that belters who have had voice training have better vocal health.

Breathy onset is generally undesirable

Breathy onset can result from a simple failure to coordinate airflow and closure of the vocal folds (i.e., exhaling air before closure of the folds). It can also be due to air flowing too fast and/or under so much pressure that the folds do not come together tightly enough to vibrate properly (Bunch, 1995).

Breathy onset is generally undesirable. It can cause intonation problems, most frequently singing sharp, due to the excessive airflow. Another problem is poor tonal quality due to the noise generated by the onset. The excessive amount of air emitted also impedes the singing of long phrases.

Although breathy onset should be generally avoided, a coordinated onset with light glottal closure to create an airy sound is entirely acceptable in many styles (e.g., pop). The choral texture can occasionally benefit from a coordinated airy onset. For example, it can be useful when a very soft or light entrance (what might be called a "feathered entrance") is needed.

Onset and younger singers

Adolescent singers may have a breathy onset due to an inability to close the posterior one-third of the vocal folds (see Chapter 2 on breathing). The onset exercises at the end of this chapter will help resolve some of this breathiness. Still, not all breathiness can be eliminated in some adolescents until they have further matured.

> ➢ De Bodt, Clement, Wuyts, Borghs, and Van Lierde (2012) studied the effectiveness of various speech rehabilitation exercises in eliminating breathiness, including one semi-occluded vocal tract exercise: humming on [m]. (See the section on SOVT exercises below.) This SOVT exercise is significantly more effective than the other exercises for improving vocal fold closure. We surmise that other SOVT exercises, such as singing through a straw, might be even more useful. The utility of straws is supported by anecdotal experiences of colleagues who direct middle school choruses.

Keep in mind that many younger singers model their vocal technique on artists they admire and may imitate breathy or glottal onsets that they hear. This may not be appropriate for their stage of vocal development. Singers should always endeavor to find their personal sound possibilities and to be conscious of their onset as part of their singing journey.

Release of sound

To finish a phrase without sound distortion (unless desired for stylistic reasons), singers need to be conscious of their release technique. The easiest way to stop the breath without closing the glottis is to inhale at the end of the phrase. With a fresh breath often needed immediately for the next phrase, this is a natural method of release. For phrases ending in consonants, singers should coordinate stopping exhalation with the end of the consonant.

Other methods of release create undesirable effects, unless appropriate for the style of singing:

- Closing the glottis is a common, often unintentional release, but in many styles it is problematic as it produces noise and alters pitch. Sometimes this is referred to as a glottal release, the release equivalent of the glottal onset. Note, however, that in styles such as rock, a glottal release may be a stylistic choice (Edwards, 2014).
- Closing the mouth is a frequently observed method of release on a vowel, but this creates a change in the vowel; unless a diphthong is desired for artistic reasons, it is best avoided. Perceived pitch alteration may also result, as movement compromises the vowel sound.
- When the final note of a phrase involves a vowel, some singers open the glottis while continuing to exhale, creating a breathy sound at the end of the vowel—the release equivalent of a breathy onset. This, too, is undesirable except when planned for artistic reasons.

Proper release also requires knowing *when* to release. Timing is crucial in a choral setting, where everyone must release at the same time. Singers must count time precisely, and conductors must be clear about the proper point of release. It is surprising how few singers, particularly those in amateur choral groups, know when they are supposed to release. Conductors should communicate clearly to their ensembles where the release should occur. For example:

- Put final consonants on the rest that follows
- When a phrase ends on a vowel, inhale on the rest that follows

Semi-occluded vocal tract (SOVT) exercises assist vocal fold vibration

In our first edition, we noted that research (e.g., Titze, 2006) has shown creating resistance to airflow during warm-up exercises supports vocal fold vibration. Semi-occluded vocal tract (SOVT) exercises create the necessary resistance. Recent research has added to our understanding of their effects by showing that backpressure from these exercises alters the vocal fold configuration to a more efficient shape (Titze, 2014). Mounting evidence supporting SOVT exercises leads us to recommend that conductors, teachers, and singers incorporate two or three as part of every warm-up session.

Beneficial effects of SOVT exercises

Benefits of SOVT exercises include:

- More comfortable singing, particularly at high pitches
- Easier register transitions
- Lower breath pressure required to initiate phonation
- Increased volume for the same level of effort (improved efficiency)
- Clearer tone
- Improved resonance

Examples of SOVT exercises

SOVT exercises you are likely familiar with include:

- Singing the voiced consonant [v]—place the top front teeth on the lower lips and hum; also, the voiced consonant [z]
- Lip trills and tongue trills
- Singing nasal consonants such as [n], [m] and [ŋ] ("ng")

Less familiar may be singing through a straw and singing vowels with the fingers over the mouth. (Place lightly closed fingers horizontally and gently resting on the lips; air will flow through the small spaces between the fingers.)

Singing through a straw

Singing through a straw or tube is an SOVT exercise with a long history in speech therapy (including placing the end of the tube in water, which is less practical for singers). More recently, there has been substantial research on the use of straws in warm-ups for singing (e.g., Titze, Finnegan, Laukkanen, and Jaiswal, 2002) and straw exercises have become more widespread, especially among professional singers.

Straws and tubes are particularly useful because the degree of airflow restriction is higher and more consistent compared to many other SOVT methods (Titze, 2006). Smaller diameter straws tend to be more effective than larger diameter straws.

- Typical coffee stirrer straws have an inner diameter of roughly 2.5 mm (3/32 inch) versus a standard soda straw with an inner diameter of approximately 5 mm (3/16 inch).
  - Smith and Titze (2017) found that diameter matters more than length for straws 2.5 mm or larger in diameter. As a practical matter there is little difference for lengths ranging from 10 to 20 cm (4 to 8 inches).

While 2.5 mm straws are difficult to use for many singers, more practical 3.5–4 mm, and 5 mm sizes can be used until they gain proficiency with 2.5 mm straws. Or, singers can use two 2.5 mm straws together.

Gently pucker the lips around a straw and vocalize through it. Hold the straw with one hand to prevent tensing the lips to hold it. Use short slides, scales and arpeggiated triads for initial exploration. (A slide involves moving up or down in pitch continuously, with no discrete steps in between.) Be sure to check that no air is escaping through the nose, diminishing the backpressure created by the straw.

Categories of SOVT exercises

Andrade et al. (2014) conducted one of the most comprehensive studies of various SOVT exercises to date. They group SOVT exercises with respect to whether they involve:

- Continuous air pressure (e.g., humming, fingers over mouth, straws)
- Pulsating air pressure (e.g., tongue trill, lip trill)
- A combination (e.g., tongue trill with fingers over mouth)

Two major benefits of SOVT exercises

Perhaps the most important benefit of SOVT exercises is the support they provide for vocal fold vibration.

- **Assistance with vocal fold vibration.** Some exercises feed energy more effectively to the glottis, thereby assisting vocal fold vibration. (See the text box on mechanisms underlying SOVT exercises.) One indicator of an exercise's ability to do this is the creation of a smaller difference in frequency between the first formant and the frequency of the sung pitch (measured in cycles per second, or Hertz [Hz], honoring the German physicist Heinrich Hertz). (The first formant is an important resonance of the vocal tract, discussed in Chapter 4.) Resonance is improved when this occurs.

Figure 3.7 illustrates the difference between the first formant frequency and the frequency of the sung pitch for most of the studied exercises, averaging over males and females (adapted from Andrade et al., 2014). The straw exercise emerges as most effective at narrowing the difference relative to normal phonation. (Straw was 12.5 cm (4.9 inches) long and had an internal diameter of 4 mm.)

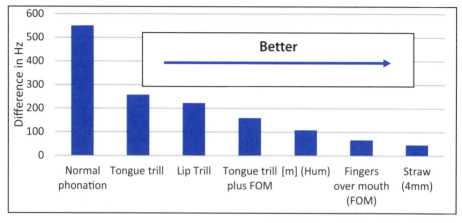

Figure 3.7. Effectiveness of various SOVT exercises relative to normal phonation. The measure is the mean difference in frequency (Hz) between the first formant and the sung pitch.

A second benefit is the possible therapeutic massaging effect of pulsating air pressure on the vocal folds. (Think of how a muscle massage involves pressing upon the muscle and subsequent release of pressure.)

- ❖ **"Massage" effect.** Exercises with pulsating pressure may increase the variability in the percentage of time the vocal folds are closed during a vibration cycle (closed quotient). One measure of variability is the range of the closed quotient—the difference between the maximum and minimum closed quotient. The more extensive the range, the more there is thought to be a massage effect on the vocal folds.
  - ➢ Andrade et al. (2014) found that pulsating/combination exercises have double the massage effect of continuous SOVT exercises.

Choosing among SOVT exercises

Based on the work by Andrade et al. and research by Maxfield, Titze, Hunter, and Kapsner-Smith (2015), the best continuous air pressure exercises are straw, fingers over mouth, and [v]. As there are no significant differences among the pulsating/combination exercises, there is no reason to prefer any one to any other for a massage effect. Nonetheless, studies show substantial variation from one participant to another, so conductors, teachers, and singers should experiment to find which exercises work best for them (though straws work well for almost everyone).

While humming (and other nasal consonants) may have some utility for supporting vocal fold vibration, they may not provide some of the other desirable effects of SOVT exercises described in the text box on mechanisms underlying their usefulness. Humming produces low air pressure within the mouth because it allows air to escape through the nasal passages, "possibly calling into question their inclusion in the SOVT category of vocal exercises" (Maxfield et al., 2015, p. 91).

Suggested order of SOVT exercises

As a general rule, SOVT exercises should start with those involving higher levels of airflow restriction, proceeding toward sustained vowels that have the highest level of oral restriction ([i] and [u]). The idea is to transfer vocal tract training from exercises that provide the most potent support for vocal fold vibration to normal singing. SOVT exercises should precede other exercises, but if you are having difficulty with a passage during rehearsal of repertoire, it may be useful to "sing" the passage using an SOVT technique such as the straw (Nix & Simpson, 2008). In this context, you may find passages requiring agility to be easier after rehearsal through a straw.

Here is a suggested order:

1) Small diameter straw (2.5–4 mm internal diameter)
2) A restricted air flow, voiced consonant such as [v] or [z]
3) Humming ([m], [n], [ŋ])
4) Lip trills, tongue trills
5) [i] or [u]

It may well be impractical to perform all these exercises in any given practice session or choral rehearsal. At a minimum, we suggest a straw exercise, lip or tongue trills, and [i] or [u]. If a straw is not available, use [v]; this produces slightly less pressure within the mouth than a small straw. While studies of SOVT effectiveness often involve 10 to 15 minutes of these exercises, our experience is that singers also benefit from just a few minutes of singing through a straw.

Singing through a straw is helpful if your voice is tired (recall its use in voice therapy). Using this device for cool-down after rehearsal of repertoire may also be beneficial. Finally, it is worth noting that using straws for a warm-up before going on stage is a quiet method that is less bothersome to fellow performers. It also allows singers to practice when traveling without disturbing others.

Carryover effects of SOVT exercises

Research shows that beneficial effects of SOVT exercises continue during singing of repertoire.

- Singers who perform straw phonation, lip trills, and tongue trills have increased sound levels after a brief rest period following performance of the three exercises (Dargin & Searl, 2015).
- Imaging studies find that favorable modifications of the vocal tract continue after straw phonation (e.g., Guzman et al., 2013; Vampola, Laukkanen, Horacek & Svec, 2011).
- A study of a women's choir found a significant increase in sound level after straw phonation (J. N. Manternach, Schloneger & Maxfield, 2019) and a study of an SATB chorus found that the chorus was perceived to sound better after use of a straw exercise (J. N. Manternach & Daugherty, 2019).

We speculate that singers who use SOVT exercises over time will likely experience cumulative gains in vocal quality. They may find improvements in their speaking voices as well, including a clearer, more resonant tone and less vocal fatigue.

Physical mechanisms underlying effects of SOVT exercises

Straw and resonance tube exercises produce physical changes in the vocal tract (e.g., Guzman et al., 2013). Two are of particular significance:

- **A narrower epilarynx tube above the glottis.** Since the glottis can be considered a thin tube through which air flows, narrowing of the epilarynx above the glottis helps to create an improved coupling of these two areas of the vocal tract. Titze (e.g., Titze, 2006) defines this improved coupling as better matching of the acoustic impedance of the glottis and the area above the glottis. Impedance matching increases sound amplitude at certain frequencies and allows for greater feedback of energy to the vocal folds (Wolfe, Garnier & Smith, 2009). This further improves vocal efficiency. (See Chapter 4 for a more detailed discussion of these issues.)
- **Alteration of glottal shape.** Titze (2014) shows that the backpressure created by a straw exercise helps to keep the upper surface of the vocal folds somewhat separated, creating a more rectangular glottal shape. This better alignment has the lowest phonation threshold pressure requirement, further easing vocal production and increasing its efficiency.

Onset and release exercises

Experiencing different methods of onset

Richard Miller (1996) suggests the following sequence of phrases to help singers experience the basic methods of onset, and particularly, to help them learn a coordinated onset. (He suggests speaking them; we recommend singing them):

Ha, Ha, Ha, Ha—linger on the "h." This gives singers the sense of a breathy onset.

Uh, Uh, Uh, Uh—close the glottis and then sing, lingering on the explosive initiation (almost like a grunt). This gives singers a sense of the glottal onset.

Between these two extremes is the coordinated onset:

Ah, Ah, Ah, Ah—we find images such as pulling a tissue gently from the box, or a scarf from out of a magician's hat to be helpful. Performing these physical actions as you sing each "ah" is particularly helpful. An extension of this might be to imagine that the tissue box is located just above the navel and performing the gesture as each "ah" is sung.

For kids and everyone! Onset/connection of breath with sound

Fffff ------------------ ah --

Fffff-ah—begin by inhaling slowly, then exhale on [f] over four beats moving seamlessly into [ɑ] or [a] as indicated. Also, try ascending and descending scales after the initial [f]. Try changing the first consonant to [s], "th," "wh," and/or changing the vowel that follows. (Adapted from Cooksey, 1999)

Exercise to vary breathiness

Sing any pitch in the middle range on [ɑ] or [a] using light vocal fold closure, creating an airy or breathy sound. If this is difficult, trying using an "h" to start the sound and keep lots of air moving as you exhale but ultimately aim for a coordinated onset. As you sustain the pitch, gradually firm the vocal fold closure to reduce the amount of air in the sound, creating a clearer tone quality. Try the exercise in reverse, starting with firmer vocal fold closure.

Good onset, good phrase!

To build upon the concept that a good onset affects how a phrase is sung, sing the same note on [e] three times with the goal of a coordinated onset. (Your first two attempts may be breathy or glottal, but by the third try, you will hopefully achieve a coordinated onset.) Immediately following the third attempt, sing a simple five-note ascending and descending scale. Once you can consistently coordinate onset, sing the exercise without the "false starts." Notice how a supported, free sound can continue through a phrase. Use a variety of vowels, particularly [i], which is one of the most difficult vowels to sing with a coordinated onset.

Encouraging coordinated onset

The following sequence provides another method to promote a coordinated onset. Choose a pitch in the middle of the singers' range. As an advanced exercise, choose a pitch in the upper portion of the range. Singers should:

- ❖ Imagine both the pitch and vowel to be sung
- ❖ Inhale without extraneous movement
- ❖ Engage the breath support muscles
- ❖ Exhale and close the glottis at the same time

Sustained notes to experiment with glottal resistance

Cottrell (2010) recommends the use of sustained tones with small changes in pitch during warm-ups to allow experimentation with both breath pressure and glottal resistance as a means of improving tonal quality. We would add that this technique also allows experimenting with how both factors affect dynamic level. The following exercise is adapted from Cottrell. *In measures three through six, experiment with breath pressure only, keeping glottal resistance constant; then experiment only with firmness of glottal closure to see how this adjustment affects dynamic level.*

Quiet head and body

Inhale and exhale as suggested in Chapter 2 on breathing. Try to keep the body relaxed without any unnecessary tension.

Add a simple vocal exercise (e.g., triad or scale passage), being conscious of the head and body during the breath cycle, onset, and release.

Teachers and conductors should monitor their singers to check periodically for any extraneous, unintentional motion. Such motion is often unconscious and thus outside of the awareness of singers. Calling their attention to the problem can help them to self-monitor.

Coordinated release

Sing an ascending triad and then a descending triad on any vowel. On beat four, finish the phrase with a clear 't' consonant. Allow the consonant to finish your exhalation and then inhale for the next phrase. Be sure to initiate the top note of the descending triad with a coordinated onset.

Repeat the exercise with no consonant. On beat four, stop the sound by closing the glottis to get a sense of a hard release. Repeat the exercise, this time ending the sound by breathing in (inhaling) on beat four. This is the coordinated release. The bonus is that you have already inhaled to sing the next phrase.

Repeat, moving up by half steps (leaving out the hard release and when using a consonant, varying it as desired).

Lip trill SOVT exercise

Lip trills involve using breath pressure to make the lips vibrate against each other—like the "motorboat" sound a child would make. *Start to say the consonant [t] but with the lips gently together, then move the tongue out of the way of the opening of the mouth and exhale with strong, steady breath pressure, allowing the lips to vibrate. If the lips don't vibrate, try gently squeezing the cheeks (to relax the lips more) or stretching them (to tighten the lips). Once the lips are vibrating, try adding a sung pitch and then varying it. Then use a lip trill with different melodic patterns.*

Chapter 4: Resonance

The human voice is capable of a fantastic range of sounds. A key to understanding how we create those sounds is the concept of resonance. Simply stated, **resonance is the tendency of a cavity (e.g., the mouth) to reinforce sounds at specific frequencies or ranges of frequencies.**

Improving and controlling resonance allows both solo and choral singers to:

- Deliver a desired tonal color
- Sing with less effort when unamplified—sound level can be increased without increased breath pressure
- Be perceived as having better intonation
- Achieve dynamic contrasts
- Negotiate the higher and lower pitches of a singer's range

Intentional use of the resonating chambers is an essential goal of the accomplished solo singer. While some assume that mindful resonance is not as crucial for choral singers, an ensemble of singers with excellent resonance will invariably produce a more satisfying and flexible sound. Furthermore, understanding the factors affecting resonance will enable conductors and singers to alter tonal color according to musical styles and artistic preferences.

Superior resonance improves tonal quality and vocal efficiency

As noted, excellent resonance control creates a broader tonal palette and allows unamplified singers to produce higher sound levels with less effort. How this occurs can be easily understood by thinking of a musical instrument such as a trumpet. The lips of the trumpet player vibrating in the mouthpiece generate only a low-intensity buzz, much like the vocal folds (Fleming, 2005), but the hollow body of the trumpet resonates at select frequencies to produce a rich tone at a much higher sound level (amplitude). Similarly, the hollow physiological structures of the vocal tract (the epilarynx, the pharynx, and the mouth) resonate to produce an improved tone and higher sound levels. These structures also act as an acoustic filter, dampening some frequencies.

Recent research indicates that the vocal tract does more than amplify and filter sound—when appropriately configured, the resonating structures of the vocal tract can feed energy back to the vocal folds, enhancing vibration (e.g., Titze, 2008b). (Recall Figure 3.1.)

❖ Note that vocal resonance does not provide higher sound levels by amplifying sound like an electronic amplifier increases sound level. Singers with good resonance are louder because they are more efficient in converting breath energy to sound.

How singers shape vocal tract structures and alter the firmness of the tissues lining the vocal tract affect the frequencies that are amplified, as well as the sound level of those frequencies. Adjustments of important vocal tract structures to improve resonance and control timbre are discussed later in this chapter.

Fundamental frequency and higher harmonics

Note to readers: For this edition we have adopted the notation system for fundamental frequency, harmonics, and formants recommended by Titze et al. (2015).

When the vocal folds are brought together and breath is exhaled, the folds vibrate in a complex manner, producing:

❖ **The fundamental frequency (f_o).** This is the frequency associated with the sung pitch. For example, A below middle-C (A_3) involves vocal fold vibration at a frequency of 220 cycles per second, abbreviated as "220 Hz."
❖ **Harmonic frequencies.** These frequencies are multiples of the fundamental frequency at higher levels. For example, when C_3 is sung (fundamental frequency of 131 Hz), harmonic frequencies (overtones) are generated at multiples of 131 vibrations per second (262, 393, 524, 655, 786, 917, etc.). The energy associated with the overtones declines substantially as frequency increases. Without amplification of some of the overtone frequencies, a singer would mostly produce a fundamental frequency and lack the richness imparted by higher harmonics. Resonance provides the amplification necessary for a richer sound.

Figure 4.1 illustrates a few harmonics generated by C_3. Note that the fundamental frequency is considered to be the first harmonic; thus the first overtone is the second harmonic.

Our nervous system interprets the fundamental frequency and associated harmonics as a single pitch. The harmonics emphasized by one singer versus another are perceived as variations in timbre.

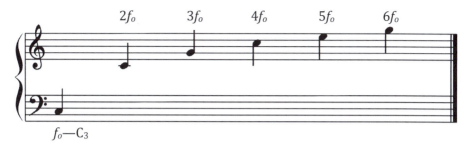

Figure 4.1 Some harmonics generated from singing C_3

Singers differ in the amplitudes (sound level) of the fundamental and higher harmonic frequencies produced by vocal fold vibration (Sundberg, 1987). The following factors also affect the sound level of harmonic frequencies:

❖ With firmer glottal closure, some higher harmonics usually have a higher amplitude than the fundamental frequency (f_o).
❖ Chest voice produces more high-amplitude, higher harmonic frequencies than head voice. In head voice, the fundamental frequency has the highest sound level. (Chest and head voice are examined in more detail in Chapter 8 on registers.)

Singers differ as well in the physiological structure of their vocal tracts above the vocal folds. These structural differences affect the frequencies that are amplified and degree of amplification. This is why no two singers sound entirely alike. While physiological differences cannot be changed, all singers can adjust and enhance their voices by learning to alter their vocal tract configuration.

Structure of the vocal tract

A basic understanding of the major components of the vocal tract and how singers can control them is essential to develop and gain mastery over timbre and sound level. (See Figure 4.2 for an illustration of the vocal tract.) The basic components include:

❖ Larynx
❖ Oral Pharynx (throat)
❖ Nasal Pharynx
❖ Mouth

As noted in Chapter 3, the **larynx** contains the vocal folds and the muscles and cartilage that control them. It is suspended from the hyoid bone, which is also connected to the tongue. This connection explains why tongue position and tension can affect laryngeal function. (Figures 3.2 and 3.3 show the suspension of the larynx from the hyoid bone; Figure 4.2 illustrates the connection of the hyoid bone to the base of the tongue.)

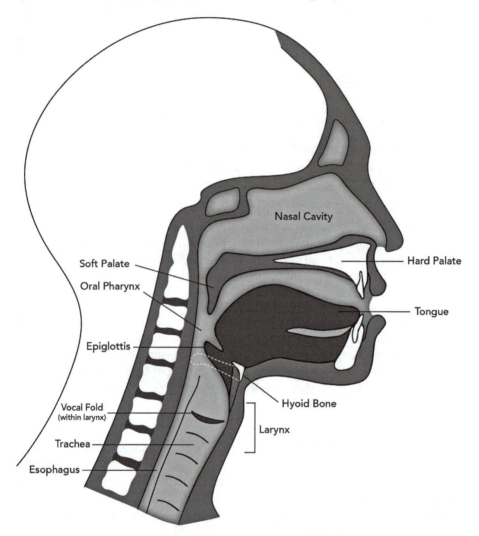

Figure 4.2 Illustration of the vocal tract

The **oral pharynx** extends from the epiglottis (the flap of tissue that folds over the space above the larynx to prevent food from entering the lungs) up to and including the back of the mouth. Jaw position has a substantial effect upon the frequencies at which the pharynx resonates. The area just above the larynx (technically known as the *epilaryngeal tube* or *epilarynx*) is thought to be a resonating space for high frequencies. (See Figure 4.5.)

The **mouth** is also an important resonator. As can be seen in Figure 4.2, the tongue occupies the majority of the mouth. Changes in tongue position affect the size and shape of the cavity, which in turn alters the frequency of resonation.

❖ When singing vowels, the tip of the tongue should rest against the lower front teeth (the lower incisors). The bottom portion of the tongue tip should just touch the gum line, as illustrated.

The **nasal pharynx** provides the resonance necessary for the production of nasal vowels (e.g., French nasals) and nasal consonants (e.g., [m], [n]). It extends from the lower portion of the soft palate through the nasal cavities. Still, for most situations, regardless of singing style, it is not a resonator and should be mostly closed off. Closure of the nasal pharynx is accomplished by raising the soft palate, closing the nasal port. The soft palate (also called the *velum*) may be lowered slightly in many contemporary styles to reduce the size of the oral pharynx and brighten the sound without noticeable nasality. Moreover, in some instances, nasality may be a stylistic choice to create a unique effect (e.g., for certain musical theatre characters). See the text box later in this chapter for further discussion of nasal resonance.

Experiment with nasal resonance by singing a scale. Pinch your nostrils with your fingers to prevent exhalation through your nose. If you experience a change in the sound, then some air has been escaping through the nose.

Resonance and formants

Topics relating to formants are among the most difficult to understand in the fields of vocal science and vocal pedagogy. Nonetheless, gaining an understanding of formants is essential to know how to:

❖ Alter vocal tract configurations to have a flexible voice in terms of timbral choices.
❖ Alter the amplitude of various harmonics, though, as noted earlier and expanded upon below, this is also affected by firmness of glottal closure.
❖ Modify vowels to change formant frequencies to improve the production of pitches at the upper end of a singer's range (and for some females in the lower portion of their range). This is examined further in Chapter 5 on vowels.
❖ Provide stable and consistent resonance throughout the range of voice for classical/legit styles (stable register transitions—see Chapter 8).

Formants amplify harmonics just below the frequency of the formant

The vocal folds generate many harmonics, but only some are amplified. The vocal tract cavities resonate most strongly within specific ranges of frequencies known as *formants*. **Formants are thus the resonances of the vocal tract,** and the harmonic frequencies that are the most amplified are the ones that are near but under the formant frequencies (Titze, Worley & Story, 2011). (Technically, a resonance of the vocal tract and a formant of the vocal tract are slightly different concepts, but for simplicity we will treat them the same.)

Because we can adjust the vocal tract, we can change the frequencies of the resonating chambers. In contrast, non-vocal instruments generally have a more fixed timbre determined by the shape of the resonance chambers and the materials employed in their construction.

When a harmonic is in the vicinity of, but below a formant, vocal tract resonance feeds energy back to the vocal folds, assisting their vibration as mentioned above. Singers can use this knowledge to increase sound level without additional effort and, as discussed in Chapter 5 on vowels, to assist with movement through pitches in more challenging areas of a singer's range. If a harmonic is allowed to cross through the formant frequency as pitch ascends, there will be an unfavorable feedback effect on the vocal folds leading to breaks and/or sudden pitch changes.

Singers typically do not have to do anything to create generally favorable vocal tract conditions until the pitch (or higher harmonic) approaches the speech value of a vowel's first formant, discussed below. Below this frequency the vocal tract is "inertant," which is favorable for vocal production (Titze et al., 2011). (Detailed discussion of inertance is beyond the scope of this book.) In the example of formant tuning for sopranos outlined in the text box, you can see that a soprano singing [e] does not need to change the first formant's frequency for notes below roughly D_5. Nonetheless, in classical singing, a soprano may wish to begin what is called *vowel modification* a few notes below to change the first formant frequency and avoid a sudden change in timbre. For lower voices the second or a higher harmonic often comes into play at this point (e.g., altos and tenors as they approach D_4). In contemporary styles the pitch at which vowel modification begins is more of an artistic choice as there is no expectation of consistent timbre.

> ➤ In practice there is some evidence that classical female singers make few changes to vowels until approaching the D_5 area.

The sound level of various harmonics is also affected by firmness of vocal fold closure and vocal register

Proximity to a formant is not the only factor affecting the sound level of the fundamental and higher harmonic frequencies. The firmness of vocal fold closure also has a significant impact. For example, firmer vocal fold closure, as occurs while belting, substantially diminishes the amplitude of the fundamental frequency and significantly increases the amplitude of the second and third harmonics, contributing to a brassier sound compared to classical/legit production.

> ➢ Guzman et al. (2015) studied females singing a variety of contemporary styles. They find higher amplitudes (greater sound levels) in the frequency region encompassing higher harmonics than in the area of the fundamental frequency. The difference in amplitude is most extensive in rock style where there is very firm glottal closure. The difference is less in jazz and least in pop styles of singing. Thus, rock has a generally brighter and louder sound than these other styles.
> ➢ Mix belt has a higher amplitude fundamental frequency than chest belt (Flynn, Trudeau & Johnson, in press). This is due to less firm glottal closure in mix belt compared to chest belt. It creates a more balanced, though still bright timbre.
> ➢ When airy production is employed, as in some pop singing, the general volume level is lower and higher harmonics have very low amplitudes. A simpler sound is created. The breathier the production, the more this is true.

More generally, regardless of style, chest voice (lower register) produces higher overall volume levels as well as higher volume levels for the higher harmonics, compared to head voice. This is due to more substantial vertical movement of the vocal folds in chest voice. Head voice emphasizes the fundamental frequency (Miller & Schutte, 2005).

The most important formants and their frequency ranges

Authorities differ in formant enumeration and labeling (listing anywhere from three to five major formants). Our experience and review of the literature suggest four to five significant formants.

The first three formants' frequencies are largely a function of the sung vowel. Changes in jaw, tongue, and lip position associated with different vowels alter the shape and volume of the vocal tract, naturally affecting the frequencies at which it resonates. The amplitudes of these formants are affected in part by how singers shape the resonating tubes/cavities.

- Thus, many resonance issues are linked inextricably with vowel formation. We discuss vowels in more detail in the following chapter but will examine in this chapter the formant frequencies of various vowels and some stylistic differences in both formant frequencies and amplitudes.

The first three formants are as follows:

- **The lowest formant (F_1)** is related mostly to the resonance of the pharynx, the largest cavity in the vocal tract. Larger chambers resonate at lower frequencies. F_1 is particularly responsive to lowering of the rear portion of the jaw. As jaw lowering increases, the volume of the pharynx closest to the larynx reduces, and the frequency of F_1 rises (Sundberg, 1977). In the range of speaking fundamental frequencies, F_1 is normally between 250 Hz and 800 Hz (B_3 to G_5) and higher for females than for males. (There are also individual differences.) See Figure 4.3. Thus, F_1 is highest when singing [ɑ] as the jaw is lowered most for this vowel. F_1 can rise above 800 Hz with further jaw lowering. A soprano singing [ɑ] can have a first formant at 1400 Hz with a substantially lowered jaw. The first formant dominates and accounts for much of the sound level in the lower (chest) register (Neumann, Schunda, Hoth, & Euler, 2005). It also dominates in chestmix (see Chapter 8 on registers concerning chestmix and headmix).
- **The next highest formant (F_2)** is most closely related to the resonance of the mouth, the second-largest cavity in the vocal tract. In the range of speaking fundamental frequencies, F_2 is generally between 800 Hz and 2200 Hz. (G_5 to D_7-flat) and is higher for females than for males. The frequency of resonance varies with tongue position and, to some extent, with lip shape. For example, F_2 is at its highest frequency when the highest point of the tongue (the arch or "hump of the tongue") is forward and the mouth opening is wide, as with [i]. General movement of the tongue in a forward direction or a general raising of the tongue can also contribute to raising the frequency of the second formant, as this narrows the area between the tongue and the palate (Hanayama, Camargo, Tsuji, & Pinho, 2009). In contrast, when singing [u], the highest point of the tongue is toward the rear of the mouth and the mouth opening is narrow, which lengthens the vocal tract. All of this lowers F_2, explaining why [u] sounds "darker" than the other vowels. Chapter 5 on vowels addresses these topics in greater detail.
- The source of the **third formant (F_3)** is less clear. Some vocal scientists say that it relates to the amount of space between the front of the tongue and the lower incisors (Sundberg, 1987; Zemlin, 1988). Others argue that

it is one of the resonances of the larynx (see below under discussion of the singer's formant). Since tongue position affects the larynx, the two perspectives are not incompatible. F_3 ranges typically from about 2200 Hz to 3000 Hz (D_7–flat to F_7#). F_3 is highest with [i] and lowest with [u]. [i] is thus the "brightest" of all vowels because the associated F_2 and F_3 formant frequencies are highest.

The fourth and fifth formants are involved with the "singer's formant." This is discussed below.

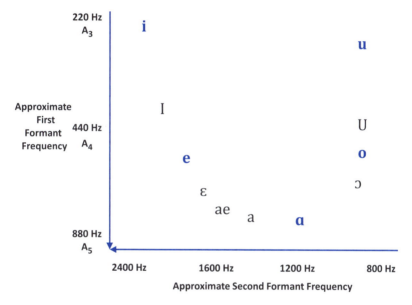

Figure 4.3 Approximate formant frequencies for common English vowels (average of males and females; frequency scales inverted to follow the Vowel Spectrum chart in Chapter 5)

Longer vocal tract lowers all formant frequencies

Formant frequencies are also affected by the length of the vocal tract from the larynx to the lip opening. If the larynx is low and the lips are protruding, the volume of the vocal tract is greater, and all formant frequencies will be lower, leading to a darker, mellower sound. Conversely, if the larynx is elevated and the corners of the lips are pulled back, the vocal tract is shortened, all formant frequencies are raised, and the sound is brighter.

Thus, vocal tract length becomes another stylistic choice. For example, a shorter vocal tract is desired in belting to help create a brighter sound. In classical and to some extent, in legit styles, a longer vocal tract is more desirable.

> ### Example of formant amplification of harmonics
>
> Above C_5–D_5, classically trained sopranos use the first formant to amplify the fundamental frequency (the first harmonic). They accomplish this by lowering the *rear* of the jaw as pitch ascends from this range. At very high pitches they add a slight smile (to shorten the vocal tract and further raise F_1). Singers should make gradual adjustments before the point where modification is absolutely necessary, but they should be careful not to over modify at lower pitches. There are three reasons for lowering the rear of the jaw as pitch ascends:
>
> ❖ Fundamental frequency is amplified somewhat when it is just below the first formant
> ❖ Pitch instabilities are avoided by preventing crossover of the first formant
> ❖ Some get a boost in higher harmonics and reduction in required airflow (Rothenberg & Schutte, 2016)
>
> The example below shows that, for the vowel [e], the first formant frequency for the spoken vowel roughly coincides with D_5 (F_1 is shown in parentheses). As classical or legit sopranos ascend the scale below, they should gradually lower the jaw to keep the first formant just above the sung pitch (f_o). Otherwise, vocal instability may occur. First formant frequencies vary by vowel (Figure 4.3). For example, F_1 is much lower for [i] and [u], necessitating lowering the jaw at lower pitches.
>
>
> Ay [e] —————————————————————————
>
> A soprano singing in a belting style should approach this situation differently. With substantial rear jaw lowering, [e] starts to sound more like [ae] or [a]. But when belting, more natural-sounding vowels are desirable for greater intelligibility and less of an operatic sound. For this style, F_1 can be raised by a modest lowering of the jaw and shortening of the vocal tract by opening the mouth with a broad smile and allowing the larynx to rise somewhat. This strategy works only up to about G_5, which is the rough upper limit for mixed belting (Titze, Worley & Story, 2011).

Resonance 73

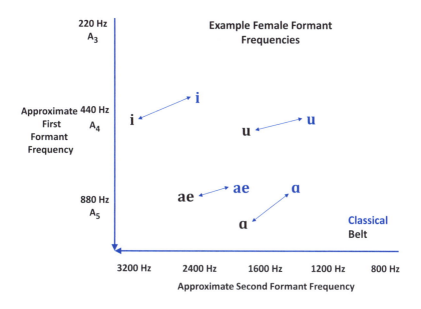

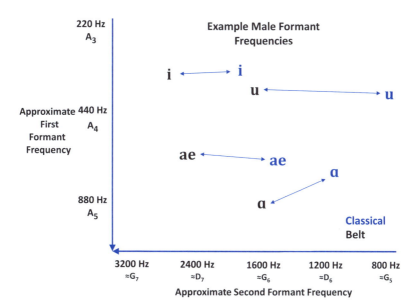

Figure 4.4. Examples of differences in formant frequencies between classical and belt styles

Differences in first and second formant frequencies between classical and contemporary styles

Timbre (tonal color) resulting from the physical alterations of the resonating chambers is often described in terms of degree of darkness and degree of brightness. In classical singing, the goal is typically a combination of both a darker, warmer sound and a brighter, brilliant sound. This is known as "chiaroscuro." In musical theatre and pop/rock styles, the goal is typically a brighter sound. Nonetheless, in some circumstances contemporary singers may choose a darker tone for artistic reasons.

Story, Titze, and Hoffman (2001) conducted one of the earliest studies of vocal tract shape and formants comparing a classical style (labeled by the authors as "yawny") and belting (labeled by the authors as "twangy"—likely mix belting). While the study involved only one female and one male due to the need to perform MRI imaging for a portion of the research, the results are consistent with many later studies. Figure 4.4 (adapted from Story et al. data) illustrates how formant frequencies differ between classical and mix belt styles. Both the female and male participants show a sizeable difference between the two styles for the second formant frequency—it is substantially higher for the belt style, creating a brighter sound. For the female there is also a slightly higher F_1 frequency for the belt style, particularly for [ɑ]. For the male this is only true for [ɑ], however, another study shows that males also tend to raise F_1 near the top of their range, particularly for chest belting and to some extent for mix (Bourne, Garnier, & Samson, 2016).

❖ A study of rock, pop, soul, and Swedish dance band (a relaxed pop style) reveals more variation in the first formant frequency than in the second formant frequency. Borch and Sundberg (2011) found that rock has the highest F_1 and F_2 frequencies, with soul having the lowest F_1 and F_2 values (creating a warmer, deeper sound). In between is pop with a higher F_1 and dance band with a lower F_1.

Singer's Formant

The singer's formant is often called the "ring" of the voice. It is mostly used to achieve a higher sound level in classical singing, where voices are unamplified. Nonetheless, elite belters often exhibit such a formant (e.g., LeBorgne, 2001). This frequency, however, may be higher than in classical singing (at the level of a "speaker's formant").

Belters do not need to rely on a singer's formant because of firm glottal closure with higher breath pressure and use of chest voice or chestmix. Also, belters almost always sing with amplification. Nonetheless, a "ring" in the voice contributes to improved tonal quality.

When a singer configures the vocal tract appropriately, the frequency of F_3 rises to create a cluster with the higher frequency formants, F_4 and F_5. The cluster is the area of the singer's formant. This clustering can create substantial sound intensity at higher harmonic frequencies (e.g., Sundberg, 1974).

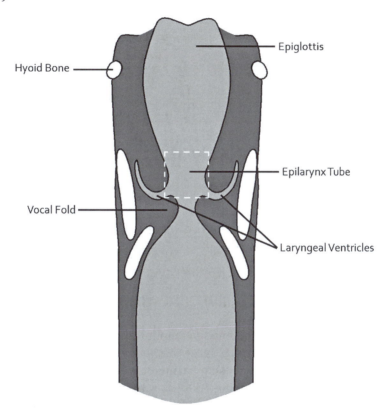

Figure 4.5 Cross-sectional illustration of the larynx with a focus on the epilarynx tube and the ventricles

The singer's formant is thought to be generated in small cavities of the larynx just above the vocal folds, an area known as the epilarynx tube. The epilarynx tube extends from the vocal folds about two to three centimeters into the laryngeal vestibule and includes portions of the laryngeal ventricles (Titze & Worley, 2009; see Figure 4.5).

A comfortably low larynx narrows the epilarynx tube (see Figure 4.5), facilitating resonance at the singer's formant frequencies when the pharynx is sufficiently wide. If the pharynx is somewhat narrower than in classical singing, it can produce the higher-frequency speaker's formant, as noted above.

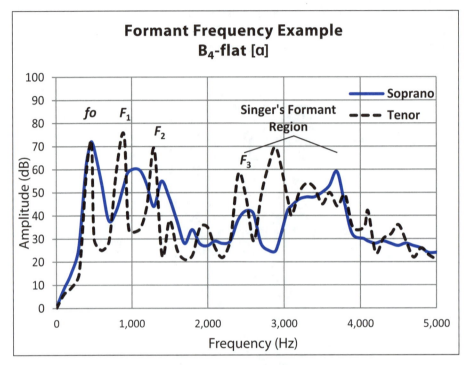

Figure 4.6 Illustration of formants

If the singer's formant has high enough amplitude, the voice can carry above musical instruments, or even a large orchestra. The orchestra's sound energy declines rapidly at increasing harmonic frequencies. Specifically, the orchestra's amplitude in the 2500–4000 Hz range will be less than that of a singer who can effectively produce the singer's formant.

➢ Vennard (1967) believes that even slight production of the singer's formant can be beneficial because the outer ear chamber of the listener is resonant in this range.
➢ Sundberg (1999) argues that sopranos depend more upon the amplitude of the fundamental frequency than that of the singer's formant. At higher pitches, the harmonic frequencies are more widely spaced, making it hard for the singer's formant to match the harmonics generated by the vocal folds. Sopranos do, however, benefit from a strong fundamental or first formant, as listeners' ears are highly sensitive to high soprano pitches. However, sopranos singing in

their chest register and in chestmix will typically exhibit and benefit from a singer's formant, or speaker's formant, as the case may be.

The amplitude of the singer's formant does not need to be extremely high to increase the perceived volume of the singer's voice.

> Hunter and Titze (2005) concur that human hearing is most sensitive in the area of 3000–4000 Hz. A classical singer with a singer's formant can achieve sound levels 15 decibels (dB) higher than those not using such a technique.
> An increase of just 6 dB is perceived to be twice as loud as a reference sound (Warren, 1970). Thus, with a singer's formant, singers can achieve dramatically increased sound levels. (Note that some say 3 dB is a doubling of perceived loudness, but this is a doubling of power in amplified signals. It is not a doubling of perceived sound level.)

The frequency of the singer's formant varies little according to pitch or vowel but does vary by gender and voice type (it is highest in sopranos). This formant (or the most prominent formant of the F_3, F_4, F_5 cluster) falls in the range of 2500 to 3200 Hz for male voices, around 3200 Hz for contraltos and mezzos, and up to 4000 Hz for sopranos (R. Miller, 1996). Elite child solo singers also exhibit a singer's formant around 4000 Hz (Howard, Williams & Herbst, 2014). Formant graphs for a tenor and soprano in Figure 4.6 also show very clearly that the most prominent formant in the singer's formant region is at a substantially higher frequency for sopranos than tenors. The higher formant frequencies of the soprano explain why a soprano sounds different from a tenor singing the same note.

Singer's formant and ensemble blend

The singer's formant can be helpful when an ensemble is singing with an orchestra. Some argue, however, that the singer's formant is not desirable in choral singing on the basis that it can be destructive to blend if only some singers have this formant. It is true that in many groups there will be a mixture of singers who do and do not exhibit a singer's formant. A conductor who perceives a vocal color standing out excessively due to a high-amplitude singer's formant can ask the singer to be more sensitive to surrounding singers and reduce the volume. Alternatively, a conductor can work with other singers to enhance their singer's formant. This should, however, rarely be a problem because studies show that both male and female singers decrease the amplitude of the singer's formant when attempting to blend in a choral setting, compared to a solo setting. Singers are particularly likely to dampen this formant when singing softly (Rossing, Sundberg, & Ternström, 1986). See Chapter 12 for more discussion of choral blend issues.

Adjusting the larynx

Controlling the vertical position of the larynx

Various muscles above and below the larynx affect its vertical position. Muscles above the larynx relate to swallowing, while those below the larynx are associated with inhalation and yawning. The dynamic balance between these muscle groups determines the position of the larynx (McKinney, 2005).

When the muscles above the larynx (constrictor or swallowing muscles) are contracted, the larynx will tend to rise.

Test this by gently placing a finger on the larynx (Adam's apple) and then swallow.

When the muscles below the larynx (yawning muscles) are contracted, the larynx is pulled downward.

Now initiate a yawn (but avoid a full yawn) and feel the larynx descend.

For classical and legit singing a comfortably low larynx is desirable. For other styles of singing a higher laryngeal position may be necessary. Still, the key is to make this a conscious choice—if singers unconsciously raise the larynx as they sing higher pitches, they may experience instability in the voice.

- Without sufficient breath pressure on high pitches, singers may unconsciously use the constrictor muscles to push air through the vocal tract, thereby raising the larynx.
- Do not assume that belting requires a raised larynx. Only heavy chest belting involves a substantially elevated larynx. With mix belting the larynx should remain flexible and buoyant; it may elevate slightly in the upper part of the range.

Vennard (1967) recommends singing classical style in the position of an incipient yawn to cause the larynx to descend by reflex action.

> Nair, Nair and Reishofer (2016) show that the rear of the mandible (lower jawbone) releases from the temporomandibular joint in just the first 10% of a yawn. It lowers the larynx, elongates the pharynx, and places the floor of the tongue lower in the mouth, all of which allows for greater resonance. Resonance is further enhanced when the entire mandible is lowered (in the back and front).
> Mercer and Lowell (in press) also show that an incipient yawn widens the vocal tract by creating greater mouth and pharynx volume.

- Vennard suggests placing a finger gently on the larynx as an exercise. Feel it drop upon an approach to a yawn and monitor its position as singing begins so that it does not rise excessively. Do <u>not</u> use your finger to control the position of the larynx.
- As noted in Chapter 2 on breathing, Sundberg (1993) has observed a phenomenon he calls "tracheal pull," which results from correct inhalation technique. The diaphragm descends, pulling on the trachea, and in so doing, causes the larynx to descend further. This can help narrow the epilarynx tube, enhancing the singer's formant.

Adjusting the oral pharynx

Recall that the oral pharynx extends from the epiglottis (which covers the larynx during swallowing) to the soft palate (velum) at the back of the mouth. Enlarging the oral pharynx improves its resonance characteristics for classical/legit styles (Vennard, 1967).

The oral pharynx can be enlarged by:

- Raising the soft palate. (See Figure 4.2. The soft palate is drawn in a lowered position in this illustration to show the opening to the nasal passages. Illustrations of the vocal tract shape associated with various vowels in Chapter 5 show the soft palate in the raised position for classical singing.)
- Lowering the back of the jaw.

Controlling the position of the soft palate

Lifting the soft palate is critical for improving the resonating qualities of the oral pharynx in classical singing. For contemporary styles, singers can relax the soft palate somewhat to reduce the volume of the pharynx, raising the frequency of the first formant (Garnier et al., 2010). This contributes to a brighter sound without obvious nasality as long as the palate is not lowered excessively.

For centuries great classical singers have recognized the importance of this vocal tract adjustment (e.g., Caruso & Tetrazzini, 1975), but it eludes many singers. Most amateur singers and even some trained singers have limited control over the relevant muscles. We want to call special attention to two of the exercises at the end of this chapter that can help singers to accomplish this "lift."

- Bah, Gah, Kah, Pah, Tah—plosive consonants followed by a vowel to raise the soft palate. The consonant creates a back pressure that forces the soft

palate into a closed position. (Singing through a straw is another way to accomplish this.)
- Hang-ah to raise the soft palate.

For now, breathe out through the nose to feel the sensation of a lowered soft palate. Next, imagine you are surprised by something and breathe in suddenly through the mouth. This will provide a sensation of a raised soft palate. Another image that helps experience a raised soft palate is to imagine blocking out a bad smell, only allowing inhalation through the mouth.

Gaining control over the soft palate is difficult because a raised soft palate is associated with only a subtle sensation of lifting. An image that may help is to imagine opening a paper cocktail umbrella inside the back of the mouth. Soft palate exercises must be practiced for some time before control is gained. They are worth the effort to achieve a better tone for classical singing and to help reduce pharynx volume for other styles without objectionable nasality.

Nasality is not an all-or-nothing phenomenon. Singers need to be able to vary the amount of nasality to create the tonal quality they desire. There are further exercises at the end of the chapter to help singers improve their control of the soft palate.

Lowering the back of the jaw for classical/legit singing; opening the front of the mouth for other styles

While lifting the soft palate is important for classical singing, lowering the jaw in the back is equally crucial. The combination of raising the soft palate and releasing the jaw at the back stretches the walls of the pharynx and enlarges the pharyngeal resonating space.

The above-described approach to a yawn is an excellent way to accomplish jaw lowering. When opening the jaw, be careful not to jut it forward to obtain space—the jaw should be lowered down and slightly back. Some classical/legit singers open the front of the mouth as opposed to releasing the jaw in back. Avoid this in classical singing. (Though, as noted elsewhere, there is a benefit for sopranos in classical singing to lowering the jaw in both the back and front at high pitches.) In many contemporary musical styles, it is, in fact, appropriate to open the front of the mouth. With this approach the vocal tract is thought of as trumpet-like as opposed to the inverted megaphone shape associated with classical singing (Titze & Worley, 2009). See Figure 4.7. Singers can use a mirror at home to ensure they are lowering the jaw properly, and conductors/teachers can watch singers during rehearsals and lessons to assist them in making necessary corrections.

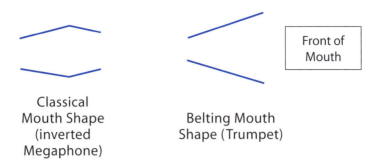

Figure 4.7 Simplified illustration of mouth shapes for classical and belting styles. Adapted from Titze, Worley, and Story (2011).

Conductors often tell choral singers to "drop the jaw" or "open the mouth," but singers sometimes open the jaw and/or mouth excessively in response to such instruction. The exercises section includes a method to help determine if the jaw has been appropriately released for classical style. (Also see Figure 5.6 in Chapter 5 on vowels for two pictures of an excessively open mouth and lowered jaw.)

Singers should experiment with the range of motion of the jaw, both up and down, forward and back, and side to side, including circular motions, to get a sense of how a comfortably open position feels. This experimentation may also relieve jaw tension, a common affliction of singers. (See Chapter 14 on reducing tension for additional methods of relieving jaw tension.)

Adjusting the mouth

Recall that the mouth is a smaller cavity than the oral pharynx, causing it to resonate at higher frequencies. (The back of the mouth, which has substantial space, is actually part of the oral pharynx.) Good mouth resonance helps to create tonal brilliance.

Resonating qualities of the mouth are affected by:

- The zygomatic majorus muscles (which lift the cheeks) and the muscles controlling the upper lip.
- Position of the tongue. This has a substantial effect upon the frequency of the second formant, as noted above.

Creating an "inner smile"

Many writers have spoken about singers needing an "inner smile." This can be thought of as creating horizontal and vertical space in the mouth. It is particularly important for resonance of the second formant. We want to be clear, that for classical style we are not advocating a "spread sound" created by a wide exterior smile, which exaggerates higher-frequency harmonics. A wide smile can be useful for other musical styles where increased sound levels of higher-frequency harmonics are desirable.

> ➢ Henderson (1979) has a wonderful explanation of the inner smile. *To get the feeling of an inner smile, she suggests closing the mouth but not the teeth, keeping an open feeling in the oral cavity. Then smile as though you were smiling at someone across the room, but you did not want other people to notice you doing so. This produces a slight lifting under the eyes and creates the sensation of a dome in the oral cavity.*

Another way to feel the sensation of an inner smile is to express surprise with a slight gasp.

A modest exterior smile is helpful for classical singing

Forming an inner smile encourages a small exterior smile, which brightens the tone. Exposing the lower portion of a *few* front teeth accomplishes this.

> ➢ Vennard (1967) has a suggestion for finding the appropriate degree of exterior smile for classical singing. He suggests smiling such that the edges of four upper teeth are visible when singing the vowel [ɑ].

A wider smile is appropriate for many contemporary styles

In musical theatre, country and pop singing, a wider mouth opening is often desirable to achieve a brighter sound. With a wider smile:

- ❖ The vocal tract shortens, raising all formant frequencies.
- ❖ More upper teeth are exposed; hard surfaces naturally emphasize higher harmonic frequencies (Vennard, 1967).
- ❖ McKinney (2005) states that pulling the lips off the teeth into a wider smile tightens the pharynx near the soft palate, contributing further to emphasis of high harmonic frequencies, thus brightening sound.

Effect of the tongue on mouth resonance

The position of the tongue alters the space in the mouth, and thus, the frequencies at which this cavity resonates. The tongue plays a major role in differentiating vowel sounds because it affects the frequency of the second formant and, to a lesser extent, the third formant.

For example, the vowel [i] is a "bright vowel" because the second and third formants associated with it are at the highest frequencies of all vowels. The hump of the tongue is high and toward the front of the mouth, creating a small space that resonates at higher frequencies.

Sing [i]. Now, lower the hump of the tongue to create the [ɑ] vowel (keeping the mouth opening unchanged, for purposes of this illustration) and the volume of space within the oral cavity is increased. Sing. Note how the tone is somewhat "darker" because the larger space resonates at a lower frequency.

Some tongue resting positions create poor quality resonance. Generally, singers should form vowels with the tongue tip resting on the line between the lower front teeth and the gums. See Chapter 5 on vowels for more detailed instructions.

Images to help create space in the mouth

The following images can help singers to create mouth space. As a bonus, the first one also helps to increase pharyngeal space for classical singers:

Place the mouth, jaw, and throat in a position as if you were attempting to swallow a medium-size boiled egg. This exercise unhinges the lower jaw, raises the soft palate, and creates an inner smile simultaneously.

Imagine opening the mouth as though biting into an extra thick sandwich or taking a bite of an apple. These images help to shape the mouth.

Classical versus contemporary resonance and vocal tract shape

In many contemporary styles of singing (e.g., in musical theatre, pop, rock), it is desirable to have a bright tonal quality. This involves several differences in vocal tract shape compared to classical production:

❖ A narrower pharynx than with classical singing, more similar to speaking. The smaller cavity size raises the frequency of the first formant and thus brightens vowels.

> ➢ Titze (2001) states that this can produce a highly resonant voice because the narrower pharynx creates an acoustical impedance that is closer to the impedance of the vocal tract below the pharynx (the epilarynx, which is quite narrow).

❖ Shortening the vocal tract by allowing the larynx to rise slightly and by widening the mouth opening and pulling back the corners of the mouth (with many upper teeth showing). A shorter vocal tract raises all formant frequencies, creating a brighter sound. Compare this to a longer vocal tract in classical production where the larynx is in a comfortably low position, and a more rounded mouth shape elongates the front of the vocal tract.

- ➢ Titze (2001) notes that combining the narrower pharyngeal shape with the aforementioned trumpet mouth shape (wider front opening than in classical singing) creates a favorable vocal tract condition for easier phonation up to roughly G_5. Beyond this pitch, however, phonation becomes difficult with such a configuration. In fact, G_5 is the rough limit for female belters using mixed registration (see Chapter 8 on registers for discussion of mixed registers).

❖ In contemporary styles that are more speech-like, the larynx may be somewhat higher, but there is no fixed position, precisely because speech involves laryngeal movement. Additionally, the larynx cannot be so high as to prevent the cricothyroids from operating in a manner that allows good control over pitches above C_5 in females and C_4 in males.

- ➢ For example, LoVetri, Lesh, and Woo (1999) found that while head voice involves a lower larynx than mix belt, chest belt often involves a lower larynx than mix belt or no change relative to mix belt.
- ➢ Guzman et al. (2015) observed in a study of pop, rock, and jazz styles that the larynx lowers as loudness increases. They speculate that this lowering helps to narrow the epilarynx tube, enhancing resonance in the region of the singer's or speaker's formant. Indeed, there is a strong relationship in that study between the amount of epilarynx tube narrowing and loudness.

❖ The size of the back of the mouth, which is the upper portion of the oral pharynx, can be reduced by slightly lowering the soft palate (velum), as noted above. The smaller cavity resonates at a high frequency compared to classical singing where the standard technique is to close the nasal port by lifting the soft palate.

Some singers of contemporary styles may actively attempt to compress the pharynx to raise the first formant frequency. Our view is that constriction should be avoided as it adds tension to vocal production and makes it more difficult to sing freely. Moreover, such an approach is not required to achieve a brighter sound.

- ➢ For example, Edwards (2014) is a strong advocate for singing rock 'n' roll with freedom and a lack of pharyngeal constriction. He states that when the pharyngeal constrictors are operative, "the voice may be sharp, flat, have an uneven vibrato, an edgy sound, and/or a forced quality" (p. 122). He suggests several excellent exercises to help with relaxation of the constrictor muscles, one of which is described in Chapter 14 on reducing tension.

An essential distinction between classical and legit styles

Legit style in musical theatre before 1960–1970 is different than modern legit style. "Golden Age" musicals featured legit singing that was close to the classical style. Modern legit singing is similar to classical singing for most aspects of vocal production, but it features a brighter sound, emphasizing mouth resonance and back vowel production that uses a more forward/elevated tongue position to raise the frequency of the second formant. Vowels like [o] and [u], which use rounded lips in classical singing, use more spread lips in the modern legit style. There may also be use of minimal vibrato with pop influences such as use of vibrato only on final notes of phrases/notes requiring emotional emphasis. (See Chapter 7 on vibrato for more detail on vibrato use according to style.)

Good resonance helps intonation

The resonating chambers of the vocal tract affect not only tonal quality but also perceived pitch. Marafioti (1922) credits Edward Scripture as the first to show through scientific experimentation that good resonance is also vital for good intonation.

- ➢ Winckel (1967) adds that a singer whose voice is rich in overtones (harmonics) will have less variability in pitch.
- ➢ Dayme (2009) states that a singer lacking in resonance of high harmonic frequencies will be perceived by listeners as flat, even though the fundamental frequency is accurate. By the same token, a singer who lacks lower harmonic frequency resonance may be perceived as sharp.

❖ Belters should consider how the deemphasis of the lowest harmonic (the fundamental frequency) might lead to a perception of their pitch as sharp. They may need to compensate by adding a little more head voice.

Resonance and the concepts of "chest voice" and "head voice"

The resonance which occurs in the vocal tract is known as cavity resonance. Two other resonance phenomena contribute to the vibrations felt in the chest and head: sympathetic resonance and conductive resonance.

An example of sympathetic resonance is the vibration of a piano string that is an octave higher than the one that is struck. Similarly, the sinuses can resonate sympathetically in response to sound resonating in the mouth and pharynx.

The violin operates in part, according to the principle of conductive resonance—the vibrations of the string are transmitted to the body of the violin through the bridge and sound peg via direct contact. In like manner, vibrations of the vocal folds and the vibrating tissues surrounding the vocal tract transmit sound conductively through the bones, cartilage, and tissues to other areas of the body.

The chest vibrates at lower frequencies; hence when singing at low pitches (D_4 and below), we feel vibrations there, particularly if we are using flow phonation, which produces the highest fundamental frequency amplitude (Sundberg, 1987). Feeling chest vibration at D_4 and below is an excellent test to see if a singer has achieved flow phonation.

The cavities of the head, particularly the sinuses and nasal passages, are smaller than the chest and so vibrate at higher frequencies. Hence when singing higher pitches, we feel vibrations there.

The terms "chest voice" and "head voice" refer to where vibrations are felt in the low and high range of a singer's voice, respectively. The listener does not hear these resonances in the chest and head; only the singer experiences them. The chest and head (other than the mouth, pharynx and nasal passages in the case of nasal consonants) are not significant resonance cavities for singing.

Resonance and "placement"

Some vocal authorities, voice teachers, and singers talk about "placing" the tone as a method of avoiding an excessively dark tone. Although images can be helpful for singers, some images are confusing and misleading; placement is a prime example.

Two placement images can be particularly problematic because of the confusion they create, along with unintended consequences:

- "place the tone in the mask"
- "forward placement"

Electronic Amplification and Processing

Most classical singing is not amplified or electronically processed (except for stadiums, broadcasts, and recordings), but singers of other styles are almost always amplified. There are three aspects of electronic processing of which singers should be aware (see Edwards, 2014 for more detail):

- **Equalization.** Various frequency bands of the voice can be emphasized or deemphasized to accommodate different microphones, performance venues, and/or the particular sound a singer would like to achieve. For example, one could choose to increase the amplitude of harmonic frequencies in the range of the second formant to help achieve a brighter sound (e.g., raise the level of sound in the range from 1000 Hz to 2200 Hz). We recommend that singers have, at a minimum, a fairly standard microphone (e.g., Shure SM58 or Beta 87A or 87C—87 is more sensitive than the 58), mixer, equalizer, and powered speakers in their practice area to experiment with producing the sound they want. Try a head-worn mic as well. When in a performance environment, the sound engineer can make adjustments to achieve the desired sound you have created in the studio.
- **Compression.** Compression reduces the difference in sound level between the lowest and highest amplitudes. Together with a "limiter," it allows for an overall higher sound level. In the music industry there has been a trend toward ever-higher levels of compression, but Croghan, Arehart, and Kates (2012) argue that listeners may not prefer this, particularly when compression limits dynamic range so much that it reduces the emotional impact of the music. In an experimental study they found that small to moderate amounts of compression are desirable, particularly for classical recordings, but also to some extent for rock recordings.
- **Reverberation.** In a performance venue there is natural reverberation or echo due to listeners hearing sound both directly and from delayed reflections from surfaces. A performance space is "dead" if there is no reverberation, "live" if there is reverberation. Both listeners and singers tend to prefer some reverberation, but if the reverberation time is too long (the time for the echo to die out), this can muddy the sound, which is particularly detrimental to diction clarity. A broadcast or recording will seem more natural if some reverberation is added to simulate a performance space. Singers who want to experiment with all these major aspects of electronic processing can purchase a relatively inexpensive stereo mixer incorporating reverb, compression, and equalization.

"Place the tone in the mask"

Some singers think nasal and sinus resonance are important for all vowels, not just French nasal vowels and nasal consonants. Thus, they speak of "placing the tone in the mask." But nasal and sinus cavity resonance are unimportant in most singing styles in English and other Western European languages (Vennard, 1967; R. Miller, 1996). Moreover, an obvious nasal tone is typically objectionable for non-nasal vowels.

While the nasal passages and sinuses resonate due to sympathetic and conductive resonance, this adds nothing to the sound heard by the audience for non-nasal vowels. In an experiment by Wooldridge (1954), singers whose nasal passages were blocked with cotton sounded the same as they normally did (on non-nasal vowels). Vennard (1967) replicated these findings.

- With nasality, the first formant is diminished in amplitude (House & Stevens, 1956), in part because of anti-resonance in this frequency range.

Considering all of this, it is best to avoid asking classical/legit singers to "place the tone in the mask," because they may respond by allowing air into the nasal pharynx to sense vibrations in the facial areas overlying the sinuses and nasal passages. It should also be avoided in most contemporary styles, except for specific stylistic uses (e.g., for a portion of a song or a particular character who should sound nasal). As Titze (2001) notes, "twang" is not inherently nasal, though, as stated earlier, a slight lowering of the soft palate may be used to increase the first formant frequency to add brightness without adding objectionable nasality.

Instead of asking singers to place the tone in the mask, strategies for improving resonance should be offered, as outlined below.

"Forward placement"

The desirability of "forward placement" is often stated.

- For example, in a book on choral singing Kemp (2009) says, "All singing should have resonance on the hard palate, forward placement" (p. 72).

"Forward placement" is misleading because resonance occurs in the mouth as a whole, not on the hard palate by itself. Singers may respond too literally to advice about placing tone. Aiming breath at the hard palate or even in front of the mouth can lead to tonal distortions, including unwanted nasality (Marchesi, 1932).

This confusion about resonance and placement has historical roots dating to the 16th century (Stark, 2003). Manuel Garcia, the great 19th-century singing teacher, initially adopted placement as a pedagogical tool. Many teachers and singers are unaware that Garcia later reconsidered and concluded that the concept of placement was a bad idea. Cornelius Reid, one of the premier singing teachers of the middle to late 20th century, reports that Garcia published a retraction of his views in the *London Music Herald* in 1894. In his retraction Garcia wrote the following:

> *I used to direct the tone into the head ... I condemn that which is spoken of nowadays, viz., the directing of the voice forward, or back and up. Vibrations come from puffs of air. All control of the breath is lost the moment it is turned into vibrations, and the idea is absurd that a current of air can be thrown against the hard palate for one kind of tone, the soft palate for another, and reflected hither and thither (cited in Reid, 1950, p. 169).*

Nonetheless, the placement concept endures. Realizing this, Vurma and Ross (2002, 2003) have endeavored to find the acoustical correlates of "forward placement" in classical singing. While there are a few differences between their two studies, both find a higher second-formant frequency and a strong singer's formant with "forward placement." This suggests singers should use a more forward/higher hump in the tongue together with a comfortably low larynx. Thus, clear advice can be provided about producing desired tonal quality without resorting to potentially misleading ideas about sound placement.

Exercises for enhancing resonance

The "surprise" breath to feel a lifted soft palate

Imagine that you have been surprised and, as a result, quickly inhale through the mouth. You should feel the soft palate lifting as you do this.

Bah, gah, kah, pah, tah—plosive consonants followed by a vowel to raise the soft palate

Using this exercise with a mirror and a flashlight to view the soft palate provides visual feedback to confirm the feeling of an elevated position.

- ❖ Recall that singing through a straw will also raise the soft palate because of the generated oral pressure.

"Hang-ah" to raise the soft palate

An exercise that combines [ŋ] (the ng in "ring") with [ɑ] (as in "father") will also help in learning to raise the soft palate. For example, *sing "hang-[ɑ]" to create a nasal sound that resolves to a non-nasal tone as* [ɑ] *is sung*. The soft palate is lowered to produce the [ŋ], and it can be felt lying against the tongue in the back of the mouth. By concentrating on the feel of the muscle pulling the soft palate up, it is possible to gain control over this important shaper of resonance (Fisher, 1966).

Note that both this exercise and the exercise with plosive consonants help more generally by focusing singers' attention on the improvement of pharyngeal space (K. Brunssen, personal communication, November 28, 2011).

Varying the position of the soft palate—Exercise 1

Sing [ng] *on any pitch in the middle range with the jaw and mouth in the position of* [ɑ]. *Gradually peel the tongue away from the roof of the mouth to the tongue position for* [ɑ]. *As you do this, intentionally keep the soft palate down and the nasal passages open. Then gradually lift the soft palate to reduce the nasality. Take your time during this exercise—if you are not sure whether the sound is nasal, try plugging your nose. If the sound continues, your soft palate is lifted (not nasal). If the sound is even partially blocked by pinching the nose, it has some degree of nasality.*

Varying the position of the soft palate—Exercise 2

Gently touch the nose just below the bridge between the thumb and forefinger. Start by relaxing/lowering the soft palate, creating a nasal sound while singing [i]. *Notice the vibrations on the bridge of the nose. Next gradually raise the soft palate. You will feel the vibrations diminish.* (N. Jordan, personal communication, April 7, 2010).

Tetrazzini's exercise for lowering the jaw for classical singers

Tetrazzini (Caruso & Tetrazzini, 1975) recognized the need to lower the jaw in the back for classical singing and suggested the following method for assuring proper release. (Be careful about doing this if you have a TMJ disorder.)

Place fingers below the temples in front of the ears, feeling the separation in the jawbones as the jaw is opened. This separation confirms that you have unhinged the jaw correctly. The mouth should not be opened excessively while doing this.

"Aiming" sound to create pharyngeal space

Sometimes it is helpful to think about "aiming" sound to find pharyngeal resonance. However, it is essential to note that this is merely a physical/image device for singers to discover resonance space in the pharynx. While singers sometimes talk about "placement," sounds cannot be aimed, placed, or projected, as noted earlier in this chapter.

Try putting one open, cupped hand just above the nape of the neck. "Aim" higher pitches toward the hand to create and access the most resonant space.

Experimenting with pharyngeal and mouth space (classical style)

Imagine you are about to bite into an apple. Notice how your mouth and jaw create space. This is a particularly useful image for classical singing.

Using a pencil to help create better mouth space

To encourage an inner smile, sing vowels with a pencil between the front teeth.

Place the pencil just behind the lower canine teeth and let the top teeth contact the pencil naturally. Keep the tongue in contact with the base of the lower incisors. Vocalize in the middle of the range on all primary vowels.

Notice how this creates a sensation of vertical space in the mouth.

"Fah" and "vah" to help develop an inner smile

Henderson (1979) suggests singing vowels preceded by [f] and [v] to help develop an inner smile *(e.g., sing "fah" and "vah")*. Singers will find that it does indeed help to create space in the mouth.

"Surprise gasp" to create an inner smile

Another way to feel the sensation of an inner smile is to express a happy surprise with a slight gasp.

Image exercises to improve mouth resonance

Place the mouth, jaw, and throat in a position as if you were attempting to swallow a medium-size boiled egg. This exercise unhinges the lower jaw, raises the soft palate, and creates an inner smile simultaneously. It is particularly useful for classical singing because it simultaneously improves mouth and pharyngeal resonance.

Imagine opening the mouth as though biting into an extra thick sandwich or taking a bite of an apple, without excessive exposure of the teeth for classical singing and more exposure for contemporary commercial styles. These images help to shape the mouth.

Alternating between [i] and [u] for classical style

Alternate [i] and [u] on one pitch, stretching the lips outward in a "Cheshire cat" smile for [i] and pulling them into pucker for [u]. The key is to create consistent resonance at the two extremes. (Note that ordinarily these extreme positions should not be used in actual singing.) This alternation will encourage flexible, relaxed facial muscles and help balance resonance between bright and dark vowels.

For kids and everyone! Tuggedy tah

On one pitch sing "tuggedy, tuggedy, tuggedy, tuggedy, tah," sustaining the final "tah." Keep the jaw lowered and use the tip of the tongue to pronounce the t's quickly. Maintain a resonant sound throughout. (Adapted from Cooksey, 1999)

Chapter 5: Vowels

Vowels are the essence of a singer's sound. Every vowel is created uniquely and imparts a slightly different timbre to the voice. Proper production of each vowel is essential for:

- Better resonance
- Intelligibility
- Achieving the desired timbre
- Consistency in tone quality, especially in classical/legit styles
- Intonation
- Blend in ensembles
- Ease of register transitions

Each vowel requires a slightly different configuration of the tongue, jaw, and lips to create the right resonance space. Many singers (particularly amateur choral singers) do not understand how each vowel should be created. Often, they fail to differentiate vowels sufficiently, resulting in a lack of tonal color variation and reduced intelligibility. Vowels are just as crucial for intelligibility as are consonants.

One ingredient of cross-training among styles is experimentation with vowel formation to explore different vocal timbres and colors. We believe that singers wishing to pursue professional careers should train across classical/legit and contemporary styles to have the flexibility to sing a variety of repertoire.

Tip of the tongue should rest at the base of the lower front teeth

Many singers do not know where to place the tip of the tongue when forming vowels. Regardless of the vowel, *the tip of the tongue should rest against the lower incisors, just above the gum line.* The portion of the tongue in contact with the teeth will vary slightly depending upon the vowel. For example, when singing [i], more of the tongue will contact the teeth. In the choral setting, a common understanding of the tongue resting position is critical for uniform production of vowels and, thus, for blending.

Resting the tongue-tip on the gum creates a dull sound

The tongue should not rest on the gum (though the bottom of the tip of the tongue will be in contact with the gum line). At rest on the gum, the tongue will be too far in the back of the mouth. Furthermore, resting on the gum will cause tension in the tongue, which can affect the larynx, as the tongue and the larynx share a common connection with the hyoid bone.

> ➤ Vennard (1967) concurs that the tip of the tongue should touch the lower front teeth and, further, that the tongue should not *press* against the teeth. This, too, will result in tongue tension and poor tonal quality. To avoid this error, remember that touching the lower front teeth is a *resting* position.

For classical/legit singing, it is essential to *immediately* return the tip of the tongue to its resting place after completing the formation of a consonant. Singers must devote a substantial amount of attention to this over time before it becomes second nature. Until this practice becomes automatic (no longer requiring conscious awareness during vocal exercises and practice), singers may let the tip of the tongue move to a position related to the preceding consonant, leading to intermediate vowel sounds. This has negative consequences for vowel differentiation, tuning, and, in the choral setting, blend. Even for contemporary styles, singers should quickly return the tip of the tongue to the base of the lower front teeth, unless a slower return to the resting position is used for artistic reasons.

The importance of leaving the tip of the tongue resting against the base of the lower incisors is easy to demonstrate:

Place the tip of the tongue at the bottom of the incisors. Sing [ɑ] and experiment with tongue position. Move the tip of the tongue forward over the lower teeth and then backward and down to the gum line below the lower teeth. The vowel sound will change.

Flick the tip of the tongue up and down to hear a different change in the sound of the vowel. This illustrates what happens to the many singers who leave the tip of the tongue partway up after singing a consonant, with disastrous effects upon intelligibility and unintentional changes in timbre of the subsequent vowel.

Basic vowel production for classical/legit styles

Consistently articulating vowels is vital for communication, and it is even more important in the choral setting than in solo singing. In the choral setting, the use of disparate vowels leads to blend and even intonation problems.

Accurate vowel production depends on proper:

❖ Degree of tongue elevation
❖ Point of tongue elevation
❖ Amount of jaw opening
❖ Lip shape

Figure 5.1 illustrates how vowels vary for all these factors in classical/legit styles. (See below for differences in how vowels should be formed in musical theatre and many contemporary styles.) The figure includes the major English vowels as well as Italian, Spanish, and Latin vowels. French and German use many of these vowels, but there are also some special vowels in these languages (see the Appendix). The figure uses the International Phonetic Alphabet (IPA) symbols to represent the vowels.

The sounds associated with some of the most important IPA vowel symbols are in Table 5.1. Cardinal vowels are in a bold, color font.

Vowel	Example
i	N**ee**d
I	H**i**d
e	G**a**te
ɛ	M**e**t
ae	C**a**t
ʌ	The emphasized form of the neutral vowel ("uh"), but one that is challenging to sing pleasingly. As in "love."
ə	The deemphasized form of the neutral vowel, known as the "schwa." As in the last syllable of "pencil."
a	Gelato—Italian "ah," brighter than [ɑ]; the Boston "ah"
ɑ	F**a**ther
ɔ	**O**ught
o	G**o**
U	B**oo**k
u	Ch**oo**se

Table 5.1 Vowel sounds associated with some IPA symbols

We do not believe that most amateur singers need to know the complete International Phonetic Alphabet. It is useful, however, for all singers to know the symbols for the major vowels. Indeed, it is often helpful to write the IPA symbol for the vowel to be sung above the staff or the lyrics. Conductors, teachers, and professional singers should have a more detailed knowledge of the IPA symbols contained in the Appendix.

Figure 5.2 illustrates how the position of the highest point of the tongue (the hump of the tongue) is most forward for [i] ("ee") and moves back in the mouth with elevation declining as vowels approach [ɑ] ("ah"). The height of the hump increases again as one sings vowels from [ɑ] to [u] ("oo"), but the hump of the tongue for these vowels is more toward the back of the mouth.

In addition, Figure 5.2 shows how the shape of the mouth opening is associated with tongue position. There is more of a lateral opening when the tongue is elevated in the front (as in [i]) and a more rounded opening when the tongue is elevated in the back (as in [u]). The relative position of the hump of the tongue and the shape of the mouth explains why the vowels from [i] to [ae] on the vowel chart are often referred to as "front vowels" or "lateral vowels," and vowels from [ɔ] to [u] are referred to as "back vowels" or "rounded vowels."

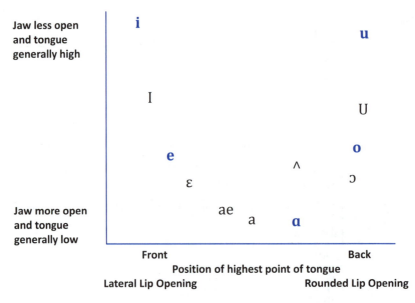

Figure 5.1 Vowel Spectrum: Tongue position, jaw opening, and lip shape for important vowels (classical style)

Vowel Spectrum for the classical style

We refer to the progression along the roughly U-shaped curve of Figure 5.1 from [i] to [u] as movement along the "Vowel Spectrum." (In the first edition we used a symmetric "U" for pedagogical simplicity. In this edition we use an asymmetric "U" to better match the reality of vowel formation.) Vowels next to each other on the Vowel Spectrum are produced similarly. It is easier for singers to develop a sense of how a vowel should feel if they can relate it to a close-by vowel because they do not have to deal all at once with the multiplicity of variables that differentiate the vowels.

A significant difference between Figures 5.1 and 5.2 versus the charts of some vocal authorities is the amount of jaw lowering as the vowel moves from [i] to [e] compared to from [e] to [ɑ] or [a]. In our view, the jaw should lower more from [i] to [e], with less additional lowering required from [e] to [ɑ] or [a]. If the jaw is not lowered enough from [i] to [e], space at the back of the mouth will be insufficient, reducing resonance and creating a shallow or brassy sounding [e]. Lowering the jaw slightly more also creates a more resonant [ɛ], which is often a dull-sounding vowel. (Note: we are speaking here of singing in the middle of a person's range.)

A small additional release of the jaw is needed from [e] to [ɑ] or [a]. If the jaw is lowered too much in the middle of a singer's range, there is a danger of failing to keep the soft palate raised, causing the pitch to be flat. Singers transitioning from [e] to [ɑ] or [a] should concentrate more on tongue position and less on lowering the jaw.

A somewhat closed jaw and rounded lips are necessary to create a resonant [u] vowel for classical singing. This lowers the frequencies of the first and second formants, creating the characteristic darker timbre of this vowel.

Some singers move their jaws excessively when transitioning from one vowel to another. Excessive jaw movement wastes energy and creates tension, but more importantly, it alters the sound of the vowel as it is sung, due to changes in the first formant that result from jaw movement.

Try the following exploration of the Vowel Spectrum, using Figure 5.2 as a guide to tongue and jaw position: Place the tip of the tongue at the base of the lower teeth. Start by singing [i] *in the middle of the range with a slight smile. The hump of the tongue should be elevated forward in the mouth. Then, lower the jaw a pinky finger's width between the molars and sing* [e]*, with the hump of the tongue moving back somewhat and decreasing slightly in height. Allow the hump of the tongue to move back further and reduce in height to sing* [ɑ]*, allowing the jaw to lower a little more. Next, increase the height of the hump and round the lips to form* [o] *while closing the jaw slightly. Finally, increase* *the height of the hump of the tongue a bit more (with the hump still toward the back of the mouth), round the lips a touch more, and close the jaw to the starting* [i] *position to sing* [u]. While an oversimplification, this device encourages singers to come to a unified understanding of vowel formation.

Figure 5.3 illustrates the exterior appearance for the five cardinal vowels for one particular classical singer. Conductors and teachers should be aware that the exterior appearance of a singer is not wholly indicative of the produced vowel. Lip position is observable, but tongue and, to some extent, jaw position are more difficult to discern.

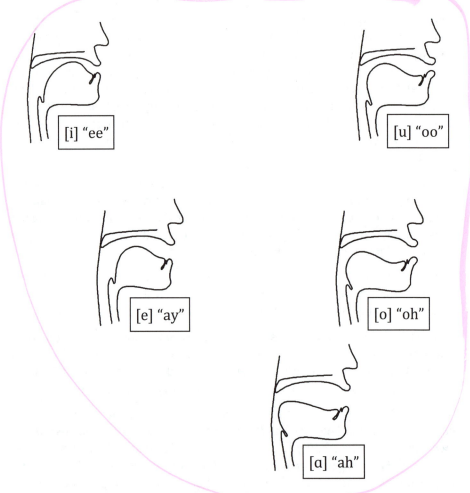

Figure 5.2 Illustration of tongue, jaw and lip positions for the cardinal vowels (classical style)

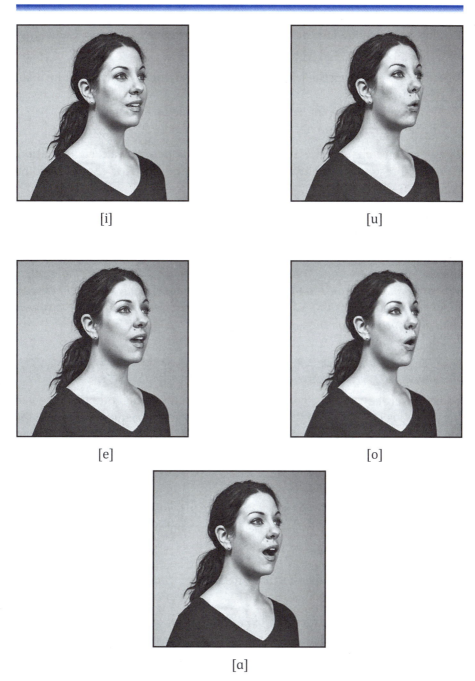

Figure 5.3 Illustration of external appearance for cardinal vowels (classical style)

Be alert to the following commonly observed problems at the end of a long-duration vowel or a long run on the same vowel:

- Raising or lowering the jaw excessively (lowers or raises the first formant frequency)
- Moving the tongue (changes the second formant frequency)
- Changing the position of the soft palate (changes F_1)

These actions change the resonating space, which can affect intonation, blend, and resonance quality. They can, however, be artistic choices in some contemporary styles.

Try singing each vowel on the same note, moving along the Vowel Spectrum from [i] through [u], then moving from [u] back to [i]. Pay close attention to tongue and jaw position.

Choose two vowels and go back and forth between them on a single pitch. Work to make the transition feel very smooth—make a quick, efficient change of jaw and tongue position as necessary. This exercise works best if the vowels used are contiguous on the Vowel Spectrum chart in Figure 5.1.

Perceptions of vowels as "bright" versus "dark"

Some vowels have a tonal color that seems "brighter" than others. Perceived brightness is largely a function of the second formant frequency, though it is also affected to some extent by the first and third formant frequencies. Vowels with higher second formant frequencies are perceived as brighter than those with lower second formant frequencies. [i] is the brightest followed by [I], [e], [ɛ], [ae], [a], and [ɑ].

The "darkest" vowel is [u], followed by [U], [o] and [ɔ]. Note that these vowels all have virtually the same second formant frequency, which is quite low (Figure 5.7, later in this chapter). What differentiates these vowels is their first formant frequency—[ɔ] has the highest first formant frequency and [u] has the lowest first formant frequency. Thus, [ɔ] is the brightest of this set of darker vowels.

Another useful exercise involves experimentation with how altering tongue and lip configurations change the tonal color of vowels. *Put your hand next to your ear and point your index finger up. Sing [ɑ] in the middle of the range. While sustaining the vowel, move your finger slowly around to a point in front of the nose, allowing the sound to brighten by increasing elevation of the hump of the tongue. Continue singing and bring the finger to the back of the head, shifting to a darker tone by depressing the hump.* This exercise helps to illustrate the possibilities of vowel color physically. For classical singing, the goal is to have a color that is neither too dark nor too light—"opposite the ear." For many contemporary styles involving belting, you will want to adopt a tonal color that is forward of the ear. For other contemporary styles, tonal color is often an artistic choice. The key is to gain control over the tonal color created by tongue shape. *Try the same approach to experimenting with lip position using [ae] or [ɑ]—rounded, almost puckered with your finger at the back, fully spread into a smile with your finger at the front.* Also, try this exercise with variations in laryngeal position and jaw position. Finally, put all the variations together to achieve the tonal quality you desire.

Vowels in contemporary styles

Intelligibility is imperative in musical theatre and many other contemporary styles, as they are often vehicles for storytelling. (Diction is also important in classical music, but in classical genres the beauty of the sound is often of slightly greater concern.)

As noted previously, in contemporary styles, the desired tonal quality is typically different than in classical singing—often brighter. Additionally, a goal of classical singing is consistent tonal quality throughout the singing range. Consistent tonal quality is not necessarily a goal in other styles, where tonal variations may be employed for artistic reasons. This means that vowels will be produced somewhat differently than as outlined above.

Pop, country, and musical theatre vowels should be pronounced more as in speech—there should be more mouth than pharyngeal resonance. Thus, the jaw is more closed in the back, the lip opening is wider, and the tongue and tongue arch more forward. For example, for [u], the jaw should be a bit more closed in the back and the lips should be less rounded. All of this creates a brighter sound that is less operatic. [e] sounds brighter as well if the tongue is a bit higher and elevated more toward the front of the mouth. Note that musical theatre uses a brighter sound than other contemporary styles, while jazz singers will tend to be less bright than most other contemporary styles. Gospel can be any timbre, though it tends to be fairly bright, yet with a more balanced set of formants than musical theatre.

Individuals who primarily sing in a classical style may have some difficulty adapting to the vowel formation methods used in musical theatre and various contemporary styles (and vice versa). Master teachers of mix belting, for example, work with singers on using front vowels such as [e] and [ae] to help access a brighter sound. Preceding these vowels with the glides [w] and [y] (e.g., "way" and "yay") seems to help create the desired sound, with more mouth resonance and less pharyngeal resonance (Roll, 2016). In contrast, [o] and [ɑ] can be helpful for contemporary singers who wish to cross-train for a classical sound.

Vowel consistency for intonation and ensemble blending

Conductors and teachers should use vocal exercises to encourage consistent vowel production by both choral singers and soloists, as this is important for intelligibility and intonation. Intonation can be affected because the perceived pitch is affected by overtone frequencies, as noted above; singing a vowel improperly can cause singers to seem out of tune. Discussions of problematic vowels appear in the following section.

Blend is enhanced when choral singers share an understanding of how each vowel feels and sounds. Remember that the first and second formant frequencies (F_1 and F_2) primarily distinguish among the vowels. If some singers in a choral group are singing a given vowel differently from other singers, then their formant frequencies will differ.

For example, when singing [ɑ] in the middle of their range, some singers may sing the vowel properly, others may sing something closer to [ɔ], others may sing something closer to [ae], and still others may sing something closer to [ʌ]. This creates dissonance among the formant frequencies, with negative consequences for blend.

> ➤ Reviewing the literature, Aspaas, McCrea, Morris, and Fowler (2004) conclude that the tuning of vowel formant frequencies among choral members is one of the most important aspects of choral blending.

See Chapter 12 for further discussion of methods to achieve choral blend.

Problematic vowels

Beware of a puckered [u]

[u] is a particularly problematic vowel. Most inexperienced singers make one or more of the following errors:

- ❖ Rounding the lips insufficiently, creating a shallow vowel with little resonance (Note, however, that in contemporary styles, there is often less lip rounding due to the desirability of a brighter [u].)
- ❖ Creating insufficient mouth space and consequent lack of resonating space

❖ Placing the hump of the tongue too far forward for this back vowel

Some choral conductors remedy these problems by asking for an excessive, forward lip-puckering, but this can create an opening that is too narrow, and reduce interior space in the mouth as the cheeks are pulled in by the tensing of the lips necessary to create a pucker. Forward puckering may be useful as an effect, but as a rule, it should be avoided, for the resulting sound has a "hooty" quality and lacks resonance.

Since [u] has the lowest first and second formants of all vowels, many singers find it difficult to achieve a resonant sound on this vowel. Further narrowing of the mouth opening will lower the first formant even more, compromising tone quality and pitch. Figure 5.4 illustrates a puckered [u].

Figure 5.4 Puckered [u]

Singers should practice moving smoothly from [o] to [u], slightly closing the jaw and slightly rounding the lips in the transition from [o] to [u]. Avoid excessive closing of the jaw. The key is to maintain the resonance of [o] in the transition to [u]. Also, try moving back and forth between [i] and [u] as suggested in the exercises of Chapter 4 on resonance. This is useful because jaw lowering is the same for [i] and [u].

Beware of making [i] too dull

The vowel [i] sounds too bright to some conductors trying to achieve a blended sound. As a result, they ask singers to modify the vowel to [I], but this modification makes words with the [i] vowel harder to understand and less resonant. We are not suggesting that vowel modification of [i] to [I] is never appropriate. As outlined below in the section on vowel modification, it is certainly desirable in the upper range of a section. For example, modification will be necessary above E_5 for sopranos, or sopranos will find the note difficult to sing, and the sound will be too brassy for classical production.

An even more problematic modification is to ask singers to sing [i] in the mouth space of [u], which creates a hooty sounding [i]. (We are not speaking about singing IPA [y] in, for example, French or German, which is approximated by singing [i] in the space of [u].) Figure 5.5 illustrates singing [i] in the space of [u].

The following factors contribute to an excessively bright [i] for classical singing:

- Excessively wide outer smile with too many exposed teeth.
- Insufficient rear jaw lowering. (Pharyngeal resonance is needed to balance the mouth resonance that is inherent with [i]).
- Nasality. Recall that nasality reduces the amplitude of the first formant, which is important for a balanced tonal color in classical style.

Darker sounds are typically easier to blend, but vowel modification toward a darker sound is a poor solution to the blending problem (see Chapter 12 on blending). Darkening vowels should only be considered after the above factors have been examined, as it may create intonation problems in the middle of the range due to formant frequency alterations. Conductors should work with ensembles to sing [i] with a balanced tonal quality, without resorting to fixes that affect vowel integrity.

In classical/legit styles beware an excessive mouth opening for [ɑ]

Classical singing does not require a wide-open mouth for [ɑ]. The key is lowering the jaw in the back, rather than opening the mouth excessively in the front. Singers are particularly prone to making this mistake when singing high pitches at high dynamic levels. Figure 5.6 illustrates two examples of excessive mouth opening. Note the tension apparent in both.

In contemporary styles a wider mouth opening can be a necessary part of achieving a brighter sound (along with a more forward tongue and higher tongue arch). Thus, the greater mouth opening in the left-hand photograph of Figure 5.6 would be appropriate for such styles. The tension and forward head position shown in these photographs is, however, undesirable for any musical style.

Figure 5.5 [i] in the space of [u] (puckered [i])

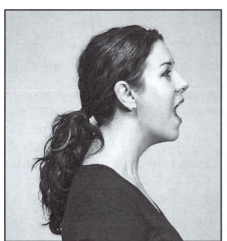 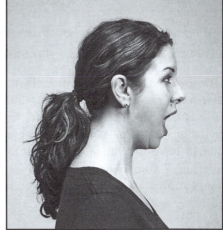

Figure 5.6 Examples of excessive mouth opening and tension when singing [ɑ]

Singing the neutral vowel "uh"

Neutral vowels can have a dull, lifeless sound. In the choral setting they also pose problems for blend, as singers can form these vowels quite differently.

There are two neutral vowels of significance:

- [ʌ], as in "but," is the accented (stressed) form
- [ə] is the unaccented (unstressed) form, commonly referred to as a "schwa" (e.g., as in the second syllable of "people")
    - Vennard (1967) argues that the neutral "uh" vowel is a muddy, dull vowel, lacking in resonance. Unlike English, it does not occur in Italian, German, or French as a stressed vowel.

To brighten the sound of the accented version [ʌ], try modifying it toward [ɑ] or [a]. For example, the word "love" when spoken often involves use of the neutral vowel, but when sung, [ɑ] or [a] could be employed. Nonetheless, in some cases an unmodified form might be employed for emphasis. For example, singing "abundant" as "abahdunt" might sound artificial; "abuhdunt" may be more appropriate.

Many English words contain [ʌ]. Table 5.2 shows examples of words that contain this vowel.

come	love	sun	done	fun
blood	son	but	the	us
just	cut	shut	tough	fluff
unto	thus	dove	just	must

Table 5.2 Examples of words containing the stressed neutral vowel [ʌ]

The unaccented form [ə], the schwa, is prevalent in French (e.g., priere) and German (e.g., liebe). It can also be heard in the final syllables of English words like "angel." In such words the schwa helps to deemphasize the last syllable. If this final syllable is sung using [ɛ] as in "angel" or [I] as in "pencil," it will have too much emphasis, and the word will sound strange to the listener. To impart some resonance to the vowel and avoid making it too neutral, singers should use something between the schwa and [ɛ], [I], or [ɑ], as the case may be.

Avoid the practice of "covering" throughout the vocal range

As we noted in our discussion of [i], it is undesirable to ask singers to create [i] in the space of [u] (or even in the space of [ɑ] except for an occasional, special effect). This is an extreme example of a more general vocal strategy known as "covering," in which vowel modifications darken vowel color. Choral conductors sometimes ask for this strategy in choral settings to create a more uniform sound—i.e., a sound with less variability in the darkness and brightness of vowels.

The term "covering" is appropriate because the epiglottis folds over the glottis as vowels move from [i] to [u] along the Vowel Spectrum. The tonal result, as aptly stated by Fleming (2005), is to "put a lid on the sound." To this we would add that if done excessively or in the middle of a singer's range, the resulting sound will strike the listener as overly dark and may make text difficult to understand. In contrast, preserving vowel integrity (with allowance for modification at high pitches) produces a broader, more pleasing tonal palette with better intelligibility. Nonetheless, this technique can be used when the artistic goal is to create a darker sound.

The use of formant frequency tuning at all pitches is a related strategy designed to boost sound level. Coffin (1980) developed a complex system of vowel modification depending upon pitch, to more closely match the frequency of the first or second formant to a nearby harmonic frequency of the sung note. Solo singers most commonly use this system in opera settings (as do some female chest belters), but it is not appropriate in most other singing. Except for what is necessary to sing the higher pitches of a singer's range, formant tuning is undesirable for two reasons:

- Vowel distortions in the lower to middle pitches of a singer's range make singing less enjoyable for audiences. Carlsson and Sundberg (1992) tested the preferences of expert listeners for three types of formant tuning versus constant formant singing across an octave from C_3 to C_4. In 98% of the comparisons, the preference was constant formant singing. Audiences do not appreciate extreme approaches to vowel modification.
- Complex systems of modification make singing more difficult.

Modification of vowels for higher pitches

Most singers must modify vowels as they sing higher pitches. Vowel modification at higher pitches:

- Prevents dangerous crossovers of the fundamental and certain higher harmonic frequencies with F_1 that destabilize vocal fold vibration (Titze, 2008b; Titze, Riede, & Popolo, 2008). When this crossover occurs, there can be a break in the voice, a sudden change in tonal quality, and/or a sudden alteration in pitch.
- Reinforces vocal fold vibration by raising formant frequencies at higher pitches, leading to less strain and lower vocal effort. There is favorable feedback of energy to the vocal folds when the frequency of a harmonic (including the fundamental frequency) is less than a formant frequency (Titze, 2004).

❖ Allows singers to maintain a relatively low larynx for classical singing.

Another benefit of vowel modification is that, for classical singers, it helps to prevent front vowels (particularly [i]) from sounding too bright or brassy at high pitches. As long as the vowel is not modified too much, it will remain understandable, particularly given the context of the lyrics. Moreover, in the choral setting, those sections not singing in the upper portions of their range will be singing the vowel in the usual manner.

Figure 5.7 illustrates the average formant frequencies in the Vowel Spectrum and how the first and second formants vary according to the vowel (approximate average frequencies of spoken vowels are shown based on a variety of studies). This chart is helpful for understanding the recommendations below for vowel modification. The chart averages over males and females, but the formants are higher for females and lower for males. (The chart shows higher F_1 and F_2 frequencies at the origin to show the correspondence of formant frequencies with the Vowel Spectrum chart of Figure 5.1.)

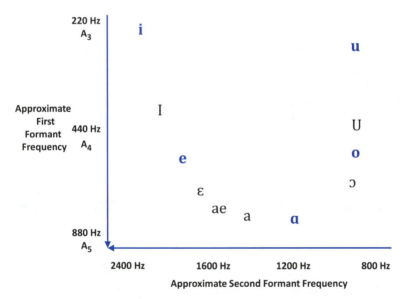

Figure 5.7 Approximate formant frequencies for common English vowels (frequencies inverted to follow the Vowel Spectrum chart)

Vowel modification for males

Contemporary strategy

As pitch ascends above roughly C_4, males should increasingly open the mouth into the shape resembling the bell of a trumpet (trumpet mouth shape). Slight lowering of the back of the jaw may also be helpful. This allows F_1 to rise as the second harmonic ($2f_o$) rises with increasing fundamental frequency, preventing a destabilizing crossover and allowing amplification of the second harmonic by the first formant. Allowing the larynx to rise and pulling back the corners of the lips also contribute to an increase in the first formant's frequency through shortening of the vocal tract.

Titze and Worley (2009) illustrate this approach with an analysis of a recording and pictures of Cab Calloway (a famous U.S. jazz singer in the 1940s). On A_4 (high male A), Calloway exhibits a strong second harmonic boosted by proximity to the first formant. A picture of him singing this note nicely illustrates a trumpet mouth shape.

Nonetheless, there are limits, particularly as pitch ascends further. As noted by Titze and Worley (2009), male belters often break into falsetto when they can no longer raise F_1. Calloway likely had extraordinary abilities to raise F_1 enough to use this strategy on a high male A.

Classical/legit strategy

Vocal science research supports a different approach to vowel modification for male classical singers that helps to maintain a more even timbre as a singer moves through register transitions (e.g., Neumann et al., 2005; Schutte, Miller, & Duijnstee, 2005; Titze & Worley, 2009). This involves three components:

- ❖ At high pitches males should limit jaw lowering by avoiding vowels such as [ae] and [ɑ]. This will keep F_1 lower than $2f_o$ so that phonation will not be disrupted by a crossing of F_1 by $2f_o$. Studies of professional classical artists show that in the first passaggio (transition between chest voice and mixed voice outlined in Chapter 8 on vocal registers), where vowel modification usually begins, there is a sudden reduction in the frequency of F_1 that avoids the destabilization problem. They reduce the first formant frequency by reducing jaw lowering. As their pitch rises further, F_1 begins to rise again as they lower the jaw more, but F_1 always stays well below $2f_o$.
- ❖ At high pitches, also avoid the vowels with low first formant frequencies, particularly [i] and [u]. Otherwise, the fundamental frequency can cross over the first formant, creating instability. Avoid the crossover by modifying [i] and [u] to [I] and [U], respectively. These vowels may even need some modification just below the first passaggio.
- ❖ Shift the arch of the tongue forward—a "fronting of the tongue" (D. Miller, 2008). Increase the amount of forward shift and the height of the arch

more as pitch increases. When done correctly, this will cause the second formant to amplify $3f_o$ for back vowels and to amplify $4f_o$ for front vowels (which naturally have a higher second formant).

> ➢ Luciano Pavarotti was a master of this technique (D. Miller, 2008). More recently, Javier Camarena may be seen using it to hit the nine high Cs of "Ah! Mes Amis" from Donizetti's *La Fille du Regiment.*

To summarize, successful vowel modification for males in classical styles involves use of mid vowels ([I], [ɛ], [e], [ɔ], [o], and [U]). These require a moderately lowered jaw plus fronting of the tongue to track higher harmonics with the second formant. Modern legit and mix belt singers might also consider this approach, but should use the brighter front vowels, or shift in their direction.

> ➢ We should note, however, there is some evidence that male musical theatre singers may, in practice, use the contemporary resonance strategy of tuning $2f_o$ to the first formant for both legit and belting styles (Bourne, Garnier, & Samson, 2016). In our experience, some classical singers do this as well.

Vowel modification for females

Classical/legit strategy

As pitch ascends above roughly C_5 and classical/legit females enter head voice (or may already be in head voice), they must raise the first formant to keep it slightly above the fundamental frequency. Otherwise, the fundamental frequency will cross above the first formant and disrupt phonation.

> ❖ As noted previously, the vocal tract is in a favorable inertant state below the speech first formant frequency; thus, classical/legit singers may do little formant tuning to amplify the fundamental frequency in this pitch range. Bourne and Garnier (2012) confirmed this in a comparison of legit to belting.
> ❖ Vowel modification should begin at somewhat lower pitches for vowels with naturally low first formant frequencies. These include [i] and [u] and even [I] and [U].

Females who properly raise the first formant have a powerful voice in their upper register because the first formant amplifies the fundamental frequency (Sundberg, 1987). This assumes, however, that they are using moderate glottal closure so that the amplitude (sound level) of the fundamental is strong.

The first formant is raised by additional jaw lowering and mouth opening as pitch ascends. Spreading the lips with a slight smile at very high pitches also helps to increase F_1 since that raises all formants by further shortening the vocal tract. In classical singing, lip spreading should not be overdone.

As a practical matter, this formant resonance strategy allows a vowel to shift slightly along the vowel chart in the direction of [ɑ]. Note that singers should *not* sing [ɑ] itself. The modification through appropriate jaw lowering is *in the direction of* [ɑ].

Try singing [i], *for example, in the standard jaw position. Then allow the jaw to lower while retaining the tongue position for* [i]. The resultant sound is [I], the next vowel toward [ɑ].

Modifying toward [ɑ] also applies to the back vowels. Lower the jaw while singing [o] and the sound will transition to [ɔ].

Above C_6 some sopranos continue to raise the first formant frequency with further mouth opening. Others transition to tuning the fundamental frequency to the second formant (Garnier et al., 2010), presumably through tongue position adjustment.

Contemporary strategy

Contemporary singers using chest or chestmix production will modify vowels to raise the first formant frequency with ascending pitch by allowing the larynx to rise somewhat, spreading the lips, and opening the mouth.

- This occurs even in the octave between roughly D_4 and D_5, whereas classical/legit singers use little vowel modification in this range.
  - Bourne and Garnier (2012) conclude that belters raise the first formant frequency in this lower portion of the female range to stay in proximity to the second harmonic (much like male contemporary singers since the fundamental frequencies are in the same range).

Vowel modification for females—easing the transition from chest voice to mixed voice around D_4

Some female voices have trouble transitioning from their lower register (chest voice) to mixed voice. (See Chapter 8 on registers for further discussion of these terms and transitional issues.)

From a resonance standpoint, this problem is similar to that experienced by males transitioning to their upper register because the pitches are in the same area. This is a more comfortable pitch area for females, however, because the thyroarytenoid muscles are not pushed as close to their limits as with males.

If female singers are having difficulty with this transition, teachers and conductors can suggest that they use the mid-vowel strategy with a fronting of the tongue (as outlined for classical/legit males).

> ### Avoid excessive modification—but sopranos are an exception with classical production
>
> Excessive modification sounds artificial, so one would rarely modify a vowel more than one or two positions along the Vowel Spectrum. Nonetheless, at the very highest pitches in classical/legit styles (roughly A_5 and above), sopranos must modify all vowels to [ae], [a], or [ɑ].
>
> To understand why, examine Figure 5.7. Notice that the normal frequency range for the first formant is between 250 and 850 Hz. Above roughly A_5, the fundamental frequency is above the first formant for all vowels. Thus, considering only the first formant frequency, all vowels will sound like [ɑ], degrading intelligibility at high frequencies.
>
> Classical sopranos who attempt to produce vowels in the upper portion of their range other than [ae], [a], or [ɑ] will experience strain and vocal instability. They should not be asked to vocalize or sing repertoire on other vowels at high pitches; [i] and [u] specifically should be avoided.
>
> Another factor affecting intelligibility is the method used to raise the first formant to accommodate rising pitch. In classical singing the jaw is lowered, but in contemporary styles the larynx may also be raised, and the lips spread, requiring less jaw lowering and thus increasing the potential for better intelligibility.
>
> > ➢ Smith and Scott (1980) studied the front vowels [i], [I], [e], and [ae]. When sung in a classical style near 880 Hz (A_5), audience members could not differentiate the vowels. Yet, when sung in a musical theatre style, vowel identification was substantially above a chance level.
> > ➢ Friedrichs, Maurer, and Dellwo (2015) found that many vowels sung by a musical theatre singer could be understood up to 880 Hz, particularly when sung in the context of words rather than in isolation.

At what pitch should vowel modification start for the classical style?

The point at which vowel modification needs to occur will vary from singer to singer because of differences in physiological structures. As a general rule, *slight* modification using second formant vowel modification principles should begin as one enters the first passaggio (the passage from chest voice to a mixture of chest and head voice). However, it may be desirable for males to modify the low F_1 formant vowels [i] and [u] slightly before entering this passaggio. (See Chapter 9 for a discussion of voice classification.)

- ❖ For most sopranos and tenors this would be in the vicinity of E_4.
- ❖ For mezzo-sopranos (second sopranos or first altos in a choral group) and baritones (first basses or even second tenors in a choral group), this would be in the vicinity of D_4.
- ❖ For contraltos (second altos) and true basses (second basses) this falls in the vicinity of C_4.

Females should begin first-formant modification toward [ɑ] as they approach their second passaggio (the passage from mixed voice to head voice).

- ❖ For most (lyric) sopranos this would be in the vicinity of E_5.
- ❖ For mezzo-sopranos (second sopranos or first altos) this would be in the vicinity of D_5.
- ❖ For contraltos (second altos) this falls in the vicinity of C_5.

Note also, that modification should occur at somewhat lower pitches for vowels with naturally low first formant frequencies.

To assist learning vowel modification for females in the higher range, start in the lower/middle range and slide up the octave allowing the jaw to lower as necessary. Allow the vowel to shift/modify without predetermining its final jaw position. Slide up and down on various vowels—observe how the vowel sound changes and how much lowering is needed. Be sure to monitor breath support as pitch ascends. For contemporary styles involving chest/chestmix production, start in the low portion of the range and open the mouth into more of a trumpet shape as pitch ascends. Allow the larynx to ascend somewhat and widen the lips as well. Experiment with various vowels, sliding up and down in the range. Mix belt will be required between D_5 and G_5. Few singers will be able to ascend above G_5 without going into head voice.

To assist learning vowel modification for men singing classical styles, start on [ɑ] in the lower/middle range. Slide up an octave modifying toward [ɔ] as the passaggio is entered. As the pitch ascends, gradually move the tongue arch forward but otherwise maintain the vocal tract in the position of [ɔ]. For a brighter modern legit style, modify from [a] toward [e]. For contemporary styles adopt an ever-larger trumpet mouth shape as pitch ascends, allow the larynx to rise somewhat, and pull back the corners of the lips.

Diphthongs, triphthongs, and glides

Diphthongs, triphthongs, and glides are combinations of two or more vowels in succession.

Diphthongs are combinations of two vowels

In words like "died," the vowel sound is composed of *two* distinct vowel sounds, [ɑ] and [i]. For classical/legit singing, the first vowel of a diphthong should be sustained ([ɑ] in this example), shifting to the second vowel (in this case [i]) at the last moment. In contemporary styles transition to the second vowel is faster and the speed of the transition is an artistic choice. (Think of how a diphthong is pronounced when speaking.) Table 5.3 lists common diphthongs, along with the primary vowel to sing for classical/legit production. [a] may be substituted for [ɑ] for a brighter sound.

Diphthong	Example—vowel receiving the most duration for classical/legit styles
ɑi	night, died—sing [ɑ] primarily
ɑu	down—sing [ɑ] primarily
ɔi	voice—sing [ɔ] primarily
ou	low—sing [o] primarily
ei	day—sing [e] primarily

Table 5.3 Examples of diphthongs

In country music, drawn-out diphthongs are common because this is characteristic of the Southern American English dialect. In addition, what are otherwise pure vowels are often spoken as diphthongs in this dialect (e.g., the vowel [e] in "face" may become [ei] with a slow transition from [e] to [i]).

Some languages, such as Italian and Latin, use mostly pure vowels with few diphthongs. German has several diphthongs, most notably [ɑi] as in *dein*, which should be sung primarily on the [ɑ] vowel.

Triphthongs are combinations of three vowels

Combinations of three vowels are known as triphthongs (Table 5.4). In most English words involving triphthongs, the third vowel is the schwa. In classical/legit styles the word should be sung on the first vowel, shifting to the second two vowels just as the word is being completed. Again, transition to these final vowels will be faster for contemporary styles.

Triphthong	Example—vowel receiving the most duration for classical/legit styles
eiə	prayer—sing [e] primarily
ɑiə	tire—sing [ɑ] primarily
ɑoə	hour—sing [ɑ] primarily
ɔiə	royal—sing [ɔ] primarily
ouə	lower—sing [o] primarily

Table 5.4 Examples of triphthongs

Glides

A glide involves two vowels, typically moving swiftly through the first vowel and singing the second vowel with greater duration. There are occasional glides in both Italian (e.g., *pianto* and *guanto*—[iɑ] and [uɑ]) and English (e.g., tune, few, and new [iu]).

Sometimes singers fail to recognize that words such as "new" can involve a glide, particularly in classical singing. [niu] is preferable to [nu] in this context. In contemporary styles [nu] is preferred as it is more like informal speech.

Avoiding problems with diphthongs and triphthongs in classical/legit styles

Diphthongs can be very tricky for classical choral singers because of a tendency to shift to the second vowel too quickly and sometimes at different rates, producing a poor choral sound. The same is true for triphthongs—where the first vowel should receive the longest duration. Remember to pronounce all the vowels to be sure the word is understood.

Shifting too quickly results from habits carried over from ordinary speech where the shift from one vowel of a diphthong or triphthong to another is quite rapid. It is often helpful for singers to write in the primary vowel to be sung. Sometimes, singers may even want to cross out the word that appears in the lyrics and write it in the way it should be sung. This advice also applies to vowels that are required to be sustained before the final consonant. Writing the vowel above the staff with a line extending to the consonant at the cutoff point can remind the singer not to move to the consonant too quickly. This is particularly important for consonants that are semi-vowels (e.g., [m] or [n]), precisely because they *are* sustainable (but should not be sustained, unless a singer desires a particular effect).

When a consonant follows a diphthong, think of the second vowel as being attached to the consonant to allow the first vowel to retain its purity and to avoid anticipating the second vowel.

Classical singers also need to avoid inadvertent singing of diphthongs when a pure vowel is required. For example, in Italian, *vivace* has the final vowel [ɛ]. English singers may inadvertently add [i] to the end of this word by closing the jaw while still singing the [ɛ] vowel, resulting in an unwanted diphthong. Keeping the jaw lowered will preserve the vowel's integrity.

Altering the tonal color of vowels

Understanding the principles outlined in this chapter allows the alteration of tonal color when desired. For example:

- For a darker tone for an [i] vowel, place the lips in the position of [a] but sing [i]. As noted above, reserve this only for special effects. Avoid singing [i] in the space of [u] for reasons outlined above.
- A brighter sounding [ɛ] involves shifting the vowel slightly toward [e].

If back vowels sound too dark

If [u] seems too dark or sung from the throat, more room in the mouth can brighten it. Less rounding of the lips will help. Also, prevent the tongue from falling back into the throat.

If [o] seems too dark or muffled, sing something closer to [ɔ] instead, shifting toward a brighter vowel. Consider less lip rounding as well.

The word "Gloria" is a good example. English singers often sing [o], when in fact, it should be sung as [ɔ] when using Italianized Latin (Church Latin). Singing [ɔ] helps to enliven the sound. However, when singing Germanic Latin, [o] is the correct vowel.

If the tone is too dark in general

McKinney (2005) provides a nice summary of factors that can lead to an excessively dark tone. We consider the following to be his most important points:

- Lowering the jaw excessively in the middle of the range. *Try singing [a] and quickly lower the jaw to imitate a full yawn.* You will readily hear a

darkening of the tone.
- ❖ Excessively low larynx. This can result from excessive jaw lowering, but it can also stem from deliberate attempts to create more vocal tract space, to artificially lower one's range. An excessively low larynx is most often an affliction of male singers, particularly baritones, who want to sing the lower notes required of bass choral singers.
- ❖ Insufficient oral space. Remember that the mouth is the resonating cavity that reinforces some of the higher harmonic frequencies.
- ❖ Flabby pharyngeal walls. Insufficient lifting of the soft palate can cause this problem.
- ❖ Tongue pulled back. This is a frequent cause of this problem.

Some singers perceive, inaccurately, that their sound is richer and resonant with a darker form of production. In reality, the sound can be lacking in resonance and be out of tune, in part because the formant frequencies are depressed. Listeners do not similarly hear a rich sound. Make and listen to recordings of your singing for a more accurate understanding of your timbre.

Teachers and conductors should give feedback to singers with overly dark production to help them balance mouth and pharyngeal resonance. This will also help with more accurate vowel production.

If the tone is too bright in general

McKinney (2005) asserts that a too-bright sound for classical singers stems from overemphasized resonance in the mouth and insufficient resonance in the oral pharynx. This problem can result from:

- ❖ Insufficient pharyngeal space due to neck/throat tension. Remember that constrictor muscles can squeeze the pharynx. See Chapter 14 on tension for an illustration of these muscles and approaches to relieving tension.
- ❖ A clenched jaw in an excessively closed position.
- ❖ Larynx rising too high. This usually results from carrying chest voice too high for classical production—the larynx rises as the thyroarytenoid muscles exert too much control at the highest pitches. It can also result from insufficient breath support and use of the constrictor muscles surrounding the vocal tract to assist airflow. (Recall that the constrictor muscles raise the larynx.)
- ❖ Excessively broad smile. This creates a wide aperture which emphasizes higher frequency harmonics. Of course, this may be desirable for many contemporary styles.

We would add that when the hump (arch) of the tongue is excessively forward and/or overly elevated for all vowels, the sound can be too bright because of a high second formant. While this is a good resonance strategy for belting and may be used to some extent in modern legit style, it is not desirable for classical style.

A summary philosophy of vowel formation

The chapters on both resonance and vowels can be summarized in the following philosophy of vowel formation:

1) In the classical style, form vowels in the context of a comfortably low larynx, an open pharynx, and good mouth space. In contemporary styles, form vowels in the context of a slightly higher larynx, a less-expanded pharynx and wider lip opening. Vowel formation is thus more speech-like in contemporary styles, including modern legit musical theatre.
2) The tip of the tongue should rest against the base of the lower incisors for all vowels in the Vowel Spectrum. In classical styles, after formation of consonants, the tongue should immediately return to its resting place prior to production of the subsequent vowel. In contemporary styles this requirement is relaxed and determined by the desired artistic expression.
3) Vowel integrity is essential to preserve intelligibility. Except for pitches in the higher portions of a singer's range, form vowels with tongue, lip, and jaw positions as shown in the Vowel Spectrum chart (Figure 5.1). This creates a broad tonal palette reflective of true differences in the sound of the various vowels. In contemporary styles, vowels should follow the patterns of the Vowel Spectrum chart, but the lip opening should be wider (in particular, less rounded for back vowels), and the tongue position more elevated with a more forward arch.
4) The tongue and jaw should not move during the singing of a vowel because doing so alters the vowel and its associated formant frequencies. In contemporary styles such as pop, rock, and jazz, singers can be more flexible and may "bend" vowels for artistic purposes.
5) Proper vowel modification is essential for singing higher pitches with ease and freedom. Without appropriate modification, singers will experience vocal instability due to a harmonic crossing over a formant frequency.
6) Within ensemble sections, singers should use a common approach to vowel modification. With different approaches to modification, there can be adverse consequences for blend.

Vowel exercises

Experimenting with tongue position

Place the tip of the tongue at the base of the incisors. Sing [ɑ] or [a] and experiment with tongue position. Move the tip of the tongue forward over the lower teeth and then backward and down to the gum line below the lower teeth. The vowel sound will change.

Flick the tip of the tongue up and down to hear a different change in the sound of the vowel.

Tongue position vocalise

Sing consonants that require tongue movement before a vowel such as [ɑ] or [a]—e.g., la, da, ta, na. Pronounce the consonant quickly and rapidly, returning the tongue to the resting place at the base of the lower incisors. Maintain vowel integrity throughout the exercise.

Vowel Spectrum

Sing [i], [e], [ɑ], [o], [u] sustaining one pitch. Progress through the Vowel Spectrum, listening to and feeling for consistency of tone and pitch.

Try moving carefully from one vowel to the next and then back to the first vowel, e.g., [i e i], while making sure jaw, tongue, and lip positions are as described in this chapter. Maintain resonance throughout. Avoid exaggerated motions—make a quick, efficient change of jaw and tongue position as necessary. Change pitches as desired, staying in the middle range. Singers should watch themselves in a mirror when practicing. Conductors should monitor singers during vocal exercises.

Continue to use the Vowel Spectrum progressing [i] through [u] and in reverse through a variety of melodic patterns, always working for consistency of sound, vibrato, and pitch.

Experimenting with vowel color

Another useful exercise involves experimentation with how altering tongue, lip, jaw, and laryngeal configurations change the tonal color of vowels. *Put your hand next to your ear and point your index finger up. Sing [ɑ] in the middle of the range. While sustaining the vowel, move your finger slowly around to a point in front of the nose, allowing the sound to brighten by increasing elevation of the hump of the tongue. Continue singing and bring the finger to the back of the head, shifting to a darker tone by depressing the hump.* This exercise helps to illustrate the possibilities of vowel color physically. For classical singing, the goal is to have a color that is neither too dark nor too light—"opposite the ear." For many contemporary styles involving mix belt, you will want to adopt a tonal color that is forward of the ear. For other contemporary styles, tonal color is often an artistic choice. The key is to gain control over the tonal color created by tongue shape. *Try the same approach to experimenting with lip position using [ae] or [ɑ]—rounded, almost puckered with your finger at the back, fully spread into a smile with your finger at the front. Also, try this exercise with variations in laryngeal position and jaw position. Finally, put all the variations together to achieve the tonal quality you want.*

Beautiful [e]

Beware of the [e] vowel. *Insert the little (pinky) finger between the back molars while singing to encourage just enough space for resonance.*

Resonant [u] for classical style

Singers should practice moving smoothly from [o] to [u], slightly closing the jaw and slightly rounding the lips in the transition from [o] to [u]. Avoid excessive closing of the jaw. The key is to maintain the resonance of [o] in the transition to [u]. Also, try moving back and forth between [i] and [u] as suggested in Chapter 4 on resonance, because the jaw position is the same for [i] and [u].

Belting vowels

This exercise focuses on creating a belt sound in the chest register (adapted from Edwards, 2014). It uses the [e] and [ae] vowels suggested by expert musical theatre teachers as useful in accessing the belt sound. An exercise focusing on mix belt is available in Chapter 8 on registers, where we discuss mixed registration in detail.

For kids and everyone! Diphthongs

Sing the phrase, "I like my bike." Each word of this phrase contains a diphthong. Sustain the first "ah" vowel for each word and move to the second vowel just before changing syllables. Use a single pitch for the whole exercise, and then proceed to a variety of melodic patterns. (Adapted from Phillips, 1996)

Vowel modification

Females—Classical/Legit

On any vowel, sing an octave, ascending and descending, sliding between the pitches. Allow the back of the jaw to be loose and slightly lowered as you ascend. The tongue should move with the jaw; lips should stay somewhat closed and relaxed. Repeat the exercise, ascending by half steps. As the pitches get higher, intentionally maintain breath energy/pressure and allow the pharynx (back of the mouth portion) to open more.

Males—Classical

Start on [ɑ] in the lower-middle range. Slide up an octave modifying toward [ɔ] as you enter the passaggio. As pitch ascends, gradually move the tongue arch forward but otherwise maintain the vocal tract in the position of [ɔ].

Females and Males—Contemporary

Using the octave slides exercises suggested for classical singing, as you ascend allow the front of the jaw to open more as you ascend in pitch; your tongue and tongue hump should be forward in the mouth. The lips should also widen as you ascend (showing more teeth). Larynx position should be flexible, allowing it to rise somewhat as needed.

Chapter 6: Consonants

Consonants certainly deserve as much attention as vowels, for they are an integral part of communicating the message of song. They are also an expressive device in all musical styles. Successful enunciation of consonants can, however, be a challenge for two significant reasons:

- ❖ Singers often compromise the preceding and subsequent vowels when they do not form consonants efficiently. We call this "vowel pollution."
- ❖ Singers often pay consonants insufficient attention because they focus on the vowels out of a desire to create beautiful tonal quality.

Singers need to learn how consonants are best formed, including which muscles and structures should and should not be involved.

The articulators

The primary players in the pronunciation of consonants are the lips, teeth, tongue, the ridge just behind the top front teeth (technically known as the alveolar ridge), the hard palate, and the soft palate (for nasal consonants). Proper jaw position is also essential. Singers should use only the articulators that are necessary to form a consonant and nothing more; otherwise, vowels preceding or following the consonant will be compromised.

Quick, efficient consonant formation in classical singing

When singing in classical style, in the vast majority of situations, consonants should be formed quickly and precisely, with the tongue returning rapidly to its resting place, lying against the lower front teeth, just touching the gum line. As noted in the preceding chapter, this practice helps to ensure vowel integrity. Production of vowels between consonants is compromised by intermediate tongue positions that occur if the tongue returns too slowly to its resting place.

The jaw also needs either to move quickly to the best position for the subsequent vowel or, whenever possible, not change its position. Guard vowel shape and resonance space! A lazy tongue or jaw risks distorting the sound of the subsequent vowel, affecting intonation, pitch stability, and/or resonance.

An unintended vowel sound (such as a schwa) can occur when consonants are sung too slowly. Consonant clusters are particularly troublesome in this respect. For example, singing [bl] in the word "blow" too slowly may cause the word to sound like "buh-lo."

- ➤ McKinney (2005) cautions that when the initial consonant of a word is formed too slowly, the pitch may be flat, forcing a singer to "scoop up" to the proper pitch on the subsequent vowel.
- ➤ This problem often occurs at the beginning of a phrase. McKinney (2005) suggests envisioning the initial consonant on the same pitch as the subsequent vowel as a solution. We would add that it is desirable to inhale with the vocal tract (pharynx space, mouth space, and tongue) in position for the vowel and pitch to be sung, whether or not a word starts with a consonant.

Excessive tongue tension/tongue rigidity makes it difficult to sing consonants quickly. Suggestions for relaxing tongue rigidity appear in Chapter 14 on tension.

Consonant length is often extended in contemporary styles

In many contemporary styles, storytelling and the expression of the text is of paramount importance. The duration of consonants is, therefore, more of an artistic choice. For example, in musical theatre, some consonants will have a somewhat longer duration while other consonants (in less important words) might be largely deemphasized.

- ➤ Sundberg and Romedahl (2009) found that elongating consonants contributes to the intelligibility of musical theatre singers.

In classical singing, certain languages will require longer consonant duration, such as the double consonant in Italian and, to some extent, in German. In English, intentionally elongating some consonants may help with expression and intelligibility, especially in art song.

Classical/legit singers should be judicious about exaggeration

Some classical vocal authorities suggest that singers should exaggerate consonants to raise their sound level closer to that of vowels (e.g., McKinney, 2005). But proper use of the tongue, lips, and jaw is usually sufficient to bring out consonants.

> As Alderson (1979) says, "Consonants are only a fraction as loud as vowels... but their high frequency energy is particularly adapted to human ears, so that crisp diction fairly crackles in a good acoustical setting" (p. 175).

Furthermore, exaggeration of jaw movements can affect resonance, vowel integrity, and tonal quality. And, exaggerated movement of any articulator can create unwanted noise and tension.

Our perspective is that classical singers simply need to understand how best to form consonants and to be mindful of the need to execute them. This is particularly important for final consonants, which are the most likely to be overlooked. (See more about final consonants later in this chapter.) In contrast, singers of contemporary styles typically need to give more attention to consonants for stylistic and intelligibility reasons, as noted above.

❖ In highly reverberant environments, regardless of style, it may be desirable to emphasize or elongate consonants to enhance intelligibility.

Finally, be careful to avoid excessive tension in emphasizing consonants. Otherwise, vowels and resonance will be compromised.

Consonants requiring special consideration

Consonants requiring substantial jaw or lip closing—b, j, m, p, s, v, z

These consonants cause problems with preceding and subsequent vowels if they are formed too slowly. For [j], [s], [v], and [z] the jaw is closed to some extent to form the consonant. The most significant source of difficulty is the jaw lowering phase—as the jaw lowers, the frequency of the first formant is raised, raising the perceived pitch. The jaw-closing phase is usually less of a problem as singers typically close the jaw quickly, but if not, the perceived pitch will lower due to the lowering of the first formant. Form consonants efficiently to avoid these unintended "scoops" in pitch. In contemporary styles scoops are often a deliberate artistic choice.

Sing bah, mah, pah sah, vah quickly and efficiently, avoiding a scoop.

As outlined below, the jaw should remain lowered to form [m], but the lips must stay closed. The jaw should also remain lowered for [b] and [p], with the lips quickly closing and opening. If the lips are slowly closed and opened for the subsequent vowel, pitch scoops can occur with these consonants as well.

Consonants requiring the tongue to seal the roof of the mouth—g, k, and ng ([ŋ])

These consonants are challenging because the obstruction of airflow makes it difficult to maintain resonance and keep a phrase moving, reducing the sense of legato. This is particularly problematic for classical/legit singing.

"God" is an excellent example of a word involving the problematic [g], because it illustrates two additional problems that occur with this consonant:

- Over pronouncing [g] generates undesirable overtone frequencies (i.e., noise). It can also distort the meaning of the word ("cod" rather than "God") if the consonant becomes unvoiced (see the section below).
- Slow production of [g] creates a diphthong. The mouth is relatively closed to generate this consonant, but then the jaw must be lowered to create the vowel [a]. Lower the jaw too slowly, and a diphthong occurs.

Consonant clusters

Consonant clusters typically require two distinct movements. With the aforementioned "bl" as in "blow," each consonant requires a separate action. The same is true of "pl" as in "plow." Singers should look for these and mark them in their repertoire for special attention.

Jaw position when singing l, k, g, t, d, m, n, ng

It is possible to sing these consonants with the jaw lowered in the back. The degree of lowering is a stylistic choice. Jaw lowering is typically greater in classical singing and the amount is determined by the vowel that follows to reduce the amount of jaw movement. This is both more efficient and helps to lessen the likelihood of interference with surrounding vowels.

Timbre of [m] varies with the extent of jaw lowering

While [m] is a nasal consonant formed with closed lips, singers can alter its timbre by changing the amount of jaw lowering in the back.

Try humming [m] with the lower jaw somewhat elevated. Then lower the jaw at the back and notice the change in resonance.

Additional difficulties associated with [l]

Singers tend to form [l] with the tongue hitting the roof of the mouth, too far behind the front teeth, which forces the tongue back in the mouth (Vennard,

1967). Also, too much of the tongue surface may contact the roof of the mouth. The *tip* of the tongue should be close to the teeth. (Vennard suggests putting the tongue on the teeth, but this is a bit extreme.)

> ➤ R. Miller (1996) indicates that classical singers should execute [l] with a flick of the tongue and a quick return to the resting position against the lower bottom teeth. Otherwise, [l] becomes "a lazy, liquid consonant that encourages transitional sounds." (Miller, p. 92) Note, however, that elongating the production of [l] may be a useful artistic device in contemporary styles.

Try saying "tele" (as in telephone) over and over, concentrating on forming both the "t" and the "l" in the same place (tongue just behind the front top teeth). Return the tongue quickly back to its resting position for the vowel. This is relatively easy because the tip of the tongue goes in the same place for both [t] and [l]. Also, try singing "blow," "clear," and "glory," combining the initial consonants into one efficient consonant cluster.

Think of [w] and "y" in terms of the vowels [u] and [i]

Although singers may think of [w] and "y" as consonants, they are actually vowels (technically, glides). By thinking of w and y as vowels, singers can improve tonal quality and expressivity:

- ❖ [w] (as in "wonder") is formed similarly to [u]—start by singing [u] with slightly more lip pucker and move quickly to the next vowel. In the transition to the following vowel, [w] will be formed.
- ❖ "y" (as in "yet"—IPA [j]) is formed similarly to [i]—start by singing [i] with the tongue closer to the hard palate and, from that position, quickly move the tongue to the place of the subsequent vowel. In the transition to the next vowel, the [j] forms.

Voiced versus unvoiced consonants

Unvoiced consonants do not involve vocal fold vibration—breath passes through the open glottis, with the sound shaped by the tongue, lips, teeth, and jaw. In contrast, voiced consonants carry pitch.

An unvoiced consonant cluster that receives insufficient attention is "wh" (e.g., as in "where"). In speaking, "wear" and "where" are not differentiated, but it is necessary to do so in some styles of singing. Shape the mouth like a puckered [u] as for [w] and increase exhalation to get the breath to rush through the lips to make the [h] portion of the sound.

Some voiced and unvoiced consonants are produced using the articulators in the same way and can, therefore, be thought of as pairs. Consider [b] and [p]. Both are formed by closing the lips and then quickly opening them. [p] is unvoiced, and [b] is voiced, but the lips work in the same way. Table 6.1 lists example pairs. A more comprehensive table is in the Appendix.

Both solo and ensemble singers can use knowledge of voiced and unvoiced pairs to great benefit. For example, when singing the word "praise," an unvoiced [s] can make the release sound strong. By using [z], the word ends on a sung pitch with a gentler tone.

When to use an unvoiced consonant even though a voiced consonant is indicated

Even when the lyrics suggest a voiced consonant, using the unvoiced version can sometimes be helpful, especially in classical choral singing. For example, when singing "joy," the unvoiced consonant "ch" can be used to add emphasis and make the word sound more joyful!

Unvoiced consonants can also be helpful when entering on a high pitch. It is complicated to coordinate glottal closure and airflow simultaneously on a high pitch. If the airflow starts on the unvoiced version, the breath is already moving when the pitch is sung.

Voiced	Unvoiced
[v]	[f]
[g]	[k]
[d]	[t]
[z]	[s]
[b]	[p]
"j" (juice)	"ch" (choice)

Table 6.1 Examples of paired voiced and unvoiced consonants

When using a microphone, singers need to be mindful of unvoiced "plosive" consonants. These can cause "pops" or distortions if sung to close to the mic or produced with the same breath pressure as without amplification. In general, when amplified, consonants should become more like natural speech. In such circumstances, singers might also consider using something between a voiced and unvoiced version of the consonant.

Additional considerations for the voiced consonants l, m, n, ng ([ŋ])

Voiced consonants [l], [m], [n], and "ng" ([ŋ]) can be sung with long duration. The same is true of "r" (addressed separately, below).

Some singers close too quickly from the preceding vowel to these sustainable consonants. This is particularly true of amateur choral singers. For example, when singing "moon," singers may give insufficient length to the [u] vowel by shifting too quickly to [n].

Nonetheless, for effect, a conductor or solo singer may choose to give additional duration to one of these consonants, particularly when they end a phrase. For example, extending [n] in "amen" will make the ending seem less abrupt. The key is to be conscious about circumstances and reasons for giving additional duration to these consonants.

"r"—a particularly problematic voiced consonant for singers

"r" has many IPA symbols depending on its pronunciation. To avoid unnecessary complexity, we use "r" to refer to a variety of articulations. Still, we are explicit in labeling the method of production (see the Appendix for specific IPA symbols). The major forms of "r" are:

- **Pre-vocal retroflex "r."** To sing "red" with a pre-vocal "r," start with the jaw closed, and the tip of the tongue curled back (the retroflex position). Move quickly to the subsequent vowel.
- **Ending retroflex "r."** This is commonly used by English speakers at the end of words such as "river," and is often referred to as the "American r." The jaw is closed but not as much as for the pre-vocal "r." Again, the tongue curls backward.
- **Flipped "r."** Flipping is almost like singing "vedy" in place of "very." The difference is that the tongue touches the alveolar ridge (the raised area behind the top front teeth) more quickly and with less firm contact than when singing "d." Make only one contact with the ridge.
- **Rolled (trilled) "r."** Place the tongue on the alveolar ridge and use a reasonably high breath pressure to make the tongue flutter.
- **Guttural "r."** Formed by the back of the tongue placed against or near the uvula. Typical of speakers in many French and German areas.

Singers who have trouble with a rolled "r"' should try to form a "d" repeatedly with the tip of the tongue against the hard palate (just behind the alveolar ridge). Next, preface the "d" with a quick "h" or an accelerated breath exhalation. The rolled "r" requires higher than usual airflow to sustain it, but when singing, the duration of the roll is very short and should not have much impact on breath management.

Singing "r" in North American English

In classical singing, a flipped "r" may be used at the beginning of a word (e.g., "praise" and "raise"). In all styles of contemporary music (including much of modern classical music), a pre-vocal retroflex "r" is more appropriate and will sound more natural.

A rolled "r" can be used for dramatic emphasis on an initial "r" (e.g., "ring") and is appropriate in much of the classical literature. Nonetheless, do not use it indiscriminately. Singers who cannot form a rolled "r" can use a flipped "r" instead.

At or near the end of words (e.g., "river" and "word"), the commonly used retroflex "r" creates a large cavity just behind the lower incisors due to the tongue tip curling back. Using the retroflex "r" dramatically lowers the frequency of the third formant. (Some people also form this ending retroflex "r" by placing the back of the tongue on the roof of the mouth, creating a rather guttural "r.") Use of the retroflex "r" should be avoided in classical music, but is appropriate in contemporary styles.

> ➢ Vennard (1967) has good advice for classical singing: concentrate on making the "r" at the end of a word silent. You will still sound it very slightly, but do not create the retroflex "r" (e.g., not "riverrr" but rather something in between "rivuh" and "rivah").

Singing "r" in Italian and Latin

Here are useful rules for forming "r" when singing Italian:

- ❖ Flip an "r" between two vowels
- ❖ Roll an "r" next to a consonant
- ❖ Roll a final "r"
- ❖ Never use a retroflex "r"

In Latin, "r" is never retroflex. A flipped or slightly rolled "r" is appropriate.

Singing "r" in German and French

In German and French, the use of a flipped or *slightly* rolled "r" at the beginning of a word (e.g., reitet) is appropriate. When "r" occurs at the end of a German or French word (e.g., sicher), leave it nearly silent.

Some singers get carried away with the rolled "r" when singing German, rendering their sound unnatural. Do not use the German or French guttural "r" except in popular or folk music because of reduced resonance.

Final consonants

As noted above, singers often give insufficient attention to final consonants (e.g., "t" in "it"). Without sufficient emphasis, a word with a final consonant may be confused with other words, or not understood at all. For example, if the "t" in "mist" is not pronounced, it sounds like "miss." Thus, in the song "Heather on the Hill," from the musical *Brigadoon,* the meaning of the phrase "when the mist is in the gloamin" could be misunderstood.

- Varying the sound of a final consonant can be a useful artistic device. For example, the word "kiss" can sound very different if a singer lengthens the "ss" with significant breath pressure. Compare this to a short "s" that is more gently expressive.
- McKinney (2005) states that a lack of attention to final consonants can cause the pitch to go flat. As noted above, because the jaw is closing during the transition from many vowels to certain consonants, the effect is to lower the first formant frequency, making the pitch sound flat. Additionally, singers may relax breath support too soon on a voiced final consonant such as [m], also causing the pitch to go flat.

Adding "uh" or "ah" to final consonants versus elision

Some singers and conductors choose to add a shadow vowel/neutral syllable after a consonant to help with intelligibility. A rousing phrase ending with a final voiced consonant can often benefit from added pitch duration. Consider "Amen"—adding a neutral syllable after the final "n" can sometimes be useful.

An added neutral syllable can also aid in the understanding of pairs of words by adding separation. Consider the text "and died"—the "ds" between the two words might be elided (combined to form one consonant sound) such as in "andied" or could be separated by a neutral syllable "anduhdied."

In some cases, eliding final and initial consonants will help with clarity. Consider the "Sanctus" by John Rutter from his *Requiem*. The repeated sanctus text could have a neutral syllable between each one "Sanctusuh, Sanctusuh, Sanctus" etc. or the conductor could choose to have the singers elide the "s" consonants to sing "SanctuSanctuSanctus." This is a personal choice based on level of enunciation and the ability of the choir.

Singers should be wary of adding too much emphasis on the neutral syllable as this can have the opposite effect, obscuring the text instead of clarifying it. Nor should it be used indiscriminately.

The choice to add a shadow vowel should take into consideration the meaning of the text and the desired degree of emphasis. With high tessituras, faster tempos, reverberant spaces, and/or many singers, elision may be the best choice.

Sometimes consonants should precede the beat

There are times when phrases begin with a consonant cluster or an unvoiced consonant. With consonants formed on the beat, listeners may perceive that singers are late. Formation of these consonants just before the beat will avoid this problem and give the subsequent vowel fuller duration. Robert Shaw applied the principle of anticipatory consonants extensively in his choral conducting (Blocker, 2004), but it is also applicable to solo singing. It is especially desirable in rhythmic music.

- ➢ Henderson (1979) argues that forming consonants just before the beat prevents singing from seeming lethargic and contributes to the sensation of a continuous, legato style of singing.
- ➢ Appelman (1986) says that "every consonant must be slightly anticipated by a proper preparation of the articulators" (p. 238). This makes it possible for the vowel to occur *on* the beat.
- ➢ Richard Miller (2004) recommends the use of anticipatory consonants primarily for unvoiced consonants, since these carry no pitch (for example, [s] and [p]; see the section on voiced and unvoiced consonants for more examples). Voiced consonants should be placed on the beat because they carry pitch.

We concur with Miller's perspective—unvoiced consonants, but not voiced consonants, should be anticipatory for classical/legit styles. We would, however, consider the anticipatory timing of consonant clusters as well because of their longer duration.

Singers can also employ anticipatory consonants expressively in any style. For example, drawing out [l] in "love" and [st] in "star" can focus audience attention on these important words.

- ➢ Sundberg and Bauer-Huppmann (2007) studied lieder recordings by eight internationally recognized artists. In most instances, consonants and subsequent vowels were timed so that the vowel onset occurred at the same time as the accompaniment, supporting the concept of anticipatory consonants. Occasionally, consonants were drawn out, or vowel onset occurred before the beat, likely for artistic purposes.

More generally, the timing of consonants is highly variable in contemporary styles depending upon the desired emotional effect. Ahead of the beat, they add a sense of tension or aggressiveness. Behind the beat ("laying back'), they create a more relaxed feeling (Shapiro, 2016).

Consonant exercises

Nasal consonants with a lowered jaw

Hang-gun-num-ee: On one pitch, move through the vowels quickly to sustain each nasal consonant ([ŋ], [n], [m]), finishing on the [i] vowel. Sustain the consonants shown in blue. Singing "hang" initially will help to lower the jaw. Be sure to maintain that lowered jaw space as you sing the remainder of the exercise.

Ha ---- **ng** ---- gu**n** ---- nu**m** ----- ee --------------

Singing consonants quickly

Hold your dominant arm in front of you and imagine you are holding a wide paintbrush in your hand with a wall in front of you. Paint a horizontal brush stroke on the "wall," moving from left to right and then changing direction quickly. Do this several times. Now sing [ta] while "painting,'" with the consonant pronounced quickly on the change of direction and the vowel sustained during the "painting." Vary the consonant and vowel.

This exercise also assists singing a legato line.

For kids and everyone! Echo consonants

Choose a group of either voiced or unvoiced consonants, e.g., [p], [t], [k]. Speak the consonants with a variety of rhythms and have singers echo these back. Increase and decrease speed.

For kids and everyone! Efficient consonants

Use nursery rhyme style phrases. Begin by speaking, then move to a variety of melodic patterns. Here are some examples:

Efficient [m]—*"Many mumbling mice, making merry music in the moonlight, mighty nice!"*

Efficient [b]—*"Baby bee, baby bee, beautiful baby bumble bee."*

Efficient [t] and [l]— *Try saying "tele" (as in telephone) over and over, concentrating on forming both the "t" and the "l" in the same place (tongue just behind the front top teeth). Return the tongue quickly back to its resting position for the vowel. This is relatively easy because the tip of the tongue goes in the same place for both [t] and [l]. Also, try singing "blow," "clear," and "glory," combining the initial consonants into one efficient consonant cluster.*

Avoiding scoops to the pitch consonants preceding a vowel

Sing bah, mah, pah sah, vah quickly and efficiently, avoiding a scoop.

Singing "y" (IPA [j]) correctly

Sing the German word "ja" on a descending triad (major or minor—ja, ja, ja). Imagine the initial consonant to be [i] and move quickly to [ɑ].

ja ---------------- ja ------------------ ja --------------------

Emphasizing initial voiced and unvoiced consonants for effect

Choose a voiced consonant and vary how long you sing it. Try singing "mother" by varying the length of [m] from a rapid enunciation to up to four beats. Try a more challenging variation by changing the length of unvoiced consonants such as [s] as in "soft" and [k] in "cool."

Classical singing of the ending retroflex (American) "r"

Sing "far" with an "American r" (farrrr). Note how the jaw is somewhat closed, and the tongue curls back slightly to form the "American r." Then sing "far," keeping the jaw lowered. First, sing "fa, fa, fa," and then sing "far, far, far," imagining a very subtle, short "r" at the end. Concentrate on keeping the tip of the tongue at the base of the lower incisors. Do not close the jaw or let the tongue curl backward to help avoid singing an "American r."

For kids and everyone! Snapping the timing of consonant release

If singers are struggling with precisely timing a final consonant, try snapping the fingers when it is time to release. It will be evident from the snap if a singer does not perceive the release accurately. Repeat until it is correct (R. Webster & S. Sivers, personal communication, August 27, 2019).

Chapter 7: Vibrato

Vibrato is an important aspect of a singer's perceived tone quality. Voices vibrate for physiological reasons—there is no such thing as a truly "straight tone," as discussed later in this chapter—but there are several factors that contribute to how the listener perceives this vibration.

Vibrato is an oscillation in pitch. There are four main vibrato descriptors—rate (number of oscillations per second), extent (how far above and below the mean pitch), jitter (variability of the rate), and shimmer (variability of the intensity). Good vibrato is part of the singer's core sound for most classical singing. It is generally moderate in extent with little jitter, and thus consistent. In other styles, vibrato is used in a variety of ways, as described later in this chapter.

Seashore conducted the first comprehensive studies on the perception of vibrato in the early part of the 20th century. He concluded, "Much of the most beautiful vibrato is below the threshold for vibrato hearing and is perceived merely as tone quality" (Seashore, 1938, p. 46). Vennard (1967) concurs, noting that the listener hears only the mean pitch, and the variations in pitch are interpreted by the audience in terms of timbre, enhancing perceived tonal quality. More recent studies confirm these findings (see Sundberg, 1995).

> ➤ Seashore (1938) asserts that vibrato helps to convey emotion, and Howes, Callaghan, Davis, Kenny, and Thorpe (2004) reach a similar conclusion. The words, in combination with sound level, provide cues to the specific emotion.

Vibrato is a natural phenomenon

Vibrato results from nerve impulses in the larynx that have a typical frequency of 5–8 pulses per second. If the laryngeal area is appropriately relaxed, the laryngeal muscles naturally pulsate in time with this frequency. Early studies showed that the cricothyroid muscles are most involved with variations in pitch and amplitude (Mason & Zemlin, 1966), though Titze et al. (2002) make a convincing case for involvement of the thyroarytenoids as well.

Some voices naturally exhibit more vibrato than others. Nonetheless, the vast majority of singers can develop a moderate vibrato, as it is a natural consequence of developing breath support and learning to relax the vocal apparatus. Even untrained singers may exhibit vibrato, especially on longer notes where they are more likely to relax.

> ➤ Nix, Perna, James, and Allen (2016) assert that vibrato tends to become more regular as posture, breath control, laryngeal coordination, and vowel formation improve.

Richard Miller (1996) observes that good vibrato also requires proper contact between the vocal folds—with a breathy method of production making vibrato unlikely. Nor will a heavily pressed method of production facilitate vibrato. Thus, singers desiring vibrato in their sound should attend to the firmness of glottal closure.

"Straight Tone"

Because there is always some variation in pitch and/or amplitude due to nerve pulses in the larynx, there is no "straight tone" at the physiological level, only *minimal vibrato*. Instead, straight tone is the listener's perception of a sound with minimal vibrato (Titze, 2008a; Walker, 2006).

Some choral conductors prefer that their singers use minimal vibrato, and many performers of early music and music historians believe that "straight tone" is desirable for music composed prior to 1750–60. We discuss these issues in later sections of this chapter.

Desirable vibrato rate and extent

Vibrato rate (how fast) and particularly, extent (how wide) are the main contributors to how vibrato is perceived. There are substantial individual differences in both production and perception of vibrato. Nonetheless, there are some general acoustical and psychological truths delineated below that can guide conductors, teachers, and singers.

Vibrato rate

Different sources recommend different "ideal" vibrato rates (number of oscillations per second), but the vast majority fall within the range of 5–8 oscillations per second (5–8 Hz). Rate is little affected by style and is difficult to control, likely because rate is determined heavily by physiology (Titze, Story, Smith & Long, 2002; Manfredi et al., 2015). Nonetheless, singers can alter rate somewhat, as outlined in a later section.

- Richard Miller (1996) argues that a pleasing vibrato rate is in the range of 6–8 oscillations per second. Above eight, the voice sounds tremulous. Below six, it begins to approach a wobble because pitch variations are discernible as separate notes, creating an unpleasant distraction.
- Anand, Wingate, Smith, and Shrivastav (2012) find that for both naïve and expert listeners a rate of 6 Hz is judged as most appropriate.
- Titze et al. (2002) note that as people age, their vibrato rate will likely slow.
- Shipp, Leanderson, and Sundberg (1980); Cecconello (2010); Guzman et al. (2012) have found that women exhibit a slightly faster vibrato rate than men.

Except for the few singers with abnormal rates below five/above eight oscillations per second, audiences take little notice of differences among singers on this parameter. As discussed below, extent of vibrato has a greater impact on audience response and, fortunately, is easier to control.

Vibrato extent

Similar to other physiological phenomena, vibrato extent exists on a continuum from a minimal vibrato ("straight tone") through a tone-quality-enhancing moderate vibrato, to a wider vibrato that is very noticeable to the listener.

Across a variety of styles, extent is often observed in the range from roughly 30–200 cents (e.g., Manfredi et al., 2015). Total variation of a half step equals 100 cents—one quarter-step above and below the sung pitch.

Vibrato extent varies among singers due to both physiology and artistic choices; it is typically greater for females and for classical singing. Recommendations for extent for classical singers range from a quarter step to a half step above and below the sung pitch. This is a total variation of 100 to 200 cents, though we believe 200 cents is excessive from an aesthetic standpoint, even for opera.

- Miller (1996) says that pitch variation should not exceed a quarter step above and a quarter step below the sung pitch (100 cents total).
- The psychologist Seashore (1936) conducted extensive studies of vibrato with listeners and concluded similarly that a moderate total variation of 100 cents is pleasing to audiences, while 200 cents is excessive.

Why do these authorities recommend moderate extent? The answer has to do with psychological fusion of the varying pitch with the fundamental frequency. With an extent of no more than roughly 100 cents, listeners do not hear the extremes of pitch, rather they hear only the fundamental frequency and interpret vibrato as a richness of tone. Thus, vibrato is not noticeable per se with moderate extent. As extent increases above this level, more listeners may attend to the pitch excursions and find them disagreeable.

> - Seashore (1938) found that some individuals have an ability to detect vibrato that is 50–100 times more sensitive than individuals with the least ability. We would venture to say that voice professionals are much more likely to notice the vibrato itself. This likely plays a role in requests for "straight tone" from some ensemble conductors.
> - Opera soloists tend to use a wider vibrato, averaging 150 cents in one study (Johnson-Read & Schubert, 2010). This extent is likely noticeable as vibrato, per se. This same study found that in lieder (art song), vibrato extents are more on the order of a moderate 100 cents.

This is not to say that optimal fused perception is always a singer's goal. In some circumstances, singers want their vibrato to be noticed as such, either for ornamental purposes or to convey stronger emotion. In the right circumstances, noticeable vibrato is not necessarily displeasing for audiences.

- *Terminal vibrato* involves adding vibrato in the middle of a note, and widening the extent as the note is sustained. Often, this is accompanied by an increase in sound level. The final note thus blossoms. Many styles use some form of terminal vibrato, particularly musical theatre. Terminal vibrato may be noticeable as a contrast to the minimal vibrato used during most of a phrase.
- Classical soloists may use wider vibrato on some words for emphasis.
- A more noticeable vibrato characterizes operatic singing. The acceptable extent has increased over the last 100 years.
- In early music, singers used a wider form of vibrato as an ornament (Jerold, 2006).

We believe that moderate vibrato in most classical and choral music is best for both audiences and singers. "Straight tone" in classical and much choral singing should be the exception rather than the rule.

- Vibrato is best for audiences because of the aforementioned perceived improvement in tonal quality.
- Vibrato is best for audiences because it improves intonation. Titze (2008a) says that the muscles controlling pitch experience irregular tremors that make it challenging to control pitch well with "straight tone"

production. Vibrato creates a more regular pulsation in pitch, allowing for a more stable perceived fundamental frequency.

❖ Suppressing vibrato can be tiring. Large and Iwata (1976) state that vibrato involves an alternating contraction and relaxation of the laryngeal muscles. Vibrato thus helps to prevent vocal fatigue. Even in contemporary styles where vibrato is not consistent, there is often vibrato at the end of a phrase, which helps to relax the muscles.

Style implications for vibrato

In most classical singing moderate vibrato is appropriate. Some argue that vibrato should be minimal for Renaissance and Baroque music, but we believe a moderate vibrato is appropriate for these periods. This is examined in greater detail in a later section.

Many contemporary styles, such as belting and pop/rock, do not involve consistent vibrato throughout the sound. The more restricted use of vibrato in contemporary styles is related to production being more speech-like, which does not generally involve vibrato unless expressing strong emotion (Roll, 2016). As noted above, contemporary singers may use noticeable vibrato at the end of a phrase and/or for expression of emotion on certain words. In styles such as folk music, vibrato may occur naturally on longer notes.

➢ LeBorgne (2001) found greater variability in both extent and rate for elite musical theatre belters compared to classical singers. This may be useful for artistic/expressive purposes in this style.

Table 7.1 illustrates some vibrato expectations by musical style, though we emphasize that vibrato is always an artistic choice in contemporary styles.

The ability to sing with varying degrees of vibrato is a valuable addition to the singer's skill set. As voices mature and achieve the ability to sing with a relaxed, tone-enhancing vibrato, singers should work towards *flexibility* of vibrato that allows them to achieve a variety of effects from a shimmering tone with minimal vibrato through a vibrant, full sound. Methods for accomplishing this are discussed later in this chapter.

Musical Style	Use of Vibrato
Most Classical*	Consistent; moderate rate and extent. Soloists may use wider extent to emphasize certain words.
Opera Solo	Consistent; slower rate and particularly, wider extent, are common.
Some 20th Century and Later Classical	No noticeable vibrato where indicated by the composer; may be used selectively.
Musical Theatre Legit	Consistent; moderate rate, sometimes less extent than in classical. Rate may be slowed and, particularly, extent widened for some notes (e.g., for emphasis/heightened emotion, at ends of phrases).
Musical Theatre Belt	Vibrato not noticeable until the end of a phrase where terminal vibrato is used. If there is a chord change in the middle of the note, vibrato will commence at that point.
Rock	Rarely used, though singers of rock ballads may exhibit vibrato for words they wish to emphasize or to convey emotion.
Country	Artistic ornament.
Pop	Sometimes, often with greater extent on the final note of a phrase for emotional expression.
Jazz	Sometimes and with narrower extent than classical. Extent increases on longer notes.
Gospel	Often used in songs with slow tempos and more generally on sustained notes. If not used throughout a song, terminal vibrato is typical (Robinson-Martin, 2017)

*Some argue that singers should use minimal vibrato in Renaissance and Baroque classical music. See below for a discussion of this issue.

Table 7.1 Use of vibrato according to musical style

Solving vibrato problems

Singers without vibrato

A person who has only recently begun to sing regularly may not exhibit vibrato initially but will likely develop it over time. It may be helpful to give such singers a sense of how vibrato feels. Moaning like a ghost or mimicking an opera singer are possible techniques. We suggest other possibilities in the exercises at the end of the chapter.

A person who sings regularly but still cannot create a vibrant sound usually has one or more of the following problems:

* Breathy or glottal onset
* Too much or too little breath pressure
* Insufficient airflow
* Tension in the vocal mechanism
* Excessively high larynx position
* Imitation of the sound of an artist who sings with minimal vibrato

Both inadequate and overly firm glottal closure are the most common culprits. Using moderate glottal closure (3, 4, or 5 on a 1 (very relaxed) to 7 (very firm) scale—see Table 7.2) creates the amount of closure necessary for vibrato. **Level 4 closure provides the highest potential for vibrato and should be the starting point for singers seeking to cultivate vibrato.**

Firmness of Glottal Closure

1 Very Relaxed	2	3	4	5	6	7 Very Firm
Breathy			Moderate			Heavy Belt

Potential for Vibrato

Table 7.2 Firmness of glottal closure for which vibrato is most likely

Another difficulty is hypo or hyper breath pressure—either too little or too much breath energy. Singers need time to learn how much breath energy is required for their voice to resonate fully and vibrantly, and it can be especially difficult to ascertain from within a chorus.

Freedom from tension throughout the entire vocal tract is also critical. With tension, the laryngeal muscles cannot relax sufficiently for natural pulsation to occur. An excessively high larynx position is also associated with a lack of vibrato (Shipp, Doherty, & Haglund, 1990).

Singers must take care to avoid forcing vibrato through artificial methods like breath pulsation, throat manipulation, or jaw movements. These methods create an inconsistent vibrato that varies excessively in pitch.

Furthermore, artificially induced vibrato involves elevated levels of tension and energy expenditure.

- ❖ Nonetheless, a number of elite musical theatre performers appear to successfully use small jaw pulsations that slow their rate on selective notes. Together with a wider vibrato extent, this helps to elicit strong emotional reactions in listeners.

To summarize, vibrato develops naturally over time as singers learn to use coordinated onset with an appropriate degree of vocal fold closure along with proper breath pressure and elimination of tension. SOVT exercises from Chapter 3 may be helpful.

Singers with unintentionally inconsistent vibrato

Inconsistent vibrato in classical singing occurs for three significant reasons:

- ❖ Glottal onset.
- ❖ Too much laryngeal tension during the phrase, relaxing only at the end or on longer pitches.
- ❖ Excessive breath pressure/airflow during the passage while reducing breath pressure on longer pitches or toward the end of the phrase. As noted in Chapter 2 on breathing, proper use of abdominal muscles to control expiration is essential for consistent vibrato.

Some singers may have a normal vibrato that becomes problematic with higher pitches and/or louder portions of a phrase. Wobble (slow vibrato with wide but inconsistent extent), often results from a lack of breath support. For those with a tremolo (excessively high vibrato rate), it is likely due to excess laryngeal tension and breath pressure.

Regular use of warm-ups prior to rehearsal is helpful in producing a moderate and even vibrato rate.

- ➢ Moorcroft and Kenny (2012) report that the warm-up process brings all singers closer to a region of more regular, moderate vibrato rates.

It is also useful to note that louder singing tends to produce more regular vibrato modulations (Guzman et al., 2012). Singers who are having difficulty creating regular vibrato may try singing at a louder dynamic (though not at the extremes of their range, as noted below).

Inconsistent vibrato is a particular problem for choral blend if some singers have vibrato only at the ends of phrases or on longer pitches. Wide-ranging vibrato at the end of a phrase is particularly important to avoid in Baroque music, where a narrow vibrato toward the end of a section is desired to make chord tuning apparent.

Unintentionally delayed vibrato

Vibrato is most likely to start at the beginning of a note with an open pharynx, raised soft palate, and comfortably low larynx. There is also some evidence that vibrato rate is more consistent when this technique is employed (Mitchell & Kenny, 2004). This is mostly an issue for certain classical styles, such as opera. Classical art song often involves a slightly delayed vibrato (Johnson-Read & Schubert, 2010).

Curing wobble

An excessively slow vibrato rate that may also be quite wide characterizes the wobble. Wobble can result from:

- Lack of proper breath support, stemming from improper breathing technique, aging, and/or general physical inactivity that affect the abdominal and rib musculature. Weak abdominal muscles are likely to be the prime problem.
  - In a study of trained singers' ability to control vibrato rate, participants stated that they could increase the vibrato rate with more breath support and decrease it with less support (Dromey, Carter, & Hopkin, 2003).
- Slackness in the vocal folds such that there is insufficient resistance to the flow of air (R. Miller, 1996). This slackness can be a consequence of aging or lack of attention to firmness of glottal closure.
- Poor condition of the laryngeal muscles due to lack of use. This is particularly problematic for older singers who also experience loss of muscle tone due to aging.
  - Titze et al. (2002) note that poor tone in the laryngeal muscles increases the time a muscle takes to contract, which could account for a reduction in the rate of 1–2 pulsations per second. Singers can reduce their wobble by performing vocal exercises and by singing at lower dynamic levels when at the extremes of their range—less mass of the thyroarytenoid muscle is involved when singing softly.
  - McKinney (2005) concurs that wobble in many amateur choral singers is due to a lack of vocal and physical exercise; they may sing only at choir practice and performances. Singers should vocalize daily and use SOVT exercises, even if only for 10 minutes a day, to maintain their breath support and keep laryngeal muscles in good shape.

Additional causes of and cures for wobble

Some other thoughts about causes and cures for wobble include:

* The cricothyroid muscles of the larynx and certain jaw muscles interconnect (Mason & Zemlin, 1966). Tensing the jaw may cause it to tremble in time with pulsations in the cricothyroid muscles. Since the jaw muscles have substantial mass, interconnection of the cricothyroids with a tense jaw will inevitably slow the vibrato rate, potentially producing a wobble.
* In a master class, Renée Fleming noted that a slow vibrato rate (in this case not involving wide pitch excursions) might occur when a singer involves the tongue and portions of the pharynx in vibrato.

Basic exercises to combat wobble

Exercises to combat wobble include onset exercises to ensure a coordinated onset. Slides extending to a fifth can be employed to make sure abdominal support is consistent throughout phonation. Physical exercise of the abdominal muscles (as outlined in Chapter 2 on breathing) is also helpful. The sibilant exercise for breathing from Chapter 2 is useful as well. These exercises are crucial as singers age. (See Chapter 13 on changing voices.)

The old saying "use it or lose it" definitely applies to singing! Keeping the muscles supple and singing more than just a couple of times a week will go a long way toward fending off the wobble.

Dealing with tremolo

A tremolo involves a fast vibrato (8–10 oscillations per second). For some singers with tremolo, the jaw and tongue exhibit a corresponding rapid shake (R. Miller, 1996). Singers who exhibit tremolo may have a strident, harsh sound usually caused by excessive breath pressure and laryngeal tension. General muscular tension may also cause tremolo (Titze et al., 2002). Tense muscles respond rapidly in so-called "twitch mode."

Tremolo is more common in younger singers and, in these cases, may result from artificial attempts to create vibrato.

Exercises to free a voice from tremolo can include breathing exercises with a particular focus on relaxing the airways during inhalation. We also recommend onset exercises to eliminate glottal attacks (in Chapter 3 on initiation, creation, and release of sound), and the tension reduction methods of Chapter 14.

Singers with vibrato problems (whether they be wobble or tremolo) can benefit from voice training. Longitudinal studies have shown that voice training results in a lowering of vibrato rates for those whose vibrato rate is initially high and raises vibrato rates for those whose rate is initially low. Furthermore, there is an increase in vibrato consistency (Mürbe, Zahnert, Kuhlisch, & Sundberg, 2007).

Vibrato is naturally less controllable at low and high ends of the range

At the low end of a singer's range, the thyroarytenoid (TA) muscles completely control pitch. At the high end of a singer's range, cricothyroid control is dominant. Given the tension of the dominant muscles at these extremes and the lack of sufficient opposition from the other set of controlling muscles, muscular pulsations may naturally be less controlled. It is thus more difficult for singers to either increase or decrease vibrato at these extremes, and there may be less stability.

Summary

The bottom line is that the best-sounding vibrato results from excellent vocal technique. Poor technique often produces inconsistent, wobbly, or tremulous vibrato.

Modifying vibrato

All singers should develop the ability to create a moderate, consistent vibrato. Once mastered, it is feasible and useful to work on modifying vibrato.

Most singers will be asked to sing with varying degrees of vibrato at some point, whether with a conductor who prefers a "straight" sound or for stylistic reasons (e.g., as in belting, pop music, etc.). While classical voice teachers may be reluctant to address singing with less vibrato in the studio (preferring to focus on the establishment of a core, vibrant sound), teachers, singers, and conductors should all be aware of techniques and exercises for healthily modifying vibrato. Voice teachers need to address the continuum of vibrato with their students, especially those who may be expected to sing with varying degrees of vibrato. A voice teacher is an ideal person to assist a singer in utilizing vocal techniques to achieve a variety of tonal colors, including vibrato.

As discussed above, the variation of vibrato focuses mainly on changes in extent (Titze et al., 2002).

- Singers who have a moderate vibrato can most easily widen it. This can be done by listening to a singer with a wide vibrato (e.g., an opera soloist or a contemporary singer who exhibits a wide, terminal vibrato) and imitating that singer.
- Singers who have a moderate or wide vibrato will find it most difficult to sing with minimal vibrato in a healthy manner. Accomplishing this is discussed below.

Singing with minimal vibrato

McCoy (2011) has found through EGG (electroglottograph) measurements in his voice science classes that when asked to sing "without vibrato," singers achieve this in three ways:

- Pressing the vocal folds together more firmly.
- Increasing airflow through the glottis by decreasing vocal fold pressure.
- Making no apparent change in laryngeal adjustments. These singers seem to sing with or without vibrato without noticeably changing their mode of production. Perhaps the changes are so subtle that EGG measurements cannot detect them.

No single technique will allow all singers to sing easily with minimal vibrato but bringing the vocal folds together more firmly or increasing airflow through a less tightly closed glottis are methods that singers should explore. In addition to fold closure, singers can experiment with varying vibrato through slight changes in breath pressure. Some singers also change their resonating space and may adjust laryngeal position (slightly higher or lower).

We advocate experimenting with vibrato through a variety of simple exercises—see the end of this chapter. Nix (2016) concurs, suggesting varying vibrato in ascending and descending slides, sustaining the final note with less vibrato. He also suggests alternating vibrato and minimal vibrato while singing one pitch, maintaining a steady air stream and a sense of freedom.

Altering vibrato in a healthy manner

When modifying vibrato, singers need to be careful to avoid excess tension in the tongue, mouth, jaw, neck, and other areas. Extraneous tension can cause fatigue, and if tension becomes a regular part of singing practice, it can contribute to vocal dysfunction. Short practice sessions in a comfortable register (mid to lower) are useful; extend both the range and length of practice sessions gradually. Using a mirror to monitor neck/facial tension and working with a trusted teacher/coach are important aids for achieving healthy vibrato modification.

Vibrato in choral singing

There is a long history of controversy about vibrato in choral singing. In this section we address the belief that vibrato is generally undesirable for choral singing. In the subsequent section we discuss the repertoire-specific issue of vibrato in early music, relevant to both ensembles and soloists.

Perception of vibrato as generally undesirable

As discussed above, some conductors who encourage their choral members to strive for "straight tone" may be particularly sensitive to the pitch variation of moderate vibrato. They may be unaware that most audience members do not notice the varying pitches when vibrato rate and extent are moderate, instead perceiving moderate vibrato to create a rich tone and hearing pitch as the average of the high and low extent of variation.

It is also possible that such conductors may be reacting to experiences with singers with a wobble or tremolo. The solution should not, however, be to suppress moderate vibrato in all members of the ensemble. Instead, wobble/tremolo should be addressed with those problematic singers, using the suggestions outlined in the section above on solutions to vibrato problems.

Other conductors may choose to suppress vibrato based on the theory that because the vibratos of singers in a group will not be in perfect phase with each other, vibrato will interfere with good intonation. This assertion is misguided because the ear perceives the pitch as the average of the high and low values, regardless of whether vibrato rates are synchronized.

- ➢ Vennard (1967) notes that in opera choruses composed of superb singers, all sing with vibrato, and there is no question of intonation problems caused by vibrato.
- ➢ Alderson (1979) states that precisely because individual singers have different vibrato rates (and hence are not in phase with each other), they will tend to balance each other out and thus contribute to the perception of vibrato as richness of tone. Ternström and Sundberg (1988) concur.

It is true that if vibrato is minimal, it is easier to tell if a choral group is in tune because the smoothing aspect of vibrato makes it harder to hear dissonant "beats." Thus, in some cases, an ensemble may wish to use minimal vibrato to show the audience that they are in tune on a final chord (e.g., in barbershop music or Baroque music). Nonetheless, demonstrating good intonation to the audience isn't the primary goal of choral singing. Instead, the key is that the audience *perceives* a choral group to be in tune.

Endorsements of vibrato in choral singing

Numerous vocal authorities endorse moderate vibrato in most choral singing.

- Robert Shaw (Blocker, 2004) argues that while a wobbling vibrato is destructive of blend, "... vibrato is as present in beautiful singing as it is in beautiful string playing" (p. 87).
- Vennard (1967) says, "When I hear concerts of choirs whose conductors have worked to eliminate [vibrato], I miss this vibrancy. It is true that they blend like one voice, and they make beautiful pianissimos. But this 'one' voice is breathy to my ears, and their fortissimos never thrill me ... When there is an assignment for a solo voice in the group, it is usually disappointing, for this weak production is inadequate" (p. 205).
- McKinney (2005) argues vigorously for the use of vibrato in a choral setting: "Vibrato is a natural concomitant of beautiful and expressive tone... There have been various movements, especially in the choral field, that have decried the use of vibrato in any form and have advocated the straight tone. Fortunately ... it has been classified not only as necessary for beauty of tone but also for physiological reasons" (p. 197).

Vibrato in the choral rehearsal

Of course, conductors can choose the tonal color that they desire for their ensemble and specific repertoire choices. But singers will be more receptive to requests for reduced vibrato if conductors demonstrate an understanding of how the voice works.

- ❖ If requesting reduced vibrato on high notes, rehearse those passages less frequently or an octave lower when learning the notes to avoid fatigue.
- ❖ Vowels such as [i] and [u] are particularly difficult to sing on high notes without vibrato, so be sure to modify the vowels appropriately, as outlined in Chapter 5 on vowels.
- ❖ Encourage more stagger breathing to provide vocal rest.

Conductors need to be aware of the implications of asking classical-style singers to modify their vibrato. For many singers, singing with less vibrato is an advanced skill, and conductors should not assume that all singers can do it easily, especially those who are actively training to be classical soloists. More generally, they should consider the ability level, training level, and goals of the singers with whom they are working and the demands of the repertoire concerning tessitura and range.

Conductors should also reflect on how long they will rehearse repertoire requiring vibrato modification. To that end, conductors should consider the way they talk about and refer to vibrato with their choirs. Words can have a considerable impact on the sound a choir achieves and the way they go about making it. Conductors use a variety of terms to refer to reduced vibrancy. Asking for "straight tone" is problematic because it seems to induce an unhealthy level of tension. Instead, we advocate encouraging singers to focus on the tone quality desired (e.g., clear, focused, bright, spinning, etc.).

> Sublett (2009) suggests that "A less problematic instruction might be, 'Sing with a pure, clear, focused tone that is right in the center of the pitch.' Emphasizing pitch accuracy is the most crucial aspect. When a choir director says, 'Straighten out your tone,' I advise my students to translate that as, 'Purify or focus the tone.' If choral colleagues can be persuaded to use different terminology, students will be far less likely to try to achieve the result by tension, and the sound itself will be more supple and flexible without losing the purity of intonation the director desires" (p. 542).

Particular issues for sopranos

Conductors frequently ask sopranos to minimize vibrato because their voice part naturally stands out in the choral texture. They may require extra support and advice about achieving a reduced vibrato, particularly when singing in the higher portions of their range where tension is highest and it is more challenging to control vibrato.

Sopranos singing classical music without vibrato and amplification will be at a particular disadvantage in larger spaces, whether they use lighter or firmer glottal closure to reduce vibrato. If they use lighter closure, their voice will have low intensity. If they use firmer vocal fold closure, this will dramatically reduce the amplitude of the fundamental frequency. But sopranos depend upon a strong fundamental frequency at the upper end of their range to be heard well—they cannot depend upon the singer's formant in this region of their voices. Singing with moderate vibrato is essential for sopranos in larger spaces (particularly those that are not resonant) unless there is electronic amplification.

Vibrato in early music

Many conductors and voice teachers assume that early music demands a sound without vibrato. Voice teachers, in particular, may therefore be reticent about asking their classical singers to perform these pieces. Yet there was much great choral (and solo) literature written in the Renaissance and Baroque eras. Not only is this music aesthetically appealing, but it is also of great pedagogical value and lends context to music written in subsequent periods.

We would suggest that early music can be sung appropriately with a moderate vibrato and that this was likely present in voices during this period. It is unfortunate if classical singers avoid this literature because of a misconception that all early repertoire was sung "without vibrato."

The degree to which singers used vibrato in Renaissance and Baroque music is unclear because no recordings exist from that time. We do, however, have historical commentary as well as intriguing information about organ stops designed to imitate the human voice during these periods. (See the section, below, concerning the Vox Humana and Voce Umana organ stops.)

Music historians who contend vibrato was absent in early music make one or more of the following arguments:

- Musicians writing about vibrato described it as objectionable; from this they infer that vibrato was generally unused. When used, it was only as an occasional ornament.
- Boys sang the high parts and did not have vibrato.
- Singing took place in small venues or resonant spaces such as churches and did not require vibrato.

Evidence from Renaissance and Baroque writers about vibrato

While writers in the 16th to 18th centuries used inconsistent terms for vocal ornaments and vibrato, the mere fact that there was commentary about vibrato suggests that it was present in singers' voices. Some contemporary vocal authorities have misinterpreted historical criticism of trills or successive, rapid re-articulations of the same pitch (now called a "trillo") to be about vibrato.

A number of writers recommended that singers have vibrato, suggesting that it was employed and viewed as desirable in early music:

> In 1598 Quitschreiber wrote, "...one sings best with a quivering voice..." (cited in Moens-Haenen, 1988, p. 158).

- In 1614 Friderici said, "The students should, from the beginning, become accustomed to singing with a refined naturalness, and, where possible, with the voice trembling...or pulsating..." (cited in Stark, 2003, p. 129).
- Praetorius listed the desirable characteristics of singers in 1619. He wrote, "...first, a singer must have a nice, pleasant vibrato..." (Praetorius, 2004, p. 215).

Indeed, some authors distinctly preferred a moderate vibrato:

- Sanford (1979, p. 9) quotes Herbst (1642): "That he have a beautiful, lovely, trembling and shaking voice (...but with particular moderation)."
- In 1592 Zacconi commended singers who have vibrant voices but said that "it should be slight and pleasing; for if it is exaggerated and forced, it tires and annoys" (cited in R. Miller, 2006, p. 93).
- Mozart detested excessive variation in pitch but prized a more natural vibrato: "The human voice vibrates naturally—but in such a way—to such a degree that it all sounds beautiful—it is the nature of the voice. We imitate such effects not only on wind instruments, but also with violins—even on the clavier—but as soon as you go beyond the natural limits, it no longer sounds beautiful—because it is contrary to nature" (cited in Spaethling, 2000, p. 157).
- In the mid-17th century Bernhard complained about "tremulo," which he compared to the singing of the elderly (Bernhard, 1973). Naturally produced, we would call this a wobble today, but it was often an artificial vibrato as noted below. In either case, it is not a normal vibrato.

Use of vibrato is also evidenced by recommendations for both string and woodwind instrumentalists to imitate the human voice by using vibrato:

- In 1636 Mersenne wrote, "... the viol ... imitates the voice in all its modulations..." (1957, p. 254).
- In 1535 Ganassi (1959) urged wind players to imitate the human voice by producing vibrato through variation of breath pressure.

Jerold (2006) argues persuasively that musical historians misinterpreted comments by writers such as Bernhard to apply to natural vibrato. Jerold states that tremulo was an artificial form of vibrato that often-involved jaw movement.

- For example, Elliott (2006) cites a number of early sources who complain about tremolo (tremulo) and about trillo as evidence for not using vibrato in early music. We do not believe that complaints about these practices are complaints about moderate vibrato.

In short, our conclusion from analyzing the historical literature is that moderate vibrato was likely prevalent. In contrast, admired singers avoided wide-ranging vibrato, just as we prefer today for most classical music. See Stark (2003) for a particularly detailed analysis of vibrato issues.

Did the boys who sang high parts have "no vibrato"?

Boys and men sang all parts in early church choirs and, in some cases, in secular performances. Some who oppose using moderate vibrato in performances of early music assume that boys would not have sung with such vibrato, and thus that early music should be performed without it (at least in the alto and soprano parts). Many countries on the continent of Europe with long choral traditions continue to utilize this tonal model. Some North American choral conductors have been heavily influenced by this tradition as well.

The idea that boys cannot sing with vibrato is a misconception. Boys who received training and sang regularly likely developed a moderate vibrato over time. Jerold (2006, p. 163) notes, for example, that in 1649, Friderici said, "From the beginning, the boys should form the voice in a naturally beautiful manner and, where possible, with a delicate trembling, wavering or quivering in the throat." Note the similarity to Friderici's earlier views about vibrato, cited above.

> Phillips (1996) concurs that children who sing freely will naturally develop vibrato. He says, "Vibrato is not taught to the students, but rather is the outcome of vocal training that frees the voice, allowing it to pulse naturally" (p. 266).

Did small or resonant spaces of the Renaissance and Baroque periods mean that vibrato was not present in early music?

Some object to vibrato on the basis that early venues were typically resonant churches or more intimate chamber spaces that would not require a resonant voice. But vibrato and resonance are separate issues. A singer can lack vibrato but produce high sound levels (e.g., through firm vocal fold closure and an appropriate vocal tract shape).

❖ Many modern performance spaces are large. Some singers who attempt to reduce vibrato will use a somewhat breathy tone as a way to diminish vibrato. A breathy production substantially decreases the sound level, making classical voices that do not use amplification harder to hear.

Moreover, diminished higher harmonics create a thin sound—even in a highly resonant space, the sound will lack a certain core level of intensity. Firmer vocal fold closure is likely to be a more successful strategy to reduce vibrato extent because the amplitude of second and third harmonics will be high. There will, however, be a reduction in the sound level of the fundamental frequency, causing problems for sopranos as outlined above.

- Jerold (2006) argues that not all performance spaces in the Baroque period were small. For example, the San Carlo Theatre in Naples (dating from 1737) seats 2400 people, mostly in boxes where the acoustics would have been poor. Light, airy production to suppress vibrato extent would not have worked in such a setting.
- Jerold (2006) also provides evidence that singers in the Baroque period likely needed loud voices even in small spaces. This was due to poor performance conditions: intemperate, noisy audiences, loud and coarse period instruments (different from their modern reconstructions), and orchestral tuning going on in the background during a vocal performance. Singers could have achieved a high sound level by performing with moderate vocal fold closure and a singer's formant. This would likely have included a moderate vibrato.

Vox Humana and Voce Umana stops in early organs suggest use of vibrato in early music

As implied by their names, organ builders designed the Vox Humana and Voce Umana organ stops to imitate the human voice (Bush & Kassel, 2006). The Vox Humana stop in most older organs uses reed pipes that resonate at slightly different frequencies, creating an undulating, vibrato-like effect. In Italy the Voce Umana (or Piffaro) stop usually involves a set of flute pipes that are mistuned from the principal flute pipes to obtain a similar vibrato effect. An accessory stop known as the Tremulant, which causes the wind pressure to vary, improves the vibrato effect. Variation in wind pressure induces both frequency and amplitude variations, as in the human voice.

If singers in the Renaissance and Baroque periods did not sing with vibrato, we would expect the Vox Humana and Voce Umana stops to be included only in organs built after 1750–60. Our review of the organ literature indicates that both the Vox Humana and the Tremulant were installed in many organs during the early music periods. They can be traced at least as far back as 1537 when the builders of an organ at the Church of Notre Dame in Alençon, France, installed both a Vox Humana stop and an accessory Tremulant (Owen, 1999). Audsley (1905) states that the Voce Umana was incorporated into three Italian organs between 1470 and 1480 in Bologna and Lucca. Stauffer and May (2000) note that Bach influenced the stop list of an organ built in Naumberg, Germany (1743–46), which has a Vox Humana. See our first edition (Davids & LaTour, 2012) for more discussion of and references on this subject or visit our web site: www.vocaltechnique.info.

Vibrato exercises

Experiencing vibrato

Singers who lack vibrato can try singing a vowel such as [i] alternating between two pitches that are a half step apart, gradually changing pitch faster and faster until the sound dissolves into "vibrato." While this is not the same as natural vibrato, it encourages relaxed laryngeal muscles and allows singers to get a sense of vibrato. Two starting pitches are illustrated below. It may also be beneficial to start using a higher pitch, such as E_5 for females and E_4 for males.

Other exercises such as moaning like a ghost or mimicking an opera singer (see above) can be used, but, in general, none of these exercises, including the one above, bring about natural vibrato. Vibrato will typically develop naturally over time as singers release tension and use proper vocal technique. Thus, we do not recommend extensive use of these exercises.

Encouraging vibrato

This exercise involves alternation of moving pitches and sustained pitches. *Encourage the flexibility of the moving notes on the sustained ones. Once you can sing with moderate vibrato, try these variations: 1) vibrato throughout, 2) minimal vibrato throughout, 3) terminal vibrato on the final, sustained note.*

Singing with minimal vibrato using good vocal technique

Encourage singers to have excellent breath support, particularly abdominal muscle support. Close the glottis somewhat more firmly than is required for flow phonation but avoid closing it so firmly that you produce a chest belting sound. Also, try a slightly breathy form of production—vary the airflow; generally, a faster flow rate will create a "straighter" sound.

Exercise to "smooth" vibrato

Sing a sustained pitch in the middle of your range on a vowel such as [a]. Sing with good breath support and a vibrant sound. Sing the passage again with a narrower vibrato (less extent). Accompany the second version with a hand gesture to help you achieve less extent—fingers outstretched, palm down, moving horizontally—like "ironing" out the vibrato. Notice how the breath and mouth/pharynx space subtly change. Now try this at a pitch toward the high end of your range (L. Abernathy, personal communication, March 7, 2019).

Terminal Vibrato

Take a relaxed, full breath and sing a pitch using [ae]. Females should choose a pitch in the middle register, males a pitch in the higher portion of chest register. Sustain the note at a medium dynamic level with minimal vibrato. Gradually crescendo, allowing vibrato extent to increase as you crescendo. Remember to maintain good breath support and avoid extraneous tension.

Messa di voce exercise with and without vibrato

Sing a messa di voce exercise (i.e., start on a vowel at a piano dynamic level; increase gradually to forte and then gradually reduce to piano). Sing first with vibrato and then without vibrato to play with the sound. Also try increasing vibrato extent as you crescendo, reducing as you diminuendo. Teachers and conductors should ask singers to think about how they produced the two different tonal colors.

Combating wobble

The following exercises are useful for combating wobble:

- ❖ Onset exercises, to make sure there is a coordinated onset (Chapter 3)

- Slides extending to a fifth, to make sure abdominal support is consistent throughout phonation
- Physical exercise of the abdominal muscles as outlined in Chapter 2 on breathing
- The sibilant exercise for breathing in Chapter 2

Reducing tremolo

Exercises to free a voice from tremolo include:

- Breathing exercises from Chapter 2 with a particular focus on relaxing the airways during inhalation
- Onset exercises to eliminate glottal onset; see Chapter 3 on initiation, creation, and release of sound
- Relaxed vocal fry, outlined in Chapter 8 on vocal registers
- Tension reduction methods from Chapter 14

Chapter 8: Negotiation of the Vocal Registers

Changes in tonal quality may occur as singers move from one part of their range to another. Our vocal mechanism has distinct registers and does not operate in the same fashion on all pitches. The term "registers" parallels the use of this word with the organ, an instrument that produces different pitches and tonal qualities with different sets of pipes.

Audible changes between registers are often desirable for purposes of contrast in certain musical styles (e.g., pop, rock, country). Composers and songwriters often take advantage of differences in registers to convey different emotions. In classical and legit, however, smooth negotiation across the registers with minimal tonal color change is the ideal. All singers, regardless of style, need to understand the various vocal registers and their transition areas in order to accomplish their artistic goals.

Knowledge of vocal registers will help singers manage register transition issues. More specifically, this knowledge will enable conductors, singers, and teachers to:

- ❖ Understand specific pitch areas that might pose difficulties for singers in various voice categories.
- ❖ Assist singers to pass through transitions smoothly by blending modes of vocal fold vibration.
- ❖ Understand how vocal tract resonance adjustment, breath pressure adjustment, and firmness of glottal closure can help with register transitions.

Working on register transitions is an essential step in enhancing singers' voices. With an intentional focus on mixing registers, areas of transition will become easier to navigate. Voice training will improve ease of production and quality of sound throughout the registers.

What are vocal registers?

Registers refer to portions of a singer's range. Pitches within a given register have the same general tonal quality.

This fundamental conception of registers has a long history, dating back to the famous 19th-century singing teacher, Manuel P. Garcia (Henrich, 2006). Garcia, the first to observe the vocal folds using a laryngoscope, noticed that the folds vibrated differently at low versus high pitches. These observations led him to develop the concept of vocal registers.

> Contemporary studies using the electroglottograph (noninvasive electrical sensors measuring changes in vocal fold activity) supply convincing evidence of differences in vibration at different points in a singer's range (e.g., Henrich, Roubeau, & Castellengo, 2003).

Two main (modal) registers

Vocal experts disagree about the number of registers and the names for specific registers. For pedagogical purposes, though, it is possible to come to a reasonably straightforward understanding of two vocal registers and the differences between them. The two registers used in most singing (modal registers) are the lower register (often called chest voice) and the upper register (often called head voice). Some of the terms singers may encounter include:

- **Lower register**—chest voice, heavy mechanism, Mode 1, TA- (thyroarytenoid) dominant.
- **Upper register**—head voice, light mechanism, Mode 2 (though some restrict Mode 2 to falsetto—see below), CT- (cricothyroid) dominant.

There has been disagreement about whether there is a middle register. Still, as we will see, recent research supports the concept that the lower and upper registers can be blended into a middle or mixed voice (French: *voix mixte*; Italian: *voce mista*). Indeed, in Chapters 3, 4, and 5 we have already discussed how use of mixed voice has transformed belting in modern musical theatre and other contemporary styles.

Lower register (chest voice)

At lower pitches, the vocal folds are thicker and come together firmly along a wide area (Bunch, 1995). The folds are thicker because the thyroarytenoid (TA) muscles, which largely govern pitch in this register, underlie the folds and bulge out the bottom part of the fold edge (Titze, 2000). For this reason, the lower register is sometimes referred to as TA-dominant production. In the lower register the nature of vocal fold vibration creates a prominent second harmonic (Titze, 2000; Miller & Schutte, 2005), producing a naturally rich sound. The lower register also has a higher closed quotient than does the upper register, further contributing to the generally greater resonance associated with chest voice. Females usually have a smaller range of pure chest voice than do males.

The term "chest voice" is often used because conductive resonance is felt most strongly in the chest at lower pitches. This term is familiar to many singers, but, as noted in Chapter 4 on resonance, the chest is not a resonating cavity that affects what is heard by the audience. (See Chapter 4 for a more detailed discussion of resonances felt in the chest and head.)

Upper register (head voice)

Recall that if the larynx stays in a relatively stable position, the cricothyroid (CT) muscles will begin to tilt the thyroid cartilage as pitch ascends. (See Figure 3.5 in Chapter 3.) This tilting action thins the vocal folds and allows for easier production of higher pitches. Moreover, as pitch ascends into head voice the vocal folds touch each other less firmly and over a smaller area because the thyroarytenoids are less involved and do not push the lower edges of the fold outward. For this reason, some refer to this mode of production as CT-dominant. The amplitude of the vibration (amount of vertical movement in the folds) is also less than in the lower register. This mode of vibration in head voice emphasizes the first harmonic—the fundamental frequency (Miller & Schutte, 2005).

Thus, at pitches where singers have a choice between lower register and upper register use, the lower register sounds louder and richer to listeners than the upper register voice. A classical/legit singer should avoid carrying the lower register too high to avoid a sudden change in timbre as pitch ascends, but in many contemporary styles this may be preferred for artistic reasons.

❖ From a different perspective, some have argued that the two main registers are chest and falsetto. Anything in between, including head voice, is understood as a mix of these two registers. We concur with this from a technical perspective, but not from a pedagogical perspective, as falsetto is generally reserved for special effects. It is not a primary mode of singing except among countertenors and some pop/rock singers. Thus, our preference is to focus on head voice as the primary upper register and treat falsetto as a unique register, discussed later in this chapter.

Figure 8.1 illustrates the vocal folds under conditions where thyroarytenoid control dominates versus conditions where cricothyroid control dominates.

Head voice still involves some TA reinforcement

While head voice mostly involves the cricothyroid muscles, recent research shows that for males, the thyroarytenoid muscles share some control, providing tensioning or bracing of the vocal folds (Georg, 2005). Consistent with this, Titze and Worley (2009) describe the upper register in males as a mixture of chest and falsetto.

Prior research had suggested that only the CT muscles are involved in female head voice (Henrich et al., 2003), while recent research shows the TA muscle supplying some tensioning at the highest pitches of a female's range (Unteregger et al., in press). Some involvement of the TA muscle does not negate the point that the cricothyroids must be allowed to take more control to stretch and thin the vocal folds to gain easier access to upper pitches (Hirano, Vennard, & Ohala, 1970).

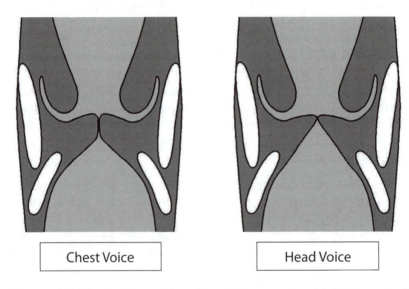

Chest Voice Head Voice

Figure 8.1 Illustration of dominant thyroarytenoid (TA) control over vocal folds (left) versus dominant cricothyroid (CT) control over vocal folds (right)

Middle register (mixed voice)

Middle register involves a blending of thyroarytenoid (TA) and cricothyroid control (CT) over the vocal folds, resulting in a distinctive tonal quality. It has a more complex sound spectrum than head voice (which is dominated by the fundamental frequency, particularly for females) but not as complex a sound spectrum as with chest voice where higher harmonics have high amplitudes.

Pitches falling between the lower and upper registers can thus be sung with a combination of lower and upper register production. As we will see below, the range of mixed voice is much less for males than it is for females.

❖ The degree of emphasis placed on lower versus upper register production in the area of mixed voice depends upon the musical context or the desired emotion. The expression of more tender emotions typically requires headmix rather than chestmix. Particularly for classical/legit singing, if the musical line is leading toward the upper register, be sure to use a lighter style of production (i.e., headmix), even on the lower notes (and vice versa). Sopranos singing in a classical style may try to avoid mixed voice and sing everything in head voice (Garnier et al., 2010), but this can lead to thin production at lower pitches.

Research supporting the existence of chestmix and headmix

Recent research supports the existence of two types of mixed voice at the level of vocal fold vibration—chestmix and headmix (Lamesch, Expert, Castellengo, Henrich, & Chuberre, 2007; Kochis-Jennings, Finnegan, Hoffman, & Jaiswal, 2012). Chestmix involves more TA control with some CT control. Headmix requires more CT control. Chestmix allows for higher volume levels, and headmix allows for softer levels as well as the ability to ascend somewhat higher in pitch.

➢ A high-speed video endoscopy study of female professional singers (Echternach et al., 2017) supplies further evidence for chestmix and headmix. Vocal fold vibrational patterns change as they transition from chest voice through the first passaggio to mixed voice and again during the transition through the second passaggio to head voice. There is also some evidence that these adjustments can be relatively continuous.

Children's registers

For most children, singing is a part of their play, and they will begin experimenting with their voices soon after birth. By the time children are ready for elementary school, their singing registration potentially includes both head and chest voices. As with adults, chest voice is achieved with the thyroarytenoid muscle (although this muscle does not finish developing until after puberty). The cricothyroid muscles stretch and thin the folds to allow for mixed and head voice, just as they do for adult voices (Brunssen, 2018).

Kenneth H. Phillips notes that many children will intuitively sing in their speaking range (chest voice) and should, therefore, be encouraged to experiment with and produce singing sounds in head voice to build that musculature.

- Only after solidifying the upper range should children be encouraged to bring that sound down into a mixed voice, to avoid children becoming "trapped in their lower voices" (Phillips, 1996, p.71).
- Singing in their upper register may be healthier/easier for young singers' voices because they cannot belt above roughly C_5 in head voice (L. Sklar, personal communication, July 1, 2019).
- "Students cannot be musical if they are 'shouting,' rather than singing with their own best voice. From day one of first grade I introduce the concept of different ways to use the voice—whisper, speak, shout, sing. After that, I never let children use their shouting voices" (E. Weismehl, personal communication, July 4, 2019).

While some prefer the English choirboy sound with its exclusive use of head voice, many styles of both choral and solo music call for a different sound. Phillips (2014) recommends middle register production with a balance of both upper (head) and lower (chest) registers. The dominance of either CT or TA in the middle register will determine the quality of sound created. For children, this technique of blending registers is best learned from the top down.

- "Exercises and vocalises must begin from the upper register and move down, permitting the natural emergence of the lower voice. Later, the voice can be exercised from the bottom up to teach the subtle shifting to the upper register on ascending vocal lines" (Phillips, 2014, p. 97).

All registers should be sung easily, never pushed or strained, at an energized, supported, medium dynamic level.

Differences in chest and head voice use in classical and contemporary styles

All singers, regardless of style, should be able to sing in all registers: chest, chestmix, headmix, and head. As noted, styles differ in terms of relative emphasis on TA versus CT control. In pitch areas where both methods of control are possible, many contemporary styles emphasize TA control while classical/legit singers emphasize CT control. Classical/legit singers blend TA and CT control to produce a smooth transition between registers without sudden changes in sound quality. This is less of an issue for contemporary styles.

- To broaden their vocal capabilities, individuals who primarily sing in a classical/legit style will need to work on chest and chestmix production (particularly females). Those who sing primarily in a belt style will need to work on head and headmix production.

Females

A heavy/chest belt only uses chest register. This generally limits the use of heavy belting to pitches no higher than C_5–D_5. Mix belting allows for more flexibility. It involves chestmix and (perhaps even headmix) at pitches above this range, increasing the upper limit for belting to roughly G_5.

❖ The advent of mix belting represented a revolution in belting because it allowed powerful singing substantially higher in the range. Female singers with this capability are highly sought after in commercial singing (Kochis-Jennings et al., 2012).

In comparison, a female classical singer will tend to use chest voice, mixed voice, and head voice in the ranges specified in Table 8.2, depending upon voice type. This allows a classical singer to maintain a more consistent timbre throughout the range. Moreover, to ascend above G_5, head voice is essential. (Above this pitch, dominant control by the cricothyroid muscles is necessary to allow the folds to vibrate at these high frequencies.)

❖ It is possible to cross register boundaries using an adjacent register. For example, as noted above, female classical singers often use head voice in the mixed voice area, but this is not desirable at the lower pitch areas of mixed voice because of the rather thin sound that is produced. For artistic reasons, contemporary singers may wish to use chest voice production in areas where a classical/legit singer would use mixed production.

In the range where female singers can choose between chestmix and headmix, contemporary singers are likely to use chestmix, while classical/legit singers are likely to use headmix.

❖ Legit singers may extend headmix higher than would a classical singer. Because they must be more intelligible than classical singers, they do not modify the vocal tract in the same way as a classical singer. For example, they will not lower the jaw quite as much and may use a somewhat wider smile to shorten the vocal tract and brighten the sound. They will not, however, generally need to sing quite as high as a classical soprano. (There are, of course, exceptions, such as the legit role of Christine in *Phantom of the Opera* requiring an E_6.)

Despite all of this, we want to emphasize that musical theatre singers, for example, do not belt every song or in all portions of a song. Indeed, within a given song, they may sing in both a legit style and a belting style, depending upon the mood they wish to create (e.g., through tonal color and dynamic level). Musical theatre singers need to have the ability to sing well in all registers to have the greatest number of opportunities (see, for example, Hall, 2014; Kayes & Welch, 2017), though they may not need the extensive range of a classical singer. If a musical theatre singer cannot sing in head voice, legit roles will typically be unattainable.

Males

Males singing in a classical style tend to use chest voice almost to the pitches of the first passaggio listed in Table 8.1. However, mixed or head voice is usually employed above C_4 since some cricothyroid involvement is required above this pitch.

Male belting in the range up to the first passaggio also employs chest voice, but with firmer glottal closure. Above C_4, belting will involve carrying chestmix to the upper limit of what is classically defined as head voice (though headmix is likely required at the highest pitches). It should be noted, however, that only elite contemporary-style male singers can carry mixed voice this high. Some elite male opera singers likely do this as well (Titze & Worley, 2009).

- ❖ As noted above, pop and particularly rock singers use a reinforced falsetto to attain pitches above the limits of head voice.

Modern singers most likely to struggle with the upper register

In the past it was thought that males tend to speak in their lower register, and women tend to speak in their upper register. Since singing is more comfortable in the register used for talking, it was widely believed that males have more trouble singing in the upper register while women struggle with the lower register. Numerous vocal pedagogy books continue to suggest this to be the case.

We believe this view is antiquated. In the last fifty years, women in Western cultures have pitched their speaking voices lower, and thus, like men, may now have greater difficulty accessing head voice. Nonetheless, because some women do speak in their higher register (as do some men), we include exercises in this chapter to aid in the acquisition of the lower register.

Transitions between registers (passaggi)

Transitions between registers are problematic for singers because the voice may abruptly change character when switching between registers. In the worst-case scenario phonation may stop, which is often referred to as a "break" or "cracking" of the voice. These transitional areas are technically known as "passaggi"—passages from one register to another.

- In contemporary styles smoothness in register transitions may also be a goal, but sudden changes in tonal character are often used for effect. For example, Steven Tyler, of Aerosmith, at the end of "Dream On," makes a sudden octave shift into falsetto.

Passaggi are not simply laryngeal phenomena; they are also acoustical phenomena resulting from the location of fundamental frequencies and their harmonics relative to formant frequencies. Hence there is a need for vowel modification to help with register transitions, as delineated below. Indeed, some authorities argue that the acoustical aspect of many passaggi is the most significant one.

Surprisingly, few vocal authorities explain the specific location of register transitions for each of the major voice types. Information about female voice types is particularly sparse. Most literature on the topic groups all voice types within a gender together. While this allows for differences in individual areas of transition, conductors, teachers, and singers can benefit from more specific knowledge about where transitions are likely to occur, for example, in basses versus tenors.

Indeed, the pitches where register transitions occur can be a useful guide to appropriate voice classification for a singer, more so than range, as developing singers typically have not developed their full range. See Chapter 9 for more discussion of voice category issues.

Formerly, authorities (based on cadaver studies) argued that subglottal resonance near E_4-flat causes the first transition for both males and females. But subglottal resonance in living people is actually around $C\#_5$ for males and E_5 for women (Lulich et al., 2012). Moreover, Wade, Hanna, Smith & Wolfe (2017) have shown that subglottal resonance does not exert a significant effect on vocal production; only resonances above the glottis (interacting with harmonics) affect the ability to transition through various areas of the vocal range.

Though subglottal resonance does not affect transition, pitches at and around E_4-flat are significant because of resonance phenomena described in Chapter 5 on vowels. As noted there, as pitch ascends through this area, there is the potential for the second harmonic frequency to cross over the first formant, destabilizing vocal fold vibration.

- This is true for both males and females, though for females the transition is usually more comfortable because there is less tensioning of the thyroarytenoids in this pitch area than is the case for males.

Register transition areas differ according to vocal classifications within genders due to differences in average formants among them. We outline below approximate register transition areas for both males and females.

Male register transitions

Table 8.1 shows approximate transitions between the lower register and mixed voice, as well as between mixed voice and the upper register for male voice types. The tenor transition range is a half-step wider than other voice types to accommodate differences between Tenor I and Tenor II. We qualify these transitions as "approximate" because they vary slightly from singer to singer.

Male Vocal Classification	Transition between Lower Register and Mixed Voice	Transition between Mixed Voice and Upper Register
Tenor	C_4–D_4	F_4–G_4
Baritone	B_3-flat–B_3	D_4–E_4-flat
Bass	A_3-flat–A_3	C_4–D_4-flat

Adapted from Alderson (1979); Miller (1996); Sell (2005); Ritzerfeld and Miller (2017)

Table 8.1 Approximate vocal register transitions for male voice types

For most males, the particularly problematic transition is the second transition (passaggio), from mixed voice into the upper register. Some males may also experience difficulties with the first transition if their voice is substantial for their vocal classification. Since mixed voice covers only a few pitches in males, some refer to the entire area between the first transition and second transition as the passaggio.

Male voices will have a strained quality in the passaggio if lower and upper register modes of production are not mixed. In addition, males who have not learned to sing in head voice will experience a dramatic change in tonal quality as they approach the second transition. Such singers will have to resort to falsetto to produce notes around and above the upper transition. Male voices can learn to access the upper register by using appropriate exercises during individual practice and choral warm-ups. They will need to focus on breath support, engagement of the cricothyroid muscles, and proper vowel modification. We discuss these and other techniques in the section below on the negotiation of the registers.

Female register transitions

Table 8.2 shows approximate vocal register transitions for the three major female voice types. As noted above, females have a much broader range in their middle voice than males, but they also have less range than males in their chest voice.

Individual singers' transitions can have substantial variability. For example, Echternach et al. (2010) observed the transition from chest register to middle voice to occur anywhere from D_4-flat to A_4 for sopranos. The transition from middle voice to the upper register occurred anywhere between D_5-flat and A_4-flat. As these are professional singers, their register transitions may be, on average, higher than amateur singers'.

Female Vocal Classification	Transition between Lower Register and Mixed Voice	Transition between Mixed Voice and Upper Register
Soprano	D_4—E_4-flat	E_5—G_5-flat
Mezzo-Soprano	C_4—D_4-flat	D_5-flat—E_5-flat
Contralto	B_3-flat—B_3	C_5—D_5

Note: Table 8.2 is based on our experience with voice classifications. However, Tarneaud and Borel-Maisonny (1961; cited by Large, 1973) list smaller differences in register transitions among female voice types than we show. Their first passaggio for sopranos is the same, but they include mezzo-sopranos at the same notes. They place contraltos only one step lower than the soprano voices. Similarly, while they agree with our placement of the soprano second passaggio, they list mezzo-sopranos and contraltos only a half-step lower. Echternach et al. (2010) place the soprano transition to mixed voice for professional singers at an average of F_4. Miller and Schutte (2005) identified two professional mezzo-sopranos with a lower register to mixed voice transition, which is similar to what we show.

Table 8.2 Approximate vocal register transitions for female voice types

Negotiating the register transitions

Four actions will help singers make transitions with minimal pitch disturbance and, in classical/legit styles, without sudden changes in tonal quality.

- Modify formant frequencies by modifying vowels and/or modifying vocal tract shape to prevent crossovers of harmonic frequencies with formant frequencies (discussed in Chapter 4 on resonance and Chapter 5 on vowels)
- Change mode of vocal fold vibration (alter the relative dominance of TA and CT muscles)
- Alter breath pressure

❖ Alter firmness of vocal fold closure

Control over the mode of vocal vibration requires control of the vertical position of the larynx. For headmix and head voice, the larynx should not be allowed to rise excessively. By monitoring laryngeal height and ensuring that the larynx rises minimally, singers have an indirect method of letting the cricothyroids take over as pitch ascends. Moreover, maintaining the larynx in a comfortably low position allows the cricothyroids to contract through their whole range.

For chestmix, the larynx is allowed to rise higher to delay the participation of the CT muscles, and preserve a more powerful sound. If the larynx rises excessively as pitch ascends, the thyroarytenoid muscle approaches 100 percent contraction. At this point the cricothyroids can increase pitch only slightly more and with great effort. If the thyroarytenoid muscle relaxes suddenly to allow the cricothyroids to take over, the vocal folds must respond to sudden tensioning by the cricothyroids (Titze, 2000). Under this circumstance singers are unlikely to have any control over pitch, resulting in the sounds that accompany register breaks. This problem is particularly likely to happen beyond the second passaggio for both female and male voices.

❖ This helps to explain why there is an upper limit to how high women can belt—at a certain point, TA control even in mixed voice is not possible for women because the TA muscle is fully stretched. As noted previously this is around G_5, though there are certainly individual differences.
❖ Because male singers are using what amounts to a headmix in the highest portion of their normal range (i.e., below falsetto), some can belt up to the limits of their range, but many cannot belt beyond F_4.

Breath pressure, firmness of vocal fold closure

Control of breath pressure and firmness of glottal closure also help to ease register transitions (Hill, 1986; Callaghan, 2014; Titze, 2014). High breath pressure does not facilitate smooth transitions. As noted in Chapter 2 on breath control, breath pressure increases as pitch increases. But as pitch ascends to the top pitch of a given register, substantially less pressure facilitates a smooth transition to the next register. Hill (1986) notes a substantial reduction in breath pressure between chest register and mixed registration for women making a successful transition. (Hill refers to the transition between chest register and head register, but it is clear from the pitches involved that the transition is to mixed registration.) A study involving a mechanical replica of the vocal folds provides further support for the utility of this technique (Lucero, Lourenço, Hermant, Van Hirtum, & Pelorson, 2012).

* Recall that in chest register the folds are thicker and touch one another along a substantially larger area than in mix or head voice. If breath pressure continues at an elevated level or even increases as a passaggio is reached, the thinner folds can be "blown apart," ceasing phonation and creating noise (a register break). Avoid this by reducing breath pressure when entering a passaggio.
* An alternative or even complementary approach is to reduce firmness of glottal closure as ascending pitch approaches a passaggio.

Additional factors to consider in register transitions

Females have substantial flexibility with vocal fold vibration strategies in the vicinity of the first passaggio, where they can use chest voice, chestmix, or headmix. Nonetheless, they should employ this flexibility wisely. For example, if the shift up from the lower register to middle voice does not involve chestmix, women can have transitional problems. Firmer closure of the vocal folds can help. Moreover, the use of chestmix in lower middle voice can help to create a more resonant female voice in this area, where some classical singers might otherwise use headmix (Stark, 2003).

Males have a similar problem in classical/legit singing if they carry lower register production too far up into the passaggio (i.e., they need to lighten production as pitch ascends).

Using nasality to assist male register transitions

A small increase in nasality can help male singers to negotiate register transitions. Think of nasality as introducing some back pressure in the vocal tract, just as with the use of nasal consonants as part of SOVT exercises. This can help stabilize vocal fold oscillation during register transitions.

> Perna (2014) and Echternach et al. (in press) find that most male classical singers use nasality to negotiate register transitions. Echternach et al. show that its use helps stabilize vocal fold oscillation as well as the open quotient (percentage of time the glottis is open during a vibratory cycle). Also, for some, there is a narrowing of the epilarynx tube, which would further contribute to resonance and assistance with vocal fold vibration. Most studies suggest this is only helpful for males, not for females, for reasons beyond the scope of this book.

While identifiable nasality is undesirable in most singing, modest lowering of the soft palate for this purpose should not be objectionable.

Jaw protrusion for classical male singers

Echternach et al. (2008) used MRI imaging of professional opera tenors to learn more about useful register transition strategies. In the transition to head voice (they label this as stage voice), they observe further widening of the pharynx, increased jaw lowering and lip opening, and interestingly, jaw protrusion. Jaw protrusion is likely related to increased pharyngeal space.

Special registers

Whistle register

A flute-like timbre characterizes the whistle register, with sound intensity mostly in the fundamental frequency and the second harmonic (Garnier et al., 2012). It overlaps with female head voice and falsetto, ranging from roughly A_5 to G_6, potentially as high as C_7 (Georg, 2005), though Garnier et al. found that some sopranos can engage the whistle register as low as D_5–E_5.

Pop music singers use the whistle register for riffs and special effects (e.g., Mariah Carey, Ariana Grande). They are unnecessary for most classical/legit soloists (except coloratura sopranos) and choral singing. Nonetheless, some believe that experimenting with the whistle register can help all women to achieve freedom of production at high pitches (Georg, 2005).

- In the whistle register the vocal folds are fully stretched and thinned with only the front portion of the vocal folds vibrating (R. Miller, 2004). However, Echternach, Döllinger, Sundberg, Traser, & Richter (2013) have high-speed video which shows vibration occurring along the entire length of folds, at least in the case of one professional soprano. This finding may contradict the idea of a distinct whistle register and deserves further study.
  - Garnier et al. (2012) verify decreased glottal contact in the whistle register. Despite this, the sound level of the register is quite loud—typically 10–15 dB higher after the transition to whistle.

To access whistle register, reduce breath pressure (Hill, 1986) and relax vocal fold closure. Stark (2003) concurs that a sense of relaxation of laryngeal muscles accompanies transition to the whistle register. Gaining pitch and dynamic control in this register may be difficult until singers gain mastery over the register.

- Limits to first formant tuning constrain use of the whistle register above roughly C_6. It is not possible to raise the first formant any further through jaw lowering. Above this pitch sopranos must typically use second-formant tuning by fronting/elevating the tongue to keep the second formant just above the fundamental frequency.

Falsetto register

While some modern authorities equate head voice with the falsetto register, we agree with Vennard (1967) that male falsetto is distinctly different. It is also distinctly different in females. Certainly, the resonance characteristics of falsetto are quite different from those of head voice.

A major difference between the male head voice and falsetto is the degree of vocal fold contact. In male head voice register, the vocal folds contact each other and vibrate along their full length. In falsetto only a portion of the vocal folds makes contact, and airflow is greater (Large, 1984).

Men can sing higher in falsetto than they can in head voice. In head voice even professional tenors can rarely exceed C_5, but almost any male voice can exceed this pitch in falsetto. At the same time, just as head voice can produce pitches in the passaggio (and lower), falsetto can also be used to achieve lower pitches.

Falsetto is generally lower in volume and thinner (higher harmonics have low sound levels) compared to head voice. It has a lower closed quotient than chest voice. Undeveloped falsetto can also sound grainy or breathy.

For most amateur and some professional choral singers, falsetto is used to sing high notes at a soft dynamic level that would be difficult in head voice. Amateur male singers tend to use the falsetto register rarely, but they should be encouraged to practice in this register so that it is readily available when needed. Falsetto is not used by most professional solo singers, except as noted below.

Reinforced falsetto

With practice, males can develop a stronger or reinforced falsetto with firmer glottal closure, some degree of resonance, and even vibrato (e.g., pop/rock singers, classical countertenors).

- Professional male singers use a reinforced falsetto in pop and particularly in rock music to reach remarkably high pitches with a clear tone and a forceful dynamic level—above the limits of head voice shown in Table 8.1. This, together with techniques involving a higher laryngeal position, an open (trumpet shape) mouth with spread lips, and a tongue raised in the back, allows them to reach pitch levels in the range of D_5 to B_5.

Examples include Freddie Mercury (Queen), Frankie Valli (The Four Seasons), Dan Reynolds (Imagine Dragons), Steven Tyler (Aerosmith).

> Guzman et al. (2014) found that even amateur rock singers successfully produce a reinforced falsetto by using the vowel [a] and raising both the first and second formant frequencies to accommodate rising pitch.

❖ A reinforced falsetto may also have been used in Italian operas in the early 1800s, where the production of pitches from D_5 to F_5 is required in certain arias (Mayr, 2017). This has been called "voce faringea," or pharyngeal voice. In this method of production there is stronger glottal closure than in unreinforced falsetto, resulting in a relatively high closed quotient and generation of harmonics with higher amplitudes.

Countertenors (classical style)

Most modern countertenors also use a reinforced falsetto. (There are a few exceptions involving countertenors with developmental differences in which the vocal folds are more like those of females.)

> Herbst, Ternström, and Svec (2009) found that a major difference between what some have termed "naïve" falsetto and professional countertenor (male alto) falsetto is firmer glottal closure among countertenors. This results in the generation of more harmonics and, thus, a more fully resonant sound.

> Echternach, Traser, Markl, and Richter (2011) conducted an MRI study to compare vocal tract configurations in tenor head voice compared to reinforced falsetto in professional countertenor singing. The following differences are of particular interest concerning the transition to reinforced falsetto versus head voice:

1) A sudden increase in lip opening versus a more gradual lip opening
2) Somewhat larger lip opening in general
3) Jaw retracted versus protruded
4) Generally higher tongue position
5) Lowering of the larynx versus increasing elevation of the larynx with higher pitches

Note that items 3) and 4) lead to a narrower pharynx in reinforced falsetto as opposed to a wider pharynx in head voice. Mayr (2017) observes similar phenomena in his efforts to duplicate the *voce faringea* of the early 1800s.

Strohbass (pulse register)

Strohbass is German for "straw bass." It refers to the crackling sound of dry straw underfoot. Some singers refer to it as "vocal fry" because it mimics the sound of crackling meat cooking in a frying pan. A more technical term is the "pulse" register.

A relaxed vocal fry can be a useful device to help chronically tense singers (including those with hyperkinetic disorders) who press the vocal folds too firmly together. It is therapeutic for such singers because the vocal folds must be relaxed for this type of vocal fry, but the effort will be counterproductive if so-called "tense vocal fry" is used. Tense vocal fry is, however, helpful in the treatment of some vocal fold disorders such as unilateral vocal fold paralysis (Cielo, Elias, Brum, & Ferreira, 2011). It may also be helpful as a therapeutic tool for breathy voices.

The role of vocal fry in classical/legit singing is limited. Relaxed vocal fry is primarily useful for basses who need to sing the low notes required by some choral composers. A breathy quality characterizes it due to minimal contact between the vocal folds.

Relaxed vocal fry with high airflow helps to create growls and similar sounds for rock, jazz, and gospel, where this sound is desirable for artistic reasons (Guzman et al., 2018). Amplification is helpful.

Register exercises

In addition to the exercises listed below, those in the next chapter on range extension may be helpful. Mastery of register transitions and range extension are closely related topics. We recommend using a straw initially for all these exercises (or [v] if a straw is not available). Afterward, you will likely find it easier to perform these exercises as written.

Ghost/siren imitation

Imitating a ghost or a siren is a relaxed and easy way to experiment with the vocal registers.

This exercise involves quick slides into the upper register and corresponding fast slides down into the lower register. It frees singers from focusing on pitch control. Singers may be pleasantly surprised at their ability to travel across the registers while doing this exercise. This exercise will help them to gain confidence in negotiating the registers while singing, as well as a sense of how the various registers feel. Vowel modification strategies outlined in Chapter 5 are an essential part of this exercise.

Strengthening head voice

Once a singer has gained some access to head voice, use exercises that start in a pitch range where head voice or falsetto is necessary. *Begin with short slides of no more than a third that stay in head voice/falsetto. Next try exercises that descend into mixed voice: a five-note descending scale, descending slides of a fifth, and an octave.* For singers less experienced with singing higher pitches, spend short periods on these exercises until muscles are strengthened.

"Ha-Ha-Ha" in head voice

Choose a pitch above the upper passaggio for females/the first passaggio for males and 'bounce' on it—sing "ha-ha-ha" with small inhalations between each bounce. Ascend and descend by half steps, maintaining a lighter tone quality. This exercise can promote less firm glottal closure and will help release tension in the upper range.

Octave slides from the lower register

A sequence of octave slides (extended portamenti) is a controlled method of guiding singers through all the register transitions. One approach is to start singing [ɑ] or [a] on a pitch that is firmly in the lower register, moving the octave slides up by half steps until the top note reaches well into the upper register. Try this exercise through a straw as a variation.

Also, sing octave slides from high to low pitches; this may involve smoother transitions than from low to high. This is especially helpful for learning to access head voice. *While singing ascending octave slides, singers should monitor laryngeal position by placing a finger gently on the larynx to be sure that it rises minimally for classical style and not excessively for contemporary styles.* Singers should be mindful of the register transition techniques outlined earlier in the chapter.

Extended arpeggios

For a more advanced exercise, try an ascending arpeggio followed by a descending arpeggio with a dominant seventh, covering the range of a twelfth. As with octave slides, start in the lower register. With classical choral groups, start singing a vowel that can be used in the upper register by both males and females, such as [ɔ] ("aw"), though women will have to modify this to [ɑ] at the highest pitches. For most contemporary groups, modify toward [ae] as in "cat."

When singing an extended ascending and descending arpeggio, imagine starting at the bottom of a Ferris wheel with the top note representing the top of the wheel. Think how the trip over the top seems effortless—strive for this same feeling when approaching the top note of an arpeggio by maintaining good breath support. Be sure to maintain support on the way down as well.

Mix belt calling exercise for register crossing

Spivey and Barton (2018) argue that belting is an extension of calling in speaking. This exercise, which is adapted from one of their exercises, helps the singer with the concept of calling by crossing normal register boundaries, starting in chest voice, and moving to mixed voice (not head voice). As written this exercise works for males (an octave lower). For females, lower the starting pitch by a half step or a whole step. (G_5 is the rough upper limit for mix belt.)

For kids and everyone! Falsetto to lower register transition

For developing male voices, start in falsetto and sing a descending arpeggio shifting into the lower register (chest voice) for lower pitches. Sing "'hah" with an aspirated "h" to begin. Imagine beginning in a yawn, then sighing as singing. (Adapted from Cooksey, 1999)

For kids and everyone! Slide whistle for experimenting with registers

Try experimenting with registers (especially head voice) by using a slide whistle instrument to demonstrate. Encourage singers to match the pitch as it rises and lowers (E. Weismehl, personal communication, July 4, 2019).

For kids and everyone! Echoing

The teacher/conductor sings simple pitches and rhythms in the various registers. Singers echo them back, modeling what is sung. Next, the teacher/conductor sings a pattern and then asks singers to sing the pattern in their heads with no humming or other sounds. After a short time, singers are directed to sing the pattern back. Try a variety of patterns and intervals. (Adapted from Phillips, 1996)

Chapter 9: Voice Classification and Improving Range

In choral singing and some styles of music such as classical, voice classification (e.g., soprano vs. mezzo-soprano) is important. For other styles such as jazz, pop, and rock, classifications are less relevant. The range of a voice (the interval between the highest and lowest pitches one can sing) is one indicator of voice classification, but there are many contributing factors. Timbre of the voice, register transition points, and the strengths of the singer are equally as important. The ability to negotiate vocal registers is essential to maximize the range of the voice, so read Chapter 4 on resonance, Chapter 5 on vowels, and Chapter 8 on registers before this chapter.

In this chapter we discuss:

- Distribution and classification of various voice types in various styles
- Practical approaches to increasing range

Many developing and amateur singers have limited ranges. Appropriate technique and use of exercises will not only help them to increase their range but will also allow them to imagine their potential.

- The typical ranges shown for various voice categories may not apply to transgender voices. For example, some transgender males may increase their range after receiving testosterone and some transgender females may have more restricted ranges. See Chapter 13 on changing voices for more details.

Distribution and classification of voice types

The determination of voice type for a developing singer is a complicated matter. Several factors should be considered (Callaghan, 2014):

- Register transition location
- Vocal range
- Timbre
- Weight and flexibility of the voice
- Tessitura—the range of most comfortable pitches
- In some musical theatre/opera castings—age and body type

Among *amateur (untrained) singers,* males tend to be baritones. There are fewer natural basses and tenors. Among females, the proportion of premenopausal females who are true sopranos is higher than the percentage of tenors among males. The proportion of mezzo-sopranos relative to sopranos increases somewhat as females age (see Chapter 13 on changing voices). Contraltos are rare.

Among *trained* singers, there are more sopranos than mezzo-sopranos in classical music (Vennard, 1967). In contemporary styles where a speech range of pitches is used for many songs, there is a wide diversity of female voices. Virtually all male singers of contemporary music need to be able to sing high pitches; they tend to be bari-tenors or tenors. In musical theatre the bari-tenor who can belt, use a lighter production for legit at higher pitches, and sing in a reinforced falsetto for pop/rock musicals is highly desirable.

Most choral music is divided into low and high parts for each gender. The result in amateur choral groups is that the tenor section includes some high baritones who may use falsetto for high notes. In contrast, bass sections have many baritones who may not be able to produce lower notes with a high sound level. Soprano and alto sections include many mezzos who face similar difficulties.

Table 9.1 lists comfortable and maximum usable ranges for the standard choral four-part voice classification. The first two columns focus on the *average, amateur choir member*. Of course, some amateurs can exceed these average usable maximums. For example, choral repertoire will occasionally demand a C_6 from sopranos, and some in the soprano section can sing this. Fortunately, given audience sensitivity to pitches in this range, not many sopranos need to be able to achieve the C_6 to create an appropriate sound level. Similarly, there are baritones in the bass section who can comfortably sing E_4 and mezzo-sopranos in the alto section who can comfortably sing E_5.

> ➢ The American Academy of Teachers of Singing (1997) is more conservative in its listings of range for average amateur choral singers. Their designated "safe range" is similar to our designation of the comfortable range for amateur singers. Our comfortable range for basses is higher than their recommended range because most amateur choral singers in the bass section are baritones.

As noted in the far-right column of Table 9.1, professionally trained singers have a somewhat greater range, particularly for the upper register. In fact, a professional mezzo-soprano could have a higher range extending to B_5-flat or higher, and a professional baritone's range could extend to A_4-flat or higher. Note that female musical theatre roles involving chest belt or mix belt will necessarily require less range than in classical/legit singing because of the pitch limitations on these methods of production (see Chapter 8 on registers).

Vocal Section	Comfortable	Maximum (Average Community Choral Singer)	Maximum (Professional Voice/Extensive Training)
Soprano	D_4–G_5	A_3–B_5	G_3–D_6*
Alto	A_3–C_5	G_3–F_5	E_3–A_5
Tenor	E_3–G_4-flat	C_3–A_4	C_3–C_5**
Bass	A_2–D_4	F_2–F_4	E_2–F_4

Note: Maximum professional voice range based on Titze (2000). *Coloratura classical/legit sopranos sing above this pitch in whistle register as do some contemporary-style singers. **In musical theatre and some other contemporary styles, tenors may have to sing to D_5 in head voice and even higher pitches in a reinforced falsetto.

Table 9.1 Comfortable and maximum ranges for general vocal classifications

Conductors and teachers should be conservative about asking singers to venture outside of their classification's vocal range, particularly on the upper end. For example, true baritones should sing in the bass section of a choir. Singing tenor can damage their voices over time because they will tend to use a highly pressed form of production.

> ➤ Henderson (1979) also cautions choral directors against asking younger, true sopranos to sing alto simply because they can read music better or are more facile at singing harmony. Developing soprano voices will rarely have the opportunity to improve upper register production if they always sing alto. Nonetheless, teachers of young sopranos who sing in choirs where directors are asking for a flute-like, straighter sound may want to advise their students to sing alto to assist the development of a more focused tonal quality.
> ➤ The American Academy of Teachers of Singing (1997) warns of "the endless temptation of choral directors to encourage young people to sing certain parts not because their voices are ready for this particular tessitura but because the chorus needs more voices on that part."

Whenever possible, do not sacrifice voices to balance sections—this can seriously limit vocal development. Instead, conductors should endeavor to choose appropriate repertoire or ask sections to alter their volume to produce balance.

Misclassification of voices in choral groups

In some choral organizations there will be singers who are singing as altos or basses when they might genuinely be sopranos or tenors. These singers are misclassified because they have not learned to access much of their head voice, a process that requires significant training and energy. An audition or voice placement process should be used to encourage singers to demonstrate their full range, even if they aren't comfortable throughout.

- Singers with sizeable vocal instruments may find gaining access to head voice difficult. In an ensemble, these singers may be comfortable in a lower voice section though they could have the potential to sing a higher part.
- Singers struggling to sing loudly on lower pitches in the bass or alto range may also be candidates for a higher voice category.
- Conductors may also assess how "heavy" or "light" singers sound. That is, do they have more low-frequency resonance or more high-frequency resonance?

The choral environment can provide an excellent opportunity for singers to experience expanding their range. Conductors should communicate with their singers to determine which voice part is a good fit in the short term and stay in touch as singers develop to re-evaluate section placement. The vocal health and development of the singer should be of prime importance when placing a singer in a section.

Tessitura versus range

As we have noted previously, tessitura refers to the average pitch of a piece of music. It can also mean the range within which most pitches fall. Compositions with high tessituras can be quite difficult for singers because higher notes require more breath pressure and involve more laryngeal tension.

The tessitura of solo and choral singing for all musical styles has vocal health implications. When singers must sing outside of their comfortable range for long periods, they may experience substantial laryngeal tension.

- For females, if many notes fall near or above the second passaggio, consider the piece to have a high tessitura
- For males, if many notes fall near or above the first passaggio, consider the piece to have a high tessitura

Faced with a high tessitura, singers need more opportunities to take a breath, including, for example, adding a rest or increasing the length of a rest where feasible. In addition, in choral groups, singers should stagger their breaths frequently. Conductors should avoid repetitive rehearsals of these types of passages to protect singers' vocal health.

The impact of high tessitura music on vocal health is a significant concern, but an unusually low tessitura can be problematic as well.

One reason that some voice teachers are reluctant to encourage their students to sing in choral organizations is the high tessitura of many choral works (American Academy of Teachers of Singing, 1997). Conductors should be sensitive to this issue, especially for younger, developing voices. The tessitura of a piece is just as important as range in selecting choral music.

In musical theatre the tessitura for parts sung by sopranos is typically lower than that in classical singing (Hall, 2014). These singers need a solid chest or at least chestmix capability for the lower notes demanded in many roles. Classically trained sopranos may not have this capability.

Classification of voices in contemporary styles

Contemporary styles rarely use formal voice classifications. For example, in musical theatre, an audition for a part may include a requirement to mix belt to a given pitch or to sing legit to a given pitch; a requirement for a female to belt to only C_5 would imply a part for a lower voice. In some cases, however, a casting director may specify a basic voice category such as soprano. In other contemporary styles, singers may alter a song's key to fit their voices best.

> ➢ "Performers are expected to know what kind of a role they are auditioning for, either because the show has been done before or because there is a description of it in the casting notice. In all of the other Contemporary Commercial Music styles, you just sing as a "vocalist." (p. 45, Jeannette LoVetri quoted in Woodruff, 2011)

Musical theatre voice requirements and show types

Insight into musical theatre voice requirements and demand levels for related styles is provided by an analysis of musical theatre audition postings in *Backstage* by Green, Freeman, Edwards, and Meyer (2014). As musical theatre draws on many contemporary styles, audition requirements are quite varied, even within show categories. The following summarizes some of their findings about show categories and the vocal requirements within each:

- **Legit** (5% of audition listings). Legit, as we have noted elsewhere, is basically classical production but with a somewhat brighter tone than some operatic approaches to classical production. Listings in this category tend to be the only ones that use classical designations for voice type (e.g., dramatic soprano). *Phantom of the Opera* is an example.
- **Traditional** (40%). These shows may include both legit and belting roles. They tend to be pre-1970 shows and revivals of the same (which are increasingly popular). Legit in these shows will tend to have a more speech-like quality. Belting style tends to be chest belting. Examples include *Oklahoma!*
- **Contemporary** (30%). Contemporary shows introduced the need for a higher belting range for female roles, accomplished by the mix belt described in Chapter 3. A speaking-style belt may be specified as a requirement for certain roles (in addition to belting). These shows require greater versatility than most Traditional shows; thus, a female lead may require both mix belt and legit capabilities. Examples include *The Lion King* and *Wicked*.
- **Pop/Rock** (25%). This category includes a wide range of styles and expectations. Range and tessitura requirements are often extensive—for example, requiring solid low notes plus a quality mix belt. Special effects such as shrieks and growls may be required. Many of the shows include the songs of well-known commercial pop and rock groups, thus requiring an ability to imitate other singers (an advanced capability that should not be pursued until a contemporary music singer has developed their own style). Producers may also have a specific artist's sound in mind even for singing that does not involve that artist's songs. Examples include *We Will Rock You* and *Jersey Boys.*

The demand for roles in these various categories will of course fluctuate over time. The key finding is the increasing need for singers to have a strong technical foundation that allows stylistic flexibility within the capabilities of a person's voice.

Singing higher pitches

Most singers want to use more of the upper part of their range and/or be more comfortable singing higher pitches. Remember that successful register transitions are key to achieving higher pitches. Recall from previous chapters that there are four primary keys to accomplishing smooth transitions:

- Vowel and/or vocal tract modification to alter resonating frequencies

(formants). See Chapters 4 and 5 on resonance and vowels.
- ❖ Upon entering a passaggio, use lower breath pressure.
- ❖ Upon entering a passaggio, reduce firmness of vocal fold closure.
- ❖ Monitoring laryngeal position—this is key to the involvement of the cricothyroids for higher pitches. If the larynx rises excessively, the CTs will not come into play. For mix belting, you can allow a modest rise and still activate the cricothyroids enough to accommodate the less demanding higher pitches of this style, while preserving a more powerful sound. For legit and particularly, classical production, the larynx should not rise very much.

Additional factors affecting attainment of high pitches

Reducing tension is key to attaining high pitches. Singers should consciously relax the muscles of the neck, jaw, and tongue. Remember that these muscles impinge on the larynx and that relaxing them will help to allow the cricothyroid muscles to tilt the thyroid cartilage. (See Chapter 14 for methods of reducing tension in the neck, jaw, and tongue.)

- ❖ The only tension that singers should experience is in the muscles of the ribs and abdomen that control and support the breath. Maintenance of appoggio can go a long way toward relaxing the vocal apparatus. (See Chapter 2 on breathing.)

Monitor vibrato use. If you are singing with minimal vibrato on every note, this will contribute tension and make it difficult to sing higher pitches. Classical and legit styles allow for continuous vibrato; at the very least, most contemporary styles allow for vibrato at the end of a phrase and/or for expression of emotion. Note that vibrato on lower pitches coupled with minimal vibrancy on higher pitches is often indicative of excess tension at higher pitches.

Use SOVT exercises, particularly singing through a straw, to assist vocal fold vibration at higher pitches. (See Chapter 3 for more detail.)

- ➢ Research (e.g., Titze, 1999) has shown that the upper portion of the vocal fold (involved in upper register production) is influenced mostly by air pressure above the glottis, while the lower part of the fold is influenced by subglottal pressure. When a partial occlusion slows airflow above the glottis, the breath pressure required for phonation reduces, making it easier for the upper portions of the folds to vibrate—precisely what is needed for mixed and head voice!

Try "singing" five-note ascending scales through a straw starting on A_3 for males and A_4 for females. Move up progressively. You may find that afterward, you can sing higher notes than you previously could. Even if you are not yet able to sing higher, your high notes will be less breathy and more focused after this exercise.

Singers should use caution when singing in a heavy voice at the upper end of their range as this can cause vocal strain, fatigue, and even granulomas/nodules on the vocal folds (Bunch, 1995). Some popular performers who sing using mostly "raw" belting have lost their voices (sometimes permanently). See Chapter 15 on vocal health.

Using falsetto to access head voice in males

Vocal pedagogy authorities disagree about the value of falsetto as a device to help male singers access head voice. Vennard (1967) is one of the strongest proponents of this method, and we agree with his perspective. This training technique certainly has a long history in voice training.

Falsetto can be helpful because the thyroarytenoid muscle relaxes in this register (the cricothyroids are primarily involved in pitch variation). By singing falsetto, male singers can gain some experience with lighter production even if they have not learned to sing in head voice. Fortunately, the vast majority of males seem to know instinctually how to sing falsetto without instruction.

Males should use descending falsetto scales that move sequentially into the passaggio area. Tenors might start on D_5, singing five-note scales downward progressively on a variety of vowels, switching to head, and chest at varying points. This technique blends falsetto with modal voice. Basses should start on C_5. Singers may find that [o] is a good vowel with which to start.

Another benefit of practicing falsetto is that it will build a more focused (i.e., less breathy) falsetto sound. Classical tenors can use this focused falsetto to produce softer sounds at A_4-flat and above. Basses can use it to produce softer sounds at F_4 and above. Such use is generally restricted to the amateur choral setting; it is not an acceptable technique for well-trained classical singers. Falsetto may, however, be used for effect in popular music; a reinforced falsetto is essential for classical countertenors and many pop/rock singers as discussed in the chapter on registers. See the preceding chapter on registers for reinforced falsetto technique.

Accessing lower pitches for female singers

Many classically-trained sopranos do not fully utilize their lower register (chest voice), but it can be a valuable addition to their tonal palette and

Voice Classification and Improving Range

range. A soprano with access to chest voice has a greater range than any other voice type.

One method of learning chest voice is to sing descending passages that cross the boundary from middle voice to the lower register.

Start on B_4, using a descending sighing slide of a fifth. Low breath pressure may help. Try downward octave slides and even leaps for further development, starting no higher than E_5. A comfortably low larynx is important because it helps to lower all formant frequencies, giving chest voice at lower pitches a rich, mellow tone. Regularly perform this exercise with a straw to build facility in accessing chest register.

> McKinney (2005) suggests a similar approach. He recommends singing descending five-note scales starting at B_5-flat.

Once sopranos gain some facility with lower register production, try descending and then ascending arpeggios in this same range (8-5-3-1-3-5-8), lowering the starting note as you progress. This will also help with developing chestmix in the range of D_4/E_4 to B_4. Firmer vocal fold closure is essential in this context. This exercise can also be helpful for mezzo-sopranos and contraltos, but they should use a lower starting pitch. If progressing down to C_4 or lower, sopranos must transition into chest voice. *Again, using an SOVT device such as a straw or [v] for this exercise will be beneficial.*

> As a more advanced exercise, McKinney (2005) suggests starting at A_3, sliding up one octave and then singing a five-note descending scale. This can be varied using different starting notes at middle-C (C_4) and below. McKinney recommends focusing on maintenance of a consistent vowel sound during this exercise.

Handling leaps in pitch

A leap of a fourth or more can be a challenge for singers, particularly when that jump transitions a vocal register boundary.

Prepare breath pressure before singing the high pitch. The key is to mentally connect the lower and higher notes and physically connect them on the same breath. Also, in classical/legit styles the lower pitch should be sung in the register of the upper pitch where feasible. For contemporary styles this is often an artistic choice.

> McKinney (2005) says that if a crescendo is indicated for an upward leap, crescendo on the lower note; otherwise, the high note will seem too loud.

A slide (an extended portamento) from the lower to upper note can be a helpful way to practice. Slides are a useful device to develop the muscle memory and breath pressure calibration necessary for negotiating a leap.

Another useful device to maintain breath support during individual practice is to use a thick physical therapy resistance band (or a large elastic such as a thick rubber balloon) that you can stretch with some difficulty. *Grab the material with hands spaced about four inches apart and hold it vertically, close to your abdomen. As you ascend in pitch, stretch the material vertically.* This device helps by assisting activation of the abdominal muscles. It also distracts singers from thinking about the larynx and from trying to control laryngeal muscles directly to make the leap. The result is less laryngeal tension and a greater likelihood of an accurate leap.

Singers also might consider lowering the chin very slightly, which helps keep the larynx low and counteracts the tendency to reach for the high note physically.

While singers usually have more problems leaping upward as opposed to down, it is common on downward leaps for singers to relax breath support too much on the lower note, leading to a sound that is flat or lacking in resonance. Breath support should be maintained whether ascending or descending.

Exercises to increase range

The following exercises are suggested for increasing range. These exercises are particularly important to maintain access to both the lower and higher limits of our ranges as we age—use it or lose it!

Image for creating space for higher pitches

For classical/legit styles, it may help to imagine biting into a large sandwich to create an inverted megaphone space. As you do this, notice how your jaw is released, the tongue lies flat but is not pulled back in the mouth, the soft palate is lifted, there is a horizontal widening of the back of the mouth, the lip and cheek muscles are raised, and the area above the upper lip is stretched horizontally.

For contemporary styles, imagine the mouth like the bell of a trumpet and open the mouth using the jaw joint as a hinge, opening the front of the mouth. Also, pull back the corners of the mouth into a wide smile.

Be sure to avoid generating too much tension as you execute these images.

Slides

Sliding is an excellent approach to range extension because it helps to maintain the correct breath pressure and weight of vocal production. In addition, it enables us to create proper space and vowel modification for upper pitches gradually. *Try sliding up and down the interval of a fifth. Start in middle voice (or upper chest voice for males) and move into the upper register. Do the exercise in reverse to work the lower end of your range. Ascend/descend by half steps. Quick slides of an octave are also helpful—try not to hesitate on the top pitch; move through it rapidly. This prevents the buildup of tension on very high and very low pitches.*

When doing these and other range exercises, singers should monitor their larynx as pitch ascends by touching it gently with a finger.

Runs

Runs (scales sung in a fast tempo) are another effective way to extend range as they too discourage tension in the extremes of the registers. *Try ascending and descending runs of a fifth or ninth. Increment the starting pitch by semitones (half steps). Be careful to start the sound with coordinated onset and appropriate pharyngeal and mouth space to ensure good resonance. Keep the abdominal muscles engaged to supply correct breath pressure and modify vowels in a fashion appropriate to the style as pitch ascends.*

Tenors and sopranos can often vocalize on runs as high as C; basses and altos can vocalize down to E. Encourage singers to experiment with their range, but not at the cost of vocal health. They should be the guardians of their own voices and never strain themselves.

Using falsetto to access head voice in males

Males should use descending falsetto scales that move sequentially into the passaggio area. Tenors might start on D_5, singing five-note scales downward progressively on a variety of vowels, switching to modal voice at varying points. This technique blends falsetto with modal voice. Basses should start on

C_5. Singers may find that [o] is a good vowel to begin with.

Using SOVT exercises to improve range

Try singing five-note ascending scales on [v] or through a straw starting on A_3 for males and A_4 for females. Move up progressively. You may find that afterward, you can sing higher notes than you previously could. Even if you are not yet able to sing higher, your high notes will be less breathy and more focused after this exercise.

Extending the lower portion of the range

To extend the lower part of the range, try singing [siɑ] or [sia]. Descend from the dominant to the tonic on [si] changing to [ɑ] or [a] on the lower pitch. This exercise can be done using a descending scale or slide. Both are illustrated. Continue descending by half steps while carefully monitoring tension. Never push the sound, but rather allow it to be released.

Low breath pressure may help. Try descending octave slides and even leaps for further development, starting no higher than E_5 for women. A comfortably low larynx lowers all formant frequencies, giving lower range chest voice a rich, mellow tone.

For kids and everyone! Darts and Frisbees

Sing [i], ascending run of a fifth, two times in quick succession. Then sing legato on [a] or [ɑ]. Pretend to throw a dart during the first two runs. Then imagine tossing a Frisbee for the arpeggiated figure. (Adapted from S. Morrison, personal communication, August 8, 2008)

Chapter 10: Improving Intonation

Excellent intonation is a primary concern of conductors, teachers, and singers. Wonderful repertoire can be sung with great conviction, but it is all for naught if it is out of tune. The good news is that attention to vocal technique can eliminate many of the causes of poor intonation.

There are certain styles where occasional detuning is intentional, such as in jazz singing, but this is a deliberate rather than accidental choice. Singers should develop excellent intonation before they attempt deliberate detuning.

Causes of poor intonation

Teachers and conductors sometimes assume that poor intonation is the result of singers not listening or not perceiving the pitch correctly. While this is true in some cases, the vast majority of singers are trying to sing on pitch. Singers can, however, find it difficult to recognize when they are out of tune because what they "hear" is not the sound that listeners hear due to bone conductance and directionality of sound (away from singers' ears). Telling singers that they are out of tune (either flat or sharp) is only part of the solution. Many singers will not know how to fix the problem.

Powell (1991) classifies poor intonation into two main categories:

- ❖ Individual, horizontal intonation problems involving melodic line
- ❖ Ensemble, vertical intonation problems involving harmony

Horizontal intonation (melodic line; relevant for both soloists and ensembles)

When singing their line, singers need to perceive the spaces between pitches (intervals) accurately. Even in the choral setting, singers should think of their part as a melody and read the intervals accurately with attention to how the key signature affects spacing. In addition, they need to develop muscle memory for the correct distance between pitches. Pitches must be learned correctly the first time—if errors are not quickly corrected, they will become a part of muscle memory and will be difficult to correct later. Leaps are especially problematic because they can be a "shot in the dark" for many singers as they guess how far to move.

Try utilizing a sliding exercise to understand how much of a leap is required—

a slide will allow for modifications in breath pressure and resonating space. Once both pitches are in tune, speed up the slide, and eventually eliminate it.

Singers may find it particularly challenging to sing descending melodic lines in tune. Awareness of this tendency goes a long way toward fixing it. **Singers should imagine that descending intervals are smaller than ascending intervals.** They should keep breath support muscles engaged and preserve resonance space as they descend.

Sing descending five-note major and minor scales on various vowels throughout the singers' ranges. Conductors and teachers should give singers immediate feedback on intonation.

Horizontal intonation problems can be related to reading rather than recognizing music. Once singers are more familiar with their music, have developed muscle memory for the line, and can use the notation to recognize the music (rather than read it), many melodic intonation problems will disappear.

Additional causes of individual intonation problems involve fundamental technique issues, previously discussed:

- ❖ Tension in the neck, larynx or tongue
- ❖ Breath pressure (too much or too little)
- ❖ Insufficient or incorrect resonance space
- ❖ Incorrect use of registers (head/chest/mix voice)

It is also essential for singers to think about the pitch of a vowel before singing it. Create the space for that particular vowel and sing any preceding consonant in that space as well.

Because singers perceive their sound differently than the actual sound they create, they must learn how it feels to sing in tune. For example, they must become used to the breath pressure and resonating space necessary to negotiate passaggi.

Vertical intonation (harmony in ensembles)

As Powell (1991) explains, a significant difference between professional and amateur musicians is that professional musicians always listen and adjust to the sounds of those around them. Choral directors encourage their singers to listen but providing guidance about how to accomplish this is crucial.

In warm-ups directors can employ numerous harmonic progressions to assist with the tuning of chords and encourage active listening to self and others. A simple Bach Chorale can be very useful.

Try sustaining a four-part major chord of your choice. Change the pitches systematically, part by part, to form new, sometimes dissonant chords. (See the exercises section of this chapter for an example.) Singers should be encouraged to notice the shifts in intervals between parts.

Powell (1991) suggests exposing and tuning octaves between parts first, then moving to fifths, etc. Singers, particularly those with some exposure to music theory, may find it helpful if their conductor points out the scale degree that they are singing, or the function of their pitch (the leading tone, the third of a major triad, a dissonant note, a four-three suspension, etc.). Whatever approach you adopt, assist the singers in correcting the problem, as opposed to just telling them they are sharp or flat.

The following corrective steps are helpful:

❖ Isolate the problematic interval (e.g., a fifth between the basses and tenors).
❖ Tune the interval—use slide exercises or adjust the vowel as necessary. For example, if a section is flat, try an adjacent brighter vowel with a higher second formant or suggest a slight fronting of the tongue to raise the frequency of the second formant. (See Figure 4.3 in Chapter 4, which shows F_1 and F_2 for various vowels.)
❖ Add in the other voice parts one by one.
❖ Have all parts sing the chord together.
❖ Finally, sing the chord in its context.

Dynamic level

Shaw advocates singing reasonably quietly at rehearsal (Blocker, 2004). He cites vocal over-singing as the basis of many vocal problems, including disturbances of intonation. He notes that every pitched musical instrument (except a few percussion instruments) can be "'forced' out of tune by too much pressure of air, bow, or fist" and that the voice is especially vulnerable to forcing (p. 87). Forcing may also be caused by high levels of breath pressure and/or pressed phonation as pitch ascends. Under such circumstances, pitch control is more difficult.

Under-singing also poses problems for intonation as the tone may become somewhat breathy, due to less than optimal vocal fold vibration and a lack of resonance. Additionally, in the choral setting, good intonation requires singers to be able to hear themselves as well as others (see the section below). Those who under-sing likely are unable to hear themselves. Since they are inconspicuous in the choral texture, they are harder for conductors to identify than those who over-sing. Conductors should observe singers and ascertain if they are inhaling properly and engaging support muscles. If not, they may be under-singing.

Vowel differences within and between ensemble sections

Conductors can eliminate many intonation problems by ensuring that singers are producing the same vowel sound in the same way. This is an example of where careful attention to uniform production of vowels in the warm-up pays off. If conductors suspect that vowels are not in agreement, they can try the following:

Isolate the word. Ask the choir/section which vowel sound(s) they should be singing. Correct them if necessary. Remember that diphthongs can be especially confusing. Have the singers sing only the vowel(s). If necessary, isolate sections (tenors, sopranos, etc.). Now ask the choir to sing the word as written (with consonants). Finally, put it back into the context of the passage.

Standing position of singers in ensembles

Ternström and Sundberg (1988) found that the ability to hear both oneself and other singers has an impact on intonation. If singers cannot perceive their own sound, it is difficult for them to know when they are singing in tune. Singers may not be able to hear themselves if they are not singing loudly enough or if someone is over-singing next to them. Additionally, intonation problems can result if a singer cannot hear the person next to them. Whenever possible, try to seat singers according to voice quality and according to height (singers cannot hear someone who is substantially taller or shorter than they are).

One useful formation that encourages excellent intonation has sopranos and altos in the front, from left to right, and basses and tenors in the back, from left to right. This formation allows the outer parts to tune to each other.

> ➢ Lamb (1988) also advocates this formation from the perspective that it emphasizes the polarity of parts.

See Chapter 12 on blend for more about the effects of standing position on choral sound.

Repertoire-specific intonation issues

If your choir sings in tune in general but experiences occasional poor intonation, consider the following aspects of the passages with which they are struggling:

Text/lyrics

Sometimes singers can successfully learn a passage of music on a pure vowel (e.g., [o]); however, once lyrics are added, or if lyrics have always been used, intonation may suffer.

Sing a problematic passage of music on only a selected vowel. If pure vowels have been established in the warm-up, singers should have a reference for how to produce these sounds.

If the intonation problems disappear, sing the same passage with the written vowels, but without consonants. In choral groups, listen carefully for places where the vowels disagree—i.e., singers do not have the same reference point for the vowel (are singing different vowels) or are not producing the vowel in the same way. Point out the correct vowel to sing and monitor how it is being produced.

Shaw advocates singing on the vowels with a single preceding consonant to learn rhythm as well (Noble, 2005).

Finally, add the consonants. Chapter 6 discusses how consonants can distort or pollute vowels, altering pitch. Remind singers to use articulators quickly and efficiently, always returning the tip of the tongue to the base of the lower front teeth, except for cases where you wish to elongate consonants for expressive purposes.

This process of correcting intonation may take some time. Be patient, and the learned skills will transfer to future singing.

In musical theatre and some other contemporary styles, the stylistic focus on text may mean that intonation is secondary. In sections of music that are out of tune, singers should consider slightly changing the way they articulate the vowel or consonant to find the correct balance of good intonation and clear text declamation.

Tessitura

In our discussion of registers in Chapter 8, we noted that some of the most challenging areas for inexperienced singers are the transition areas or passaggi. If a piece of music lingers in a pitch (has a tessitura) in or near a passaggio, intonation can suffer unless there is careful attention to breath support and relaxation techniques. Simply reminding singers about the technical demands of singing in a passaggio will help. Singers can also try more frequent stagger breathing in ensembles, or inhalations of slightly longer duration than usual to give the vocal mechanism more time for recovery.

The following technique is helpful for both choral and solo singers:

Practice the recovery portion of the breath cycle by elongating it. *Sing the passage in question. Singers should release the abdominal and rib muscles so that the subsequent inhalation can be complete and relaxed. For soloists and ensemble group-breaths, the breath should be significantly longer (e.g., a quarter rest becomes a half rest by reducing the duration of the preceding note). Then continue to sing the passage. Repeat the exercise with slightly shorter breaks for the breath cycle (dotted quarter/two seconds etc.). Finally, sing in time.*

This technique will build stamina and encourage awareness of the breath cycle.

Register use may also cause intonation issues, most notably when singers chest belt or have too much TA dominance in the mid to upper register. This may create tension and intonation instability. Attention to the mix voice (headmix, chestmix) and choosing which to use in various contexts will fix many intonation issues in all styles.

Key of the piece

Some keys are more difficult to sing than others, likely because of their tessitura, but also because of the unique relationship of intervals (the space between pitches) in the singing voice. The voice is not a fixed pitch, equal-tempered instrument. Thus, conductors can create intonation problems for their choirs by programming *a cappella* music that moves from flat keys to sharp keys. If the choir is singing in tune with itself, but the entire piece consistently sinks in pitch by a half step (or goes sharp), conductors should consider lowering (or raising) the key of the piece by a half step. In early music, spirituals, folk songs, show tunes, and some other genres, small variations in key can go a long way toward allowing an ensemble to "settle" their intonation. However, in classical music notated since the mid-18th century, this solution is not appropriate, as composers wrote in specific keys for particular reasons.

For solo singers, especially in contemporary styles such as jazz and pop, key selection must be done with care to make sure the qualities of the voice match the desired emotional expression of the song. If a singer consistently sings a song out of tune, consider changing the key.

Extraneous factors affecting intonation

Solving intonation problems can involve other "nonmusical" considerations.

These apply particularly to ensembles, but they also apply to solo singers.

Energy level

A tired singer will struggle to sing in tune. A singer who is pumped full of adrenaline will also have intonation problems. Conductors should anticipate where the choir might be in terms of energy and plan rehearsals accordingly. For example, planning slow, sustained a cappella repertoire for long periods of rehearsal time may result in the choir learning to sing a piece out of tune because of fatigue. Whenever possible, assist the choir in learning a piece in-tune so that muscle memory will help rather than hinder at performance time.

Method of supplying a starting pitch

The way you provide a starting pitch can have a surprising influence on the initial intonation of *a cappella* music. This has the strongest implications in the teaching of pitch matching and intonation for developing singers.

> - A starting pitch provided by a piano or organ is not ideal. A recent study has shown that less experienced adult singers can better match a pitch supplied by a live singer (Granot, Israel-Kolatt, Gilboa, & Kolatt, 2013).
> - Several studies have investigated pitch matching among children. In general, these studies find that children better match pitches to female or child models (e.g., Green, 1987; Price, Yarbrough, Jones, & Moore, 1994).
> - Another study found that male adolescents achieved their best intonation when matching a baritone model (Demorest & Clements, 2007).

Acoustics of the room

Ternström and Sundberg (1988) ascertained that acoustical feedback received from the singing space could affect intonation. Some spaces offer helpful information to singers by way of modest reverberation. These environments permit singers to hear themselves and others, encouraging good intonation and singing with a full sound. Others provide too much or too little information—either so reverberant or acoustically dry as to interfere with good intonation.

Thus, the space in which a soloist or ensemble rehearses can substantially influence intonation and overall sound. Of course, the acoustics of the rehearsal space may differ from the acoustics of the performance space.

Teachers and conductors should help singers build muscle memory in rehearsal. Singers should trust that memory (and teacher/conductor feedback) when singing in different spaces.

Conducting pattern

An experimental study (Brunkan, 2013), comparing a standard conducting pattern to a high pattern using a circular hand gesture and a low pattern using a circular arm gesture, shows the low pattern to have the following benefits:

- Better intonation
- More balanced tone quality

A high conducting pattern generally has unfavorable effects on both intonation and tone quality.

Concluding thoughts about intonation

Proper vocal technique will always improve intonation. When individuals sing with resonance and excellent breath support, their sound is more in tune. Ekholm's (2000) study of singing styles in the choral setting (solo, soloistic, and blended) found that the majority of listeners (who were voice teachers) reported problems with intonation when singers consciously attempted to blend with those around them. When they did this, the quality of their technique suffered. Singing in a "trained mode," that is, with proper technique, is the most consistent defense against poor intonation. Conductors should not ask singers to attempt to blend with their neighbors; instead, they should use the blending techniques suggested in Chapter 12 (e.g., consistent production of vowels within sections, voice matching).

With careful monitoring, teachers and conductors can assist their singers to take an active role in anticipating, avoiding, and fixing intonation issues.

Exercises to improve intonation

Paying attention to the spacing of intervals for a given key, developing muscle memory for pitches, and proper vocal technique go a long way toward improving intonation. A few intonation-specific exercises may be helpful, as well.

Slides to help with leaps in pitch

Try utilizing slides to accurately perceive how far a leap is—a slide will allow for modifications in breath pressure, registration, and resonating space. Once both pitches are in tune, speed up the slide, and eventually eliminate it. Experiment with different intervals. Also, practice downward leaps in pitch.

Major and minor scales to learn intervals

Sing descending five-note major and minor scales (fifth—tonic) on various vowels throughout singers' ranges. Vary the key. Give singers immediate feedback on intonation.

Pivot note exercise for horizontal intonation

Sing [di] on a given pitch in the middle of the range. Use this pitch as the 'pivot' note—move up a half step and return to the original pitch, then move down a half step and return to the starting pitch. Breathe and repeat, but this time move a whole step above and below the 'pivot' pitch. Add repetitions using wider intervals. Continue to work on this so that the singer(s) can easily sing all intervals above and below the pivot pitch, from a half step through a perfect fifth, with excellent horizontal intonation.

Vertical and horizontal intonation

The following exercise concentrates on vertical intonation but involves horizontal intonation as well. Notice that sopranos and basses must tune octaves at the start of each of the first two measures. Encourage the singers to notice the shifts in intervals between parts and to note which part of a chord they are singing (root, third, suspension, etc.). A chorale is another possible choice. Sing these types of exercises in a variety of keys.

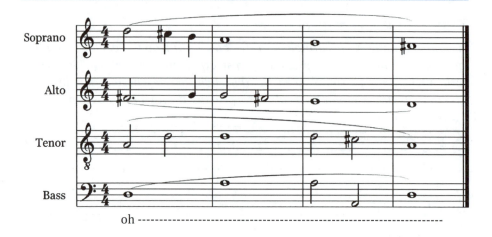

Chapter 11: Legato, Staccato, Accents, Melismas/Riffs, Dynamic Control, and Special Vocal Effects

Several articulation choices present challenges for many singers:

- **Legato** creates continuous sound. This should be the fundamental method of vocal production for classical/legit styles, but it is useful for all singers to have this capability. Contemporary styles use a more nuanced legato, as outlined below.
- **Staccato** is correctly created by releasing a sound quickly. Unfortunately, many singers think that staccato involves a glottal onset to create a short, crisp sound.
- **Accents** are created by the nature of the onset or the way the sound begins. Numerous singers create accents with problematic tension.
- **Melismas** (runs/riffs), or passages of rapid pitch changes, are the bane of many singers. They are relevant for both classical and contemporary styles. Agility is a difficult skill to acquire, particularly for heavier voices within a given vocal classification. Nonetheless, some helpful techniques can make these fast passages less of a trial.
- **Dynamic control** involves the ability to sing with a full range of sound levels throughout one's publicly usable range. Singing softly on high pitches can be especially tricky.
- **Special vocal effects** may include growls, yells, grunts, speak-singing (Sprechstimme, Sprechgesang, parlando, recitative, patter, belt speaking), slides (portamenti), among others. Sometimes vocal effects are called for by the composer in the music/score; other effects are characteristic of an individual style and it is the performer's choice about when to use them.

This chapter is designed to help singers gain mastery over these advanced techniques.

Legato involves vowel-to-vowel continuity

The term *legato* comes from the Italian verb *legare,* which means "to join." In a legato vocal line, the singer joins together all the words in a phrase to produce a continuous sound. For this reason, legato is generally the most preferred method of vocal production for classical style singing.

- ❖ Essential to legato is consistent breath support. Unless breath is well-connected to sound, there can be no legato.
- ❖ Knowing where the phrase is going is also essential for a legato line. For example, it is crucial to maintain the intensity of expression through the most important word or syllable in a phrase.

Legato involves truly connected sound: regardless of pitch changes and vowel changes, resonance is consistent, breath support and energy are consistent, and consonants interfere minimally with breath or resonance. This is essential for classical production, in part because legato is the sound distinctive of the style, and in part, because classical singers typically do not use amplification. The expectation in classical singing is total tonal consistency.

- ❖ In other styles there may be varying degrees of legato. Certainly, in legit singing, legato is quite prevalent. It may also be expected in at least some portions of pop and jazz songs (e.g., power ballads).
- ❖ Some styles, such as classical recitative, some art songs, pop, jazz, and legit musical theatre, do require legato, but not with the unrelenting intensity of sound associated with operatic singing. Singers in these styles use legato as a lyrical articulation that is heavily nuanced according to the text. A largely legato line may also include uneven weighting of syllables, glottal strokes (a slight glottal separation of syllables), elongated consonants, and/or relaxed/adapted rhythms including pauses, all motivated by text.

Try singing an ascending and descending scale (major or minor) with a continuous, legato sound. Next, try varying the intensity (dynamic) of every other note—heavy/light/heavy/light. Try reversing the intensity pattern. Then, try a more subtle variation by varying the tempo. Apply this technique to repertoire by choosing a phrase and singing it legato, then with a legato that is flexible and informed by the text stress.

Consonants and legato

Quick, efficient enunciation of consonants is essential to prevent consonants from intruding upon the legato line. If consonants are formed too slowly, there can be noise, intonation issues, changes in resonance, lack of continuous sound, and even vocal fatigue.

- ➤ Vennard (1967) suggests that singers think in terms of slight crescendo from one syllable to the next. This may help maintain breath energy and consistent resonance.

Eliding consonants to aid legato

Eliding consonants is particularly important for the creation of a legato line. This involves connecting the final consonant of the preceding word with the word that follows. For example, sing "mist on the moor" as "mi ston the moor." In this example there should be no stopping of the vowel sounds except to pronounce the consonants quickly.

Even complex consonant clusters can be elided. Consider, for example, this phrase from Haydn's *Creation*, "The wonder of his works displays the firmament." Singers can elide "works displays" as follows: "wor—ksdi—splays."

As noted in Chapter 6 on consonants, sometimes a glottal stroke or perhaps a slight pause before a vowel may be desirable in preference to slavish adherence to legato. For example, singing "his eyes" as "hi—seyes" would sound strange. Instead, sing "his {eyes" where the bracket indicates a slight glottal separation (glottal stroke).

Be sure to maintain or accelerate the breath pressure on consonants that consume a lot of air (unvoiced consonants) to keep the sense of legato and the musical line going. For example, when singing "king," do not interrupt exhalation or close the glottis after you form the "k."

Again, in contemporary styles, there may be a frequent interruption of the legato line – a flexible form of legato that is more inflected by consonants.

Language requirements that necessarily interrupt the legato line

The language being sung may require an interruption of the legato line. For example, Chapter 3 discusses the use of a soft glottal for words beginning with a vowel within a German phrase. This will necessarily interrupt the legato line.

Italian may be the most natural language for legato production because it has fewer consonants than English and other Germanic languages. Nonetheless, some Italian words have double consonants, and for correct pronunciation and understanding, it is important to stop very briefly on the first occurrence before forming the second consonant. For example, if *notte* is pronounced [no]-[te], it will mean "note," not "night."

Images to help with achieving legato articulation

Singers can imagine vowels of a vocal phrase as a flowing river. Consonants are dropped precisely and quickly into the river so that they do not interrupt the flow.

Singers can hold their dominant arm in front of them and imagine they are holding a wide paintbrush in their hand with a wall in front of them. *Paint a horizontal brush stroke on the "wall," moving from left to right and then changing direction quickly. Do this several times; it will provide a physical sensation of making fast, barely perceptible transitions that keep the sound going. Now, sing a phrase, quickly reversing the brush between the syllables of words in the phrase.*

Staccato

Stop the tone by ceasing exhalation to sing staccato properly

Staccato is a release gesture. Accomplish it by stopping the breath. It is not a hard, glottal onset followed by a tight glottal closure. While singers may think that staccato has to do with onset, it is all about a quick release after a coordinated onset.

> ➢ Sundberg (1993) adds that to produce a staccato sound, breath pressure must reduce to zero in the spaces between notes, and the vocal folds must open. The singer must then immediately create the correct breath pressure for the next note based on pitch and dynamic level. Without the right pressure, intonation will suffer. His analysis illustrates why staccato singing is so difficult and again emphasizes the critical need for control over breath support. With, for example, an upward-moving staccato line, singers must use one level of breath pressure for the starting note, go to zero, then suddenly increase pressure by just the right amount for the next note. This is technically very difficult.

An aid to learning staccato production is to breathe in very slightly after each note—this makes it easier to stop the sound, and there is less likelihood of closing the vocal folds to cease the sound.

Singers must take care to prevent the breathing mechanisms from collapsing during the singing of staccato notes. After inhalation, the intercostal and abdominal muscles should maintain the expanded position of the ribcage and abdomen for as long as possible.

Abdominal musculature and diaphragm should pulsate

Henderson (1979) used a fluoroscope to observe the diaphragm of a trained singer. She observed that during a staccato passage, the diaphragm pulsated. Pulsing of the abdominal muscles accomplishes this; it is a particularly valuable technique with a grouping of staccato notes.

Accents

While staccato is all about the release of sound, an accented pitch is all about onset. The method of onset will depend upon the composer's markings and the context of the accented note. Accented pitches sometimes require a glottal onset, but singers should usually try using higher breath pressure at the start of the note followed by a sudden reduction in pressure. This increase in breath pressure at the start of a note applies both to words that begin with vowels and to those that start with consonants. Singers may feel this as a little bounce in the abdomen, which creates a sudden increase and decrease in breath pressure. The result is a louder sound at the beginning of the note, followed by a decay of intensity. This is one way of achieving a tenuto accent (–). Tenuto can also mean emphasis in duration—a slight elongation of the pitch (rubato). A commonly used musical notation for a marcato accent (>) illustrates rapid dynamic change very nicely. A martellato (hammered) accent (^) combines a glottal onset with a staccato release.

Choose any simple exercise and vary the articulation of the pitches for each repetition. Make conscious choices/suggestions about the way to achieve each type of accent. Include staccato, staccatissimo (very short staccato), tenuto, marcato, and martellato.

Vocal ornaments and embellishments

Many styles of singing require the singer to perform ornaments or vocal embellishments. Certain types of classical music feature extensive use of ornaments, such as Baroque literature (which has the expectation that the singer will add these, even if not explicitly identified by the composer). Later periods in classical music did not typically involve extensive embellishment but in many contemporary styles such as gospel and jazz, runs, riffs, and scat singing are expected to be added by the singer as improvisatory embellishments. As with classical styles, we see periods in which certain types of ornaments are in vogue and then fall out of favor. For example, in pop music, melismas/runs were common in the 1990s and early 2000s, but by 2010 the expectation for these ornaments was greatly diminished (Browne, 2010).

Ornaments take the form of adding notes such as suspensions (holding a note while the chord changes), trills, or riffs. The style of music might also encourage varying the rhythm, the duration of pitches, the timing of entrances or releases, or changing the actual melodic line (e.g., as in jazz). Ornaments and embellishments generally serve to highlight something an individual singer does well (fast or high notes, long notes, etc.) or heighten the emotion of the text. Riffs on vowels are often used in rhythm and blues, gospel, and jazz. They can involve ascending or descending lines as well as sudden register crossings (large jumps up or down in pitch) for dramatic effect. Singers do not generally perform riffs/melismas in traditional or contemporary musical theatre; they may, however, appear in pop/rock musicals. Scat singing (primarily used in jazz and gospel) is similar in some aspects to vocal runs but can integrate consonants and will generally cover longer melodic phrases—as opposed to ornamenting individual pitches or small groups of pitches.

In general, ornaments should sound spontaneous or improvised. This does not mean that they should be a spur-of-the-moment decision! Singers should practice various ornaments so that they can determine which patterns their voices can best execute and perform consistently and in a healthy manner.

Technique for singing melismas in classical and contemporary styles

The key to singing melismas in classical styles is relaxation of all muscles that impinge on the larynx plus slight pulsation of the central abdominal muscles.

> ➢ Richard Miller (1996) has a helpful image. He says that the epigastric area of the abdominal wall (the upper middle portion of the abdomen just below the sternum) should move similarly to what occurs during rapid, silent panting. Thus, melismas are like a quick staccato incorporated into a legato line.

If singers' larynxes move excessively as they sing melismas, they likely lack breath support. Excessive movement of the larynx may also indicate they are attempting too much direct control over laryngeal muscles to change pitch. Laryngeal movement may also indicate extraneous tension. Singers can gently touch the larynx to create the awareness necessary for stabilizing its height.

Contemporary singers may use jaw and tongue movement to assist with the articulation of runs (e.g., Mariah Carey, Ariana Grande). Some modern classical singers at times also exhibit tongue and jaw movement (e.g., Cecilia Bartoli, Vivica Genaux).

One argument against using jaw, tongue, and lip movement in the articulation of melismas/runs is that for many singers, the added tension is fatiguing. We advocate utilizing a foundation of epigastric pulsation; add additional methods of articulation only as needed.

Richard Miller's approach to learning melismas

Richard Miller (2004) provides an extended discussion of a strategy for learning melismas through initial staccato execution of passages. Here is a simplified summary of his recommendations:

- To gain a sense of bouncing the abdominal wall (pulsing the abdominal muscles), sing a rapid "hm, hm, hm, hm, hm" as though engaged in stifled laughing. Singers should be sure that the upper area of the abdominals is bouncing. Raise and lower the pitch while doing this, ending with a descending five-note scale.
- Sing [ɑ] using this same pattern. If singers have difficulty, *as a learning device*, they can sing "ha, ha, ha, ha, ha." As outlined below, this is not a suitable method for singing melismas. Discard as quickly as possible.
- Using five-note ascending and descending scales, first sing a sequence using [ɑ] with staccato production; then sing the scales legato but retain a sense of the small abdominal pulsations of staccato.

Developing muscle memory for melismas

Learn melismas by singing slowly to build muscle memory for the pitch sequences. As soon as you know the patterns, sing short sections (e.g., one or two beats) at performance speed. Once sections are learned, they can be combined and sung at performance speed.

Avoid continued use of the "ha-ha-ha-ha" crutch

Some conductors advocate singing runs with the assistance of [h] to differentiate the notes (e.g., "ha-ha-ha-ha"). As noted above, this can be a useful learning device if used with moderation—a tiny [h]—but in general, it is a poor device that creates noise and reduces vowel resonance due to interruption of the legato line. (Recall that the vocal tract resonates best during the closed phase—deliberate glottis opening reduces the amount of time during the melisma the glottis is closed.) This method of singing melismas has other problems as well:

- It creates tension and makes it difficult to sing the notes quickly
- The constant opening and closing of the glottis create a series of collisions

between the vocal folds that can be damaging (Sundberg, 1987)
- ❖ It is inefficient due to loss of breath associated with aspirated onset (R. Miller, 2004)

Using "ha, ha, ha" to sing melismas can be considered an aspirated glottal articulation. Sherman and Brown (1995) recommend a non-aspirated glottal articulation. That is, they suggest rapid opening and closing of the glottis to sing the notes of a run. They argue that this creates a cleaner separation of pitches than is attainable with abdominal pulsation. And, they find that choral groups can learn this method more easily than abdominal pulsation. While we agree that glottal articulation methods (whether aspirated or non-aspirated) can assist learning, they are undesirable endpoints—both have problems of noise, reduced resonance, and excessive airflow. This noise can be seen in the sound waveforms of the glottal articulation method; Sherman and Brown themselves acknowledge the higher airflow. In short, advocates of glottal articulation methods overlook problems with the resulting quality of sound. A staccato-like legato singing of melismatic passages using epigastric pulsation produces the most pleasing sound.

Singing choral melismas

For most choral singers, singing melismas is a requirement. In a choral environment, singers are generally not expected (and should not try) to sing every note of a melisma. If they attempt this, they may easily fall behind the tempo. Instead, singers should work toward maintaining tempo and accuracy, and taking time out to breathe (stagger breathe) and re-enter in time. (See an exercise for singing melismas at the end of this chapter.) With practice, all singers can contribute positively to group melismas without sacrificing their vocal health.

Not all can sing with agility

All singers need to practice diligently and with patience to build and hone the skills that will enable them to sing with agility. Nonetheless, it is important to note that not all singers can sing easily with agility. Some may find singing trills or melismas quite simple; at the same time, others, even with considerable practice, may be challenged by these tasks. We are all built differently. Consider those who play sports; even if physically gifted, there is no expectation that they will be able to play all sports with ease.

Dynamic control

Most singers who use flow phonation and have developed balanced resonance can sing relatively loudly, as can singers who use a belting style of production. Singing softly with a supported sound can be more difficult, particularly at high pitches.

> Coleman (1994) found that a significant factor in the greater dynamic range of trained versus untrained choral singers is the ability of trained singers to sing more softly.
> Cooksey (1999) suggests that singing at medium-loud dynamic levels (*mf* and *f*) is indicated for young voices, as these dynamic levels require less physical manipulation. Fine dynamic control (*pp* in particular) can be developed later as a more advanced skill.

Messa di voce is an excellent exercise for learning how to gain better dynamic control. *Start in the middle of the range on a vowel such as* [o], *singing very softly. Crescendo to a forte sound, then back down to pianissimo.* This exercise is most difficult at high pitches. In the exercises for this chapter, we include a standard *messa di voce*, plus a reverse *messa di voce* that may be easier to sing at high pitch levels.

> Vennard (1967) believes that *messa di voce* is an excellent exercise for the development of breath control. Also, it helps to develop a desirable approach to onset because one can easily hear a glottal attack, and a breathy onset will not produce a clear tone at soft dynamic levels. He notes that this exercise forces the singer to coordinate the vocal registers—starting with a light production incorporating head voice (or headmix) and shifting into more of a lower register (chest or chestmix) production approaching the forte section of the exercise. (This assumes that the exercise is sung in the middle register [i.e., in mixed voice]). The most difficult aspect of the exercise is the decrescendo—shifting from TA-dominant production to CT-dominant production to soften the sound.

Soft production at high pitches

As noted, singing softly at high pitches is one of the most challenging tasks for singers. A major culprit is a tendency to relax breath support too much. Subglottal pressure indeed needs to reduce to produce softer dynamic levels, but unless support is maintained, singers will tend to tighten the larynx and strangle softly-produced high pitches.

> As Henderson (1979) says: "Keep energy in your 'piano' dynamic so that it will be alive and intense and will be supported" (p. 179).

Some singers relax the arytenoids to open the glottal space slightly as a method for softly singing high pitches. Although this method reduces the amplitude of vibration of the vocal folds, it is a poor technique because it produces a breathy sound (unless desired as an effect).

Special vocal effects

Speech-like singing

Many styles of music utilize a type of singing that closely mimics speech. Some terms that refer to this are Sprechgesang, Sprechstimme, parlando, recitative, patter, rapping, and speech-like belting.

- ❖ Singers need to be aware of breath management when producing speech-like singing—managing the balance of airflow and pressure to avoid extraneous tension/to keep other muscles relaxed (constrictors, tongue, jaw, etc.)

In opera and some musical theatre, recitative (or sung dialogue) is notated in the score with specific pitches yet requires more flexible/approximated rhythms than written. In still other musical theatre scores, there may only be text, and the singer will decide pitch and pacing. In certain styles, such as some 20th and 21st-century art song, there will be a loose notation (only a contour).

Tonal requirements for speech-like singing vary based on style and emotion. Techniques such as Sprechstimme require a lighter, more sing-song quality (more breath escaping between the folds, lighter vocal fold adduction) while in some musical theatre contexts, singers may need to produce a clear, belt-like quality.

Patter singing occurs especially in comedic musical theatre roles such as the Major-General in Gilbert and Sullivan's *Pirates of Penzance*. Patter singing requires rapid delivery of sung text. This makes breathing the biggest challenge. Singers should carefully plan the places where they will take full, relaxed breaths (after having exhaled completely), as well as breathing spots for small "top-ups."

Non-sung effects

In contemporary styles, grunts, growls, screams, squalls, and yells may be an essential part of artistic interpretation.

Screams, yells, and squalls typically involve high breath pressure and firm vocal fold closure. Most screams and yells start with an abrupt glottal onset and are loud.

A growl is characterized by a rough sound (relaxed vocal fry with high airflow) that is followed by a clearer vocal quality. (A squall also uses this texture to start but finishes like a yell.) A growl is generally used in places of heightened emotion, especially in Gospel or rock singing. In some circumstances, the rough sound might be maintained throughout an entire phrase or longer. (See, for example, Robinson-Martin, 2016.)

There are no standard symbols for these effects—in fact, their production is often the performer's decision, and they may not be indicated explicitly in the musical score. Singers who want to use these types of vocal sounds should plan and practice their use so that they can produce these effects in the healthiest manner possible. This is particularly important for screams, yells, and squalls.

The combination of excessive breath pressure, pressure on the vocal folds, tension in the larynx, high volume, and hard onset can be vocally damaging if not executed carefully and intentionally. Singers should consider a healthier approximation of these techniques by:

- ❖ Focusing on abdominal support
- ❖ Using coordinated onset or a gentle glottal onset when possible
- ❖ Maintaining good body alignment
- ❖ Relaxing non-essential muscles such as the pharyngeal constrictors
- ❖ Fronting the tongue and opening the front of the mouth to vary resonance instead of relying on high breath pressure to produce volume
- ❖ Letting the microphone and amplification do some of the work

Singers who frequently utilize extended special vocal effects may be especially vulnerable to acute injury such as vocal fold hemorrhage. This appears particularly likely after screams and yells at high pitches. Constant use of these techniques over time can result in chronic conditions such as polyps and granulomas. Numerous famous contemporary singers who use these techniques have required surgery, experienced periods during which they could not perform, or have had their careers shortened.

Exercises for legato, staccato, accents, melismas, and dynamics

Legato—singing text using only the vowels

One method to create a legato line is to sing a piece of music using only the vowels. (You may wish to start by singing on only one vowel to make this easier.)

With no consonants to interrupt the flow of tone, the sound will be continuous. This is trickier than it seems for some singers because they may not be accustomed to thinking about vowels outside the context of the words themselves. Thus, until singers are comfortable with this approach, it is best to write in the IPA symbols for the vowels above the staff. This is particularly important for diphthongs and words with the stressed neutral vowel ([ʌ]) that should be sung using [a] or [ɑ]. A variation on this exercise is to sing the phrase through a straw (no vowels are possible with the straw), paying careful attention to the continuity of the line/breath.

After singing the music with only the vowels, sing the words with the consonants, concentrating on maintaining sound production with no stops between words. Quick, efficient production of consonants will help immensely with creating legato.

For kids and everyone! Legato image

Think about the story from Winnie the Pooh, where Pooh and Piglet are playing "Pooh Sticks." They stand together on one side of a bridge and toss pinecones into the water, then race to the other side of the bridge to see whose pinecone emerges first. Imagine the water as the vowel sounds and the pinecones as the consonants, dropped quickly into the ever-present, ever-moving water.

Staccato and tenuto

Sing two notes staccato on the same pitch, then start a five-note ascending scale ending with staccato notes. Substitute other vowels.

Sing a legato arpeggio followed by a staccato arpeggio, followed by a tenuto arpeggio. Start with [i] and then substitute other vowels.

Contrasting accents

Sing an ascending run of five notes. Sing the first note martellato (glottal onset and quick release) and the following four notes staccato.

Getting a sense of melisma

The following exercise makes it easy to gain a sense of what a melisma should feel like. Singers should execute the run as though they were giggling (T. Stalter & J. Brueck, personal communication, April 5, 2011).

For kids and everyone! Melismas

On a five-note ascending and descending scale, sing "bubble, bubble, bubble, bubble, bubble, bubble, bubble, bubble, bubble"—two eighth notes on each pitch. Add additional consonants such as "bubble, trouble, bubble, trouble." (Adapted from Cooksey, 1999)

Complex melismas

This exercise breaks apart a melisma from Handel's "And He Shall Purify" into two components. *Rehearse each portion slowly until learned, moving as soon as possible to performance speed (quarter-note = 92–96). Then sing the entire melisma, slowly at first if necessary, again moving to performance speed once learned. (Parts should sing down octaves as appropriate.). Also, try singing this exercise through a straw.*

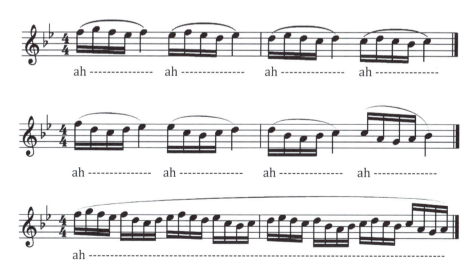

Messa di voce exercises to learn dynamic control

Sing a messa di voce exercise in the middle range (i.e., start on a vowel at a piano dynamic level; increase gradually to forte and then gradually reduce to piano). Try varying the beginning and ending dynamic levels (e.g., start pianissimo and crescendo to fortissimo). Less experienced and younger singers can try the exercise at first without specific start and end dynamics. For these singers, start at a comfortable, medium dynamic, and crescendo a bit, then come back down gradually to the starting dynamic level. Work to begin more softly and crescendo more, little by little.

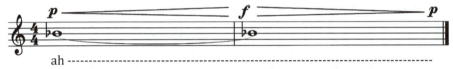

ah ------

Sing a reverse messa di voce in the upper register, followed by a standard messa di voce in the upper register. We recommend starting the reverse messa di voce in the upper register because it is more difficult to initiate a pitch at a low dynamic level in the upper register. (Upper note is for upper voices; lower note is for lower voices; tenor and bass are an octave lower than written.)

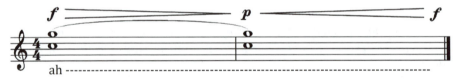

ah ------

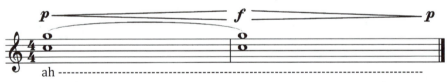

ah ------

Try singing a mid to low range messa di voce (as above) but start the sound with a growl (un-pitched, relaxed vocal fry with plenty of air) and then move into a clear, pitched sound. Keep the growl as gentle as possible by exhaling in a relaxed, consistent manner. Monitor tension in the larynx. Try practicing this with amplification; it is your friend for this type of special effect.

Practice yells by making them musical—almost a sung effect. Focus on good breath support, the vowel shape, and remember to consider the pitch level (not too low, not too high!).

Melissa Cross (2007) has developed a popular and highly regarded DVD/CD (*The Zen of Screaming*) that provides information about producing growls, screams and similar effects in a healthy manner.

Chapter 12: Improving Choral Blend

Blend in choral singing can be defined as perceived homogeneous sound—the combining of disparate voices into one uniform-sounding ensemble. Goodwin (1980) defines blend as "an ensemble sound in which individual voices cannot be separately discerned by a listener" (p. 25). Conductors and singers are always searching for ways to produce better choral blend. Vowel and consonant production, rhythm, timbre choice including use of falsetto, voice matching, and positioning of singers are some of the strategies that can be considered.

Blend philosophies

Numerous sources discuss how to select voices for a choral ensemble that will be flexible and easily blend with others (e.g., Basinger, 2006; Eskelin, 2005; Noble, 2005). The presumption is that conductors should not include singers who do not fit their tonal model. The reality is that most conductors of amateur ensembles cannot pick and choose voices—and *should not* do this! All singers can benefit from and all should have the opportunity to experience ensemble singing.

The earliest, most fully articulate proponent of a blended choral sound was F. Melius Christiansen, director of the choir at St. Olaf College from 1912 to 1943. His ideas about blend have influenced many conductors, including ideas about precise enunciation of consonants and consistent production of vowels. Nonetheless, his approach to choral blend tended to produce an artificial sound that was not always well received by audiences. Latimer and Daugherty (2006) describe a *New York Times* review of a 1927 concert of the St. Olaf Choir that characterized the sound of the female choir members as "so impersonal in character that it suggested the voices of boys" (Downes, 1927, p. 17).

This approach to blend that produces an artificial sound often involves use of two techniques:

❖ Asking singers (female voices in particular) to use covered vowel production (shifting vowels toward darker versions with a lower second formant frequency—see Chapter 5 on vowels)
❖ Requesting "straight tone" (minimal vibrato)

Not only are these methods artificial and unreflective of the full tonal quality of female voices, requesting minimal vibrancy causes vocal tension, as outlined in Chapter 7 on vibrato. Even in Christiansen's day many vocal pedagogues argued that his approach to choral singing "caused unnecessary and unhealthy tension in the vocal mechanism" (Latimer & Daugherty, 2006, p. 19).

Many credit the Robert Shaw Chorale (1948-1965) for "opening the door to a much wider range of possibilities for choral tone" (Basinger, 2006, p. 4). Nonetheless, some choral directors continue to attempt to achieve blend by altering the production of individual voices, which fuels the argument by some voice teachers that developing voices should not participate in choirs (Ekholm, 2000).

We maintain that blend can be achieved without sacrificing individual vocal integrity. Research supports the move away from requesting all singers to sound the same or sacrifice individual tone quality to achieve choral blend (Knutson, 1987). The techniques in this chapter are intended to assist ensembles in moving toward a good blend without "neutralizing idiosyncrasies of individual singers" (Smith & Sataloff, 2006, p. 182). As previously stated, however, we encourage all singers to develop flexibility in their production to allow for comfortable tonal variation in ensembles.

Choral sound

Conductors' concepts of desired choral sound can have a substantial effect on how they seek to achieve blend. One preference is for a homogeneous sound from the highest through the lowest voices. Another is for blend within vocal sections, while allowing distinctive colors for each section. A third perspective is to use blend across or within sections as appropriate to the repertoire. Such a conductor may seek to create a wall of even sound on an eight-part chord in, for example, an Eric Whitacre piece, while encouraging the distinctive warm, resonant quality inherent in the soloistic bass and alto voices in repertoire by Brahms. As noted in Chapter 4 on resonance, the quality of sound can be subtly influenced in a number of ways, allowing the voice parts to maximize or minimize their inherent differences.

Keys to a blended sound

Smith and Sataloff (2006) suggest the following as essential elements for creating a blended sound:

- Color (no individual voices identifiable, distinctive color for each section, distinctive color for the ensemble as a whole)
- Balance (individual sections are balanced within the ensemble)
- Tuning
- Diction (vowels and consonants performed uniformly)

This is a helpful set of issues to keep in mind, but we would suggest that the ingredients for blend are more numerous and multifaceted. The following are our recommendations for improving and refining blend.

Uniform vowel production within sections

Robert Shaw cites "distortion of voweling" as a major reason for a failure to achieve sectional unison (Blocker, 2004, p. 87). As noted in Chapter 5 on vowels, if singers within a section produce vowels differently, the first and second formant frequencies will differ excessively, creating a lack of uniformity in sound. Singers can be helped to achieve uniformity of tone quality if conductors take time in the warm-up to establish the desired vowel colors and review the preferred method of achieving them.

Uniformity of vowels is important for all singers in an ensemble, but we especially emphasize uniformity *within a choral section*. When sections are called upon to sing notes near the top of their range for instance, those sections will need to modify their vowels in a fashion according to the style of the piece. Singing a slightly modified vowel in these sections will not harm the sound—it will actually contribute to better blend, provided all singers share the same concept of the desired modification and understand how to execute it.

Precise, quick consonants

Weston Noble (2005) describes what he calls "the 'original sin' of the amateur vocalist" (p. 57)—closing too quickly on the vowel by anticipating the consonant that follows, shortening the length of the beauty of the vowel. Also, if some choral group members are lazy in their production of consonants, a less than cohesive sound will result, with some singers appropriately moving quickly to the next vowel while others are creating consonant noise. Refer to Chapter 6 on consonants for strategies and exercises to improve individual and group production of consonants.

Precise rhythms

Noble (2005) quotes Robert Shaw as saying, "The bottom line of blend is rhythm! You directors work so hard at unifying the vowel and never arrive at the vowel together—how can you achieve blend?" (p. 57).

Often, the underlying problem is the singer's perception of time or rhythm. Singers need constant encouragement to watch the conductor and to find ways of physically incorporating the beat and subdivisions of that beat. Long, sustained pitches are particularly difficult. It does not take long for singers to lose the sense of where they are rhythmically if they are not paying close attention.

Try subdividing sustained pitches, either audibly or mentally. Sing a passage on a neutral syllable and rearticulate each subdivision (da-da-da-da on eighth notes, for example). Another technique is to tap the pulse (or a subdivision of it) with your toe or finger. Avoid tapping the foot as this can be distracting to others.

Highly rhythmic passages can also cause difficulties. A lack of blend will occur if choral singers are moving through the musical line at different times. In such cases rehearsing to the rhythm without the pitches can be helpful.

Either chant the passage in a high pitched, sing-song tone quality (more easily linked to the singing voice than regular speaking) or sing it slowly on one constant note. After a couple of repetitions sing the correct pitches and increase the speed so that muscle memory does not occur at a slow tempo. This can be difficult to correct! Rather, practice shorter sections up to performance tempo and systematically link sections as facility increases. Finally, practice singing the passage as written.

Precise cutoffs/releases

All singers have experienced poor cutoffs, particularly when they involve noisy consonants like [s]. Sometimes singers fail to watch the conductor's indication of a cutoff and sometimes conductors fail to indicate clearly when the release is to occur. A singer's individual perception of the passage of time may be at fault as well. Regardless, conductors should endeavor to explain clearly where final consonants are to be placed and where the sound should stop. They should use a gesture that communicates the cutoff as clearly as possible, and help their singers practice efficient releases in order to maintain blend right through the ends of phrases. The "snap fingers" exercise from Chapter 6 on consonants may be helpful.

Attention to dynamics

Blend is improved when all singers within a section produce the same dynamic level. Intensity of sound will also be heavily influenced by the choice of registration/mode of production, as discussed below.

❖ Singers often do not accurately perceive the level of sound that they produce. One singer's *mp* may not be the same as another's. One way to get a sense of your own sound level is to sing facing a wall.

> ➢ Robert Shaw emphasizes the perils of over-singing (see Chapter 10 on intonation), noting that both "distortion of voweling" and "disturbances of vocal color" are results of singing too loudly (by some or all singers). He states that they "impede sectional unison—which is the *sine qua non* of good choral discipline" (Blocker, 2004, p. 87).

Many blend problems related to dynamic level disappear if singers listen to each other. Indeed, when singers are in groups and do listen to each other they will naturally adjust their dynamic level, as well as pitch and formant frequencies (Titze, 2008a). This is something that amateur singers need to work on assiduously; recall that they are less likely to listen to other singers than are professionals,

Of course, balancing of dynamic level across the entire choir is also important when the same dynamic level is indicated in the music for each section.

Sopranos and dynamics

Remember that sopranos sing at pitch levels in a range where the human ear is keenly sensitive, thus chastising them for their louder perceived volume is unproductive. If sopranos are asked to reduce their volume, a reduction in sound quality, and intonation, as well as blend may result. If perceived soprano volume is an issue, consider encouraging the other sections to sing out more.

Developing singers and soft dynamic levels in a choral setting

Developing singers are encouraged by their voice teachers to sing with a full sound to facilitate the development of supported, resonant singing. Singing softly is, simply put, a more advanced skill. Offering helpful techniques for, and reminders about, soft singing can be beneficial:

❖ Learn very soft passages at a slightly louder dynamic than at which you would ultimately perform them so that the mechanics of the rhythms, pitches, and words are under control before attending to issues of dynamic levels
❖ Suggest more frequent stagger breathing
❖ Using *messa di voce* exercises is an excellent method for helping singers to

learn how to sing softly. (See exercises for Chapter 11.)

For the most part, however, allowing a comfortable level of production is the best approach with developing voices.

The role of timbre in blending

Another element in achieving blend is how consistently singers create the sound. As outlined in previous chapters, there are various methods that singers use to create resonance, sing in the different registers, and create vibrato. If not all choral members are creating sound in the same way, problems in blend will arise.

Choristers who are belting, for example, will often be singing more loudly than those who are not, and will also have both a fundamental frequency lower in amplitude than the other singers, along with a higher level of certain harmonic frequencies (Sundberg, Thalén, & Popeil, 2012). If the musical piece is a show tune requiring belting, then everyone needs to belt. If it is not a belting piece then everyone needs to use a classical or legit form of production, as the case may be.

When performing an opera chorus such as the Finale of Beethoven's Ninth Symphony with full orchestra, the director of a choir of accomplished singers may choose to have singers utilize the singer's formant both to aid in blend and for projection. If all singers are able to do this, the sound will be blended. If some are not, both balance and blend will be compromised.

The role of covering to produce blending

Some conductors favor a slightly darker tone for an ensemble as a whole because darker voices are easier to blend—brighter voices tend to stand out. Some conductors use a covered style of vowel production as a default to accomplish this. (See Chapter 5 on vowels.) Use of a covered method of production is also one way to achieve blend when a specific part stands out more than is desired. For example, if most parts are in the lower portion of their range during a *piano* section but one section is asked to ascend the scale, that part may stand out too much. If this is the case, you can ask singers in that section to use a covered approach to production, particularly if a bright vowel such as [i] is being sung (e.g., sing [i] with the mouth formed to sing [o] or [ɔ]).

A covered method of production may be a useful effect at times but if sustained, is ultimately an unhealthy method of production. It should be used sparingly because an improper alignment of the vocal tract relative to the vowel to be sung will produce undesirable tension.

The role of falsetto to produce blending

Choral literature frequently asks tenors to sing in a high tessitura. Many untrained tenors (especially younger singers) will find it difficult to sing A_4-flat or even G_4 and above in modal head voice without breaking or without a pressed mode of production. In such cases, suggesting they use falsetto may help to blend their sound with other sections. This is particularly true for quiet passages. For this to work, tenors need to practice falsetto periodically and to work on improving its quality, otherwise their falsetto will be too grainy or inconsistent to serve as an effective blend device. (Professional/well-trained amateur tenors will have more control over their head voice but may still choose to utilize falsetto for higher, lighter passages.)

The need for basses to use falsetto is rarer, because they are more likely to act as the anchor in the chord structure. Falsetto can be helpful, however, when basses must sing E_4 and above for an extended period or at a soft dynamic level. For this, they too will need to practice falsetto periodically.

Voice positioning

Conductors know that the arrangement of singers within a chorus can definitely influence blend (Smith & Sataloff, 2006). Nonetheless, only recently has research been conducted to ascertain scientifically the benefits of various approaches to the positioning of singers.

There are three levels of consideration when arranging a choral ensemble:

1) Placement of sections
2) Placement of individual singers within sections
3) Distance between individual singers

Section placement

Chapter 10 on intonation mentions some of the benefits of placing basses and sopranos in near proximity. A common arrangement of singers places basses behind sopranos and tenors behind altos, with the conductor immediately in front of the sopranos/altos.

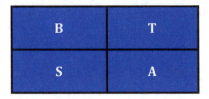

A variation of this formation would be to mix sopranos among basses and altos among tenors.

Another standard arrangement puts singers within their sections in columns that run from the back of the ensemble to the front. Soprano columns are placed on the left, followed by bass, tenor and alto columns. Conductors of choirs with fewer male singers favor this arrangement, which again allows good contact between the outermost parts (sopranos and basses):

S	S	B	T	A	A
S	S	B	T	A	A
S	S	B	T	A	A
S	S	B	T	A	A
S	S	B	T	A	A

Mixing singers in quartets (SBTA) throughout the choir is a popular arrangement in ensembles with strong, independent singers. This arrangement takes advantage of an improved self-to-other loudness ratio that allows singers to hear themselves and others better (Daugherty, 1999):

S	B	T	A	S	B
T	A	S	B	T	A
S	B	T	A	S	B
T	A	S	B	T	A
S	B	T	A	S	B

If singers need support from each other, consider using this formation with groups of two singers on the same part.

Daugherty's (1999) "circumambient formation" is another arrangement that allows an improved self-to-other loudness ratio. Singers are placed two feet apart (shoulder to shoulder) on risers with one riser row empty between rows. Both audience and singers prefer this formation to closer formations, and singers feel a greater freedom of production. However, this amount of spacing can be impractical with larger groups.

Interestingly, until recently, most studies have identified few acoustical differences among these formations (but see below about singer spacing). That said, singers and conductors definitely perceive each of these formations differently and have preferences (Aspaas et al., 2004). Singers sing more or less freely and confidently depending on where they stand, which has a potentially significant impact on choral blend. How often have ensembles gone from rehearsal to a performance venue that necessitates a different standing formation, only to find that their careful work on blend was all for naught!

- ❖ A reminder to sing in the same way as in rehearsal, regardless of the acoustical feedback in the performance space, can be helpful.

Our suggestion is that conductors use these formations as a guide to good possibilities, but each ensemble needs both to find its preferred arrangement for positioning of sections and to practice being flexible as performance spaces may demand.

Positioning singers within sections

Positioning singers within sections is one important way to achieve blend without altering healthy vocal production. Ekholm (2000) notes that Weston Noble and others advocate elaborate voice-matching trials. One approach starts with an anchor, "ideal" voice (based on conductor preference) plus one other voice, or with a pair of voices that have a natural blend. Singers then perform a simple vocal exercise together. One by one, other singers are asked to join the singing, removing those whose sound does not have a favorable effect on the whole and keeping those who do blend.

Jordan (2007) uses the visual image of a comb to illustrate voice matching. Combs vary in their thickness and spacing of teeth. As such, some combs can interlock. Put another way, the formant amplitudes and frequencies of some singers fit together better than others. Singers whose formant amplitudes and frequencies do not mesh well will create a combined sound that is too loud, out of tune, strident, etc. Eventually all singers are placed within a block or a sideways line. This should allow the section to sound blended and give individual singers the freedom to sing naturally. See Noble (2005) and Jordan (2007) for more detailed descriptions of approaches to voice placement.

Although this method is impractical for large choruses because it is so time-consuming, it does take into account factors of blend between singers such as tone color, vibrato, pitch, physical height, size of tone, and individual perception/execution of rhythm. All these factors can be perceived by the conductor when listening to voices together. Gardiniere's (1991) study of more than 100 choral conductors' perceptions of the blend produced by Noble's methods of voice matching led to the conclusion that matching has a perceptible benefit that "transcended individual taste or preference" (cited in Ekholm, 2000, p. 125). A recent study by Killian and Basinger (2007) further verifies the utility of voice matching. This suggests that even if elaborate voice matching strategies are not viable for a large chorus, conductors are well served by using their listening skills to seek to place complimentary voices close together.

Distance between individual singers (singer spacing)

Recall that Daugherty (1999) observed advantages to a circumambient formation in which singers are spaced 24 inches apart, shoulder to shoulder. Daugherty has recently found that spacing has more of an impact on the sound of the ensemble than the formation in which singers stand (Daugherty 2018). While some ensembles may find 24-inch spacing impractical, smaller/more advanced groups may find the spacing of singers to be a powerful tool when working towards blend.

- When singers are spaced 24 inches apart, Daugherty, Grady, and Coffeen (2019) observe a decrease in high-frequency acoustical energy. This improves blend without singers having to modify significantly their personal vocal production (e.g., through techniques such as covering).
- They also report that 96% of studied singers say their vocal production is most efficient when singing in a choral formation using 24-inch spacing.

Concluding thoughts on blend

Conductors need to consider carefully their aesthetic goals for blend in their ensembles. Whenever possible, they should choose strategies that are founded on proper vocal technique. These include efficient consonant production, uniform vowel production within sections (with appropriate vowel modification for higher pitches), precise rhythms, precise cutoffs, and balanced dynamic levels among sections. Placement of sections, voice matching/placement of singers within sections, and particularly, spacing of singers are also good possibilities. All these techniques allow for creation of a more natural, blended sound that eliminates the need to use more artificial methods such as extensive covering or "straight tone singing." Conductors can achieve blend goals without compromising individual voices and singers can use healthy methods of vocal production—a win-win!

Chapter 13: Changing Voices

This chapter discusses why and how voices change during adolescence, gender transitions, and as singers age. We also discuss vocal technique issues during these changes. Conductors, teachers, and singers will benefit from knowing what happens to voices during these transitions and how to respond to the changes that occur.

Overview of voice change during childhood and puberty

Voice changes occur during adolescence because of increases in hormones associated with sexual maturation. A significant effect of these hormones is an increase in vocal fold length for both females and males and an increase in vocal fold thickness for males. The percentage of increase in vocal fold length is much higher for males than it is for females and is associated with the development of the "Adam's apple." These changes lead to a lowering of both speaking and singing pitches during childhood and adolescence.

Other important changes during adolescence include:

❖ Lengthening of the vocal tract, which is somewhat more for males than females. A significant change occurs from about ages 9 to 14, with some further lengthening in females to about age 16 and in males to about age 18 (Fitch & Giedd, 1999). Recall from Chapter 4 on resonance that a longer vocal tract lowers all formant frequencies. This leads to a change in timbre during adolescence that might be characterized as "deeper" or "richer."
❖ The larynx, pharynx, and mouth increase in size, leading to the potential for improved resonance.
❖ Lung capacity increases, improving the ability to sustain notes for more extended periods.

This list includes many positive aspects of adolescent development that will ultimately lead to a singer's adult voice. However, the process of change is often difficult. Young singers no longer have the childhood voice with which they have become comfortable. Instead, their voices have transformed into what has been called a "cambiata" voice category.

Difficulties with vocal change

When voice change occurs in boys, some will experience it more gradually than others. Certain boys have little difficulty with the lowering of their voices—many may ultimately be tenors as adults (Phillips, 1996). Others will experience a faster change from one stage of development to another and thus may experience sudden instabilities in their voices. They may be more likely to sing the bass choral part as adults.

Since the amount of change in singable pitches is less for girls' voices, little attention was paid to their experience of voice maturation until recently. Nonetheless, girls experience many of the same problems as boys with changing voices. Briefly, some of the most challenging aspects of the vocal maturation process are:

- Loss of previously singable high notes, particularly for boys, but also for girls
- Reduced range at certain stages of development
- Difficulties with pitch control and pitch matching
- Breathiness or "huskiness" related to incomplete closure of the rear portion of the glottis during puberty and even late adolescence (While breathiness is perhaps more common with girls, it occurs with boys as well. The laryngeal muscles have not developed sufficiently to close the newly enlarged vocal folds.)
- Difficulty with achieving coordinated onset, which is related to the glottis closure problem
- Abrupt register transitions, or "breaks in the voice" (Gackle, 2006)

We analyze these issues in detail in a later section of this chapter.

Voices are changing at younger ages

Since the 1940s the average age at which vocal change begins has been decreasing in the United States and likely in other countries as well. This trend has accelerated in the last 40 years and is associated with further decreases in the age of onset of sexual maturation (Herman-Giddens et al., 1997; Herman-Giddens, Kaplowitz, & Wasserman, 2004). While earlier sexual maturation since the 1940s is in part due to improved nutrition, the causes are not fully understood. Some studies suggest a connection to increased obesity and the use of certain plasticizers that mimic estrogen effects (e.g., BPA, phthalates), but the data are too sparse for firm conclusions.

For an overview of the timing and rate of vocal change in recent years, see Figure 13.1, which contains a chart of age and speaking fundamental frequency (SFF). (Where lines are very close together, they are at roughly the same SFF.) The chart is based on two studies, one that involved U.S. data from around 1996, another that used data collected in Germany 2010 to 2018 (labeled at the mid-point year of 2014 for convenience).

SFF is the average frequency of the speaking voice. It is commonly used as an indicator of vocal change. SFF is strongly related to the lowest singing pitch, typically 3–4 semitones (half steps) below the SFF after initial voice change (Cooksey, 1999). We want to emphasize, however, that the pitches shown for the various age groups and genders are averages. There is substantial variability in the age of vocal change onset and the specific pitches associated with each age. At the individual level, the observed *change* from childhood baseline provides the most useful clues about the stage of vocal development.

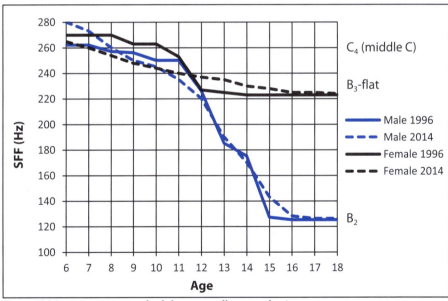

Note: 1996 curves are smoothed due to smaller sample size.

Figure 13.1 Age and average speaking fundamental frequency (SFF)

1996 data are from an analysis by Lee, Potamianos, and Narayanan (1999). The chart shows smoothed means because of modest sample sizes for each age/sex group. (The data set was originally announced in 1996, hence we label the time as 1996.) Figure 13.1 shows that the SFF for both boys and girls in 1996 changed little up to age nine. Between ages 9–10 and continuing to age 11, both boys and girls decreased to B_3. Further change continued to age 12 where both sexes decreased to B_3-flat and girls reached a level close to their adult SFF (adult female average SFF is roughly A_3-flat). Boys then declined precipitously to G_3-flat at age 13, reaching close to their adult-mean SFF of B_2 at age 15. (A little further decrease in SFF after age 18 is likely for both sexes.)

- ❖ Patterns of maturation mean that female voices at age 18 will have a degree of maturity that is far greater than that of males who have been undergoing more substantial change over a more extended time.

The 2014 data are from Berger et al. (2019). The sample is a very large one from Germany (2626 participants), hence no smoothing has been necessary. The curves represent the findings for the median SFF for "classroom voice," since this most closely matches the 1996 U.S. data at younger and older ages where there is more stability. (The 2014 data set also includes SFF for conversational voice. Had we used these values, the pitch levels would have been noticeably lower.)

- ❖ The 2014 data reveal a more gradual change in SFF compared to 1996 for both girls and boys, though boys show the same precipitous drop in SFF from age 12 to 15–16.
- ❖ 2014 data show girls' voices declining more slowly after age eleven than in 1996. This is likely due to differences in the studied countries. The 1996 data are for U.S. girls; the 2014 data are from a European country. A recent comprehensive study of age of pubescence for girls shows that European females begin puberty roughly one year later than females in the U.S. (Eckert-Lind et al., in press).

Studies by Killian and research by Fisher provide additional information about male vocal change. For example, 46% of boys were exhibiting vocal change in grade four (ages 9-10; Fisher, 2010). In grade five (ages 10-11), 56% were showing change, and 74% were showing change in grade six (average of results from Killian, 1999, and Fisher, 2010).

- ❖ Both this data and the SFF age chart (Figure 13.1), changing voices may be seen as young as 9–10. Even in grade 3, music teachers may encounter voices that are starting to change.

Timing of voice change compared to the 1940s and 1970s

How does this timing of voice change compare with earlier studies? One point of comparison is a 1940 study, which showed that boys' SFF was the same at ages 10 and 14 (Fairbanks, 1940). Thus, the voice of the average boy in 1940 started to mature after age 14. Based on the 1996 and 2010–2018 data, male voice maturation starts substantially earlier today.

Another point of comparison is Titze's (2000) composite summary of two studies published in 1976 and 1980. His chart shows females not declining to B_3-flat until about age 14 (compared to age 12–13 in these more recent studies). Males did not reach F_3 until about age 16 (compared to age 14 in the studies in Figure 13.1). Thus, voices reached a level of near-adult SFF about two years earlier in the mid-1990s compared to the late 1970s.

Vocal development in adolescent males

The most accepted and studied approach to categorization of the characteristics of changing boys' voices is that of John Cooksey. He wrote an influential series of articles in the *Choral Journal* (1977a, 1977b) in which he proposed a system of categorization that has been extensively validated both by him and others (see Freer, 2010). Cooksey's book, *Working with Adolescent Voices*, summarizes his study of boys' voices and provides guidance concerning girls' voices as well (Cooksey, 1999). It also contains numerous suggestions for working with changing adolescents, including methods of determining changing voice categories, seating plans for changing voices, and repertoire. We highly recommend this book to anyone working with adolescents. Another valuable resource is a comprehensive treatment of adolescent male voices by Dilworth (2012).

Cooksey describes five maturational stages in boys, in addition to a pre-change stage (Cooksey, 1977a, 1999). These stages along with some comments about them are summarized below. Where adult choral parts are indicated, the boy's voice is not the equivalent of the adult version, rather it is an indication of the part that might be sung during this stage, with a recognition that range and resonance characteristics will often be limited.

- **Unchanged Voice (pre-change).** This is the boy soprano, though some are altos. Just prior to puberty, boys reach their maximum childhood range. There is good dynamic range, and voices are agile.
- **Mid-Voice I ("Alto").** Loss of high notes begins. Breathiness occurs, particularly on upper pitches. Range decreases by about four half steps to 16–17 half steps. Lowest singing pitch and speaking pitch reduce only a half step. Height and weight begin to increase.
- **Mid-Voice II ("Tenor").** Adam's apple becomes apparent. The speaking voice lowers two half steps below the unchanged voice. However, our analysis of the data from Cooksey (1999), Killian (1999), and Killian and Wayman (2010) suggest that the decrease in lowest singing pitch is somewhat more noticeable, i.e., three half steps below the unchanged

voice. Range further reduces by a half step. Cooksey (1999) describes the voice as "husky," but "thicker" than Mid-Voice I. Height and weight increase further, and lung capacity increases. Falsetto register starts to develop.

- **Mid-Voice IIA ("Tenor")**. The lowest pitch lowers substantially (four half-step reduction from Mid-Voice II). Range is similar to Mid-Voice II, but upper pitches are often strained and breathy; obvious register breaks occur. Additional weight gain and increase in height are noticeable. There is greater difficulty matching an intervallic fifth in this stage than in any other stage (Willis & Kenny, 2008). Cooksey cautions that boys in this stage may use chest voice excessively as they experiment with their new lower notes (Cooksey, 1999). Changing voices in this and other stages should continue to vocalize using head voice/falsetto to explore their full range of possibilities. Nonetheless, they should be moving toward their new, lower voice (Freer, 2010).
- **New Voice (New "Baritone")**. The lowest sung pitch lowers an additional four half steps. Range is similar to Mid-Voice II and IIA. Baritone quality is somewhat light. Notes may be missing between head voice and falsetto. We suggest downward scales starting in the falsetto register to help with bridging to head voice and lower registers. This will also help with the development/retention of head voice. Weight and height increase further as do chest and shoulder development. Vocal agility is limited. As with Mid-Voice IIA, there is a tendency toward heavy production. The suggested falsetto exercises can help with this problem.
- **Emerging Adult Voice (Developing "Baritone")**. This stage involves a further three half-step lowering of lowest sung pitch, but range increases 3–4 half steps. Sound quality improves, becoming clearer and more focused. Cooksey (1999) uses the term "emerging adult voice" to recognize that not all individuals in this stage will become baritones; some will develop into tenors and basses. Even at this point some may have ranges that better fit the tenor or bass classifications. However, those ranges will be restricted relative to the comparable adult category. Physical development continues in this stage, with vocal tract cavities approaching final volumes, further increasing the opportunity for improved resonance.

As male and female voices mature from junior into senior high school, they take on more of the characteristics of adult voices, though with less range (Phillips, 1996).

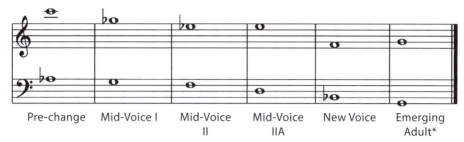

Note: Mean highest pitch is for the choir group in Killian and Wayman (2010). Mean lowest pitch averages over findings from Cooksey and Killian. *E_5 is actually the mean high pitch for emerging adult voice choir members in Killian and Wayman (2010). This was likely falsetto. We have estimated the high end of the modal voice for the emerging adult range based on other trends in their data.

Figure 13.2 Mean lowest and highest pitches for Cooksey male stages of vocal development

Figure 13.2 illustrates the vocal range associated with each of Cooksey's stages. The lower pitch is an average of Cooksey (1999) and studies by Killian (Killian, 1999; Killian & Wayman, 2010). These studies have similar findings for the low end of the range. Studies are more variable concerning mean high pitch, which in part reflects how variable the highest singable pitches are during development. We have shown the result for Killian and Wayman's (2010) choir group, which generally had higher upper-range limits than a group of band members who did not sing in a choir. These choir members seem particularly accomplished, especially considering the upper mean pitch for the pre-change voice group (C_6). (Cooksey says that the upper pitch for unchanged voices is likely to be G_5, which is consistent with our experience.) As a result, the choir members in Killian and Wayman's study exhibit more change in range across the stages than described by Cooksey.

Vocal development in adolescent females

Gackle (1991; Huff-Gackle, 1985; Gackle, 2008) proposed four stages of development for adolescent females. She now refers to these as "phases" to emphasize the gradual nature of girls' voice development (Gackle, 2006).

Although Gackle bases her phases and their characteristics on her extensive experience working with female adolescent choirs, no systematic program of research has been published to date to validate these phases and their characteristics. Nonetheless, her ideas have been influential and may assist those working with young female voices. Unlike boys, girls exhibit little change in the average highest singable pitch and only small changes in average SFF and lowest singable pitch. Gackle suggests that vocal development in girls can be thought of as involving shades of change, like shades of colors. The voice is still treble, but the color becomes richer, warmer, and has greater depth (i.e., resonance characteristics change over time). Listed below are summaries of Gackle's phases.

- **Phase I—Prepubertal (pre-change).** Phase I is a light, flexible soprano voice. Gackle describes the tonal quality as "flute-like." Qualities similar to the pre-change boy's voice are present, but there is less potential to achieve high sound levels than boys. There are no obvious register transitions. The comfortable range is D_4 to D_5. First soprano would be a common part.

- **Phase IIA—Pubescence.** Average speaking and lowest singable pitch both decrease by a half step. Perhaps the most noticeable change is the development of breathiness, particularly when singing high notes. Some may experience register transitions in the vicinity of F_4 to B_4-flat, and agility is reduced. Interestingly, Gackle shows an increase in range due to an expansion of the upper singable pitch by two half steps along with the aforementioned decrease in the lowest singable pitch. (This is quite different from the initial stage of change for boys, who experience a reduction in range.) Part assignment might be second soprano though some may still be able sing first soprano. Breast development begins, and height starts to increase.

- **Phase IIB—Puberty/Post-menarche.** This is the most unstable and challenging phase of girls' voice development. Average SFF may lower an additional semitone. Comfortable range reduces by three half steps at the lower end of the range and by two half steps at the upper end of the range (now roughly B_3 to C_5), but the changes can be highly variable. Breathiness can occur throughout the range. Register transitions appear in the vicinity of both F_4 to B_4-flat (chest voice to middle voice) and D_5 to G_5-flat (middle voice to head voice). (The indicated areas of register transition seem quite large but may accurately reflect the highly variable nature of this stage.) Singing the alto part may be most comfortable during this phase, but girls should not be categorized arbitrarily. They should have the opportunity for vocal exercises that extend into the upper parts of the range that are comfortable for them. Similar to boys in Cooksey's Stage IIA, some girls may want to sing only in their newfound chest voice, but this should be avoided. Part assignments may be second soprano or alto, but what is comfortable may vary over time. Girls should be encouraged to switch parts as they feel necessary.

- **Phase III—Young Adult.** The female voice begins to stabilize upon entering this phase. Breathiness decreases, though in our experience, some degree of breathiness may persist for a few more years. Timbre becomes richer due to increased vocal tract length and size of resonating cavities. The transition between middle voice and the upper register stabilizes at the adult level. Average SFF lowers an additional half step. Range and comfortable range both increase substantially (A_3 to A_5 and A_3 to G_5, respectively). Vocal agility improves. All part assignments are possible depending upon comfort and vocal character.

	Phase I Pre-pubertal	Phase IIA Pubescence	Phase IIB Puberty	Phase III Young Adult
Range	B_3-flat to F_5/G_5	A_3 to G_5/A_5-flat	A_3 to E_5/F_5	G_3/A_3 to A_5
Comfortable Range	D_4 to D_5	D_4 to D_5	B_3 to C_5	A_3 to G_5
SFF	D_4-flat	C_4	B_3	B_3-flat
Age range 1980s	8–11	11–13	13–15	14–16
Mean age 1996	9.5	10.5	11.5	12.5

Notes: Range and comfortable range are from Gackle (2008). SFF is the average speaking pitch based on the midpoint of the pitch range estimated by Gackle (1991) for each phase. 1980s age range from Gackle (1991). Mean age in 1996 associated with Gackle's SFF for each phase is estimated from Lee et al. (1999).

Table 13.1 Selected characteristics of adolescent girls during the phases of the Gackle classification system

It is instructive to consider the age ranges proposed by Gackle for each phase in relation to the average SFF observed in recent research (Table 13.1). Gackle's age ranges are based on her experience with adolescent girls in the 1980s (Gackle, 1991). Comparing her age ranges to the approximate mean age for the average SFF in the 1996 data (Lee et al., 1999) provides evidence that female vocal development may be starting earlier. Compare the ages in the bottom row of the table (1996) to the row above (1980s).

❖ Note how the age with the SFF for Gackle's Phase IIA, which marks the start of voice change, is roughly 1.5 years earlier than in the 1980s (10.5 in 1996 vs. a midpoint of 12 in the 1980s). Observe, also, that females are moving from Pubescence to Young Adult voices more rapidly (in roughly 2 years rather than 3 years). (We do not include the 2014 data because European females commence puberty about one year later than in the

U.S., as noted above.)
- ❖ More recent U.S. data suggest that the age of female pubescence may have decreased further to ages 9–10 (Eckert-Lind et al., in press).

We caution that SFF is not a perfect indicator of vocal phase. The key takeaway is to be alert for earlier/faster vocal maturation and to encourage students to change voice parts as needed.

Part assignment during vocal change

Choral conductors should be sensitive to the need to move adolescents whose voices are changing to lower parts as necessary. Also, singers should feel free to move to a higher part on days when their voice feels more comfortable at that level. Girls should be encouraged to rotate parts as they are comfortable to enable continued access to head voice and to gain more experience with chest voice at lower pitch levels.

Cooksey (1999) outlines a time-saving group audition method that conductors and teachers can use for part assignment. We describe this below for each sex, with some simplification. Given the embarrassment that adolescents are prone to during his period, it is best if possible, to do this separately for boys and girls. For both groups, choose a song with limited range in the key of C, such as "America" or "Kum-ba-yah" ("Come By Here").

Boys

1) Identify boys who are singing an octave lower than the treble singers.
2) These are "baritones" (bass part in SATB arrangements). Listen to this group again to check for any who can sing in the treble octave—these are "tenors" (at least in this stage of their development). Be sure, however, that these are not lower voices singing up the octave in falsetto.
3) Move the key up to F and ask the remaining boys to sing again. (You can push the key up to G, if necessary.)
4) Assign to the soprano part boys who sing easily in the upper octave. But see below about labeling and seating issues to avoid embarrassment.
5) Those who sing the highest notes less easily can be placed in the alto section, or perhaps the tenor section for repertoire that does not require low tenor pitches.
6) Assign those who cannot sing the highest notes in this key to the tenor part.
7) Listen carefully to be sure some baritones singing in falsetto register

have not slipped through to the tenor group.

Boys whose voices have not changed may need to be assigned to the alto or even tenor parts for social reasons, particularly in junior high school (Cooksey, 1977b). Phillips (1996) suggests referring to boys whose voices have not changed as "first tenors." Seat them near the alto section and have them sing the alto part. Alderson (1979) suggests seating boys who still sing soprano or alto between girl sopranos/altos and boy tenors/basses so that they are not separated from those boys whose voices have changed. Dilworth (2012) and others have noted that it is important to avoid labeling adolescent boy voices with feminine terms (unless they have specifically requested this as part of gender transition—see below).

Girls

1) Ask girls to sing the song in the keys of both C and F. (Again, G can be used for the higher key if necessary, to assist in discernment.) Identify girls who sing clearly and easily in each of these keys.
2) Girls who sing clearly and easily in both keys can be divided evenly between soprano and alto parts (and should alternate those parts periodically).
3) Girls who can sing clearly and easily in only the lower or higher keys should be assigned accordingly to alto or soprano.
4) Girls who do not sing clearly in either key can be divided between the two parts depending upon which is most comfortable.

Given the short time periods over which young voices can change, repeat this procedure at eight-week intervals to ensure that no one has changed in the interim.

Finally, conductors and teachers of adolescents should always be alert to facial and bodily signs of tension that may indicate a need for a possible move to a different vocal section (e.g., chin rising in an attempt to sing high notes that were previously comfortable).

Vocal technique issues in child and adolescent voices

Registers in unchanged voices

Although Gackle describes unchanged girls' voices as not having registers (or at least lacking noticeable register transitions), Phillips argues that children do have lower and upper registers (and mixed voice). It is Phillips' contention that, similar to adults, children can extend chest register into middle voice, and often remain in middle voice for higher pitches that are more appropriate for head voice. Phillips contends that many children are not taught how to access head voice and, as a consequence, rely on chest production and do not develop their vocal range. See Chapter 8, Negotiation of the vocal registers, for more detail.

Teaching children and adolescents about vocal technique

We think that virtually all the vocal techniques addressed in this book should be taught to children and adolescents over time. This is not to say that they should be taught with the same depth or with as much technical information as might be communicated to adults, but the techniques are as useful for children and adolescents as they are for adults.

- ➢ Both Phillips (1996) and Sell (2005) believe children and adolescents should be informed about vocal technique. Sell argues that they should also learn the proper terminology. As she argues, if they can learn musical concepts such as pitch, rhythm, and notation, they can also absorb the language of vocal technique.
- ➢ Sell (2005) argues further that how to sing well should not be a mystery for children. Teaching children almost *exclusively* through imagery, as is often done, does them a disservice. We agree.
- ➢ Cooksey (1999) supports teaching vocal technique through a variety of exercises outlined in his book. These cover many of the topics included in this book. He presents exercises for posture, breath control, vowel consistency, resonance, articulation, development of vocal agility, register transitions, and dynamic control, among others. Adaptations of some of these exercises appear in this book.
- ➢ Brunssen (2018) states that vocal technique for and expectations about adolescents need to be flexible because adolescent bodies are changing so rapidly. "The goal is to move as smoothly as possible into their more adult vocal instrument with its new sounds, sensations, and coordination" (p. 107).

Inform and support adolescents undergoing vocal change

Sell (2005) argues that the process of voice change should be explained to adolescents and that if this is done, they find periodic testing of where they are in the process of change to be interesting. Cooksey (1977a) concurs, and we agree.

Talking with adolescents about what is happening to both girls' and boys' voices and the paths they may take to vocal maturity can be helpful. Unless adolescents are supported and encouraged both to sing during this period and to be patient with their changing voices, they may stop singing. They need reassurance that voice change is a normal part of maturation, connected to the other physical changes they are experiencing. Adolescents are impatient by their very nature—a year seems like a lifetime—so they must be helped to understand that vocal change takes time. Knowing what will happen can encourage them to keep singing through this challenging period.

One of the joys and benefits of choral singing is that changing voices can be socially and vocally supported by those around them. While social support may seem evident for girls, the social aspect of a singing ensemble can also be encouraging and reassuring for boys as their voices change. Solo singing can be frustrating and embarrassing while going through these vocal changes, but choral singing allows adolescents to continue to sing and develop their voices without focusing on the flaws or limitations of their current instruments.

Adolescence is a challenging time, full of raw emotion and self-doubt. Singing in a choral group can give adolescents a sense of peace and happiness as exemplified by this comment from an anonymous seventh-grade student:

> "All of the ugliness binding me disappears ... suddenly I feel beauty all around as I open my lips ... and my heart ... and my mind ... simultaneously to a song!" (Williams, 2006, p. 124).

Keep boys singing during the period of change

Some vocal authorities argue that boys who are going through dramatic vocal changes should wait until their voices have stabilized before singing. Indeed, this has been the historical practice in the Church of England choir program. This approach has several problems:

- When boys do sing again, most will have only lower register capability with limited access to the upper register. Continuing to sing through the period of vocal change can help male voices achieve a fuller range when they stabilize.
- While they are singing, boys are continuing to learn about music. Removing them from choral groups means that they are no longer progressing with their musical abilities. Even if they are having difficulty with pitch control and register breaks, they can still improve breathing, resonance, articulation, language skills, music literacy skills, repertoire, etc.
- This approach contributes to the phenomenon of decreasing male participation in choral groups. Cooksey (1993) argues that if boys are

encouraged to sing through the period of vocal change, more will continue to sing as adults.

- As Freer (2010) notes, "The careful application of theory and research can help the choral conductor guide all boys ... Ultimately, the goal is that these boys understand their voices and expand their musicianship so that they can partake in choral singing throughout their lifetimes, whenever and wherever they choose" (p. 34).
- Williams has conducted extensive studies of boys in the British cathedral choir system (e.g., Williams, Welch, & Howard, in press). She and her colleagues have found that boys transitioning to puberty sing with greater comfort and less tension if they are allowed to follow their voices down as opposed to continuing to sing mostly in head voice. She argues that asking boys in pubertal transition to sing extensively in their former higher pitch range risks sudden voice loss.

Vocal models and adolescents

Adolescents often model their tonal quality on popular artists. Popular performers may have a breathy quality or may sing in a range that is inappropriate for developing voices. Other performers may have a heavy belting style, which some adolescents may be tempted to imitate to sound more mature. Both breathy singing and raw belting can have severe consequences for the young voice—young voices are particularly prone to damage from the use of inappropriate technique.

- Conductors and music educators should consider identifying young singers in their groups who can be models for their peers (instead of modeling themselves) to provide an age-appropriate "ideal" (R. Dilworth, personal communication, February 27, 2020).

Breathiness of adolescent females

It is particularly important to help adolescent females to develop a more focused tone with better resonance. In mixed-gender middle school and high school choral groups, it is often difficult to achieve a dynamic balance among sections because females have excessively breathy voices and males are trying out their emerging chest voice.

As noted in previous chapters, it is challenging to eliminate breathiness among adolescent females; there are physiological limitations on their ability to fully close the glottis. Nonetheless, SOVT exercises such as singing through straws can aid immensely.

- In this context, conductors and teachers should advise adolescent girls to avoid excessive use of hard glottal attacks as a solution to breathiness. The cost of doing this can be vocal fold injury. See Chapter 15 on vocal health.

Avoid excessive vocal loading

In Chapter 15 we explain the concept of vocal loading, which can be measured according to the amount of time that singers engage in various vocal activities during the day (including talking). Adolescents are developing rapidly and are vulnerable to injury; thus, they should avoid excessive vocal loading.

- ➢ As Dilworth (2012) notes, conductors and teachers should watch for signs of strain, and encourage singers to rest their voices when they are fatigued.

Orthodontics

It is common practice to treat teeth and jaw alignment issues during childhood and adolescence. Palate expanders, as well as fixed and removable orthodontic appliances, can cause discomfort and may change the way singers form vowels and consonants in both speech and singing. While most research focuses on the duration of treatment, even a brief orthodontic intervention can cause persistent articulatory issues. Consider an eight-year-old who has spent a formative year of growth with a palate expander across the roof of the mouth. Even after the expander is removed, the muscle memory created while the expander was in place may cause a lack of clear articulation. For example, the child may avoid placing the tongue firmly on the hard palate for consonants requiring this tongue position (e.g., [d], [t]).

- ➢ Brunssen (2018) notes that teachers of adolescent singers must determine if issues with sounds, vowels, and consonants are due to growth and development, orthodontics, or muscle memory, among other possible causes.

Vocal exercise issues specific to adolescents

While virtually all the exercises in this book can be useful for adolescents, some exercises are of particular value during this period:

- ❖ Onset exercises can reduce breathiness and the related difficulty of starting sound. They are not, however, a panacea for these problems, as muscles controlling glottal closure will be weak for some time.
- ❖ Legato exercises can help with creating sustained sound throughout a

musical phrase.
- ❖ Staccato exercises can provide further assistance with coordinating glottal closure and opening.
- ❖ Register bridging. Register transitions are particularly difficult during the period of vocal development.
- ❖ For males, falsetto exercises can help to develop a lighter approach to higher pitches to avoid carrying chest voice too high.
- ❖ SOVT exercises—in particular, the use of straw phonation, can be immensely helpful in clarifying tone. See Chapter 3 for an explanation of the benefits for developing voices.

Cooksey (1999) suggests confining most vocal exercises for a mixed choir during the years of vocal change to what he calls the "Composite Union Range." Girls in all developmental phases and boys in the Mid-Voice IIA stage or earlier can sing together between roughly B_3-flat and A_4, though this range may need to be lowered to B_3 to G_4. Boys in the New Voice and Emerging Voice categories can sing in the same range an octave lower. This does not apply, however, to register bridging and falsetto exercises, which need to go beyond these boundaries.

Transgender singers

Communication is at the heart of what conductors, teachers, and singers do. Expression of gender in singing is an important topic that is gaining more attention. First, we need to distinguish between "sex" and "gender." "Sex" is assigned at birth, while "gender" is self-determined by the individual (Hearns & Kremer, 2018, p. 5). Gender identity is "who I am," gender expression is "how I show it," and gender perception is "how I am seen" (p. 6). Voice teachers and conductors need to recognize their singers as individuals who do not necessarily fit into a binary (male/female) system of gender identity, expression, and perception.

As of 2014, roughly 1.4 million individuals in the United States ages 18 and over identified themselves as transgender (Flores, Herman, Gates, & Brown, 2016). Since younger adults are more likely to identify as transgender, this number is likely to increase over time. Moreover, this estimate does not include transgender adolescents. Thus, voice teachers and choral conductors are increasingly likely to work with transgender singers.

While the intricacies of gender eclipse the scope of this book, we encourage voice teachers and conductors to develop a practice of self-reflection and to familiarize themselves with inclusive language to respect and support the singers with whom they work.

- Avoid binary classifications—instead, use voice categories when referring to singers in an ensemble. Use "trebles/sopranos and altos" instead of "ladies/women/girls" and "tenors and basses" instead of "men/guys/boys".
- Invite singers to share their gender pronouns and promote the use of those pronouns by other singers.
- Choose repertoire in consultation with the voice student, making sure to consider both the vocal range and gender expression of the individual.

Voice teachers and conductors who are working with transgender singers must educate themselves about special considerations for these individuals. Body-shaping garments, hormone replacement therapies, and surgeries all have a significant effect on the voice and the way people sing.

Singing can be a source of stress for singers navigating the discomfort that accompanies gender dysphoria (discomfort with one's assigned gender). Nonetheless, these individuals often feel disenfranchised, so singing can be a way to create bonds and community through a shared love of music. Additionally, singing may allow transgender individuals to express who they are and feel heard. A 23-year-old transgender female expresses it this way:

> "I think that music has always been front and center to my transition. I mean, it was thanks to music I had the courage to come out, and it's thanks to the people who love and support me and are connected to me through music that I have the courage to continue to transition. If it weren't for the people I have met [through] my involvement with classical music, I would not have been brave enough . . . to ask if I could wear a dress at choir concerts. And not only has music helped me that way, it is also thanks to music that I am able to express who I am" (B. Manternach, 2017, p. 210).

We encourage voice teachers and conductors to consult the growing body of literature, communicate respectfully and sensitively with their singers, and strive to be inclusive and supportive. This will allow singers to feel safe and encouraged to communicate with their voice teachers and conductors.

Voice changing methods for transgender males

Some transgender people will consider hormone therapy as a method for aligning their physical characteristics with their gender identity. Trans males may choose testosterone therapy, which will most notably cause facial hair, redistribution of fat throughout the body, vocal fold changes, and the ceasing of menstruation. This process can be compared to adolescence except that in the case of testosterone therapy for people later in life, the changes are much more sudden. The effects on the voice include:

- Thickening of the vocal folds; this will lower the average fundamental frequency of both the speaking and singing voice
- Lengthening of the vocal folds, though not as much as during adolescence because cartilages are not able to grow as much (Constansis, 2008)
- Testosterone causes a more abrupt and early ossification of the laryngeal cartilages, which can restrict vocal fold movement and thereby limit dynamic range and pitch control, creating a sound that is hoarse, weak, or rough (Hearns & Kremer, 2018)

Transgender males often wish to obtain a more masculine appearance as quickly as possible to confirm their gender identity. However, initial high doses of testosterone can create substantial vocal instability and even reduce the long-term gain in vocal range. In one study, singers ages 20-29 increased their range by an average of six half steps with a large starting dose of testosterone, whereas those with gradual escalation in dose achieved an average gain of nine half steps (Constansis, 2008). Improvements in range decreased as age increased, but greater average range improvements were always seen with gradual dose escalation. It is essential to be aware that the effects of testosterone therapy on the voice are irreversible, even after stopping testosterone (Hearns & Kremer, 2018).

Voice changing methods for transgender females

In addition to the utilization of body shaping garments, trans females may decide to take estrogen to feminize their appearance. This is not, however, an effective method of feminizing the voice and may have detrimental effects such as vocal fold swelling and interference with tissue repair mechanisms.

- Standard voice therapy should always be the first choice for raising speaking pitch and helping with other aspects of female vocal patterns (Gelfer & Tice, 2013), though it is not always effective and requires ongoing effort.
- Kawitzky and McAllister (2020) have developed a promising new method using biofeedback to train transgender females to raise their second formant frequency. They observe a subsequent increase in perceived femininity by others.

Dissatisfaction with voice therapy (and the effort required to maintain elevated pitch) may lead some transgender females to seek surgery for a more permanent raising of SFF and perhaps the upper limit of the singing range.

Well-controlled studies of the effects of surgery are limited, but the following are some indicative findings:

- **Anterior Web Formation** involves removal of some tissue from the front (anterior) portion of the vocal folds, followed by closure of the front portion—sometimes called a glottoplasty. This shortens the vibrating part of the vocal folds and is often successful in raising speaking pitch. Exact procedures vary, but recent studies show little or no reduction in pitch range, though some singers experience unfortunate reductions in dynamic range (Kelly, Hertegård, Eriksson, Nygren, & Södersten, 2019; Meister et al., 2017).
- **Cricothyroid Approximation** creates permanent contraction of the cricothyroid muscles, thereby raising pitch. There are numerous problems with this procedure (e.g., substantially reduced range, problems with long-term efficacy, permanent fusing of the cricothyroid joint). Thus, this surgery is now performed less frequently (e.g., Kelly et al., 2019).

Surgical techniques will continue to evolve, hopefully with improved results as refinements occur. Transgender singers can always benefit from voice therapists and voice teachers who have experience working with transgender individuals. Voice teachers should help transgender students make informed decisions about what is best for them.

Aging voices

As we age, so do our voices. Many physiological changes affect the larynx:

- Women's ovaries secrete less estrogen, particularly after menopause. While the ovaries continue to produce some estrogen (estrone) after menopause, they also secrete testosterone (Fogle, Stanczyk, Zhang, & Paulson, 2007). These changes in hormonal balance are associated with increases in the density of vocal fold tissues, resulting in lowered speaking pitch (Gilbert & Weismer, 1974). This generally translates into a lowering of the singing range. Conductors should keep this in mind when programming pieces involving high pitches and high tessituras. For example, Beethoven's Ninth can be problematic for some older singers.
- In males there is a decline in testosterone level that is associated with a slight increase in speaking pitch, raising the lowest singable pitch by a small amount though not appreciably increasing the highest singable pitch.
- Over time, portions of the laryngeal cartilages may calcify and even transform into bone (ossify). This can limit range and may affect high pitches the most.

- Muscles atrophy with age, and laryngeal muscles are not exempt. For example, in some older individuals, the thyroarytenoid muscles atrophy, with the vocal folds exhibiting a characteristic bowed appearance. The result is incomplete closure of the glottis, producing a breathy or hoarse sound. This problem can also be caused by degradation in neuromuscular control.
- Mucus and other secretions that help to lubricate laryngeal tissues decrease in quality and quantity (Ramig et al., 2001). Perhaps related to this is a reduction in hydration of the mucosal tissue at the edges of the vocal folds (Abitbol, Abitbol, & Abitbol, 1999). Older singers need to be particularly vigilant about staying hydrated. See Chapter 15 on vocal health.
- Accumulation of fluid in the tissues (edema) is a frequent problem associated with aging, particularly in females (Ramig et al., 2001). Vocal folds are affected like any other tissue, and the puffiness created by edema will produce a hoarse sound.

While the effects of aging on the larynx are important, vocal scientists are now also paying attention to its impact on breath control. A recent study shows an association among aging, diminished respiratory capacity, and reduced vocal quality (Awan, 2006). It certainly makes sense that aging would affect the muscles controlling breathing, such as the intercostals and the abdominals. Given the importance of breath support for singing well, maintenance of muscles supporting breath control is essential for preserving vocal function as we age. Respiratory muscle training, breathing exercises, and physical exercises for the abdominals outlined in Chapter 2 on breathing are critical for older singers.

Finally, loss of hearing can affect a singer's ability to control the voice, with respect to both pitch and amplitude. Older singers who seem to be having such problems may benefit from referral to an audiologist.

What characterizes the aging voice?

One way to answer this question is to ask middle-aged and older singers about their experience with their voices as they aged. Boulet and Oddens (1996) interviewed male and female professional singers ages 40–70 about their experiences and perspectives. Roughly 75% stated that the voice changes around age 50, but only 29% of females and 28% of males experienced negative changes. When negative changes were mentioned, they most frequently included:

- Loss of high notes—both sexes, but particularly females
- "Less supple vocal cords"—both sexes, but mostly females

- Change in timbre
- Less steady voice
- Breathiness/huskiness—reported mostly by females

The change in timbre described by both sexes is notable. In the past this was reported only for females because the changes in vocal fold tissues related to menopause were connected with some loss of higher-frequency harmonics. These new findings suggest that aging alters vocal tissue composition in at least some singers of both sexes.

Another approach is to compare younger and older singers on various physiological and acoustical measures. Research suggests the following are characteristics of aging voices (Unteregger et al., 2017; Luchsinger & Arnold, 1965; Biever & Bless, 1989; Ramig & Ringel, 1983; Ferrand, 2002; Awan, 2006):

- Reduced thyroid cartilage flexibility due to ossification, making it more difficult to produce higher pitches
- Incomplete closure of the glottis and associated breathiness
- Increased acoustical noise and shimmer, heard as vocal roughness
- Reduced amplitude of vibration of the vocal folds (lower sound level)
- Less control over pitch
- Less range
- Wobble—see Chapter 7 on vibrato for solutions to this problem

Singers can delay vocal aging

Singers can slow the aging of the voice by adopting healthy practices. Foremost is to keep physically fit. Many studies have demonstrated that vocal quality and sound level can be preserved into the seventies and even into the eighties for those whose physiological age ("real age") is younger. Regular exercise, both aerobic and strength training, along with a well-balanced diet and weight control, contribute to the continued ability to sing well into old age. Given that reduced blood flow is thought to be a significant cause of the laryngeal dysfunction associated with aging, it is no surprise that these are also the behaviors related to the prevention of cardiovascular disease.

- For example, Ramig and Ringel (1983) examined physical condition and measures of vocal quality and range in three age groupings of males: 25–35, 45–55 and 65–75. Males in good physical condition had better vocal quality and greater range than those in poor physical condition. This difference was more pronounced in the older age group.

Other actions that singers can take to prevent premature aging or cope with the aging of their voices include (adapted in part from Heman-Ackah, Sataloff, Hawkshaw, & Divi, 2008):

- Perform exercises that help prevent atrophy of breathing muscles, such as the sibilant exercise. Respiratory training devices are also helpful.
- Avoid excessively pressed phonation that can damage the vocal folds over time.
- Onset exercises may help older singers who have excessively breathy voices for the style they are singing (Chapter 3).
- Always warm up before singing. Use straw phonation and other effective SOVT exercises such as [v] as part of the warm-up.
- Use techniques to enhance resonance, thereby increasing the efficiency of singing.
- Use good vocal technique, not only in singing, but also in everyday speech.
- Stay well-hydrated and take preventive measures to avoid gastric reflux (see Chapter 15 on vocal health).
- Do not smoke (tobacco or marijuana) or use vaping products. These injure the vocal folds, causing swelling and changes in the tissues. They also damage the lungs.
- Avoid ingesting marijuana as well, as it interferes with cognitive function and muscle control.

As we noted earlier, singing at one rehearsal per week and one performance per week is insufficient. Singers should strive to sing at least 10–15 minutes per day to stave off the atrophy of muscles important for singing.

> Supporting the idea that ongoing voice use helps to preserve vocal quality is a study by Lortie, Rivard, Thibeault, and Tremblay (2017). They find that frequent singing improves the stability of aging voices.

Chapter 14: Reducing Tension

Muscle tension is necessary to accomplish many of the tasks of singing. For example, muscles controlling the vocal folds must be contracted to enable closure of the glottis; abdominal muscles must be recruited to maintain breath pressure. But excessive and extraneous tensions may compromise desired tonal quality and compromise vocal health in both the short and long term. The most problematic tensions involve the:

- Neck/larynx/pharynx
- Jaw
- Tongue
- Lips
- Shoulders
- Legs

Recall from Chapter 1 that proper body alignment is key to reducing tension. In this chapter we focus in more detail on specific manifestations of tension in these areas and how to minimize them.

Larynx and neck/pharynx tension

As noted in Chapter 3 on initiation and creation of sound, muscles that control the vocal folds are not under direct, conscious control, except for the cricoarytenoids and interarytenoids, both of which control the opening and closing of the glottis. Nonetheless, singers may try to control directly the muscles of the larynx in the mistaken belief that this will adjust pitch, leading to inappropriate and unnecessary tension in the vocal tract.

> McKinney (2005) states that a pressed, edgy, strained sound results from tension in the vocal folds and in other muscles of the larynx and neck. If breath pressure is excessive, the combination can be particularly disastrous. He describes the resulting sound as harsh, strident, and grating.

Some singers use neck and/or constrictor muscles of the pharynx to help control their sound. This is virtually guaranteed to impair vocal function and produce poor tonal quality (Bunch, 1995).

When the constrictor muscles of the pharynx are tense, the diameter of the pharynx decreases. Recall that this can cause intonation problems, vibrato problems, and a tight, edgy sound (Edwards, 2014). The potential for the pharyngeal constrictors to compromise the vocal tract can be seen in Figure 14.1, which illustrates the upper, middle, and lower constrictors. The upper constrictor is attached to a ligament at the sides of the rear portion of the jaw, forming a muscular wall on the sides and back of the throat. The middle constrictor is attached to the hyoid bone. Since the larynx suspends from this bone, constriction of this muscle will affect the larynx as well as the pharynx. The lower constrictor muscle is attached to the oblique ridge of the thyroid cartilage and thus can have a direct effect upon the larynx.

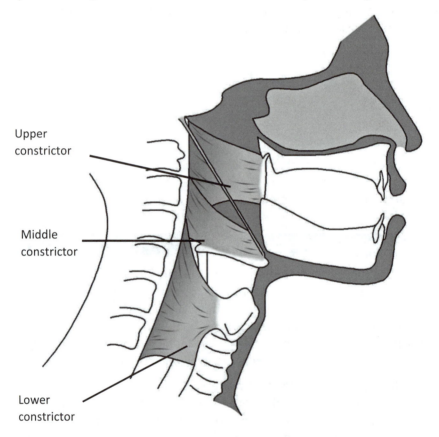

Figure 14.1 Illustration of oropharynx and laryngeal-pharynx constrictor muscles

Pharyngeal constriction in contemporary styles

In most contemporary styles, singers do not attempt to create the wide pharynx of classical singing unless they are producing a darker or mellower tone for artistic reasons. While a brighter sound can be achieved, in part, by active constriction of the pharynx, a better approach is modest relaxation of the soft palate, elevating/fronting the tongue, plus shortening the vocal tract by allowing the larynx to rise naturally and widening the lips. This avoids the tension of active constriction and offers the benefit of a better quality of sound. Singers can also experiment with jaw retraction, but they must be careful not to do this in a way that creates tension.

> Edwards (2014) suggests several excellent exercises to help with relaxation of the constrictor muscles. One involves singing while looking at the ceiling as though taking a drink from a tipped-back water bottle. This stretches the pharyngeal constrictors to a point where they have difficulty contracting.

Sing short patterns in the drinking-from-a-water-bottle position using [a] or [ɑ] to experience singing without constriction. Compare this with the sensations you experience singing the same patterns with your head in a normal position. Be sure to sing some notes at high pitches as these often involve tension. Alternate back and forth between the two head positions until you can sing without constriction (Adapted from Edwards, 2014).

Neck/pharynx tension can be a carryover from speech production that lacks good breath support

Some singers have a poor approach to speech production that they carry over to singing. Speaking without proper breath support is relatively easy, and many of us do this. We may, for example, engage in upper chest breathing and tightening of the pharynx when we lack enough breath at the end of a spoken sentence. This method forces out enough breath to complete what we want to say—though with poor production. When we use this approach while singing, the results are much worse. Efforts to improve breath support will help. In addition, conductors and teachers should model proper speech production, being mindful of breath support when speaking.

Jaw tension

Jaw tension is common among singers: sometimes it is unintentional, and sometimes it is due to an incorrect understanding of how far the jaw should lower. Some singers drop the jaw excessively and, as a result, must tense the jaw muscles to keep it lowered. This can also induce laryngeal tension.

❖ Recall from Chapter 4 on resonance that for classical singing, just the first

10% of an approach to a yawn is sufficient to release the rear of the mandible (jaw bone). In contemporary styles there is more of a focus on lowering the front of the jaw. See the exercises in Chapter 4 for Tetrazzini's exercise for singers of classical music on jaw release.

Jaw tension may also be created by holding the jaw in a fixed position in an attempt to improve resonance by stretching the tissues in the mouth and pharynx. Tension can accumulate, and the position of the jaw may become rigid and tight.

Try sustaining [ɑ] or [ae] while gently massaging the jaw joints in front of the ears with a finger. Also, massage the masseter muscle (chewing muscle) which controls jaw movement. Singers often carry tension in this muscle.

> Vennard (1967) believes that jaw freedom is critical and that there is a strong relationship between pharyngeal tension and jaw tension. "A tight jaw is a symptom of a tight throat" (p. 117–118).

Figure 14.2 illustrates neck, jaw, and facial tension associated with excessive lowering of the jaw and opening of the mouth when singing [ɑ]. Note, however, this amount of mouth opening may be appropriate for a number of contemporary styles involving belting at higher pitches. What is inappropriate is the obvious tension in the neck and face and the jutting forward of the head.

Figure 14.2 Illustration of problematic neck, jaw, and facial tension

Temporomandibular joint (TMJ) disorder

Some singers experience pain in the jaw joints and/or grating or clicking of the joints that interfere with easy jaw movement. A number of factors can cause this:

- Teeth grinding (often during sleep but even during the day)
- Excessive gum chewing
- Improper teeth alignment
- Improper bite adjustment

Home treatments such as ice packs, joint massage, and/or non-steroidal anti-inflammatory medications (aspirin, ibuprofen, naproxen sodium) are often helpful. Stress reduction is also essential as is avoidance of gum chewing. If these remedies are insufficient, consult a dentist with experience in the treatment of TMJ disorders. Treatments can include bite adjustment through teeth resurfacing and the creation of a custom mouthguard worn at night.

Tongue tension

The tongue is a large muscle with many connections to vocal tract structures, including the pharynx. Of particular importance is the connection of the tongue with the hyoid bone, from which the larynx is suspended (Figure 14.3). Tongue tension can easily change the resonance characteristics of the vocal tract.

Holding the tongue back/excessive tongue flattening creates a throaty sound

When the tongue is too far back in the mouth, it lowers the larynx excessively and, as discussed in Chapter 4 on resonance, alters the resonating characteristics of the pharynx. Lower frequency harmonics can bypass this constriction, but high-frequency harmonics cannot. In addition, tongue tissue crowding the pharynx can absorb high-frequency harmonics. Depression of the larynx also lowers all formant frequencies, a problem for most contemporary styles, and often for classical singing as well.

> - Fisher (1966) and Tetrazzini (Caruso & Tetrazzini, 1975) both describe the sound resulting from excessive tongue flattening as "throaty." Fisher adds that allowing the tongue to fall back creates vowels that sound too dark.
> - Fleming (2005) notes that even during her years in a master's degree program at Juilliard, she still struggled with her tongue falling back,

strangling her high notes, and sometimes cutting them off. To help, one of her teachers placed a honey drop on the center indentation near the tip of the tongue. Reflexively, the tongue rises somewhat and remains in a forward position. Only exercises using [ɑ] or [a] can be performed when doing this, but these are the vowels for which this type of tongue problem is most likely.

Place your finger gently on the larynx. Move the tongue backward from its normal resting position and feel how this pushes the larynx down.

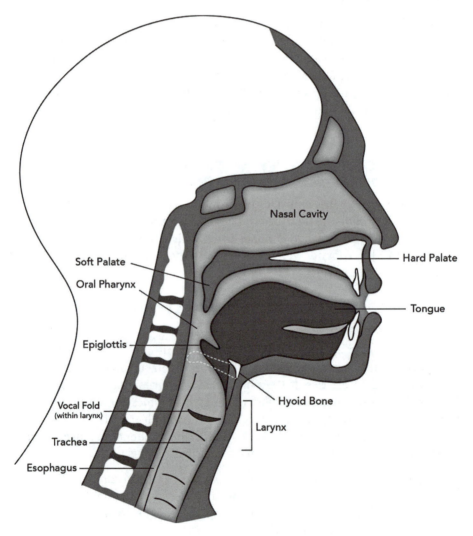

Figure 14.3 Illustration of the vocal tract

It is worth noting in this context that singers should not deliberately flatten the tongue as a way of creating pharyngeal space.

> Bunch (1995) says that this creates a shortened and narrowed resonance chamber, resulting in a strident tone.

Sing [ɑ] in the middle of the range with a relaxed tongue and then depress it or force it back. You will hear a dramatic change in tone.

Tetrazzini's test for tongue tension

One of Tetrazzini's talks on singing addressed the "Mastery of the Tongue" (Caruso & Tetrazzini, 1975). She views the tongue as a significant problem for most singers because it is such a large muscle whose roots, even with slight movement, can affect the larynx unfavorably.

Singers who have any tendency toward tongue tension (and most singers do at one time or another), can use a technique advocated by Tetrazzini to check for its presence. *Feel the underside of your jaw behind the chin—if your tongue is tense (and particularly if it is depressed) you will feel a lump or hardness in that area.*

Tongue groove—is it a sign of tension?

A groove running from the front to the back of the tongue is most obviously seen when someone sings [ɑ] or [a] on a high pitch. Some vocal pedagogy authorities believe the creation of a subtle groove is a natural development, while others claim that it is a sign of muscular tension.

Vennard (1967) asserts that a modest tongue groove develops naturally as singers' voices develop over time. Our experience is in accord with this perspective. Vocal production that is free of tension will often naturally result in a small groove. The key is to avoid trying to create a groove, as attempts to do so will likely result in tension and alter resonance.

> Tetrazzini argues that there should be a slight furrow in the tongue, which naturally increases in depth as pitch ascends (Caruso & Tetrazzini, 1975).
> Marafioti (1922) believes that a groove in the tongue is helpful because it increases oral space. He stipulates that the proper groove is created through complete relaxation of the tongue on the floor of the mouth. He warns explicitly against a stiff, contracted tongue.

Lip tension

McKinney (2005) cites several indicators of lip tension:

- Holding the lips rigidly in one position
- Pulling the lips back into a continuous, forced smile.
- Holding the lips against the teeth, creating a dark, muffled sound

Some singers also make the mistake of pushing the lips too far forward. Even when singing [u] in a classical style, the lips should not be puckered excessively. (See Chapter 5 on vowels.)

For classical singing, we do recommend raising the upper lips and cheek muscles slightly to create a pleasant smile. If only four upper teeth show, the lips have not been raised excessively for this style (Vennard, 1967). For contemporary styles seeking a brighter sound, form a wider smile with more upper teeth showing.

Figure 14.4 illustrates a forced smile. Note the associated lip and facial tension.

Figure 14.4 Illustration of a forced smile

Shoulders

Shoulder tension invariably affects the neck and thus the larynx. Raised shoulders are a common problem. Some singers keep their shoulders in a fixed, raised position while others unconsciously lift the shoulders when they inhale, particularly if they are engaging in upper chest breathing. Instead, shoulders should be relaxed comfortably in their sockets. Shoulder tension can also occur from holding a music folder; conductors and teachers need to remind singers to relax their shoulders and maintain excellent posture—the shoulders do not hold music!

Hunched shoulders (shoulders pushed forward) are another common source of muscular tension. Hunched shoulders lower the sternum and rib cage, reducing the area available for the lungs to expand during inhalation. Singers who concentrate on expanding the back of the ribs to maximize lung expansion should be careful to avoid inadvertently hunching their shoulders to accomplish this while inhaling.

Legs

Leg tension can be a serious problem. Leg muscles that are tensed for too long will cause the legs to tremble and even shake. Locked knees are a common sign of tensed leg muscles, as both the lower and upper leg muscles must be contracted to accomplish this posture. We offer several stretching exercises at the end of the chapter to help reduce leg tension.

- ❖ Knee locking limits the return flow of blood to the heart and thus to the brain. This is a major cause of fainting, often when choir members are standing on risers (McKinney, 2005). Do not overcompensate, however, with excessive knee bending.

Concluding thoughts on tension

Voice teachers and conductors should listen and look for signs of tension in their singers and endeavor to help them with appropriate exercises. For example, an edgy sound may be due to pharyngeal constriction or an excessively high larynx. Both airiness and a chest-belt sound can be signs of tension when these are not the intended sounds. Sometimes, as discussed in the section on onset in Chapter 3, singers exhibit tension by unconscious body movement (e.g., swaying, moving the arms, raising the chin—not to be confused with intentional movement).

Tension often compensates for something that is missing in vocal technique. It can also be a way that our bodies attempt to support or energize sound. Focusing on the desired sound can allow us to wean ourselves from the sensation of energy or support we derive from nonproductive tension. Concentrate on what *does* need to happen, and much of the extraneous tension will disappear.

Exercises to reduce tension

Neck relaxation

Head tilt and rotation. This exercise is one that we recommended in Chapter 1 as part of a set of exercises to release tension and create good body alignment. *Tilt the head from side to side; then tilt the head forward and move it slowly in a half-circle to the back and then to the front again; repeat to the right.*

Backward neck stretch (Fisher, 1966). *Place a chair near a wall such that when sitting with your head tilted back, your head just touches the wall.* This stretching of the neck muscles can help to relax them, just as a runner relaxes calf and hamstring muscles by stretching them.

Side neck stretch. *Lean your head to the left. Place your left hand on the top right side of your head. Gently pull the head to the left. It should require very little movement of the head before you feel the muscles on the right side of your neck stretching. Do the same with your head tilted to the right with the right hand gently pulling on the top left side of your head.*

Jaw freedom exercises

Jaw wiggle. *Vennard (1967) suggests wiggling the jaw from side to side while vocalizing. Singers can also look at themselves in a mirror at home and move the jaw slowly up and down within a limited range. Then increase the range of movement until you feel tension. Now sing an ascending and descending octave scale, lowering the jaw when ascending and closing it somewhat when descending. (Males should reduce jaw lowering as they ascend into the first passaggio but can increase jaw lowering past the passaggio as discussed in the vowel modification section of Chapter 5.) Monitor to be sure there is no tension when you do this.*

Hum and chew. *Hum and chew at the same time, moving the jaw gently in circular motions in all directions. Imagine a cow chewing grass while singing!*

Tongue relaxation

Lax vowels (Fisher, 1966). A number of vowels are considered "lax" because they require minimal tongue tension. *Sing lax vowels such as [ɛ], [ae], and [U] to experience less tension. Then sing neighboring vowels in the Vowel Spectrum and see if you can keep the same relaxed sensation.*

Tetrazzini (Caruso & Tetrazzini, 1975) suggests pushing the tongue forward out of the mouth (without stiffening it) and withdrawing it slowly. (Singing is not necessary for this exercise, but you could also try singing vowels such as [a] *or* [ɑ].*)*

Vowel exercises to bring the tongue forward

Springboard exercise. Fisher (1966) lists a variety of words that use front vowels. Each word starts with a consonant that requires the tongue to contact the area near the alveolar ridge on the roof of the mouth. *Sing the consonant quickly, using the contact with the ridge area as a springboard to keep the tongue forward on the subsequent vowel. Sample words include:*

- tea, deep
- tick, tin
- tail, day
- den, net

Tip of tongue slightly in front of the lips. *If you have trouble with the tongue falling back into the throat, try singing a short scale on* [ɑ] *or* [a] *with the tip of the tongue slightly in front of the lips. Then return the tip of the tongue to its normal resting place at the base of the lower incisors and sing the scale again.*

There are additional exercises to help with tongue placement in Chapter 5 on vowels.

Shoulder relaxation

Raise the arms over the head and stretch toward the ceiling. Then shrug the shoulders several times. Finally, roll the shoulders in a circle to the back and then to the front, letting them relax into their sockets.

Scapular retraction is an exercise to help reduce hunching. *In a standing or sitting position, attempt to pull your shoulder blades together in the back. Hold the position for ten seconds. Repeat several times.* This, of course, is an extreme backward shoulder position, which helps counteract forward hunching, but it is not the position you want for singing.

Leg muscle relaxation

Calf muscle stretch. *If your calf muscles are tense, a variation on the runner's stretch is an excellent exercise. Stand facing a wall with your feet about one foot from it. Place your hands on the wall at head height to brace yourself. Move one foot back about two feet. Straighten that leg until you feel your calf muscle stretch. Hold for 30 seconds and repeat with the other leg.*

Quadriceps stretch. *If your front upper leg muscles are tight, stand sideways next to a chair or wall. Brace yourself with the hand closest to the wall. Lift the foot of your leg farthest from the wall behind you. Grasp it with your free hand and pull it as close as is comfortable to your buttock. You should feel a stretch in your quadriceps but do not overdo the stretch. Hold for 30 seconds and repeat on the opposite side.*

Hamstrings stretch. *Stand close to a bed or sofa with a height that allows you to lift one leg onto it. Place your left leg on the surface such that it is stretched out with the heel reasonably close to the edge (but avoid locking the knee). Lean forward slightly to place your right hand on the surface to help provide balance. You should feel a stretch in the hamstrings (muscles on the back of the thigh). Increase the stretch as desired by reaching for your toes with your left hand. Rotate your foot to the left and right, and you should feel stretching in different areas of the hamstrings. Do this for 30 seconds and repeat on the opposite side.*

Hips/glutes stretch. *Sit in a chair, place your right ankle on your left knee. Slowly lean forward until you feel a gentle stretch. Hold for 30 seconds and repeat on the opposite side.*

Chapter 15: Guarding Singers' Vocal Health

As noted in Chapter 3 on initiation and creation of sound, the human vocal instrument is composed of small structures capable of producing incredible sound. Keeping our instruments functioning well requires keeping our bodies in good health through a well-balanced diet, regular exercise, good sleep habits, and avoidance of harmful substances. This includes not smoking (tobacco or marijuana) or using vaping products. As noted earlier, these products injure the vocal folds, causing swelling and changes in the tissues. They also damage the lungs.

Singers also need to understand how to use their voices without causing physical harm to their vocal folds. Many of the preceding chapters have included approaches to vocal technique that will help ensure healthy singing throughout the lifetime. This chapter focuses in more detail on health issues specific to singers and their vocal instruments:

- ❖ Vocal fold hydration and factors affecting hydration
- ❖ Vocal stamina and fatigue
- ❖ Stress, anxiety, and vocal health
- ❖ Meal consumption before singing
- ❖ Mucus
- ❖ Gastric reflux
- ❖ The common cold; coughing
- ❖ Medications that may cause vocal fold bleeding
- ❖ Hormonal factors affecting the voice
- ❖ Surgical considerations
- ❖ Vocal health concerns of professional singers
- ❖ Vocal health concerns of amateur singers
- ❖ Choral conductor's role in vocal health

Studies have revealed that untutored singers are more likely to develop vocal dysfunction, both because of their lack of accurate information about vocal production, and because of as their limited awareness of the need to protect vocal health (Neto & Meyer, 2017). Many singers in contemporary styles have been mostly self-taught, in part because voice lessons have traditionally focused on classical training (more recently on musical theatre as well). As more voice teachers are trained to teach singing in a variety of styles, we encourage all singers to add voice lessons to help them learn vocal health-preserving singing techniques.

> Recall from Chapter 3 that Lawrence (1979) found belters who have had voice training have better vocal health.

This chapter is intended to provide general information about health issues particularly relevant to singers. It is not meant to provide diagnosis or treatment information for specific individuals. Singers should consult their healthcare providers for such advice.

Hydration

We noted in Chapter 3 that when our bodies are not adequately hydrated, the mucus coating of the vocal folds is more viscous, making it challenging to get the folds vibrating. Higher pitches are exceptionally difficult to sing without sufficient hydration. There can also be more noise in the voice and pitch instability.

A comprehensive review of the effects of hydration on voice quality (e.g., tone clarity, pitch stability, sound level stability) was conducted by Alves, Krüger, Pillay, van Lierde, and van der Linde (2019). They conclude that voice quality is impaired by:

- Systemic dehydration due to insufficient intake of fluids or fasting
- Vocal fold surface dehydration due to mouth breathing (e.g., while sleeping)

In contrast, the following improve voice quality:

- Systemic hydration from fluid intake (This also increases maximum phonation time.)
- Vocal fold surface hydration from inhalation of steam

Nebulizers are relatively inexpensive devices that singers can use to inhale cool mist, which may also be helpful. Tanner et al. (2010) find that inhaling a mist containing saline is more effective than inhaling a plain-water mist.

Singers need to be consistently hydrated. If you feel thirsty, you are likely already dehydrated. Drink plenty of fluids throughout the day, well before singing. Fluids consumed just before or during rehearsal will not immediately assist hydration but may help wash away irritants. **Fluids do not flow over the vocal folds**, a misconception held by some singers.

On waking, your body is dehydrated, so drink a couple of glasses of water soon after rising, particularly if singing in the morning. Singing a few vocalises while showering also helps because of the inhalation of warm, moist air.

Singers who live in a dry climate (including winter in a temperate climate) should have a humidifier. Dry air passing over the vocal folds contributes to their dehydration. If you do not have central air humidification, use a portable humidifier, preferably in the room where you sleep.

Another benefit of well-hydrated vocal folds is that they are less prone to injury from use and recover more quickly if injured (Verdolini-Marston, Sandage, & Titze, 1994).

Effects of caffeinated beverages, alcohol, and antihistamines

The table summarizes what is known about the effects of various substances on hydration (see Verdolini et al., 2002; Sataloff & Hawkshaw, 2006 for more information about antihistamines and diuretics).

Substance	Effect on Vocal Fold Hydration
Alcohol	Dehydrating—drink extra water
Antihistamine	**Diphenhydramine hydrochloride (Benadryl)**: No dehydration of vocal folds, no effect on amount of breath pressure required to initiate phonation; use with caution due to potential for drowsiness **Other antihistamines:** Little is known, but some singers use loratadine (Claritin) without problems. In fact, clinical trials report very low percentages experiencing dry mouth or thirst with loratadine.
Antihistamine plus Decongestant	May thicken mucus on the folds
Caffeine/coffee	No dehydration for most regular drinkers
Diuretics	Dehydrating and require increased breath pressure for phonation

Table 15.1 Effects of various substances on vocal fold hydration

Coffee and other beverages containing caffeine were once thought to be dehydrating. Recent research has shown, however, that caffeinated drinks have a diuretic effect similar to that of water at moderate levels of consumption (Armstrong et al., 2005; Killer, Blannin, & Jeukendrup, 2014).

Alcohol is dehydrating. If you consume alcoholic beverages, be sure to compensate by consuming additional amounts of water.

Allergies lead to sneezing, coughing, swollen tissues, and excess mucus. All these interfere with singing. Many singers with allergies find that taking an antihistamine is helpful and can make the difference between singing easily and struggling to sing. Yet they are often cautioned against taking antihistamines such as diphenhydramine hydrochloride (Benadryl) due to a supposed dehydration effect. In the case of Benadryl there is no scientific basis for the assertion (Verdolini et al., 2002).

Vocal stamina and fatigue

Individual practice and group rehearsals help to build muscles important for vocal production. Gradual increases in practice periods and their intensity are necessary to accomplish this without damage. Just as with physical exercise, "muscles need to be worked beyond what they are used to for them to continue to develop" (Hoch & Sandage, 2018, p. 80). At the same time, singers need recovery periods after intense vocal use. Warm-ups are also vital to improving performance while preventing damage.

The safe amount of daily singing depends in part on the style of production that a singer uses. A singer who carries a lot of tension in areas affecting the larynx will be able to sing for only short periods without risk of developing hoarseness. Hoarseness occurs because of excessive friction between vocal folds and consequent swelling. An overly pressed style of production can similarly cause problems.

Even singers who use good vocal technique should limit *continuous* rehearsal to two hours. A three-hour rehearsal will require a 15-minute break to allow singers to recover. Brancaccio (2015) has developed a point system to create an awareness of vocal use and the potential for vocal fatigue. This system can be thought of as a scale for measuring the amount of vocal loading.

- ❖ Every half hour of choral rehearsal, voice lessons, individual practice, loud talking (e.g., in a noisy environment) is worth 10 points, as is every hour of relaxed, intermittent talking. We would add that points for singing could be higher or lower depending upon the tessitura and technical difficulty of the music.
- ❖ Aim for a total of no more than 100 points per day; use a 50-point or lower limit if you are not feeling well or are vocally fatigued. A three-hour choral rehearsal (including a break) plus talking throughout the day could easily reach the 100-point limit.
- ❖ Professional singers often exceed 100 points and thus need to be especially aware of the need for opportunities to avoid voice use.

Singers and other voice users should consider taking what Brancaccio calls "vocal naps" at various points in the day to allow for vocal recovery. Remember that speaking during breaks does not constitute resting the voice.

Some other suggestions to lessen vocal fatigue include:

- When speaking, be sure to use an appropriate pitch; speaking at an excessively low or high pitch is much like singing for long periods at the low or high end of one's range.
- Sing through a straw as part of your warm-up and cool-down, or whenever you feel vocally fatigued. A vibrating SOVT exercise such as a lip trill can be helpful as well.
- Use "marking" strategies to reduce vocal load for passages with difficult tessituras (e.g., singing up or down an octave, reducing volume, using falsetto, singing through a straw) when needed and appropriate. For example, sing up or down an octave during staging/blocking rehearsals in musical theatre/opera, though never during the dress rehearsal.

Astaxanthin may help prevent vocal fold damage

Antioxidants have long been thought to help reduce tissue damage. Kaneko, Kishimoto et al. (2017) reasoned that a potent antioxidant might help reduce damage caused by vocal loading. In a pilot study they found that 24 mg/day of the supplement, astaxanthin, taken for 28 days reduces vocal fold inflammation and prevents deterioration in various vocal quality measures. Astaxanthin is present in certain algae and pink/red seafood such as salmon. It is available without a prescription in the U.S., but more research is necessary to prove its efficacy.

Stress, anxiety, and vocal health

Stress has well-known detrimental effects on health in general. Holmqvist, Santtila, Lindström, Sala, and Simberg (2013) provide insight into how stress affects vocal production. They argue that because the primary evolutionary function of the larynx is to protect the airway rather than to create sound, when someone is under stress or is anxious, the muscular system may revert to its primary function. This can create an imbalance in muscular tension, which can cause the voice to become strained, tremble, and/or crack. Holmqvist et al. (2013) add the following common symptoms of stress: hoarseness, throat clearing or coughing while talking, sensation of muscle tension or a lump in the throat. Muscular tension problems can also affect the muscles of inhalation and breath support, further contributing to vocal production difficulties.

If singers have ongoing issues of stress, anxiety, or depression affecting their voice, recurrence of difficulties is likely unless they also receive psychological counseling (Tezcaner, Gökmen, Yıldırım, & Dursun, 2019).

The good news is that singing is extolled for its mental and physical health benefits and is, for many people, a significant way to reduce stress and anxiety. Kang, Scholp, and Jiang (2018) list some of the benefits of singing (particularly ensemble singing) observed in various studies:

- A heightened sense of well-being (and less depression); a greater sense of connectedness associated with singing in ensembles—higher than playing a team sport
- Improved immune function as measured by Secretory Immunoglobulin A
- Higher endorphin levels—endorphins enhance mood and reduce pain

Amateur singers have less jitter and more intensity in their speaking voices, compared to non-singers (Prakup, 2012). As a result, singers are judged as significantly younger than non-singers when speaking.

Meal consumption prior to singing

Timing of meals before singing

Eating before singing is important because of the energy required for what is truly an athletic endeavor. Nonetheless, eating too close to performance is problematic because incomplete digestion can result in burping and/or reflux. A full stomach also interferes with breathing because the diaphragm has less room to descend. Most authorities recommend eating an hour and a half to three hours before singing. Henderson (1979), for example, suggests two to three hours, and Fleming (2005) recommends an hour and a half (and a moderate meal).

A small amount of alcohol may relax a nervous singer, but too much alcohol is dehydrating and detrimental to cognitive function.

Mucus

In excess, mucus interferes with singing. We suggest waking at least two hours before singing to allow time for the sinuses to drain (a source of excess mucus) and mucus on the vocal folds to thin. Good hydration helps to thin mucus—as noted above, drink extra water after waking. Singers experiencing problems with mucus due to respiratory illness may find that guaifenesin, an over-the-counter product (found, for example, in Mucinex), is helpful.

Do dairy products contribute to mucus problems?

Many people believe that dairy products increase mucus. This belief may be due to how dairy products coat throat surfaces, creating a sensation similar to that of mucus. Formal studies have discovered that objective measurements of mucus production show no evidence of increased mucus production after consumption of dairy products (Wuthrich, Schmid, Walther, & Sieber, 2005). Nonetheless, a recent double-blind experimental study concludes that people with *persistent* nasal/pharyngeal mucus problems may benefit from a dairy-free diet (Frosh, Cruz, Wellsted, & Stephens, 2019).

Gastric reflux

Gastric reflux is a well-known cause of what is commonly referred to as "heartburn." However, gastric reflux can damage the larynx without associated heartburn symptoms. In fact, this is considered a different condition called laryngopharyngeal reflux—LPR (Selby, Gilbert, & Lerman, 2003).

LPR can cause subtle changes in the voice, inability to sing for extended periods, hoarseness, coughing, and in some cases, laryngitis. Additional possible symptoms include bad breath, the need for extended warm-up time (especially in the morning), the sensation of a lump in the throat, and chronic sore throat (Sataloff & Hawkshaw, 2006; Koufman, 1991).

LPR is more prevalent than previously thought (Koufman, 1991). Every singer should take preventive measures, including the avoidance of food and alcohol consumption within three hours of sleeping (alcohol tends to relax the sphincter in the esophagus that prevents reflux). Weight control is also an important preventive measure.

Singers who experience reflux should adhere to the above recommendations and sleep in an upper-body-elevated position on an adjustable bed or with a high-quality wedge pillow. They should also avoid acidic beverages such as coffee and soft drinks, citrus fruits, chocolate, fatty foods, onions, spicy foods, and tomato-based foods (National Institute of Diabetes and Digestive and Kidney Diseases, 2020). Treatment with antacids, H2 histamine blockers (which reduce acid secretion), and proton pump inhibitors may also be useful. Examples of H2 histamine blockers include famotidine (Pepcid), and cimetidine (Tagamet). Examples of proton pump inhibitors include lansoprazole (Prevacid), omeprazole (Prilosec), and esomeprazole (Nexium).

One study of treatment with proton pump inhibitors (PPIs) for eight weeks in combination with dietary restrictions observed a reduction in hoarseness associated with laryngopharyngeal reflux (Selby, Gilbert, & Lerman, 2003). However, a comprehensive review casts doubt on the utility of PPIs for treating LPR, as other studies show no effect, and those that do are mostly uncontrolled (Spantideas, Drosou, Bougea, & AlAbdulwahed, in press). Indeed, PPIs do not help a sizeable percentage of people, in part because while they may reduce acid production, they do not help with reflux itself (e.g., Reimer, Lødrup, Smith, Wilkinson, & Bytzer, 2016).

- ❖ Gaviscon Advance does, however, reduce reflux. It contains sodium alginate (a natural seaweed derivative) and potassium bicarbonate. The alginate reacts with stomach acid to create a gel, while the potassium bicarbonate reacts with stomach acid to create bubbles that float the gel. This creates a physical barrier to reflux for 3–4 hours. Reimer et al. (2016) conducted a controlled study showing that Gaviscon Advance liquid formulation reduces reflux events in those taking PPIs. Other studies have shown that it is also superior to a placebo in reducing reflux events. Note that Gaviscon Advance is a U.K. product and is not available in U.S. pharmacies. You can purchase it, however, on internet sites such as Amazon. Do not confuse this with U.S. versions since these are less effective in reducing reflux.

If a combination of prevention and pharmaceutical treatment is ineffective, there is the possibility of gluten sensitivity affecting reflux. In such cases, it may be worth trying a gluten-free diet (Jaworek & Sataloff, 2019).

While all the above-listed examples of medications for LPR are available over the counter, singers should consult a healthcare provider if symptoms last for more than a short time. Surgical options that aim to tighten the lower esophageal sphincter are available for treatment-resistant reflux and may be a viable alternative to long-term medication for voice professionals. As surgical methods are continuing to evolve, be sure to explore them carefully.

Singing and the common cold

A cold is a viral infection (rhinovirus) of the upper respiratory tract (nose and throat) that generally resolves within one to two weeks. Colds typically do not involve fever and are, therefore, distinct from the flu and other infections of the respiratory tract. While preschool children (and the people around them) are most at risk for contracting colds, even healthy adults will suffer a few colds each year (Mayo Clinic, 2020).

Because both the nose and throat are affected by a cold, singers will experience some distress. If singing is not necessary, a week of vocal rest (no singing and minimal speaking) will help. That said, people are often able to sing through colds, depending on symptoms. Sinus congestion can be uncomfortable, but as long as the soft palate mostly closes the nasal port, congestion will not affect the sound of the voice to listeners, despite the altered perception of the singer! Swelling in the throat and tonsils, however, can be problematic because pharyngeal resonance will be compromised. Imagine the change in sound in a resonant room if you added shag carpet—soft, swollen surfaces absorb sound.

A cold may also result in coughing. When the upper airway structures become irritated, the body responds by coughing to clear the airways of the irritants. A cough is physically created when the vocal folds are quickly pushed together and then blown apart by expulsion of breath, much like glottal onset but more extreme. Extended coughing and even clearing of the throat can irritate the vocal folds. To avoid harm, try swallowing instead of attempting to clear the throat. If the problem is mucus in the lungs, keep the glottis open and use a forceful contraction of the abdominals to expel mucus. Nonetheless, if the vocal folds have excess/thick mucus on them, Bonilha et al. (2017) find that the only effective method to clear them/reduce mucus thickness (aside from increased hydration) is hard throat clearing (essentially, coughing). Singers should avoid singing when suffering from a cough or if frequent coughing is needed to clear mucus from the folds.

Postnasal drip can cause a cough, which is usually much worse in the morning. Hoarseness and/or difficulty in phonating can develop. If this is the case, vocal rest is best.

Singers who suspect that their vocal folds are swollen/retaining fluids must rest their voices. Singing with inflamed vocal folds risks laryngitis and possibly vocal fold polyps (Sundberg, 1987). Indications of swelling in the folds include an inability to phonate in one area of the voice (typically, loss of upper register production), breathiness in the sound (folds not coming fully together), and difficulty with onset—often a delayed onset. Physical fatigue can be another red flag. Singing will be tiring for a body fighting illness.

A good test of the ability to phonate is to sing "Happy Birthday," staccato, in head voice or falsetto. Also, try vocal fry—if the folds are inflamed, this will be difficult (M. Blanks, personal communication, Dec. 2, 2019). If these things are easily accomplished, the singer should be able to continue safely singing. If not, rest the voice.

The most treacherous time for singers' vocal health may be as they are recovering from illness. The vocal folds and surrounding tissues often heal more slowly, and since we cannot see them, it is tempting to resume full singing before everything is mended. Not only can singers develop compensatory bad habits, they can also do permanent damage to their vocal folds (granulomas, nodules, etc.). Keep testing the ability to sing before returning to full production.

Treatment of colds and coughs

Recommended treatments for a cold are rest and plenty of fluids. Gargling with warm water mixed with salt can be effective in relieving and shortening the period of irritation in the throat. High-volume, low-pressure nasal irrigation is safe and usually remarkably effective (e.g., neti pot and other commercially available nasal irrigation systems). This is essentially a saltwater gargle for the nasopharynx that can shrink mucosal swelling, promote sinus decompression, and even remove irritants (Playe, 2010). Saline nasal sprays can also be helpful. Reduction of irritants by consuming soothing beverages such as warm tea can also be of benefit. The use of a cool-mist humidifier is recommended as well.

Many people advocate the use of zinc lozenges or throat sprays at the onset of a cold. While there have been conflicting findings (Jackson, Lesho, & Peterson, 2000; Caruso, Prober, & Gwaltney, 2007), a systematic review of thirteen clinical trials finds support for zinc lozenge efficacy (Singh & Das, 2011). The review authors conclude that zinc, used within 24 hours of experiencing symptoms, reduces both the duration and severity of symptoms. Avoid sucking zinc lozenges on an empty stomach to prevent stomach upset.

Antibiotics are generally prescribed for bacterial infections. If the infection involves the vocal tract, it is best to suspend singing until you finish the entire dose of antibiotics. Rest and plenty of fluids will assist the antibiotics in doing their job.

Medications for coughs include cough suppressants such as dextromethorphan and expectorants such as guaifenesin. (Expectorants aid productive coughs in removing phlegm from the lungs.) If a cough is productive, it is wise to avoid suppressing it so that problematic excretions can be ejected from the body. But rather than coughing, use the technique involving an open glottis and forceful contraction of the abdominals to expel mucus.

Guidelines for the treatment of coughs associated with the common cold have been updated since our first edition (Malesker, Callahan-Lyon, Ireland, & Irwin, 2017). The American College of Chest Physicians now recommends the use of OTC cough and cold medicines in both adults and children as well as the use of NSAIDS in adults. They also suggest that honey is a possible treatment for children, though it is not better than dextromethorphan (ages 2-18). In our view, honey might also work for adults, but its use has not been studied in older individuals. For persistent/chronic coughs, an inhaled corticosteroid (budesonide) used twice daily for one month may be helpful (Tuzuner et al., 2015).

Prevention of colds

Finally, prevention of colds and other respiratory diseases is one of your best defenses for your voice. Zinc supplements, taken for at least five months, have been shown in two clinical trials to reduce the frequency of colds (Singh & Das, 2011). Studies have also shown that frequent handwashing with soap and water or hand sanitizers with 60–95% alcohol is an effective defense against infection, including gastrointestinal illnesses (Bloomfield, Aiello, Cookson, O'Boyle, & Larson, 2007). It is also helpful to clean devices used by multiple persons, such as television remote controls and telephone handsets in hotel rooms with disinfecting wipes. In addition, when singers have colds, they should cough or sneeze into a tissue or the crook of their elbow rather than into the air or their hands.

Medications with the potential to cause vocal fold bleeding

Singers are frequently warned against using nonsteroidal anti-inflammatory medications (NSAIDs) such as aspirin, ibuprofen, naproxen, and celecoxib (Celebrex), which have the potential to lead to vocal fold bleeding. While this danger might be overstated for products such as celecoxib and ibuprofen, it is a real possibility if higher than normal doses are taken, particularly if a singer is also taking Vitamin E or another supplement or medication with blood-thinning properties. For example, the combination of aspirin and a class of anti-depressants known as SSRIs increases the risk of bleeding (Labos, Dasgupta, Nedjar, Turecki, & Rahme, 2011). It is particularly important to be cautious if taking NSAIDS at high dosage levels or taking multiple NSAIDs. Singers should use caution drinking alcohol while using

NSAIDs, as alcohol dilates the blood vessels. For a safer alternative, use acetaminophen (Klein & Johns, 2007).

Increasingly, middle-age and older singers diagnosed with cardiovascular disease are receiving antiplatelet therapy. This therapy reduces the chance of a clot forming in a blood vessel, which could result in a heart attack or stroke. Warfarin (Coumadin) is the classic therapy, but it has a remarkably high risk of hemorrhage (Shehab, Sperling, Kegler, & Budnitz, 2010). In fact, there is a case study of a singer who experienced vocal fold hemorrhage while on warfarin therapy (Neely & Rosen, 2000). Although warfarin is still prescribed, newer antiplatelet therapies have become more common. One is apixaban (Eliquis); another is "dual antiplatelet therapy," involving combinations of aspirin and clopidogrel (Plavix) or aspirin and rivaroxaban (Xarelto). The risk of bleeding with these therapies is substantially less than with warfarin, but there is still a risk (see Shehab et al., 2010). Singers on such therapies should be careful to avoid chest belting and extended periods of singing involving high tessituras.

Sometimes medications that singers might not associate with the potential for bleeding have significant risks. An example is erectile dysfunction medication, which has seen a meteoric rise in use among men and even among some women (Korkes, Costa-Matos, Gasperini, Reginato, & Perez, 2008). These medications cause dilation of the blood vessels, which can enhance the potential for bleeding. The risk is exemplified by a published case study (Singh et al., 2010) of a 31-year-old male singer who lost his voice due to a vocal hemorrhage after using vardenafil (Levitra).

Hormonal factors affecting the voice

Female menstrual cycle

The vocal fold mucosa contains receptors for sex hormones (estrogen/progesterone), which affect laryngeal function. For females during reproductive years, hormones fluctuate systematically with the menstrual cycle.

Women's menstrual cycles can cause variation in voice quality. The premenstrual phase (4–5 days before menstruation, when estrogen levels are at their lowest) may be associated with fluid retention in the vocal folds. Fluid retention in the folds alters vibration characteristics, which can cause reduced range, fewer harmonics, and reduced sound levels, as well as vocal fatigue. This may affect up to one-third of female singers (Abitbol et al., 1999). Female singers who use diuretics in an attempt to compensate for fluid retention in the vocal folds during the pre-menstrual period should be aware that this fluid is bound; diuretics will not aid its excretion (Sataloff & Hawkshaw, 2006).

- ❖ It is worth noting that some European opera houses offer pre-menstrual cycle leave.

Other phases of the menstrual cycle (menstruation, after menstruation, mid-cycle) do not appear related to vocal limitations for most women (Çelik et al., 2013; Tatar et al., 2016; Arruda, da Rosa, Almeida, Pernambuco, & Almeida, 2018). Findings over time have been conflicting concerning the mid-cycle days of ovulation, but Çelik et al. observe no effect on the voice during this period.

Oral contraceptives

Modern oral contraceptives with a lower progesterone percentage are less likely to affect the voice compared to older formulations. Thompson (1995) states that oral contraceptives do not have a significant effect on the voice. Recent studies actually suggest beneficial effects:

- ❖ A small-scale study suggests that low-dose, monophasic oral contraceptives improve premenopausal women's vocal quality (Amir et al., 2003). Specifically, less variation in amplitude and fundamental frequency occurred among women using oral contraceptives in comparison to a control group. (Monophasic oral contraceptives involve a fixed daily hormonal dose for 21 days followed by seven days of a nonactive pill.)
- ❖ The above-cited study by Arruda et al. (2018) confirms the findings of Amir et al.
- ❖ Another small-scale study suggests that young women using oral contraceptives have a richer harmonic voice spectrum (Kunduk, Vansant, Ikuma & McWhorter, 2017).

Nonetheless, individual responses to such medications can vary. Women who notice a deleterious effect may wish to consult a healthcare provider about alternative formulations or an alternative contraceptive method.

Pregnancy and in-vitro fertilization

There appear to be few vocal changes during the first two trimesters of pregnancy, but during the third trimester breath capacity is diminished, reducing maximum phonation time (Saltürk et al., 2016). In our view, the possibility of increased gastric reflux during the third trimester and vomiting during the first trimester also have the potential to cause vocal problems.

In-vitro fertilization has the potential to affect the voice due to the associated use of hormonal treatments, but there is limited information about its effects. One study (Amir, Lebi-Jacob, & Harari, 2014) found that an increase in estrogen increases the mass of the vocal folds, leading to a reduction in speaking fundamental frequency (SFF). There are also some effects on acoustic measurements, but these are within the normal range and perceived by listeners as normal.

Menopause

Hormone replacement therapy (HRT) has been used to help maintain laryngeal function and reduce mucus thickening as women progress through menopause. Some research indicates that estrogen therapy, a type of HRT, also prevents the lowering of pitch range associated with menopause (Murry, McRoy, & Parhizkar, 2007). Other research with non-professional singers indicates that while HRT maintains a higher SFF, it does not prevent lowering of maximum pitch. Instead, without HRT, the lower end of the range is slightly lower (one half step; D'haeseleer, Depypere, Claeys, Baudonck, & Van Lierde, 2012). Whether this would be true for professional singers is an open question. On balance, we would say that HRT may help some women retain their familiar voices. If desired vocal outcomes are not achieved, estrogen HRT can be discontinued, though singers may still wish to use it for other desired physical and psychological results, for example:

- ❖ A clinical trial of HRT (Schierbeck et al., 2012) shows that women who start HRT early in menopause have reduced cardiovascular risk and no increased risk of cancer. The study was conducted over 10 years, and benefits persisted for another six years—after which the investigation was concluded.
- ❖ Currently, the North American Menopause Society position statement recommends that for women under the age of 60 who are within ten years of menopause onset, HRT can have a favorable benefit/risk ratio for certain symptoms of menopause (Pinkerton et al., 2017). Singers approaching menopause or in the early years of menopause may wish to consult with their healthcare providers concerning the value of HRT. Of course, specific health conditions or family history may pose unacceptable risks for some singers.

Women over the age of fifty are more susceptible to hypothyroidism (low thyroid hormone levels) than are men or younger female singers. Prevalence increases with each decade. Hypothyroidism can lead to a thickening of the vocal folds and, consequently, a lowering of vocal range. The symptoms of hypothyroidism are often very subtle and diverse, making it difficult to diagnose based on symptoms alone. Symptoms may include fatigue, unexplained weight gain, hair loss, swelling in the hands/feet, hoarseness, and cognitive effects such as difficulty concentrating or memory lapses. Fortunately, the TSH (thyroid-stimulating hormone) blood test can readily detect this condition. If diagnosed, levothyroxine therapy is an effective treatment.

Additional medication considerations

Nemr, Di Carlos Silva, de Albuquerque Rodrigues, and Zenari (2018) comprehensively review medications that may cause vocal problems. They also conducted a study to determine which drugs are associated with difficulty phonating (dysphonia). In addition to medications discussed above, their review and research suggest that the following commonly used medications are problematic:

- Anti-anxiety products such as Diazepam (Valium) and Clonazepam (Klonopin)—difficulty with articulation and in some cases loss of voice
- Some angiotensin-converting enzyme (ACE) inhibitors for high blood pressure such as Enalapril (Vasotec)—coughing, hoarseness
- Inhaled asthma medication, formoterol plus budesonide (Symbicort)—hoarseness

Singers taking these medications should be aware of the potential for problems and may wish to discuss alternative dosages or medications with their prescriber.

If surgery is contemplated

General surgery

Some types of surgery require general anesthesia, necessitating intubation. This involves passing a tube through the glottis into the trachea to assist breathing. If the tube is too large or placed inappropriately, or if the balloon holding the tube in place is inflated excessively, singers may be at risk for vocal fold trauma. Indeed, singers often complain of hoarseness or even inability to phonate after surgery involving general anesthesia. Be sure to consult with your anesthesiologist before surgery to discuss the possibility of using a small-diameter tube (e.g., pediatric-size tube). You may also wish to discuss alternatives such as conscious sedation combined with local anesthesia. If assisted breathing is necessary, a laryngeal mask airway

(LMA), which sits above the glottis, is a possible alternative to intubation. Of course, the LMA device cannot be used for vocal fold surgery.

Vocal fold surgery

Singers who must undergo vocal fold surgery will be happy to know that more modern operative techniques are associated with reduced tissue trauma. Newer procedures ensure the removal of damaged/diseased tissue with minimal effect upon healthy tissue. Nonetheless, submucosal scarring that can affect voice quality can occur (Sataloff & Hawkshaw, 2006).

Singers who have contact granulomas, contact ulcers, vocal nodules, polyps, or cysts affecting their singing should avoid surgery until they have pursued a course of voice therapy. One reason for doing this is that voice therapy is often effective by itself.

- Cohen and Garrett (2007) report it to be effective for 49% of singers across cysts and all types of polyps, for 82% of those with translucent polyps
- Saltürk et al. (2019) observe 88% full or partial efficacy for nodules

Another reason is that unhealthy vocal practices are a primary cause of vocal fold abnormalities.

- For example, individuals with muscle tension dysphonia (inability to vocalize), vocal fold nodules, and/or cysts use a relatively high frequency of hard glottal attacks on words beginning with vowels, compared to controls with no vocal fold pathology (Andrade et al., 1999). The frequency of hard glottal attacks is particularly high for females with vocal disorders and may reflect, in part, efforts to overcome breathiness.

An initial course of voice therapy is also recommended because recurrence is highly likely when treatment involves only surgery (Bloch, Gould, & Hirano, 1981). Moreover, unsuccessful surgery may diminish the subsequent effectiveness of voice therapy.

- Ylitalo and Lindestad (1999) note a recurrence rate for contact granuloma after surgery of 92%. The cure rate for vocal therapy alone was 51% but was less (35%) for those who received therapy after failed surgery. Individuals who previously had surgery required twice as much vocal therapy as those who did not have surgery, and they took twice as long to recover.
- Emami, Morrison, Rammage, and Bosch (1999) report that a combination of voice therapy and treatment of gastric reflux is

effective in treatment of vocal fold contact ulcers and granulomas. They reserve surgical and injection treatment for those who are not helped by voice therapy and gastric reflux treatment.

Otolaryngologists often recommend seven days of vocal rest after vocal fold surgery, but some believe that only three days of vocal rest is better because early mechanical stimulation of the folds activates cellular processes that aid healing. A controlled study by Kaneko, Shiromoto et al. (2017) shows that three days of rest, followed by voice therapy, results in better long-term voice quality.

Non-surgical physical treatments of vocal fold lesions

An alternative to surgery is acupuncture. There is now evidence from a well-controlled study that acupuncture can reduce the size of vocal lesions and increase maximum pitch for individuals with dysphonia (Yiu et al., 2016).

Another useful alternative may be transcutaneous electrical nerve stimulation (TENS). When combined with tongue trills, this reduces vocal roughness and improves phonation comfort among individuals with nodules (Santos, Silvério, Oliveira, & Gama, 2016).

Tonsillectomy

Some singers, particularly younger ones, may have tonsils and/or adenoids that are chronically infected and swollen. These swollen tissues compromise sound quality because they reduce space in the oral pharynx and absorb high-frequency sound waves. Enlarged tonsils can also create turbulence in airflow, cause difficulty with articulation, and may result in hypernasality due to interference with nasal port closure (Mora, Jankowska, Mora, Crippa, Dellepiane, & Salami, 2009).

While tonsillitis caused by bacteria is often well treated with antibiotics, singers who experience multiple episodes of tonsil infection each year may wish to consult with an otolaryngologist (ENT) about the desirability of a tonsillectomy. This is typically a same-day-surgery procedure.

Avoid academic medical centers and teaching hospitals with ENT surgical residency programs unless they will guarantee that the surgery will be performed by a faculty member, rather than a resident. (It may be challenging to obtain such a guarantee.) You want an experienced otolaryngologist. One who specializes in treating singers is a plus. Ask about the surgical technique they propose to use. Bovary cautery may cause thermal damage to pharyngeal tissues; coblation is an example of a preferred technique. Let your surgeon know that singing is important to you if you are an amateur and is your livelihood if you are a professional. While scarring is less prevalent today, ask how they propose to minimize scarring and about their post-surgery recommendations to help prevent scarring. Scarring will cause pharyngeal tissues to stiffen and become less pliable (S. Kim, personal communication, January 13, 2020).

After recovery, singers will need to stretch stiffened pharyngeal tissues gradually and regain control over raising the soft palate (Dayme, 2009). They will also need to adjust to their improved pharyngeal space, but that should be a joyful experience. Tonsillectomy in those cases for which it is appropriate solves most of the problems identified above and reduces problems with jitter and shimmer as well (Mora et al., 2009).

> Improvement in the volume of the pharynx after a tonsillectomy also leads to improvements in the amplitude of certain formants. The first formant amplitude increases (recall it is most strongly associated with the pharynx), and the fourth formant appears for the first time in singers who did not have it before tonsillectomy.

Vocal health concerns of professional singers

For professional voice users, vocal health is a life-long pursuit. Vocal dysfunction could result in the loss of productivity and therefore, loss of income and the potential end to a singing career. A study of theatre students found that combining education about anatomy, physiology, and vocal health with a program of exercises in respiration, posture, relaxation, warm-ups, and vocal resonance, resulted in the maintenance of vocal quality (Sezin, Özcebe, Aydinli, Köse, & Günaydin, in press).

Nonetheless, professional singing places a high burden on the voice. In fact, professional singers of all styles have a higher risk for voice problems than non-professional singers (Kwok & Eslick, 2019). Common problems are:

- Gastric reflux (perhaps related to eating late and drinking alcohol after performances)
- Vocal fold swelling (possibly associated with reflux but also with over-singing)
- Hoarseness (often related to swelling)
- Vocal fold polyps

There are also some issues of particular significance for musical theatre performers. The following are among the challenges cited by D'haeseleer et al. (2017) in their study of college students preparing for musical theatre careers, though many could apply to all professional singers:

- ❖ Physical environment—dust, smoke, heavy/hot costumes, makeup, masks
- ❖ Stress and anxiety from limited downtime
- ❖ Insufficient sleep
- ❖ Use of hard onsets
- ❖ Imitating sounds or other singers
- ❖ Using the voice with an uncomfortable pitch level for extended periods
- ❖ Using a high speech rate
- ❖ Speaking with irregular breathing or breaks
- ❖ Talking for more than an hour without a break
- ❖ Performing while sick
- ❖ Singing and acting with poor technique

Musical theatre performers, in particular, have a high vocal load as they combine singing, acting, and dancing with many of the elements from the above list. Rehearsals are long, and, once into performance, there are often eight shows a week. In addition, vocal habits such as screaming, habitual use of a loud voice, speaking with a tensed voice, and shouting above background noise are problematic (D'haeseleer et al., 2017).

Worship/song leaders who sing contemporary Christian music often lack voice training and may belt in an untutored style. Such belting can also occur in an environment with less than ideal acoustics and poor-quality sound systems. A recent survey of 614 such singers revealed substantial percentages with vocal problems, including vocal fatigue, sore throat, laryngitis, and loss of upper range. At the same time, these singers assert that their overall vocal health is good, even though, objectively, there are problems. Many also appear to lack knowledge of good vocal hygiene practices, including warming up prior to singing (Neto & Meyer, 2017).

Vocal health of amateur singers

Even though the vocal demands faced by amateur singers are substantially less than those faced by professional singers, a study has shown that roughly 20% frequently experience two or more vocal symptoms, a prevalence similar to that among professional singers (Ravall & Simberg, 2020). Also, roughly 50% may be at high risk for vocal health problems, particularly females and singers who use their voice extensively in their daily activities (Rosa & Behlau, 2017).

Part of the problem may be that amateur choral singers have limited knowledge about vocal production and harmful vocal habits.

> Ravall and Simberg (2020) find that over 80% of the more than 300 participants in their study are interested in increasing their knowledge of the voice.

All singers can benefit from education on how their vocal instrument works as well as best practices for voice care. Voice teachers and conductors are the most obvious individuals to provide vocal education for amateur singers, either integrated into lessons and rehearsals or as a supplement in workshops and other educational opportunities.

Choral conductor's role in maintaining vocal health

The conductor's appearance and gestures

The way a conductor physically appears to an ensemble has a direct influence on the vocal production and health of singers. Nonverbal communication has a strong and often unconscious effect. Conductors should use gestures that encourage good vocal technique with special attention to connecting their gestures to singer's breathing. They should consider the space in front of their bodies (between their arms and their bodies) and the freedom of their gesture, avoiding rigidity and tension. Some additional gestural considerations include:

- ❖ **Posture**—Practice what you preach. Stand with good alignment, balanced on two feet. Avoid unnecessary physical motions and tension, especially in the neck and shoulders. Try not to lean in toward the ensemble, tipping the torso forward in an effort to engage the singers—instead, have the singers produce energy in their sound to bridge the gap to you.
- ❖ **Conducting pattern**—Conducting with a very large pattern all the time will make everyone feel tense and tired, especially you. Make sure that your conducting pattern does not sway your body out of good postural alignment. Consider the height of your conducting pattern—a lower pattern will encourage singers to use low, supported breaths. A gesture that consistently moves above the conductor's head will do the opposite and create tension in both singer and conductor.
- ❖ **Cues**—Prepare the singers' breaths and infuse your cues with a grounded inhalation whenever possible. Opening your mouth for the choir's inhalations is helpful. Breathing in through the shape of the vowel to follow is useful, so try showing the vowel shape yourself as you inhale with the choir.

- **Cutoffs**—Cutoffs/releases should be clear and prepared. Whenever possible, avoid a rapid clamping shut of the fingers. Singers may respond to this gesture by closing their glottises or their mouths—a poor-sounding means of release in most styles, as we established in Chapter 3. Instead, prepare the cutoff a beat ahead with a gesture and simply show the place for the singers to sound the final consonant, or inhale to stop the sound if it is a vowel.
- **Handshape**—When conducting without a baton, choral conductors should look carefully at the shape of their hands. The shape can affect the tone quality produced. For example, fully extended tense fingers may result in a more intense, strident sound. Try to remind singers of pharyngeal space with your hand and mouth shapes. Generally, you want to create a shape that looks relaxed yet engaged (e.g., a gently rounded handshape).
- **Facial expressions**—Attempt to stay relaxed in your face as you conduct. Show your intensity and connect with your singers, but avoid demonstrating tension, especially in the jaw and lips. When difficult sections of the music approach, show confidence in the ensemble on your face!
- **Difficult passages**—Conductors often do precisely the opposite of what their singers need to see in technically difficult sections of the repertoire. For example, for higher pitches, keep gestures low and grounded near the abdominal/rib support muscles to encourage your singers to stay on their breath support. If the repertoire is fast and rhythmic, keep gestures more precise with little extraneous motion. Be careful not to over-conduct to help your singers avoid unnecessary tension. Be a model of physical engagement without tension whenever possible.

While not part of a conductor's repertoire of gesture, use a healthy, supported sound for your speaking and singing. You don't need to have the tonal quality of a top-notch soloist, but you should use your voice in a healthy manner. A short personal warm-up for you before rehearsal, including SOVT exercises, will go a long way toward helping you stay vocally healthy, too!

Sight-singing

Sight-singing (sight-reading) is a vocally fatiguing activity for singers. When sight-singing, singers are fully occupied with achieving pitch and rhythmic accuracy and have few thoughts about vocal technique. Pitches and rhythms are frequently achieved "at all costs," including singing without consistent support. Often the articulators (teeth, lips, tongue) are overly involved, and breath pressure, as well as space for resonance, is incorrect. Moreover, singers may experience substantial tension.

The result is that extended periods of sight-singing can leave singers vocally fatigued. It is difficult sometimes to avoid this—the first rehearsal of a concert of new repertoire will necessarily involve a great deal of sight-reading. The goal then is to help singers progress rapidly through "reading" the music as quickly as possible and move toward "recognizing" the music as quickly as possible. Some methods of achieving this include:

- Using a neutral syllable (e.g., "ba") or a straw on early exposures to music eliminates the difficulty of reading words and music at the same time. You can use Solfège if it is familiar to the singers. It is frustrating and time-consuming to "unlearn" a passage. Better to learn it well the first time.
- Encouraging the development of muscle memory by singing difficult intervals and passages slowly and concentrating on vocal technique while learning pitches.
- Looking for patterns or repetitions in the music and pointing these out to the singers so that there can be more immediate recognition.
- Rehearsing together sections of the choir that sing similar or complementary lines. During this time, other parts can mentally rehearse or rest.

Standing, sitting, and taking breaks

Encouraging good posture is essential. Make sure you remind your singers to sit and stand, as discussed in Chapter 1 on posture/alignment. Although it may seem obvious, varying whether the group sits or stands at various points during the rehearsal is desirable.

Taking breaks for vocal rest is crucial to maintaining good vocal health. That said, vocal breaks do not need to be mental breaks—keeping singers engaged and invested in the rehearsal is important. Conductors can make some of the following choices in rehearsal to preserve their singers' vocal health:

- Instruct a voice part to rehearse their line mentally while another section sings.
- Have the accompanist play through a chord progression for the singers to hear.
- Ask the singers to speak a line in a sing-song, well-supported sound.
- Allow sections to change the range of a passage, for example, by having the sopranos sing down an octave while learning a high-pitch portion of music.

- Encourage the group to sing at a comfortable dynamic, especially when learning new music or with sections at the extremes of the range.
- Use straws or other SOVT techniques ([v], lip trills etc.) to sing through a passage to reinforce good technique and allow singers to use a method of production that is less vocally taxing.

Mental breaks are also necessary—take time to talk with the choir briefly about the music, tell a story, share a laugh. These moments, rather than distracting the choir from your goal, will allow the singers to connect with you, and relax, increasing their enjoyment of rehearsal.

Full breaks are essential as well. Encouraging singers to get up, stretch, and talk with each other will build community as well as give minds and voices a change of pace.

Never skip the warm-up and consider a cool-down!

A thoughtful, well-planned warm-up, even as short as five to ten minutes, can make a significant difference in the vocal health of the ensemble. (See Chapter 16 for guidance on building useful warm-up sequences.)

- For many amateur singers, the choral rehearsal is the only singing they do each week. Conductors should spend some time establishing the foundations of vocal technique and practicing these principles at every rehearsal. Technique and stamina will improve, and so will the sound of the ensemble. Choose a piece of repertoire to bridge the warm-up and the rehearsal—this should be a piece of music that allows singers to focus on and transfer the skills they have been working on in the warm-up.

A cool-down is also important for promoting good vocal health. See Chapter 16 for cool-down suggestions. If a cool-down is not possible within the confines of a choral rehearsal, conductors should encourage singers to do this on their own.

Plan and pace rehearsals carefully

The order of rehearsal is crucial to an ensemble's success and their vocal health. As mentioned above, it is a good strategy to start with repertoire that resembles an extension of the warm-up as a chance to apply the foundations of vocal technique.

The first piece should avoid extremes of range and be simple enough to allow singers to continue to think about their vocal production. Following this, an alternation of easier versus more technically demanding pieces throughout rehearsal is desirable. As a rehearsal progresses, singers tire both physically and mentally. Finishing rehearsals with more familiar repertoire is encouraging to singers and helpful for reinforcing proper vocal technique. Moreover, if this a memorable piece, it will stay with singers, bringing them inspiration and supporting psychological well-being throughout the week.

Some specific elements of musical works to consider in planning the order of practice for a rehearsal sequence are:

- Tempo
- Key
- Accompanied vs. a cappella
- Tessitura
- Range
- Prevailing dynamic
- Language (familiar vs. unfamiliar)

Tessitura deserves special mention since a sustained high (or low) tessitura can result in tension and vocal fatigue. High tessitura is often a problem for the tenor and soprano sections. Remind singers to modify vowels when appropriate. Encourage excellent breath support and body alignment. Provide adequate time for rest and recovery by allowing the singers to sing a passage down an octave occasionally and by planning breaks in the singing.

Conductors' sensitivity to vocal health can make a real difference

Be patient with singers experiencing vocal health issues or on vocal rest. While singers are ultimately responsible for their own vocal health, conductors play a crucial role in their return to singing. Finally, knowledge of the voice and careful planning will maximize what an ensemble can accomplish and minimize vocal health problems for individual singers.

Chapter 16: A Productive Warm-Up

Why are warm-ups important?

All voice teachers advocate a sequence of exercises to facilitate vocal warm-up and development of technique during individual practice. Choral directors vary in their use of warm-ups, but we believe the choral warm-up process should both physically ready the singers to sing and focus on vocal technique to develop and preserve healthy voices. This chapter presents the elements of an effective warm-up and provides comprehensive sequences of exercises to assist that process.

Importance of choral warm-ups

If you are opposed to choral warm-ups, you might say, "Why bother? Trained singers have probably warmed up already." Or, "Amateur singers are there to sing good music, not sing exercises! Besides, warm-ups waste valuable rehearsal time."

We argue, however, that warming up is a critical part of the choral rehearsal process and it is a mistake to assume that trained singers have performed warm-up exercises before rehearsal. Singers need a warm-up in the same way that warm-ups are desirable before full engagement of muscles in physical training and athletics. This is essential as part of every singer's intentional vocal hygiene.

Most singers who have experienced singing without a warm-up can attest to vocal fatigue a mere 20 minutes into a rehearsal of repertoire. Individual practice sessions and choral rehearsals are more productive when prefaced by a proper warm-up. See the next section for specific warm-up benefits.

Importance of a well-constructed warm-up sequence

A thoughtful warm-up process that addresses important aspects of vocal technique is essential for the vocal development of singers. The warm-up is also the time to continue to practice and reinforce techniques that have previously been mastered. In addition, ensemble conductors can establish rehearsal expectations (e.g., vowel colors) during the warm-up.

As noted in the Introduction, singers benefit from multiple repetitions of warm-up exercises over time – both for skill development and for fatigue resistance. This is essential for the development of muscle memory. Both massed practice (multiple repetitions within a given warm-up) and spaced practice (repetition over time) are necessary to learn and retain proper vocal technique.

Specific benefits of a thoughtful warm-up sequence

Warm-up time provides an opportunity for teaching vocal technique through a careful selection of exercises that will dramatically improve the sound of developing soloists and choral singers. Some of the benefits of a thoughtful warm-up sequence include:

- Warming up the vocal apparatus is essential for reducing tension and creating free production of higher pitches. Warm-ups help with the production of higher pitches because the warm-up process makes muscles more extensible. This is particularly important for developing and aging voices.
- Warm-ups increase blood flow, which improves oxygenation of muscle tissue. Oxygenation is essential for proper muscle functioning.
- Warm-ups are essential for good vocal health. Mindful singing with a focus on tension-free production will allow singers to sing more challenging repertoire for longer periods and recover more quickly.
- Warm-ups improve tonal quality. Amir, Amir, and Michaeli (2005) found that warm-ups reduced noise in the voice as well as disturbances in frequency and amplitude. The amplitude of the singer's formant also increased.
- Moorcroft and Kenny (2012) demonstrated that warm-ups enhance vibrato rate regularity and help to create a more stable rate from one note to the next. They also help to reduce vibrato rates that are too fast and increase vibrato rates that are too slow.
- Warm-ups help singers to sing more efficiently. Semi-occluded vocal tract (SOVT) exercises, in particular, can significantly improve the ease with which singers produce their sound.
- Warm-ups with the proper exercises improve resonance and vowel formation. In the choral setting vowel exercises will help to ensure that all singers produce their vowels in the same way, which enhances choral tuning and blend.
- Warm-ups can provide an opportunity to prepare for more difficult repertoire passages such as those requiring smooth onset of phrases beginning with vowels, staccato passages, and passages with melismas.
- A combination of physical and vocal warm-up procedures improves the sound levels of SATB choral groups across the entire frequency spectrum.

Vocal-only warm-up is similarly effective; physical-only is not. A replication of the study with children/adolescents produced similar findings (Cook-Cunningham & Grady, 2018; Grady & Cook-Cunningham, in press).

Warm-up sequence

The sequence of exercises is almost as important as the exercises themselves. Think of preparing for a game of tennis—you would not start your warm-up by hitting serves as hard as you can. Start with basic exercises and move to the more complicated.

1) Physical stretches to relieve tension
2) Breathing awareness
3) Semi-occluded vocal tract exercises (can also be incorporated in steps 4, 6, 7 and 8 as desired)
4) Connect breath with sound (address onset throughout or in detail here)
5) Vowels and resonance
6) Range reinforcement and extension
7) Linking and mixing of registers
8) Articulation, repertoire-specific exercises (address consonants here or throughout)

Stretching/body awareness

Stretching and body awareness can involve simple, small stretches or more rigorous activity. Children might need to work off some steam, while adults might need to release tension in the neck and shoulders. Everyone needs a reminder to find their best body alignment for singing.

Breathing awareness

Breathing awareness can be as simple as taking a few deep, low breaths with reminders to open at the mouth and glottis, release the abdominal muscles, and expand the ribs for inhalation. For exercises focused on exhalation, remind singers to engage the abdominals and intercostals. More elaborate exercises without pitch can also be included.

Semi-occluded vocal tract exercises

Because SOVT exercises have been shown to have such a positive impact on both solo and choral singing, we have included them here in a category of their own. That said, they can and should be combined with many other steps of the warm-up sequence. A general guideline is to start with SOVT exercises with the highest levels of airflow restriction (e.g., a straw) and move toward more sustained vowels that have the highest levels of oral resistance ([i] and [u]). Lip trills or tongue trills are also useful for their "massage effect" on the vocal folds. See Chapter 3 for a discussion of SOVT exercises and their benefits.

SOVT exercises can help protect the laryngeal muscles and mucosal layers of the vocal folds as they are being prepared for more strenuous singing to follow. In many respects they are like the stretching and flexing exercises that precede vigorous physical exercise (Titze, 2008a).

Connect breath with sound

Use simple exercises, lower register to mixed voice, such as singing through a straw, [v], humming, lip trills/tongue trills, alternating vowels such as [i u i u i u] and slides.

During these exercises, singers should think about a coordinated, flow-phonation onset and work for a steady sound without too much breath escaping. Think about creating appoggio—the breath support governed by the abdominal and rib muscles that is essential for free vocal production.

If the style of singing to follow requires the use of other types of onset (e.g., airy, mix belt), practice their coordination with breath flow as well.

Vowels and resonance

Conductors and teachers should establish expectations for vowels—where they resonate (tongue, jaw, and lip position), the preferred tone color for various styles, etc. Work mainly with cardinal vowels [i], [e], [a] or [ɑ], [o], [u] in this order (the Vowel Spectrum) or, occasionally, the reverse. Sing in the middle range. One or two vowels needing special attention can also be isolated. For ensembles, listen for uniformity in pitch and vowel sound/color but do not fret about minor differences in the external appearance of the singers.

Resonance will work hand in hand with vowels. If a singer lacks proper vowel formation, resonance will be affected. Remember that vowel formation can vary somewhat depending upon the style. Solo singers will generally want to strive toward developing consistent tone quality(ies) for the style(s) of singing to follow. Consider the extent of vibrato as well, including minimal vibrato followed by terminal vibrato in many contemporary styles. The key is to develop tonal flexibility for a variety of styles. Finally, vary the dynamic level to work toward a free, resonant sound regardless of dynamic.

Range reinforcement/extension

Use simple exercises with a small to moderate range to stretch the voice up and down. Generally, work in a rapid, sequential manner to avoid taxing the voice for prolonged periods. Begin with ascending exercises for upper range extension and descending exercises for the lower portions of the range. As singers become experienced and accomplished, try the reverse (begin on a higher pitch and descend). Use vowels that are comfortable—generally [a] or [ɑ] works for women and men, but with males modify to [ɔ] or [ae] in the upper portion of their range, depending upon style. Be sure to use continuous pressure SOVT exercises here!

Linking and mixing of registers

Arpeggios, scales covering an octave or more, octave slides, etc. are all good exercises that will encourage singers to prepare to traverse registers. Singers should consider the variables (heavier versus lighter production, vowel modification, space, breath support, amount of glottal tension) as they ascend or descend. Don't forget to use continuous pressure SOVT exercises to help with navigating register shifts.

Special techniques

The sky is the limit! Choose exercises that address specific issues related to the repertoire to be sung or general skills that a singer or ensemble needs for further development. Some possibilities include articulation, consonant pronunciation, agility/melismas, special effects such as growls, leaps, part independence in ensembles, intonation, dynamics, etc. SOVT exercises can be helpful for agility and leaps.

When creating and selecting exercises, our philosophy is that if the concept and/or technique is challenging, the exercise should be as simple as possible. Simple exercises permit singers to focus on the technical demands instead of being distracted by complicated composition.

Concluding thoughts about exercise selection

Vary vocal exercises from rehearsal to rehearsal, but the underlying concepts (foundations and enhancements of vocal technique) should always govern the choice of exercises. The goal is to use exercises over time to develop singers' voices. Thoughtful repetition is the best way for singers to progress, so do not hesitate to keep certain exercises in warm-ups for more extended periods.

Sample warm-up sequences

The following sample sequences use brief descriptions of the exercises. See the exercises at the end of this chapter or in the body of previous chapters for notation on staves, where relevant.

Sample sequence one (approximately 12-15 minutes)

1) Gently roll the shoulders both frontward and backward. Tip head forward, then upright, then back. Do the same side to side to stretch the neck.
2) Inhale slowly through the nose, then exhale through the mouth. Repeat. Listen to make sure both phases are silent.
3) Beginning on a D, sing through a straw an ascending and descending major third, sliding between the pitches. Concentrate on staying connected to the breath. Repeat the exercise up a half step. Repeat again through the area of mixed voice, and then come back down to the starting pitch. You can switch to humming afterward ([m], [n], or "ng.")
4) Work through the Vowel Spectrum using pairs. Start with [i] to [e]. Sustain one pitch and move seamlessly from [i] to [e] and back to [i]. Concentrate on a fluid motion with no interruption of the resonance. Lower the back of the jaw and allow it to lower a little when singing [e]. Move up and repeat. Then try [e] to [a] or [ɑ], [a] or [ɑ] to [o], and [o] to [u].
5) Sing an ascending and descending fifth on a cardinal vowel quite rapidly. Use a variety of vowels, modifying appropriately according to style as you move through a passaggio. Work to maintain abdominal support throughout, sustaining the intensity of sound and resonance from top to bottom.
6) Starting around C_4/C_5, sing a stepwise descending fifth. Use [i] for the first four notes moving smoothly to [a] or [ɑ] for the final pitch. Continue descending by half steps well into the lower range.
7) Starting in C major, sing legato arpeggios on [o]. Ascend by half steps, modifying as necessary.
8) Sing "mamamia, mamamia, mamamia ma" using the following pitch sequence: do re mi do, re mi fa re, mi fa so mi do. Ascend and descend by half steps. Vary the tempo. Substitute different consonants. Concentrate on maintaining the correct vowel space and using quick,

efficient articulation of the consonants.

Sample sequence two

1) Stretch the arms overhead. Bring the arms down and roll the shoulders slowly, both forward and back. Slowly bend forward, allowing the arms to hang naturally. Slowly straighten the torso, rolling up to a position with the sternum in a comfortably high position. Roll both shoulders slightly back into their sockets to assume excellent standing posture.
2) Inhale over four beats. Suspend the breath for four beats without closing the glottis and without inhaling or exhaling. Exhale over four beats. Repeat over five beats, then six. Singers should maintain rib and abdominal expansion during suspension and resist collapse during exhalation.
3) Using lip or tongue trills (or humming if not able to do trills), start in the lower register and move up and down in whole steps. Ascend and descend back to the starting pitch.
4) In the middle of the range, sing an ascending and descending major scale of a fifth. Sing on "ng" for the first four ascending pitches, then open to [a] or [ɑ] at the top and for the descent. Concentrate on making sure the palate is in the correct position for the style (up for classical, somewhat down without obvious nasality for contemporary). Ascend and descend by half steps, modifying across a passaggio as appropriate to the style. Vary the vowel to [e] and [o].
5) Sing a descending major or minor triad on "ja, ja, ja." Imagine the initial consonant to be an [i] vowel to increase focus and resonance. Work down by half steps.
6) Sing an ascending major scale plus a second, and then descend rapidly. Move up and down by half steps.
7) On a single pitch, sing a messa di voce—crescendo and diminuendo. Pace each phase over a number of counts—4, 6, 8, etc. Vary vibrato extent.

Vocal cool-down

Exercise science indicates that cool-down/stretching after physical activity is important for both physical development and recovery. Currently, there is little scientific research applying this concept to singing. Still, the anecdotal experience of singers and voice teachers indicates it is wise to include a cool-down sequence as part of good vocal health practice.

There are benefits to devoting a few minutes at the end of a choral rehearsal or vocal lesson to relaxed phonation. During this time, singers should focus on easy, tension-free production—though still maintaining breath support. For all singers this can help to relieve fatigue and muscle tension from the entire vocal tract. Also, a soft dynamic can reveal hidden fatigue, information that the singer can use to plan appropriate vocal loading for future practice and performance. This can help move the voice back towards the speaking range, particularly if the rehearsal has involved classical/legit singing with an expansive range.

> ➤ Ragan (2015) found that singers who utilized a consistent vocal cool-down perceived a strong sense of vocal well-being. They experienced a faster recovery time, faster return to baseline speaking voice, and less vocal fatigue.

Cool-down sequence

A cool-down sequence should include SOVT exercises, especially lip and tongue trills—recall the massage effect these can have on the vocal folds (see Chapter 3).

Ensemble directors might also consider a "cool-down song" for their ensembles—a simple piece with legato lines and modest range—to function as a closer for rehearsals.

Here is a suggested cool-down sequence:

1) Shoulder rolls and neck stretches.
2) Straw phonation with ascending and descending slides throughout the range; if a straw is not available use [v] followed by a vowel such as [ae] or [ɑ].
3) Perform lip trills or tongue trills in the middle of the range.
4) Short descending scales on [u]. Concentrate on singing with a coordinated onset designed to produce flow phonation (moderate glottal closure).

Compendium of suggested exercises for warm-up

This section contains a variety of exercises for each part of the warm-up sequence. Many are exercises presented in earlier chapters, but there are some new exercises as well. If you are looking for exercises geared explicitly toward younger singers, these are at the end of most chapters. Sources for adapted exercises are identified where they first appear and are not generally included here.

It is important to note that many of these exercises are basic starting places. We strongly advocate encouraging singers to vary the method of production (e.g., classical, modern legit, belt, light fold closure, narrow or wide vibrato extent, etc.). Choose and develop exercises to meet the needs of your singers. Be creative as long as you are continuing to practice good technique and protect vocal health. Modify any of these exercises by varying starting pitch, vowels, consonants, articulations, melodic patterns, adding straws, etc.

Physical stretches

McKinney (2005) and Henderson (1979) emphasize the importance of physical warm-ups before vocal warm-ups and have many suggestions for exercises. Here are a few that we have found most helpful:

- Expand by reaching the arms out to the sides and spread the legs into a 'sea star' pose, tip the head back and lift the chin towards the ceiling. Then tuck the head, arms, and legs in, contracting. Expand again, then come to a centered, aligned position, ready for singing.
- Lift and lower the shoulders three times in a relaxed fashion. Inhale as you lift, exhale as you lower.
- Pull the shoulder blades back slowly as though trying to make them touch.
- Slowly roll the head around in circles, three times clockwise, three times counterclockwise.
- Move the shoulders around in circles, first one direction and then the other.
- Move the jaw up and down freely while saying "yah."
- Rag doll—let the body fall forward from the waist, keeping the knees flexed. Inhale and raise the trunk easily, exhaling slowly after returning to a standing position. Keep the sternum comfortably high.

During this period of the warm-up you can also use exercises for reducing tension from Chapter 14.

Breathing awareness

- Try taking a noisy breath. Then contrast with a silent inhalation. Notice the sensations associated with each.
- Inhale through the nose then out through the mouth. Repeat. This exercise will slow the inhalation phase and allow singers to more easily sense the passage of air into the lungs. (Breathe through the mouth when singing.)
- Place both hands on the upper abdomen, thumbs touching lower ribs, little fingers near the waist, and middle fingers just touching. Then

release the abdominal muscles and expand the ribs to fill the lungs. The middle fingers should part slightly. This is a good sign that abdominal muscles are allowing the diaphragm to descend correctly. If some rib expansion is felt, this is a further good sign that the intercostal muscles are engaged.
- ❖ Hold this expanded position briefly and observe how it feels. Maintain this expanded position while saying "s" and, ultimately, while singing. Make the "s" hissing sound with a minimum of breath pressure and a metered flow rate, while trying to keep the abdominal and rib area expanded (i.e., holding fingers on the abdomen apart), allowing collapse only at the very end. For an extension of this exercise, try the voiced consonant [v]. This is more like singing and requires more engagement of the support muscles.
- ❖ Take a "snap-like" or quick breath, letting the abdomen spring out quickly (but naturally) for the intake of air. Then meter the air on exhalation as in the sibilant exercise. Breathe in silently when doing this exercise, as quick breaths are often associated with constriction in the vocal tract.

Semi-Occluded vocal tract exercises

For all categories of exercises, try also using:

- ❖ Small diameter straw (2.5–4 mm internal diameter)
- ❖ A voiced, restricted-airflow consonant such as [v]
- ❖ Humming ([m], [n], [ŋ])
- ❖ Lip trills, tongue trills
- ❖ [i] or [u]

Connect breath with sound

- ❖ Using intervals of a third, fifth, arpeggiated triads, etc., slide up and down engaging the support muscles throughout. Listen and feel for consistent breath pressure.
- ❖ Focusing specifically on onset:

    Sing "Ha, Ha, Ha, Ha"—linger on the "h." This exercise gives singers the sense of a breathy onset.

    Sing "Uh, Uh, Uh, Uh"—close the glottis and then sing, lingering on the explosive initiation (almost like a grunt). This exercise gives singers a sense of the glottal onset.

    Between these two extremes is the coordinated onset:

    Sing "Ah, Ah, Ah, Ah"—Images such as pulling a tissue gently from the box, or a scarf from out of a magician's hat are helpful. Performance of these physical actions while singing each "ah" can be beneficial. An extension of this exercise would be to imagine that the tissue box is located just above the navel and to perform the gesture as each "ah" is sung. Try this with moderately firm glottal closure, then with airy and mix belt degrees of closure.

- Good onset, good phrase—sing a pitch three times, concentrating on the onset. Immediately following the third attempt, sing a simple five-note ascending and descending scale. Once onset is consistently coordinated, sing the exercise without the "false starts." Use a variety of vowels, particularly [i], which is one of the most difficult for achieving a coordinated onset.

- Sing an ascending triad and then a descending triad on any vowel. On the top note of the ascending triad, stop the tone by closing the glottis to obtain a sense of a hard release. Then sing the ascending triad and stop the tone on the top note by breathing in. This is the coordinated release. A bonus is that you have already inhaled to sing the descending triad. Be sure to initiate the top note of the descending triad with a coordinated onset.

Vowels and resonance

- Start in the lower/middle portion of the range, slide up the octave and down again, allowing the jaw to lower as necessary. Allow the vowel to shift/modify without predetermining its final jaw lowering. Slide up and down on various vowels.
- Put your hand next to your ear and point your index finger up. Sing [ɑ] in the middle of the range. While sustaining the vowel, move your finger slowly around to a point in front of the nose, allowing the sound to brighten by increasing the elevation/forward position of the hump of the tongue. Continue singing and bring the finger to the back of the head, shifting to a darker tone by depressing the hump/moving it back. This

exercise helps to illustrate the possibilities of vowel color physically. For classical singing, the goal is to have a color that is neither too dark nor too light—"opposite the ear." For many contemporary styles involving belting, you will want to adopt a tonal color that is forward of the ear. For other contemporary styles, tonal color is often an artistic choice. The key is to gain control over the tonal color created by tongue shape. Try the same approach to experimenting with lip position using [ae] or [ɑ]— rounded, almost puckered with your finger at the back, fully spread into a smile with your finger at the front. Also, try this exercise with variations in laryngeal position and jaw position. Finally, put all the variations together to achieve the tonal quality you desire.

- Sing "tele" (as in telephone) over and over on one pitch, concentrating on forming both the "t" and the "l" in the same place (tongue just behind the front top teeth). Return the tongue quickly back to its resting place for the vowel.
- Sing consonants that require tongue movement before a vowel such as [ɑ]—e.g., "la," "da," "ta," "na." Pronounce the consonant quickly and rapidly, returning the tongue to the resting place at the base of the lower incisors. Maintain vowel integrity throughout the exercise. Start on a single pitch, progress to more complicated melodic patterns. Vary the vowels. Try the spectrum in reverse.

- Sing [i], [e], [ɑ], [o], [u], sustaining one pitch. Progress through the Vowel Spectrum, listening to and feeling for consistency of tone and pitch.
- Move from one vowel to the next on the Vowel Spectrum and then back to the first vowel, e.g., [iei], while optimizing jaw lowering, tongue position, and lip position.
- Alternate [i] and [u] on one pitch, stretching the lips outward in a "Cheshire cat" smile for [i] and pulling them into slight pucker for [u]. Strive for consistency of resonance.
- Place a pencil just behind the lower canine teeth and let the top teeth contact the pencil naturally. Keep the tongue in contact with the base of the lower incisors. Vocalize in the middle of the range on all primary vowels.
- Focus on creating a belt sound in the chest register. This exercise uses the [e] and [ae] vowels suggested by expert musical theatre teachers as useful in accessing the belt sound.

Hey, hey yeah ———— yeah!

- Sing [ng] on any pitch in the middle range with the jaw and mouth open in the position of [ɑ] or [a]. Gradually peel the tongue away from the roof of the mouth to the tongue position for [ɑ]/[a]. As you do this, intentionally keep the soft palate down and the nasal passages open. Then gradually lift the soft palate to reduce the nasality. If you are not sure whether the sound is nasal, try plugging your nose.
- Sing "hang-gun-num-ee." On one pitch, move through the vowels quickly to sustain each nasal consonant ([ŋ], [n], [m]) finishing on the [i] vowel. The consonants to sustain are shown in blue. Maintain the jaw position while singing the remainder of the exercise. Change the final vowel to [e], then to [a]. Next, try the exercise quickly. Then add an ascending and descending five-note major scale at the end.

Ha ---- **ng** ---- gu**n** ---- nu**m** ---- ee ----------------

- Ming, ming, ming—change vowels. Same on "kah, fah, vah." The last set helps to create mouth space.
- Ng-ah—start on the top note of a descending arpeggio. Sustain the "ng" nasal. Then slowly peel the tongue away from the roof of the mouth, close the soft palate, and feel the sound resonating in the pharynx. Descend through the rest of the arpeggio on [ɑ].
- Sing the German word "ja" on a descending triad (major or minor—ja, ja, ja). Imagine the initial consonant to be an [i] and move quickly into [ɑ].

ja ---------------- ja ------------------ ja ------------------

Range reinforcement and extension

Slides of a fifth— Start in middle voice (or upper chest voice for males) and move into the upper register. Do the exercise in reverse. Try varying the method of modification—for classical modification, remind females to allow the back of the jaw to lower. Males should close the jaw slightly upon moving into the passaggio and gradually shift the tongue arch forward. For contemporary modification, allow the front of the jaw to lower more as you ascend in pitch. The hump of the tongue should be fairly forward and the lips should widen. Keep the larynx position flexible, but don't allow it to ascend excessively.

- Runs of a fifth ascending and descending, as above
- Try the above exercises using a straw or [v]
- See-ah descending:

See ---------------------- ah ------------- See --------------- ah ---------------

- Runs of a ninth ascending and descending:

ah --

Linking of registers

- Arpeggios, ascending, descending or both – a reminder to try varying the modification strategies as above.
- Runs of a ninth, ascending and descending (see above).
- Arpeggios detaching each note, preparing the space and breath pressure in between pitches.
- Arpeggio releasing after the top pitch, then descending.
- Slides of an octave, ascending and descending.
- For a more advanced exercise, try an ascending arpeggio followed by a descending arpeggio with a dominant seventh, covering the range of a twelfth. As with octave slides, start in the lower register. With classical choral groups, start singing a vowel that can be used in the upper register by both male and female voices, such as [ɔ] ("aw"), though female voices will have to modify this to [ɑ] at the highest pitches. For most contemporary groups, modify toward [ae] as in "cat.'

aw---
ae---

Articulation, dynamic control, and repertoire-related exercises

- Vee-ah. Sing staccato descending as shown below.

- Articulated runs—combine a run with onset and release. Release between each group. Quick tempo.

- Darts and Frisbees—on [i], ascending run of a fifth, two times in quick succession. Then sing legato on [ɑ].

- Rhythmic trill to gain a *sense* of vibrato—move slowly up a half step and back, repeat faster and faster. This is not an exercise to *achieve* vibrato.

- Ascending run of a fifth, staccato on the top pitch, repeat the top pitch staccato, then descending run of a fifth.
- Ascending run of a ninth with repetition of top two pitches.

- Mamamia, tatatia, zazazia, etc.

- Sing a *messa di voce*—gradually increase to forte and decrease. You can vary this exercise by minimizing vibrato, adding moderate extent, and adding wide extent.

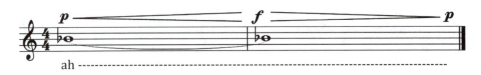
ah

- Try singing a mid- to low-range messa di voce (as above) but start the sound with a growl (un-pitched vocal fry with plenty of air) and then move into a clear, pitched sound. Keep the growl as gentle as possible by exhaling in a relaxed, consistent manner. Monitor tension in the larynx. Be sure also to try practicing this with amplification.
- Sing a sustained pitch in the middle of your range on a vowel such as [a]. Sing with excellent breath support and a vibrant sound. Sing the passage again with a narrower vibrato (less extent). Accompany the second version with a hand gesture to help you achieve less extent—fingers outstretched, palm down, moving horizontally—like "ironing" out the vibrato.
- Choose a voiced consonant and vary how long you sing it. Try singing "mother" by varying the length of [m] from a rapid enunciation to up to four beats. Try a more challenging variation by changing the length of unvoiced consonants such as [s] as in "soft" and [k] in "cool."
- Practice yells by making them musical—almost a sung effect. Focus on good breath support, the vowel shape, and remember to consider the pitch level (not too low, not too high!).
- Spivey and Barton (2018) argue that belting is an extension of calling in speaking. This exercise helps the singer with the concept of calling by crossing normal register boundaries, starting in chest voice, and moving to mixed voice (not head voice). As written, this exercise works for males (an octave lower). For females, lower the starting pitch by a half step or a whole step. (G_5 is the rough upper limit for mix belt.)

Go   a - way   cat!   Hey!   Hey!   ta - xi!

Appendix: IPA Symbols for Important Vowels and Consonants

IPA Symbol	English Example	French Example	Italian Example	German Example
[i]	Feet	bistro	piccolo	Bieder
[ɪ]	Hip	—	—	Dritte
[e]	Base	éclair	repubblica	spähen, sehr
[ɛ]	Pet	neige	bello	Engel
[ae]	fact, cat	papillon	—	—
[a]	Boston (New England, U.S.)	la	gelato	—
[ɑ]	Father	Paques	affare	Vater
[ɒ]	pot (New England, U.S.)	—	—	—
[ɔ]	modern, rod	plomb, bonne	voglia	Knopf
[o]	Tote	tôt, faux	cotone	Tod
[ʊ]	Shook	—	—	Mutter
[u]	Pool	loup	fortuna	Gut
[ʌ]	money, shrug	—	—	—
[ə]	taken (schwa)	demandé	—	Edel
[y]	[i] space of [u]	fumer, lucide	—	Für
[ʏ]	[ɪ] space of [ʊ]	—	—	Tüchtig
[ø]	[e] space of [o]	Joyeux	—	Blöd
[œ]	[ɛ] space of [ɔ]	heure	—	Götze

Table A.1. IPA symbols for important vowels

IPA Symbol (Voiced)	Example	IPA Symbol (Unvoiced)	Example
Pairs of Voiced and Unvoiced Consonants			
[b]	*B*orn	[p]	*p*ower
[d]	*D*oor	[t]	*t*ape
[g]	*G*o	[k]	*c*all
[dʒ]	*j*ump	[tʃ]	*ch*ore
[ʒ]	Le*s*ion	[ʃ]	*sh*ot, *s*ure
[ð]	*Th*e	[θ]	*th*rough
[v]	*V*ery	[f]	*f*our
[z]	*Z*ebra	[s]	*s*ea, *c*ease
[dz]	La*ds*	[ts]	*ts*ar
[w]	*W*eek	[hw]	*wh*ere
Other Consonants			
[m]	*M*en	[ç]	*ich* (German)
[n]	*N*ote	[x]	*ach* (German)
[ŋ]	Si*ng*	[h]	*h*eart (aspirate)
[l]	Fu*ll*	[j]	*y*ou
[r] (retroflex)	*r*ed (pre-vocal) playe*r* (ending)	[ʁ]	*r*ester (French guttural)
[r] (rolled)	Pe*rr*o (Spanish)	[ɾ] (flipped)	Ca*r*o (Italian)

Notes: Technically [ɹ] is the symbol for the "American" retroflex "r," but [r] is commonly used. The guttural [ʁ] is not used in cultured singing.

Table A.2. IPA symbols for selected voiced and unvoiced consonants

References

Abitbol, J., Abitbol, P., & Abitbol, B. (1999). Sex hormones and the female voice. *Journal of Voice, 13*, 424–446.

Alderson, R. (1979). *Complete handbook of voice training*. West Nyack, NY: Parker Publishing Company.

Alves, M., Krüger, E., Pillay, B., van Lierde, K., & van der Linde, J. (2019). The effect of hydration on voice quality in adults: A systematic review. *Journal of Voice, 33*, 125.e13–125.e28.

American Academy of Teachers of Singing (1997). *Tessitura in choral music.pdf* Retrieved February 6, 2020 from americanacademyofteachersofsinging.org.

Amir, O., Amir, N., & Michaeli, O. (2005). Evaluating the influence of warmup on singing voice quality using acoustic measures. *Journal of Voice, 19*, 252–260.

Amir, O., Biron-Shental, T., Muchnik, C., & Kishon-Rabin, L. (2003). Do oral contraceptives improve vocal quality? Limited trial on low-dose formulations. *Obstetrics & Gynecology, 101*, 773–777.

Amir, O., Lebi-Jacob, N., & Harari, O. (2014). The effect of *in vitro* fertilization treatment on women's voice. *Journal of Voice, 28*, 518–522.

Anand, S., Wingate, J. M., Smith, B., & Shrivastav, R. (2012). Acoustic parameters critical for an appropriate vibrato. *Journal of Voice, 26*, 820.e19–820.e25.

Andrade, A. A., Wood, G., Ratcliffe, P., Epstein, R., Piper, A., & Svec, J. G. (2014). Electroglottographic study of seven semi-occluded exercises: LaxVox, straw, lip-trill, tongue-trill, humming, hand-over-mouth, and tongue-trill combined with hand-over-mouth. *Journal of Voice, 28*, 589–595.

Andrade, D. F., Heuer, R., Hockstein, N. E., Castro, E., Spiegel, J. R., & Sataloff, R. T. (1999). The frequency of hard glottal attacks in patients with muscle tension dysphonia, unilateral benign masses and bilateral benign masses. *Journal of Voice, 14*, 240–246.

Appelman, D. R. (1986). *The science of vocal pedagogy: Theory and application*. Bloomington, IN: Indiana University Press.

Armstrong, L. E., Pumerantz, A. C., Roti, M. W., Judelson, D. A., Watson, G., Dias, J. C., . . . Kellogg, M. (2005). Fluid, electrolyte, and renal indices of hydration during 11 days of controlled caffeine consumption. *International Journal of Sport Nutrition and Exercise Metabolism, 15*, 252–265.

Arruda, P., da Rosa, M. R. D., Almeida, L. N. A., Pernambuco, L. A., & Almeida, A. A. (2018). Vocal acoustic and auditory-perceptual characteristics during fluctuations in estradiol levels during the menstrual cycle: A longitudinal study. *Journal of Voice, 33*, 536–544.

Aspaas, C., McCrea, C. R., Morris, R. J., & Fowler, L. (2004). Select acoustic and perceptual measures of choral formation. *International Journal of Research in Choral Singing, 2*, 11–26.

Audsley, G. A. (1905). *The art of organ building (Volume I)*. New York, NY: Dodd, Mead, and Company.

Awan, S. N. (2006). The aging female voice: Acoustic and respiratory data. *Clinical Linguistics & Phonetics, 20*, 171–180.

Basinger, L. (2006). *Acoustical analysis of choral voice matching and placement as it relates to group blend and tone* (Unpublished doctoral dissertation). Texas Tech University, Lubbock, TX.

Berger, T., Peschel, T., Vogel, M., Pietzner, D., Poulain, T., Jurkutat, A., . . . Fuchs, M. (2019). Speaking voice in children and adolescents: Normative data and associations with BMI, Tanner Stage, and singing activity. *Journal of Voice, 33*, 580.e21–580.e30.

Bernhard, C. (1973). (W. Hilse, Trans.). The treatises of Christoph Bernhard. In W. J. Mitchell, & F. Salzer (Eds.), *The Music Forum, Volume 3* (pp. 1–196). New York, NY: Columbia University Press.

Biever, D. M., & Bless, D. M. (1989). Vibratory characteristics of the vocal folds in young adult and geriatric women. *Journal of Voice, 3*, 120–131.

Björkner, E. (2008). Musical theater and opera singing—why so different? A study of subglottal pressure, voice source, and formant frequency characteristics. *Journal of Voice, 22*, 533–540.

Bloch C. S., Gould W. J., & Hirano M. (1981). Effect of voice therapy on contact granuloma of the vocal fold. *Annals of Otology, Rhinology & Laryngology, 90*, 48–52.

Blocker, R. (Ed.) (2004). *The Robert Shaw reader*. New Haven, CT: Yale University Press.

Bloomfield, S. F., Aiello, A. E., Cookson, B., O'Boyle, C. & Larson, E. L. (2007). The effectiveness of hand hygiene procedures in reducing the risks of infections in home and community settings including handwashing and alcohol-based hand sanitizers. *American Journal of Infection Control, 35*, S27–64.

Bonilha, H. S., Gerlach, T. T., Sutton, L. E., Dawson, A. E., McGrattan, K., Nietert, P. J., & Deliyski, D. D. (2017). Efficacy of six tasks to clear laryngeal mucus aggregation. *Journal of Voice, 31*, 254.e11–254.e15.

Borch, D. Z., & Sundberg, J. (2011). Some phonatory and resonatory characteristics of the rock, pop, soul, and Swedish dance band styles of singing. *Journal of Voice, 25*, 532–537.

Boulet, M. J., & Oddens, B. J. (1996). Female voice changes around and after the menopause—an initial investigation. *Maturitas, 23*, 15–21.

Bourne, T. & Garnier, M. (2012). Physiological and acoustic characteristics of the female musical theater voice. *Journal of the Acoustical Society of America, 131*, 1586–1594.

Bourne, T., Garnier, M., & Samson, A. (2016). Physiological and acoustic characteristics of the male music theatre voice. *Journal of the Acoustical Society of America, 140*, 610–621.

Bourne, T., & Kenny, D. (2016). Vocal qualities in music theater voice: Perceptions of expert pedagogues. *Journal of Voice, 30*, 128.e1–128.e12.

Brancaccio, T. (2015). Staying on track: Vocal use points tracker. *Inter Nos, 48,* 8.

Browne, D. (2010, December 26). Trilling songbirds clip their wings. *The New York Times*, p. AR25.

Brunkan, M. C. (2013). The effects of watching three types of conductor gestures and performing varied gestures along with the conductor on measures of singers' intonation and tone quality: A pilot study. *International Journal of Research in Choral Singing, 4,* 37–51.

Brunssen, K. (2018). *The evolving singing voice: Changes across the lifespan.* San Diego, CA: Plural Publishing, Inc.

Bunch, M. (1995). *Dynamics of the singing voice* (3rd ed.). Wien, Austria: Springer-Verlag.

Bush, D. E., & Kassel, R. (Eds.) (2006). *The organ: An encyclopedia.* New York, NY: Routledge.

Callaghan, J. (2014). *Singing and science: Body, brain & voice.* Oxford UK: Compton Publishing Ltd.

Cardoso, R., Lumini-Oliveira, J., & Meneses, R. F. (2017). Associations between posture, voice, and dysphonia: A systematic review. *Journal of Voice, 33*, 124.e1–124.e12.

Carlsson, G., & Sundberg, J. (1992). Formant frequency tuning in singing. *Journal of Voice, 6*, 256–260.

Caruso, E., & Tetrazzini, L. (1975). *Caruso and Tetrazzini on the art of singing.* New York, NY: Dover Publications, Inc. (Original work published 1909, New York, NY: The Metropolitan Company)

Caruso, T. J., Prober, C. G., & Gwaltney, J. M. (2007). Treatment of naturally acquired common colds with zinc: A structured review. *Clinical Infectious Diseases, 45*, 569–574.

Cecconello, L. A. (2010). Caracteristicas acusticas del vibrato en coreutas. *Árete. 10*, 17–25.

Çelik, Ö., Çelik, A., Ateşpare, A., Boyacı, Z., Çelebi, Ş., Gündüz, T., . . .Yelken, K. (2013). Voice and speech changes in various phases of menstrual cycle. *Journal of Voice, 27*, 622–626.

Cielo, C. A., Elias, V. S., Brum, D. M., & Ferreira, F. V. (2011). Thyroarytenoid muscle and vocal fry: A literature review. *Revista da Sociedade Brasileira de Fonoaudiologia, 16*, 362–369.

Coffin, B. (1980). *Coffin's overtones of bel canto*. Lanham, MD: Scarecrow Press, Inc.

Cohen, S. M., & Garrett, C. G. (2007). Utility of voice therapy in the management of vocal fold polyps and cysts. *Otolaryngology–Head and Neck Surgery, 136*, 742–746.

Coleman, R. F. (1994). Dynamic intensity variations of individual choral singers. *Journal of Voice, 8*, 196–201.

Conable, B. (2000). *The structures and movement of breathing: A primer for choirs and choruses*. Chicago, IL: GIA Publications, Inc.

Constansis, A. N. (2008). The changing female-to-male (FTM) voice, *Radical Musicology, 3*, 32 pars.

Cook-Cunningham, S. L., & Grady, M. L. (2018). The effects of three physical and vocal warm-up procedures on acoustic and perceptual measures of choral sound. *Journal of Voice, 32*, 192–199.

Cooksey, J. M. (1977a). The development of a contemporary, eclectic theory for the training and cultivation of the junior high school male changing voice. Part II: Scientific and empirical findings; some tentative solutions. *Choral Journal, 18 (3)*, 5–16.

Cooksey, J. M. (1977b). The development of a contemporary, eclectic theory for the training and cultivation of the junior high school male changing voice. Part III: Developing an integrated approach to the care and training of the junior high school male changing voice. *Choral Journal, 18 (4)*, 5–15.

Cooksey J. M. (1993). Do adolescent voices 'break' or do they transform? *Voice, 2*, 15–39.

Cooksey, J. M. (1999). *Working with adolescent voices*. Saint Louis, MO: Concordia Publishing House.

Cottrell, D. (2010). Support or resistance? Examining breathing techniques in choral singing. *Choral Journal, 50*, 53–59.

Croghan, N. B. H., Arehart, K. H., & Kates, J. M. (2012). Quality and loudness judgments for music subjected to compression limiting. *Journal of the Acoustical Society of America, 132*, 1177–1188.

Cross, M. (2007). *The zen of screaming* (DVD). Van Nuys, CA: Alfred Music.

D'haeseleer, E., Claeys, S., Meerschman, I., Bettens, K., Degeest, S., Dijckmans, C., . . . Van Lierde, K. (2017). Vocal characteristics and laryngoscopic findings in future musical theater performers. *Journal of Voice, 31*, 462–469.

D'haeseleer, E., Depypere, H., Claeys, S., Baudonck, N., & Van Lierde, K. (2012). The impact of hormone therapy on vocal quality in postmenopausal women. *Journal of Voice, 26*, 671.e1–671.e7.

Dargin, T. C., & Searl, J. (2015). Semi-occluded vocal tract exercises: Aerodynamic and electroglottographic measurements in singers. *Journal of Voice, 29*, 155–164.

Daugherty, J. F. (1999). Spacing, formation, and choral sound: Preferences and perceptions of auditors and choristers. *Journal of Research in Music Education, 47*, 224–238.

Daugherty, J. F. (2018). Choir spacing vs choir formation: Long-term average spectra comparisons. *Journal of the Acoustical Society of America, 143*, 1842.

Daugherty, J. F., Grady, M. L., & Coffeen, R. C. (2019). Effects of choir spacing and riser step heights on acoustic and perceptual measures of SATB choir sound acquired from four microphone positions in two performance halls. *Journal of Research in Music Education, 67*, 355–371.

Davids, J., & LaTour, S. (2012). *Vocal technique: A guide for conductors, teachers, and singers*. Long Grove, IL: Waveland Press, Inc.

Dayme, M. B. (2009). *Dynamics of the singing voice* (5th ed.). New York, NY: SpringerWienNewYork.

De Bodt, M. S., Clement, G., Wuyts, F. L., Borghs, C., & Van Lierde, K. (2012). The impact of phonation mode and vocal technique on vocal fold closure in young females with normal voice quality. *Journal of Voice, 26*, 818.e1–818.e4.

Demorest, S. M., & Clements, A. (2007). Factors influencing the pitch-matching of junior high boys. *Journal of Research in Music Education, 55*, 190–203.

Dilworth, R. (2012) Working with male adolescent voices in the choral rehearsal: A survey of research-based strategies. *Choral Journal, 52*, 22–33.

Downes, O. (1927, February 9). The St. Olaf choir. *The New York Times*, p. 17.

Dromey, C., Carter, N., & Hopkin, A. (2003). Vibrato rate adjustment. *Journal of Voice, 17*, 168–178.

Echternach, M., Burk F., Köberlein M., Selamtzis A., Döllinger M., Burdumy, M., ... Herbst, C. T. (2017). Laryngeal evidence for the first and second passaggio in professionally trained sopranos. *PLoS ONE, 12*, e0175865.

Echternach, M., Döllinger, M., Sundberg, J., Traser, L., & Richter, B. (2013). Vocal fold vibrations at high soprano fundamental frequencies. *Journal of the Acoustical Society of America, 133*, EL82–EL87.

Echternach, M., Högerle, C., Köberlein, M., Schlegel, P., Döllinger, M., Richter, B., & Kainz, M-A. (in press). The effect of nasalance on vocal fold oscillation patterns during the male passaggio. *Journal of Voice*.

Echternach, M., Sundberg, J., Arndt, S., Breyer, T., Markl, M., Schumacher, M., & Richter, B. (2008). Vocal tract and register changes analysed by real-time MRI in male professional singers—a pilot study. *Logopedics Phoniatrics Vocology, 33*, 67–73.

Echternach, M., Sundberg, J., Arndt, S., Markl, M., Schumacher, M., & Richter, B. (2010). Vocal tract in female registers—a dynamic real-time MRI study. *Journal of Voice, 24*, 133–139.

Echternach, M., Traser, L., Markl, M., & Richter, B. (2011). Vocal tract configurations in male alto register functions. *Journal of Voice, 25*, 670–677.

Eckert-Lind, C., Busch, A. S., Petersen, J. H., Biro, F. M., Butler, G., Bräuner, E. V., & Juul, A. (in press). Worldwide secular trends in age at pubertal onset assessed by breast development among girls: A systematic review and meta-analysis. *JAMA Pediatrics*.

Edwards, M. & Hoch, M. (2018). CCM versus music theater: A comparison. *Journal of Singing, 75*, 183–190.

Edwards, M. (2014). *So you want to sing rock 'n' roll: A guide for professionals*. Lanham, MD: Rowman & Littlefield.

Ekholm, E. (2000). The effect of singing mode and seating arrangement on choral blend and overall choral sound. *Journal of Research in Music Education, 48*, 123–135.

Elliott, M. (2006). *Singing in style: A guide to vocal performance practices*. New Haven, CT: Yale University Press.

Emami, A. J., Morrison, M., Rammage, L., & Bosch, D. (1999). Treatment of laryngeal contact ulcers and granulomas: A 12-year retrospective analysis. *Journal of Voice, 13*, 612–617.

Emmons, S., & Chase, C. (2006). *Prescriptions for choral excellence: Tone, text, dynamic leadership*. New York, NY: Oxford University Press, Inc.

Eskelin, G. (2005). *Components of vocal blend. Plus: Expressive tuning.* Woodland Hills, CA: Stage Three Enterprises.

Fairbanks, G. (1940). Recent studies of fundamental vocal pitch in speech. *Journal of the Acoustical Society of America, 11,* 373–374.

Ferrand, C. T. (2002). Harmonics-to-noise ratio: An index of vocal aging. *Journal of Voice, 16,* 480–487.

Fisher, H. B. (1966). *Improving voice and articulation.* Boston, MA: Houghton Mifflin Co.

Fisher, R. A. (2010). Effect of ethnicity on the age of onset of the male voice change. *Journal of Research in Music Education, 58,* 116–130.

Fitch, W. T., & Giedd, J. (1999). Morphology and development of the human vocal tract: A study using magnetic resonance imaging. *Journal of the Acoustical Society of America, 106,* 1511–1522.

Fleming, R. (2005). *The inner voice: The making of a singer.* New York, NY: Penguin Books.

Flores, A. R., Herman, J. L., Gates, G. J., Brown, T. N. T. (2016). *How many adults identify as transgender in the United States?* Los Angeles, CA: The Williams Institute.

Flynn, A., Trudeau, J., & Johnson, A. M. (in press). Acoustic comparison of lower and higher belt ranges in professional Broadway actresses. *Journal of Voice.*

Fogle, R. H., Stanczyk, F. Z., Zhang, X., & Paulson, R. J. (2007). Ovarian androgen production in postmenopausal women. *The Journal of Clinical Endocrinology & Metabolism, 92,* 3040–3043.

Freer, P. K. (2010). On the voice: Foundation of the boy's expanding voice: A response to Henry Leck. *Choral Journal, 50,* 29–35.

Friedlander, C. (2018). *Complete vocal fitness: A singer's guide to physical training, anatomy, and biomechanics.* Lanham, MD: Rowman & Littlefield.

Friedrichs, D., Maurer, D., & Dellwo, V. (2015). The phonological function of vowels is maintained at fundamental frequencies up to 880 Hz. *Journal of the Acoustical Society of America, 138,* EL36–EL42.

Frosh, A., Cruz, C., Wellsted, D., & Stephens, J. (2019). Effect of a dairy diet on nasopharyngeal mucus secretion. *The Laryngoscope, 129,* 13–17.

Gackle, L. (1991). The adolescent female voice: Characteristics of change and stages of development. *Choral Journal, 31,* 17–25.

Gackle, L. (2006). Finding Ophelia's voice: The female voice during adolescence. *Choral Journal, 47,* 29–37.

Gackle, L. (2008, Oct.–Nov.). *Adolescent voice: A framework for understanding.* Presented at the 2008 Wisconsin State Music Conference, Madison, WI.

Gagné, J. (2015). *Belting: A guide to healthy, powerful singing.* Boston, MA: Berklee Press.

Galante, B. (2011). Vibrato and choral acoustics: Common voice science issues for the choral conductor. *Choral Journal, 51*, 67–78.

Ganassi, S. (1959). *Opera intitulata fontegara, Venice 1535.* H. Peter, (Ed.), (D. Swainson, Trans.). Berlin-Lichterfelde: Robert Lienau.

Gardiniere, D. C. (1991). *Voice matching: A perceptual study of vocal matches, their effect on choral sound, and procedures of inquiry conducted by Weston Noble* (Unpublished doctoral dissertation). New York University, New York, NY.

Garnier, M., Henrich, N., Crevier-Buchman, L., Vincent, C., Smith, J., & Wolfe, J. (2012). Glottal behavior in the high soprano range and the transition to the whistle register. *Journal of the Acoustical Society of America, 131*, 951–962.

Garnier, M., Henrich, N., Smith, J., & Wolfe, J. (2010). Vocal tract adjustments in the high soprano range. *Journal of the Acoustical Society of America, 127*, 3771–3780.

Gelfer, M. P., & Tice, R. M. (2013). Perceptual and acoustic outcomes of voice therapy for male-to-female transgender individuals immediately after therapy and 15 months later. *Journal of Voice, 27*, 335–347.

Georg, K. (2005). Unifying the voice through registration: Reid's two-register concept of the voice versus Miller's vowel modification techniques. In A. Bybee & J. E. Ford (Eds.), *The modern singing master: Essays in honor of Cornelius L. Reid* (pp. 101–111). Lanham, MD: The Scarecrow Press, Inc.

Gilbert, H. R., & Weismer, G. G. (1974). The effects of smoking on the speaking fundamental frequency of adult women. *Journal of Psycholinguistic Research, 3*, 225–231.

Gilman, M., & Johns M. M. (2017). The effect of head position and/or stance on the self-perception of phonatory effort. *Journal of Voice, 31*, 131.e1–131.e4.

Goodwin, A. W. (1980). An acoustical study of individual voices in choral blend. *Journal of Research in Music Education, 28*, 119–128.

Grady, M. L., & Cook-Cunningham, S. L. (in press). The effects of three physical and vocal warm-up procedures on acoustic and perceptual measures of choral sound: Study replication with younger populations. *Journal of Voice.*

Granot, R. Y., Israel-Kolatt, R., Gilboa, A., & Kolatt, T. (2013). Accuracy of pitch matching significantly improved by live voice model. *Journal of Voice, 27*, 390.e13–390.e20.

Green, G. A. (1987). *The effect of vocal modeling on pitch matching accuracy of children in grades one through six* (Unpublished doctoral dissertation). Louisiana State University, Baton Rouge, LA.

Green, K., Freeman, W., Edwards, M., & Meyer, D. (2014). Trends in musical theatre voice: An analysis of audition requirements for singers. *Journal of Voice, 28*, 324–327.

Guzman M. A., Dowdall, J., Rubin, A. D., Maki, A., Levin, S., Mayerhoff, R., & Jackson-Menaldi, M. C. (2012). Influence of emotional expression, loudness, and gender on acoustical parameters of vibrato in classical singers. *Journal of Voice, 26*, 675.e5–675.e11.

Guzman, M., Acevedo, K., Leiva, F., Ortiz, V., Hormazabal, N., & Quezada, C. (2018). Aerodynamic characteristics of growl voice and reinforced falsetto in metal singing. *Journal of Voice, 33*, 803.e7–803.e13.

Guzman, M., Barros, M., Espinoza, F., Herrera, A., Parra, D., & Lloyd, A. (2014). Resonance strategies revealed in rock singers during production of high notes. *Journal of Singing, 71*, 183–192.

Guzman, M., Lanas, A., Olavarria, C., Azocar, M. J., Muñoz, D., Madrid, S., . . . Mayerhoff, R. M. (2015). Laryngoscopic and spectral analysis of laryngeal and pharyngeal configuration in non-classical singing styles. *Journal of Voice, 29*, 130.e21–130.e28.

Guzman, M., Laukkanen, A. M., Krupa, P., Horacek, J., Svec, J. G., & Geneid, A. (2013). Vocal tract and glottal function during and after vocal exercising with resonance tube and straw. *Journal of Voice, 27*, 523e19–523.e34.

Hall, K. (2014). *So you want to sing music theater: A guide for professionals.* Lanham, MD: Rowan & Littlefield.

Hammer, G. P., Windisch, G., Prodinger, P. M., Anderhuber, F., & Friedrich G. (2010). The cricothyroid joint-functional aspects with regard to different types of its structure. *Journal of Voice, 24*, 140–145.

Hanayama, E. M., Camargo, Z. A., Tsuji, D. H., & Pinho, S. M. R. (2009). Metallic voice: Physiological and acoustic features. *Journal of Voice, 23*, 62–70.

Hearns, L. J., & Kremer, B. (2018). *The singing teacher's guide to transgender voices.* San Diego, CA: Plural Publishing, Inc.

Heman-Ackah, Y. D., Sataloff, R. T., Hawkshaw, M. J., & Divi, V. (2008). How do I maintain longevity of my voice? *Journal of Singing, 64*, 467–472.

Henderson, L. B. (1979). *How to train singers: Featuring illustrated "natural" techniques and exercises.* West Nyack, NY: Parker Publishing Company, Inc.

Henrich, N. (2006). Mirroring the voice from Garcia to the present day: Some insights into singing voice registers. *Logopedics Phoniatrics Vocology, 31*, 3–14.

Henrich, N., Roubeau, B., & Castellengo, M. (2003, Aug.). *On the use of electroglottography for characterisation of the laryngeal mechanisms.* Paper presented at SMAC 03: Stockholm Music Acoustics Conference. Stockholm, Sweden.

Herbst, C. T. (2017). A review of singing voice subsystem interactions—toward an extended physiological model of "support." *Journal of Voice, 31*, 249.e13–249.e19.

Herbst C. T., Ternström S., & Svec J. G. (2009). Investigation of four distinct glottal configurations in classical singing—a pilot study. *Journal of the Acoustical Society of America, 125,* EL104–EL109.

Herman-Giddens, M. E., Kaplowitz, P. B., & Wasserman, R. (2004). Navigating the recent articles on girls' puberty in *Pediatrics*: What do we know and where do we go from here? *Pediatrics, 113*, 911–917.

Herman-Giddens, M. E., Slora, E. J., Wasserman, R. C., Bourdony, C. J., Bhapkar, M. V., Koch, G. G., & Hasemeier, C. M. (1997). Secondary sexual characteristics and menses in young girls seen in office practice: A study from the Pediatric Research in Office Settings network. *Pediatrics, 99*, 505–512.

Hill, S. (1986). Characteristics of air-flow during changes in registration. *The NATS Journal, 43*, 16–17.

Hirano, M., Vennard, W., & Ohala, J. (1970). Regulation of register, pitch and intensity of voice: An electromyographic investigation of intrinsic laryngeal muscles. *Folia Phoniatrica et Logopaedica, 22*, 1–20.

Hixon, T. J., & Hoffman C. (1978). Chest wall shape during singing. In V. Lawrence (Ed.), *Transcripts of the Seventh Annual Symposium, Care of the Professional Voice* (pp. 9–10). New York: The Voice Foundation.

Hoch, M., & Sandage, M. J. (2018). Exercise science principles and the vocal warm-up: Implications for singing voice pedagogy. *Journal of Voice, 32*, 79–84.

Holmqvist, S., Santtila, P., Lindström, E., Sala, E., & Simberg, S. (2013). The association between possible stress markers and vocal symptoms. *Journal of Voice, 27*, 787.e1–787.e10.

House, A. S. & Stevens, K. N. (1956). Analog studies of the nasalization of vowels. *Journal of Speech and Hearing Disorders, 21*, 218–232.

Howard, D. M. (1995). Variation of electrolaryngographically derived closed quotient for trained and untrained adult female singers. *Journal of Voice, 9*, 163–172.

Howard, D. M., Williams, J., & Herbst, C. T. (2014). "Ring" in the solo child singing voice. *Journal of Voice, 28*, 161–169.

Howes, P., Callaghan, J., Davis, P., Kenny, D., & Thorpe, W. (2004). The relationship between measured vibrato characteristics and perception in western operatic singing. *Journal of Voice, 18*, 216–230.

Huff-Gackle, L. (1985). The adolescent female voice (ages 11–15): Classification, placement and development of tone. *Choral Journal, 25*, 15–18.

Hunter, E., & Titze, I. R. (2005). Overlap of hearing and voicing ranges in singing. *Journal of Singing, 61*, 387–392.

Jackson, J. L., Lesho, E., & Peterson, C. (2000). Zinc and the common cold: A meta-analysis revisited. *Journal of Nutrition, 130*, 1512S–1515S.

Jaworek, A. J., & Sataloff, R. T. (2019). Gluten sensitivity. *Journal of Singing, 75*, 303–308.

Jerold, B. (2006). Distinguishing between artificial and natural vibrato in premodern music. *Journal of Singing, 63*, 161–167.

Johnson-Read, L., & Schubert, E. (2010, August). Lieder singers delay vibrato onset: some acoustic evidence. *Proceedings of the International Symposium on Music Acoustics,* 1–5. Associated Meeting of the International Congress on Acoustics, Sydney and Katoomba, Australia.

Jordan, J. (2007). *Evoking sound: The choral rehearsal. Volume one: Techniques and procedures.* Chicago: GIA Publications, Inc.

Kaneko, M., Kishimoto Y., Suzuki, R., Kawai, Y., Tateya, I., & Hirano, S. (2017). Protective effect of astaxanthin on vocal fold injury and inflammation due to vocal loading: A clinical trial. *Journal of Voice, 31*, 352–358.

Kaneko, M., Shiromoto, O., Fujiu-Kurachi, M., Kishimoto, Y., Tateya, I., & Hirano, S. (2017). Optimal duration for voice rest after vocal fold surgery: Randomized controlled clinical study. *Journal of Voice, 31*, 97–103.

Kang, J., Scholp, A., & Jiang, J. J. (2018). A review of the physiological effects and mechanisms of singing. *Journal of Voice, 32*, 390–395.

Kawitzky, D., & McAllister, T. (2020). The effect of formant biofeedback on the feminization of voice in transgender women. *Journal of Voice, 34*, 53–67.

Kayes, G. & Welch, G. F. (2017). Can genre be "heard" in scale as well as song tasks? An exploratory study of female singing in western lyric and musical theater styles. *Journal of Voice, 31*, 388.e1–388.e12.

Kelly, V., Hertegård, S., Eriksson, J., Nygren, U., & Södersten, M. (2019). Effects of gender-confirming pitch-raising surgery in transgender women: A long-term follow-up study of acoustic and patient-reported data. *Journal of Voice, 33*, 781–791.

Kemp, M. (2009). *The choral challenge: Practical paths to solving problems.* Chicago, IL: GIA Publications, Inc.

Killer, S. C., Blannin, A. K., Jeukendrup, A. E. (2014). No evidence of dehydration with moderate coffee intake: a counterbalanced cross-over study in a free-living population. *PLoS One. 9*, e84154.

Killian, J. (1999). A description of vocal maturation among fifth- and sixth-grade boys. *Journal of Research in Music Education, 47*, 357–369.

Killian, J. N., & Basinger, L. (2007). Perception of choral blend among choral, instrumental and nonmusic majors using the continuous response digital interface. *Journal of Research in Music Education, 55*, 313–325.

Killian, J. N., & Wayman, J. B. (2010). A descriptive study of vocal maturation among male adolescent vocalists and instrumentalists. *Journal of Research in Music Education, 58*, 5–19.

Klein, A. M., & Johns, M. M. (2007). Vocal emergencies. *Otolaryngologic Clinics of North America, 40*, 1063–1080.

Knutson, B. J. (1987). *Interviews with selected choral conductors concerning rationale and practices regarding choral blend.* Dissertation Abstracts International, 48, 3067A.

Kochis-Jennings, K. A., Finnegan, E. M., Hoffman, H. T. & Jaiswal, S. (2012). Laryngeal muscle activity and vocal fold adduction during chest, chestmix, headmix, and head registers in females. *Journal of Voice, 26*, 182–193.

Korkes, F., Costa-Matos, A., Gasperini, R., Reginato, P. V., & Perez, M. D. (2008). Recreational use of PDE5 inhibitors by young healthy men: recognizing this issue among medical students. *The Journal of Sexual Medicine, 5*, 2414–2418.

Koufman, J. A. (1991). The otolaryngologic manifestations of gastroesophageal reflux disease (GERD): A clinical investigation of 225 patients using ambulatory 24-hour pH monitoring and an experimental investigation of the role of acid and pepsin in the development of laryngeal injury. *Laryngoscope, 101*, 1–78.

Kunduk, M., Vansant, M. B., Ikuma, T., & McWhorter, A. (2017). The effects of the menstrual cycle on vibratory characteristics of the vocal folds investigated with high-speed digital imaging. *Journal of Voice, 31*, 182–187.

Kwok, M., & Eslick, G. D. (2019). The impact of vocal and laryngeal pathologies among professional singers: A meta-analysis. *Journal of Voice, 33*, 58–65.

Labos, C., Dasgupta, K., Nedjar, H., Turecki, G. & Rahme, E., (2011). Risk of bleeding associated with combined use of selective serotonin reuptake inhibitors and antiplatelet therapy following acute myocardial infarction. *Canadian Medical Association Journal, 183*, 1835–1843.

Lamb, G. H. (1988). *Choral techniques* (3rd ed.). Dubuque, IA: William C. Brown, Publishers.

Lamesch, S., Expert, R., Castellengo, M., Henrich, N., & Chuberre, B. (2007, August 15–19). Investigating voix mixte: A scientific challenge towards a renewed vocal pedagogy. In K. Maimets-Volt, R. Parncutt, M. Marin & J. Ross (Eds.), *Proceedings of the third conference on interdisciplinary musicology (CIM07)*, Tallinn, Estonia.

Lamperti, F. (1877). *A treatise on the art of singing*. (J. C. Griffith, Trans.). London, UK: Ricordi.

Large, J. W. (1973). *Vocal registers in singing*. The Hague, Netherlands: Mouton.

Large, J. W. (1984). Male high voice mechanisms in singing. *Journal of Research in Singing, 8,* 1–10.

Large, J., & Iwata, S. (1976). The significance of air flow modulations in vocal vibrato. *The NATS Bulletin, 32*, 42–46.

Latimer, M. E., & Daugherty, J. F. (2006). F. Melius Christiansen: "Attitude of the director toward the composer: Personal opinion," an annotated edition with discourse analysis of an unpublished manuscript. *Choral Journal, 47*, 7–36.

Lawrence, V. L. (1979). Laryngological observations on belting. *Journal of Research in Singing, 2,* 26–28.

LeBorgne, W. D., & Rosenberg, M. D. (2019). *The vocal athlete* (2nd ed.). San Diego, CA: Plural Publishing, Inc.

LeBorgne, W. L. D. (2001). *Defining the belt voice: Perceptual judgments and objective measurements* (Doctoral dissertation). ProQuest Dissertations and Theses (Accession Order No. 3028707).

Lee, S., Potamianos, A., & Narayanan, S. (1999). Acoustics of children's speech: Developmental changes of temporal and spectral parameters. *Journal of the Acoustical Society of America, 105*, 1455–1468.

Lehmann, A. C., Sloboda, J. A., & Woody, R. H. (2007). *Psychology for musicians: Understanding and acquiring the skills*. New York, NY: Oxford University Press, Inc.

Lortie, C. L., Rivard, J., Thibeault, M., & Tremblay, P. (2017). The moderating effect of frequent singing on voice aging. *Journal of Voice, 31*, 112.e1–112.e12.

LoVetri, J. (2008). Editorial: Contemporary commercial music. *Journal of Voice, 22*, 260–262.

Lovetri, J., Lesh, S., & Woo, P. (1999). Preliminary study on the ability of trained singers to control the intrinsic and extrinsic laryngeal musculature. *Journal of Voice, 13*, 219–226.

Lucero, J. C., Lourenço, K. G., Hermant, N., Van Hirtum, A., & Pelorson, X. (2012). Effect of source–tract acoustical coupling on the oscillation onset of the vocal folds. *Journal of the Acoustical Society of America, 132*, 403–411.

Luchsinger, R., & Arnold, G. E. (1965). *Voice-Speech-Language*. Belmont, CA: Wadsworth.

Lulich, S. M., Morton, J. R., Arsikere, H., Sommers, M. S., Leung, G. K., & Alwan, A. (2012). Subglottal resonances of adult male and female native speakers of American English. *Journal of the Acoustical Society of America, 132*, 2592–2602.

Malesker, M. A., Callahan-Lyon, P., Ireland, B., & Irwin, R. S. (2017). Pharmacologic and nonpharmacologic treatment for acute cough associated with the common cold: CHEST expert panel report. *CHEST, 152*, 1021–1037.

Manfredi, C., Barbagallo, D., Baracca, G., Orlandi, S., Bandini, A., & Dejonckere, P. H. (2015). Automatic assessment of acoustic parameters of the singing voice: Application to professional western operatic and jazz singers. *Journal of Voice, 29*, 517.e1–517.e9.

Manternach, B. (2017). Teaching transgender singers. Part 2: The singers' perspectives. *Journal of Singing, 74*, 209–214.

Manternach, J. N., & Daugherty, J. F. (2019). Effects of a straw phonation protocol on acoustic and perceptual measures of an SATB chorus. *Journal of Voice, 33*, 80–86.

Manternach, J. N., Schloneger, M., & Maxfield, L. (2019). Effects of straw phonation and neutral vowel protocols on the choral sound of two matched women's choirs. *Journal of Research in Music Education, 66*, 465–480.

Marafioti, P. M. (1922). *Caruso's method of voice production: The scientific culture of the voice*. New York, NY: D. Appleton and Company.

Marchesi, B. (1932). *The singer's catechism and creed*. London, UK: J.M. Dent & Sons.

Mason, R. M., & Zemlin, W. (1966). The phenomenon of vocal vibrato. *The NATS Bulletin, 22*, 12–17.

Maxfield, L., Titze, I., Hunter, E., & Kapsner-Smith, M. (2015). Intraoral pressures produced by thirteen semi-occluded vocal tract gestures. *Logopedics Phoniatrics Vocology, 40*, 86–92.

Mayo Clinic (2020). Common Cold. Retrieved 2/8/2020 from mayoclinic.org/diseases-conditions/common-cold/symptoms-causes/syc-20351605.

Mayr, A. (2017). Investigating the Voce Faringea: Physiological and acoustic characteristics of the bel canto tenor's forgotten singing practice. *Journal of Voice, 31*, 255.e13–255.e23.

McCoy, S. (2011). The choir issue, part I. *Journal of Singing, 67*, 297–301.

McKinney, J. C. (2005). *The diagnosis & correction of vocal faults: A manual for teachers of singing and for choir directors.* Long Grove, IL: Waveland Press, Inc.

Meister, J., Hagen, R., Shehata-Dieler, W., Kühn, H., Kraus, F., & Kleinsasser, N. (2017). Pitch elevation in male-to-female transgender persons—the Würzburg approach. *Journal of Voice, 31*, 244.e7–244.e15.

Mercer, E., & Lowell, S. Y. (in press). The low mandible maneuver: Preliminary study of its effects on aerodynamic and acoustic measures. *Journal of Voice.*

Mersenne, M. (1957). *Harmonie universelle: The books on instruments.* (R. E. Chapman, Trans.). The Hague, Netherlands: M. Mijhoff.

Miller, D. G. (2008). *Resonance in singing: Voice building through acoustic feedback.* Princeton, NJ: Inside View Press.

Miller, D. G., & Schutte, H. K. (2005). 'Mixing' the registers: Glottal source or vocal tract? *Folia Phoniatrica et Logopaedica, 57,* 278–291.

Miller, R. (1993). *Training tenor voices.* Belmont, CA: Schirmer Books.

Miller, R. (1996). *The structure of singing: System and art in vocal technique.* Belmont, CA: Schirmer Wadsworth Group.

Miller, R. (2004). *Solutions for singers: Tools for every performer and teacher.* New York, NY: Oxford University Press, Inc.

Miller, R. (2006). Historical overview of vocal pedagogy. In B. Smith & R. T. Sataloff (Eds.), *Choral Pedagogy* (2nd ed.) (pp. 91–115). San Diego, CA: Plural Publishing, Inc.

Mitchell, H. F., & Kenny, D. T. (2004). The impact of 'open throat' technique on vibrato rate, extent and onset in classical singing. *Logopedics Phoniatrics Vocology, 29*, 171–182.

Moens-Haenen, G. (1988). *Das vibrato in der musik des barock.* Graz, Austria: Akademische Druck-u. Verlagsanstalt.

Moorcroft, L. & Kenny, D. (2012). Vocal warm-up produces acoustic change in singers' vibrato rate. *Journal of Voice, 26*, 667.e13–667.e18.

Mora, R., Jankowska, B., Mora, F., Crippa, B., Dellepiane, M., & Salami, A. (2009). Effects of tonsillectomy on speech and voice. *Journal of Voice, 23*, 614–618.

Mürbe, D., Pabst, F., Hofmann, G., & Sundberg, J. (2002). Significance of auditory and kinesthetic feedback to singers' pitch control. *Journal of Voice, 16,* 44–51.

Mürbe, D., Zahnert, T., Kuhlisch, E., & Sundberg, J. (2007). Effects of professional singing education on vocal vibrato—a longitudinal study. *Journal of Voice, 21,* 683–688.

Murry, T., McRoy, D. M., & Parhizkar, N. (2007). Common medications and their effects on the voice. *Journal of Singing, 63,* 293–297.

Nair, A., Nair, G., & Reishofer, G. (2016). The low-mandible maneuver and its resonential implications for elite singers. *Journal of Voice, 30*, 128.e13–128.e32.

Nakao, M., Yano, E., Nomura, S., & Kuboki, T. (2003). Blood pressure-lowering effects of biofeedback treatment in hypertension: A meta-analysis of randomized controlled trials. *Hypertension Research, 26*, 37–46.

National Institute of Diabetes and Digestive and Kidney Diseases (2020). *Acid reflux (GER & GERD) in adults.* Retrieved February 9, 2020 from niddk.nih.gov/health-information/digestive-diseases/acid-reflux-ger-gerd-adults.

Neely J. L., & Rosen C. (2000). Vocal fold hemorrhage associated with coumadin therapy in an opera singer. *Journal of Voice, 14*, 272–277.

Nemr, K., Di Carlos Silva, A., de Albuquerque Rodrigues, D., & Zenari, M. S. (2018). Medications and adverse voice effects. *Journal of Voice, 32*, 515.e29–515.e39.

Neto, L., & Meyer, D. (2017). A joyful noise: The vocal health of worship leaders and contemporary Christian singers. *Journal of Voice, 31*, 250.e17–250.e21.

Neumann, K., Schunda, P., Hoth, S., & Euler, H. A. (2005). The interplay between glottis and vocal tract during the male passaggio. *Folia Phoniatrica et Logopaedica, 57*, 308–327.

Nix, J., & Simpson, C. B. (2008). Semi-occluded vocal tract postures and their application in the singing voice studio. *Journal of Singing, 64*, 339–342.

Nix, J., Perna, N., James, K., & Allen, S. (2016). Vibrato rate and extent in college music majors: A multicenter study. *Journal of Voice, 30*, 762.e15–762.e21.

Noble, W. H. (2005). *Creating the special world: A collection of lectures.* S. M. Demorest (Ed.). Chicago: GIA Publications, Inc.

Opila, K. A., Wagner, S. S., Schiowitz S., & Chen, J. (1988). Postural alignment in barefoot and high-heeled stance. *Spine, 13*, 542–547.

Owen, B. (1999). *The registration of Baroque organ music.* Bloomington, IN: Indiana University Press.

Perna, N. (2014). Nasalance and the tenor passaggio. *Journal of Singing, 70*, 403–410.

Phillips, K. H. (1996). *Teaching kids to sing.* New York, NY: Schirmer Books.

Phillips, K. H. (2014). *Teaching kids to sing* (2nd ed.). Boston, MA: Schirmer Cengage Learning.

Phyland, D. J., Oates, J., & Greenwood, K. M. (1999). Self-reported voice problems among three groups of professional singers. *Journal of Voice, 13*, 602–611.

Pinkerton, J. V., Aguirre, F. S., Blake, J., Cosman, F., Hodis, H., Hoffstetter, S., . . . Utian, W. H. (2017). The 2017 hormone therapy position statement of The North American Menopause Society. *Menopause: The Journal of The North American Menopause Society, 24*, 728–753.

Playe, S. J. (2010). You came to the ED for a cold? *Emergency Medicine News, 32*, 21.

Powell, S. (1991). Choral intonation: More than meets the ear. *Choral Journal, 77*, 40–43.

Praetorius, M. (2004). *Syntagma musicum III.* J. T. Kite-Powell (Ed. and Trans.). New York, NY: Oxford University Press. Original work published 1619.

Prakup, B., (2012). Acoustic measures of voices of older singers and nonsingers. *Journal of Voice, 26*, 341–350.

Price, H. E., Yarbrough, C., Jones, M., & Moore, R. S. (1994). Effects of male timbre, falsetto, and sine-wave models on interval matching by inaccurate singers. *Journal of Research in Music Education, 42,* 269–284.

Ragan, K. (2015). Impact of vocal cool-down exercises: A subjective study of singers' and listeners' perceptions. *Journal of Voice, 30,* 764.e1–764.e9.

Ramig, L. A., and Ringel, R. L. (1983). Effects of physiological aging on selected acoustic characteristics of voice. *Journal of Speech and Hearing Research, 26*, 22–30.

Ramig, L. O., Gray, S., Baker, K., Corbin-Lewis, K., Buder, E., Luschei, E., . . . Smith, M. (2001). The aging voice: A review, treatment data and familial and genetic perspectives. *Folia Phoniatrica et Logopaedica, 53*, 252–265.

Ravall, S., & Simberg, S. (2020). Voice disorders and voice knowledge in choir singers. *Journal of Voice, 34*, 157.e1–157.e8.

Ray, C., Trudeau, M. D., & McCoy, S. (2018). Effects of respiratory muscle strength training in classically trained singers. *Journal of Voice, 32*, 644.e25–644.e34.

Reid, C. L. (1950). *Bel canto: Principles and practices.* New York, NY: Joseph Patelson Music House.

Reid, C. L. (1983). *A dictionary of vocal terminology: An analysis.* New York, NY: Joseph Patelson Music House.

Reimer, C., Lødrup, A. B., Smith G., Wilkinson, J., & Bytzer, P. (2016). Randomised clinical trial: Alginate (Gaviscon Advance) vs. placebo as add-on therapy in reflux patients with inadequate response to a once daily proton pump inhibitor. *Alimentary Pharmacology and Therapeutics, 43*, 899-909.

Ritzerfeld, W. G. J., & Miller, D. G. (2017). Formant tuning and feedback in the male passaggio. *Journal of Voice, 31*, 506.e7–506.e17.

Robinson-Martin, T. (2016). *So you want to sing gospel: A guide for performers*. Lanham, MD: Rowman & Littlefield.

Robison C., Bounous, B., & Bailey, R. (1994). Vocal beauty: A study proposing its acoustical definition and relevant causes in classical baritones and female belt singers. *Journal of Singing, 51*, 19–30.

Roers, F., Mürbe, D., & Sundberg, J. (2009). Predicted singers' vocal fold lengths and voice classification—a study of x-ray morphological measures. *Journal of Voice, 23*, 408–413.

Rollings, A. (2018). The effects of heel height on head position, long-term average spectra, and perceptions of female singers. *Journal of Voice, 32*, 127.e15–127.e23.

Rosa, M. & Behlau, M. (2017). Mapping of vocal risk in amateur choir. *Journal of Voice, 31*, 118.e1–118.e11.

Rossing, T. D., Sundberg, J., & Ternström, S. (1986). Acoustic comparison of voice use in solo and choir singing. *Journal of the Acoustical Society of America, 79*, 1975–1981.

Rothenberg, M. (1981). Acoustic interaction between the glottal source and the vocal tract. In K. N. Stevens & M. Hirano (Eds.), *Vocal Fold Physiology* (pp. 305–328). Tokyo, Japan: University of Tokyo Press.

Rothenberg, M., & Schutte, H. K. (2016). Interactive augmentation of voice quality and reduction of breath airflow in the soprano voice. *Journal of Voice, 30*, 760.e15–760.e21.

Rubin, H. J., LeCover, M., & Vennard, W. (1967). Vocal intensity, subglottic pressure and air flow relationships in singers. *Folia Phoniatrica (Basel), 19*, 393–413.

Saltürk, Z., Kumral, L. T., Bekiten, G., Atar, Y., Ataç, E., Aydoğdu, I., . . . Uyar, Y. (2016). Objective and subjective aspects of voice in pregnancy. *Journal of Voice, 30*, 70–73.

Saltürk, Z., Özdemir, E., Sari, H., Keten, S., Kumral, T. L., Berkiten, G., . . . Uyar, Y. (2019). Assessment of resonant voice therapy in the treatment of vocal fold nodules. *Journal of Voice, 33*, 810.e1–810.e4.

Sanford, S. (1979). *Seventeenth and eighteenth century vocal style and technique* (Unpublished doctoral dissertation). Stanford University, Palo Alto, CA.

Santos, J. K. O., Silvério, K. C. A., Oliveira, N. F. C. D., & Gama, A. C. C. (2016). Evaluation of electrostimulation effect in women with vocal nodules. *Journal of Voice, 30*, 769.e1–769.e7.

Sataloff, R. T., & Hawkshaw, M. (2006). Medical care of voice disorders. In B. Smith & R. T. Sataloff (Eds.), *Choral Pedagogy* (2nd ed.) (pp. 29–59). San Diego, CA: Plural Publishing, Inc.

Schierbeck L. L., Rejnmark, L., Tofteng, C. L., Stilgren, L., Eiken, P., Mosekilde, L., ... Jensen, J-E. B. (2012). Effect of hormone replacement therapy on cardiovascular events in recently postmenopausal women: Randomized trial. *British Medical Journal, 345*, e6409–6419.

Schutte, H. K., Miller, D. G., & Duijnstee, M. (2005). Resonance strategies revealed in recorded tenor high notes. *Folia Phoniatrica et Logopaedica, 57*, 292–307.

Schutte, H. K., & Miller, D. G. (1993). Belting and pop, nonclassical approaches to the female middle voice: Some preliminary considerations. *Journal of Voice, 7*, 142–150.

Sears, T. A. (1977). Some neural and mechanical aspects of singing. In M. Critchley & R. A. Henson (Eds.), *Music and the brain* (pp. 78–94). London, UK: Heinemann Medical Books.

Seashore, C. E. (1936). *Psychology of the vibrato in voice and instrument*. Iowa City, IA: The University Press.

Seashore, C. E. (1938). *Psychology of music*. New York, NY: The McGraw-Hill Book Company, Inc.

Selby, J. C., Gilbert, H. R., & Lerman, J. W. (2003). Perceptual and acoustic evaluation of individuals with laryngopharyngeal reflux pre- and post-treatment. *Journal of Voice, 17*, 557–570.

Sell, K. (2005). *The disciplines of vocal pedagogy: Towards an holistic approach*. London, UK: Ashgate.

Sezin, R. K., Özcebe, E., Aydinli, F. E., Köse, A., & Günaydin, R. Ö. (in press). Investigation of the effectiveness of a holistic vocal training program designed to preserve theatre students' vocal health and increase their vocal performances; a prospective research study. *Journal of Voice*.

Shapiro, J. (2016). *So you want to sing jazz: A guide for professionals*. Lanham, MD: Rowman & Littlefield.

Shehab, N., Sperling, L. S., Kegler, S. R., & Budnitz, D. S. (2010). National estimates of emergency department visits for hemorrhage-related adverse events from clopidogrel plus aspirin and from warfarin. *Archives of Internal Medicine, 170*, 1926–1933.

Sherman, J., & Brown, L. R. (1995). Singing *passaggi*: Modern application of a centuries-old technique. *Choral Journal, 36*, 27–36.

Shipp T., Leanderson R., & Sundberg J. (1980). Some acoustic characteristics of vocal vibrato. *Journal of Research in Singing, 4*, 18–25.

Shipp, T., Doherty, E. T., & Haglund, S. (1990). Physiologic factors in vocal vibrato production. *Journal of Voice, 4*, 300–304.

Singh, M., & Das, R. R. (2011). Zinc for the common cold. *Cochrane Database of Systematic Reviews 2011*, Issue 2.

Singh, V., Cohen, S. M., Rousseau, B., Noordzij, J. P., Garrett, C. G., & Ossoff, R. H. (2010). Acute dysphonia secondary to vocal fold hemorrhage after vardenafil use. *Ear Nose Throat Journal, 89*, E21–22.

Sliiden, T., Beck, S., & MacDonald, I. (2017). An evaluation of the breathing strategies and maximum phonation time in musical theater performers during controlled performance tasks. *Journal of Voice, 31*, 253.e1–253.e11.

Smith, B., & Sataloff, R. T. (2006). Choral singing: The singing voice and choral tone. In B. Smith & R. T. Sataloff (Eds.), *Choral Pedagogy* (2nd ed.) (pp. 171–187). San Diego, CA: Plural Publishing, Inc.

Smith, L. A., & Scott, B. L. (1980). Increasing the intelligibility of sung vowels. *Journal of the Acoustical Society of America, 67*, 1795–1797.

Smith, S., & Titze, I. R. (2017). Characterization of flow-resistant tubes used for semi-occluded vocal tract voice training and therapy. *Journal of Voice, 31*, 113.e1–113.e8.

Spaethling, R. (Ed.) (2000). *Mozart's letters, Mozart's life: Selected letters.* New York, NY: W. W. Norton & Company, Inc.

Spantideas, N., Drosou, E., Bougea, A., & AlAbdulwahed, R. (in press). Proton pump inhibitors for the treatment of laryngopharyngeal reflux. A systematic review. *Journal of Voice*.

Spivey, N., & Barton, M. S. (2018). *Cross training in the voice studio: A balancing act.* San Diego, CA: Plural Publishing, Inc.

Stark, J. (2003). *Bel canto: A history of vocal pedagogy.* Toronto, Canada: University of Toronto Press.

Stauffer, G. B., & May, E. (Eds.) (2000). *J. S. Bach as organist: His instruments, music and performance.* Bloomington, IN: Indiana University Press.

Story, B. H., Titze, I. R., & Hoffman, E. A. (2001). The relationship of vocal tract shape to three voice qualities. *Journal of the Acoustical Society of America, 109*, 1651–1667.

Sublett, V. (2009). Vibrato or nonvibrato in solo and choral singing: Is there room for both? *Journal of Singing, 65*, 539–544.

Sundberg, J. (1974). Articulatory interpretation of the "singing formant." *Journal of the Acoustical Society of America, 55*, 838–844.

Sundberg, J. (1977). The acoustics of the singing voice. *Scientific American, 236,* 82–91.

Sundberg, J. (1987). *The science of the singing voice.* DeKalb, IL: Northern Illinois University Press.

Sundberg, J. (1993). Breathing behavior during singing. *The NATS Journal, 49,* 49–51.

Sundberg, J. (1995). Acoustic and psychoacoustic aspects of vocal vibrato. In *Vibrato* (P. H. Dejonckere, M. Hirano, & J. Sundberg, Eds.) (pp. 35–62). San Diego, CA: Singular Publishing Group, Inc.

Sundberg, J. (1999). The perception of singing. In D. Deutsch (Ed.), *The psychology of music* (pp. 171–214). San Diego, CA: Academic Press.

Sundberg, J., & Bauer-Huppmann, J. (2007). When does a sung tone start? *Journal of Voice, 21,* 285–293.

Sundberg, J., & Romedahl, C. (2009). Text intelligibility and the singer's formant—a relationship? *Journal of Voice, 23,* 539–545.

Sundberg, J., Thalen, M., & Popeil, L. (2012). Substyles of belting: Phonatory and resonatory characteristics. *Journal of Voice, 26,* 44–50.

Tanner, K., Roy, N. R., Merrill, R. M., Muntz, F., Houtz, D. R., Sauder, C., . . . Wright-Costa, J. (2010). Nebulized isotonic saline versus water following a laryngeal desiccation challenge in classically trained sopranos. *Journal of Speech, Language, and Hearing Research, 53,* 1555–1566.

Tarneaud, J., & Borel-Maisonny, S. (1961). *Traité pratique de phonologie et de phoniatrie. La voix, la parole, le chant.* Paris, France: Moloine.

Tatar, E. C., Sahin, M., Demiral, D., Bayir, O., Saylam, G., Ozdek, A., & Korkmaz, H. M. (2016). Normative values of voice analysis parameters with respect to menstrual cycle in healthy adult Turkish women. *Journal of Voice, 30,* 322–328.

Ternström, S., & Sundberg, J. (1988). Intonation precision of choir singers. *Journal of the Acoustical Society of America, 84,* 59–69.

Tezcaner, Z. C., Gökmen, M. F., Yıldırım, S., & Dursun, G. (2019). Clinical features of psychogenic voice disorder and the efficiency of voice therapy and psychological evaluation. *Journal of Voice, 33,* 250–254.

Thompson, A. R. (1995). Pharmacological agents with effects on voice. *American Journal of Otolaryngology, 16,* 12–18.

Titze, I. R. (1989). On the relation between subglottal pressure and fundamental frequency in phonation. *Journal of the Acoustical Society of America, 85,* 901–906.

Titze, I. R. (1992). Acoustic interpretation of the voice range profile (phonetogram). *Journal of Speech & Hearing Research, 35*, 21–34.

Titze, I. R. (1999). The use of low first formant vowels and nasals to train the lighter mechanism. *The Journal of Singing, 55*, 41–43.

Titze, I. R. (2000). *Principles of voice production* (Second printing). Iowa City, IA: National Center for Voice and Speech.

Titze, I. R. (2001). Acoustic interpretation of resonant voice. *Journal of Voice, 15*, 519–528.

Titze, I. R. (2004). A theoretical study of F_0-F_1 interaction with application to resonant speaking and singing voice. *Journal of Voice, 18*, 292–298.

Titze, I. R. (2006). Voice training and therapy with a semi-occluded vocal tract: Rationale and scientific underpinnings. *Journal of Speech, Language, and Hearing Research, 49*, 448–459.

Titze, I. R. (2008a). Getting the most from the vocal instrument in a choral setting. *Choral Journal, 49*, 34–41.

Titze, I. R. (2008b). Nonlinear source-filter coupling in phonation: Theory. *Journal of the Acoustical Society of America, 123*, 2733–2749.

Titze, I. R. (2014). Bi-stable vocal fold adduction: A mechanism of modal-falsetto register shifts and mixed registration. *Journal of the Acoustical Society of America, 135*, 2091–2101.

Titze, I. R., Baken, R. J., Bozeman, K. W., Granqvist, S., Henrich, N., Herbst, C. T., ... Wolfe, J. (2015). Toward a consensus on symbolic notation of harmonics, resonances, and formants in vocalization. *Journal of the Acoustical Society of America, 137*, 3005–3007.

Titze, I. R., Riede, T., & Popolo, P. (2008). Nonlinear source-filter coupling in phonation: Vocal exercises. *Journal of the Acoustical Society of America, 123*, 1902–1915.

Titze, I. R., Story, B., Smith, M., & Long, R. (2002). A reflex resonance model of vocal vibrato. *Journal of the Acoustical Society of America, 111*, 2272–2282.

Titze, I. R., & Worley, A. S. (2009). Modeling source-filter interaction in belting and high-pitched operatic male singing. *Journal of the Acoustical Society of America, 126*, 1530–1540.

Titze, I. R., Worley, A. S., & Story, B. H. (2011). Source-vocal tract interaction in female operatic singing and theater belting. *Journal of Singing, 67*, 561–572.

Tuzuner, A., Demirci, S., Bilgin, G., Cagli, A., Aydogan, F., Ozcan, K. M., & Samim, E. E. (2015). Voice assessment after treatment of subacute and chronic cough with inhaled steroids. *Journal of Voice, 29*, 484–489.

Unteregger, F., Thommen, J., Honegger, F., Potthast, S., Zwicky, S., & Storck, C. (2017). How age and frequency impact the thyroid cartilages of professional singers. *Journal of Voice, 33*, 284–289.

Unteregger, F., Wagner, P., Honegger, F., Potthast, S., Zwicky, S., & Storck, C. (in press). Changes in vocal fold morphology during singing over two octaves. *Journal of Voice*.

Vampola, T., Laukkanen, A. M., Horáček, J., & Švec, J. G. (2011). Vocal tract changes caused by phonation into a tube: A case study using computer tomography and finite-element modeling. *Journal of the Acoustical Society of America 129*, 310–315.

van den Berg, J. W. (1958). Myoelastic-aerodynamic theory of voice production. *Journal of Speech and Hearing Research, 1*, 227–244.

Vennard, W. (1967). *Singing: The mechanism and the technic* (Rev. ed.). New York, NY: Carl Fischer.

Verdolini, K., Min, Y., Titze, I. R., Lemke, J., Brown, K., van Mersbergen, M., ... Fisher K. (2002). Biological mechanisms underlying voice changes due to dehydration. *Journal of Speech, Language, and Hearing Research, 45*, 268–281.

Verdolini, K., Titze, I. R., & Fennell, A. (1994). Dependence of phonatory effort on hydration level. *Journal of Speech and Hearing Research, 37*, 1001–1007.

Verdolini-Marston, K., Sandage, M., & Titze, I. R. (1994). Effect of hydration treatments on laryngeal nodules and polyps and related voice measures. *Journal of Voice, 8*, 30–47.

Verdolini-Marston, K., Titze I. R., & Druker, D. G. (1990). Changes in phonation threshold pressure with induced conditions of hydration. *Journal of Voice, 4*, 142–151.

Vurma, A., & Ross, J. (2002). Where is a singer's voice if it is placed "forward"? *Journal of Voice, 16*, 383–391.

Vurma, A., & Ross, J. (2003). The perception of 'forward' and 'backward' placement' of the singing voice. *Logopedics Phoniatrics Vocology, 28*, 19–28.

Wade, L., Hanna, N., Smith, J., & Wolfe, J. (2017). The role of vocal tract and subglottal resonances in producing vocal instabilities. *Journal of the Acoustical Society of America, 141*, 1546–1559.

Walker, G. (2006). Good vibrations: Vibrato, science, and the choral singer. *Choral Journal, 47*, 37–48.

Ware, C. (1998). *Basics of vocal pedagogy: The foundations and process of singing*. Boston, MA: McGraw-Hill.

Warren, R. M. (1970). Elimination of biases in loudness judgments for tones. *Journal of the Acoustical Society of America, 48*, 1397–1403.

Wells, B. (2006). Belt technique: Research, acoustics, and possible world music applications. *Choral Journal, 46*, 65–76.

Williams, J., Welch, G. F., & Howard, D. M. (in press). Which sung pitch range is best for boys during voice change? *Journal of Voice.*

Williams, S. B. (2006). Turn the world around at the middle level. *Choral Journal, 47*, 123–124.

Willis, E. C., & Kenny, D. T. (2008). Effect of voice change on singing pitch accuracy in young male singers. *Journal of Interdisciplinary Music Studies, 2*, 111–119.

Winckel, F. (1967). *Music, sound and sensation: A modern exposition.* (T. Binkley, Trans.). New York, NY: Dover Publications.

Wolfe, J., Garnier, M., & Smith, J. (2009). Vocal tract resonances in speech, singing, and playing musical instruments. *HFSP Journal, 3*, 6–23.

Woodruff, N. W. (2011). Contemporary commercial voice pedagogy applied to the choral ensemble: An interview with Jeannette LoVetri. *Choral Journal, 52*, 39–53.

Wooldridge, W. B. (1954). *The nasal resonance factor in the sustained vowel tone in the singing voice* (Unpublished doctoral dissertation). Indiana University, Bloomington, IN.

Wuthrich, B., Schmid, A., Walther, B., & Sieber, R. (2005). Milk consumption does not lead to mucus production or occurrence of asthma. *Journal of the American College of Nutrition, 24*, 547S–555S.

Yiu, E. M. L., Chan, K. M. K., Kwong, E., Li, N. Y. K., Ma, E. P. M., Tse, F. W., . . . Tsang, R. (2016). Is acupuncture efficacious for treating phonotraumatic vocal pathologies? A randomized control trial. *Journal of Voice, 30*, 611–620.

Ylitalo R., & Lindestad, P. A. (1999). A retrospective study of contact granuloma. *Laryngoscope, 109*, 433–436.

Zemlin, W. R. (1988). *Speech and hearing science: Anatomy and physiology* (3rd ed.). Englewood Cliffs, NJ: Prentice Hall.

Index

A

Abdominal muscles 22–23, 25–28, 32–34, 142, 144, 156, 186–187, 202, 205, 245, 290
   obliques 27
   rectus abdominus 27
   transverse 27
Acupuncture 273
Adolescents 12, 53, 227, 232–237
Agility 58, 199, 206, 230, 285
Aging 143, 242–243
Airy sound 45–46, 60, 284, 291
Alcohol 259, 262–263, 267
Alignment 9, 17–18
Allergies 259
Altos 68, 113, 152, 178–180, 187, 192, 219–220, 227, 230, 232–233
American Academy of Teachers of Singing 178–179, 181
Amplification 64–65, 74, 128, 149, 152, 173, 200, 209, 212, 296
Anesthesia, general 271
Angiotensin-converting enzyme inhibitor (ACE) 271
Anterior Web Formation surgery 240
Anti-depressants 267
Antihistamines 259
Antiplatelet therapies 267
Anxiety 13, 257, 261, 274
Appoggio 25–26, 29, 183
Arms 13, 15, 17–18, 28, 35, 253, 255, 276, 287, 289
Arrangement of ensemble singers 219–221
Articulators 123, 125, 128, 132, 193, 277
Aspirin 249, 267–268
Astaxanthin 261

B

Balance
   choral 30, 147, 179, 215, 218, 236
   hormonal 241
   of inhalation and exhalation muscles 25
   postural 9–10, 12–13
   resonance 92, 104
Baritones 113, 117, 166, 177–178, 228, 232

Baroque period 152–153
Basses 41, 165–166, 173, 178, 180, 184, 187, 191–192, 197, 212, 219–220, 228
Belt
   chest 47, 51–52, 69, 74, 84, 178, 182, 268
   mix 46, 49, 52, 69, 74, 78, 84, 120, 159, 163, 169, 175, 178, 181–183
   sound 120, 292
Belting 46–47, 50–52, 69, 71–72, 74, 78, 139, 145, 163–164, 182, 184, 218, 292, 296
   raw 51, 236
   styles 46, 72, 81, 110, 163, 182, 207
   vowels 120
Benadryl 259
Bernoulli Effect 38
Biofeedback 42, 48, 240
   auditory 48
   kinesthetic 48
Blend 77, 93–95, 100, 102, 104–105, 118, 148, 192, 196, 213–219, 221–222, 282
Body
   alignment 9, 12, 14, 17–18, 280
   movement 15, 31
Breaks
   for breathing 31, 194
   in phonation 35, 46, 68, 107, 109, 165, 224
   register 168–169, 228, 235
   from singing 260, 278–280
Breath
   cycle 31, 62, 194
   energy 29, 39, 141, 200
   metering 29, 31, 33
   pressure 23, 25–26, 28–29, 32, 47, 61–62, 141–142, 167–170, 183, 185, 190–191, 201–203, 245, 259
   support 15, 18–19, 25, 27, 29, 31, 35–36, 46, 142–143, 186, 200, 202, 204, 284–285
   support muscles 33, 35, 50, 61, 190, 192, 290
Breathiness 30, 48, 53, 60, 224, 227, 230–231, 236–237, 265, 272
   of adolescent females 30, 236

Breathing
    clavicular 23, 31
    contemporary styles 31
    muscles 19, 51, 243
    staggered 31, 148, 193, 206, 217
Breath pressure
    control and firmness of glottal closure 168
    correct 187, 202
    high 43, 129, 168, 208–209

C

Caffeine 259, 263
Cambiata voices
categories 223
Composite Union Range 238
Cartilages 40, 65, 86, 240
    thyroid 40, 42–43, 159, 183, 246
CCM (Contemporary Commercial Music) 1, 181
    and musical theatre 1–2
Celecoxib (Celebrex) 267
Chairs 17
Changing voices 2–3, 144, 177–178, 224, 227–228, 234–235
Cheeks 62, 186, 252
Chest and head voice differences 162
Chestmix 70, 77, 111, 161–164, 168–169, 194
Chest voice 69, 85–86, 109, 111, 113, 158–161, 163–164, 167, 169, 171, 175, 184–185, 228, 230
    newfound 230
Chiaroscuro 74
Children 5, 12, 152, 161–162, 195, 227, 233–234, 266, 283
Chin 10, 12–14, 18, 35, 186, 233, 251, 253, 289
    position 12, 18
Choral
    blend 102, 142, 213–214, 221
    singer positioning 219–222
    warm-ups 36, 166, 281–296
Choral singing 7, 77, 138, 147–148, 170, 177, 180, 213–214, 235–236, 283
    classical 128
Classical production 47, 83, 104, 112, 117, 182–183, 200
Classical/legit production 31, 46, 52, 69, 80, 94, 110, 114, 124, 159, 161–163, 169, 173, 179
Classical style 6, 8, 78, 81–82, 91–92, 96–99, 101, 110, 112–113, 118, 120, 172, 174, 203–204
Clavicles 22–23
Closed quotient 47–48, 57

Coffee 259, 263
Colds 264, 266–267
Conducting pattern 196, 276
Conductors 4–7, 12–13, 34, 54–55, 102–104, 131, 147–150, 179–181, 189–192, 194–196, 213–216, 221–223, 236–239, 275–280
Conscious control 42–45, 48, 245
Consonants 7, 62, 93–94, 115–116, 118–119, 123–133, 192–193, 200–201, 203–204, 209–210, 215–216, 237, 286–287, 292–293
    anticipatory 132
    clusters 124, 126–127, 132, 134
    double 124, 201
    duration 124
    eliding 201
    elongating 124–125, 193
    final 54, 115, 125, 131, 134, 201, 216, 276
    voiced 131
    initial 124, 127, 131, 134, 287, 293
    plosive 79, 89, 128
    release 134
    unvoiced 127–128, 132–134, 201, 298
    length of 134, 296
    voiced 33, 55, 58, 127–129, 132, 134, 290, 296
    problematic 129
    voiced and unvoiced pairs 128, 298
Constrictors, pharyngeal 84, 209, 246–247
Contemporary Commercial Music. See CCM
Contemporary styles 1–3, 12, 67–69, 100–102, 112–113, 115, 117–118, 120, 139, 162, 178–179, 181, 185–186, 248–249
    singers of 6, 84, 125, 246
Contraceptives, oral 269
Contraltos 41, 77, 113, 167, 185
Cooksey's stages 229–230
Cool-down sequence 287–288
Coughing 51, 257, 259, 261, 263, 265–267, 271
Countertenors 159, 172, 184
Cricoarytenoids, lateral 45
Cricothyroid Approximation surgery 241
Cricothyroids (CT) 40, 42–43, 51, 84, 135, 144, 158–160, 162–163, 166, 168, 183–184, 241
    control 52, 145, 159–162
    CT-dominant production 207
    tilt 13–14, 28, 159, 183, 254
Cutoffs 216, 222, 276

D

dB (decibels) 29, 77, 170
Dehydrating substances 259, 262
Dextromethorphan 266
Diaphragm 19–21, 25, 27–29, 34, 79, 202, 262, 290
Diphenhydramine (Benadryl) 259
Diphthongs 54, 114–116, 121, 126, 192, 210
    contemporary styles 114
Diuretics 259, 268
Dynamic control 170, 199–212, 234, 294
Dysphonia 271, 273
    muscle tension 272

E

Early music 138, 150, 152–153, 194
Ears 10, 23, 76, 90, 100–101, 119–120, 147–148, 189, 248, 291–292
Elastic reversion 38
Electroglottograph 146, 158
Electronic processing 87
Emotion 135, 138, 157, 183, 204, 208
    expressing strong 139
English choirboy sound 162
ENT (otolaryngologist) 272–273
Epilarynx 47, 59, 63, 66, 75, 79, 83–84, 169
Estrogen 240–241, 269
Exhalation
    ceasing 202
    control of 27–28
    muscles 25
Expansion 21, 33–34, 36, 230
    abdominal 21, 33, 287
    rib 34, 290
Expectorants 266

F

Facial muscles 15, 92
Falsetto 158–160, 165–166, 168, 170–172, 174–175, 178, 184, 187, 213, 219, 228, 232, 261, 265
    reinforced 3, 164, 171–172, 178–179, 184
Fatigue 148, 184, 195, 257, 260, 270
Feet 10, 17–18, 216, 255–256
Female menstrual cycle 268
Flow phonation 45, 86, 155, 206, 288
Fluid retention 268
Fluids 242, 258, 266, 268
Formant 48, 67–70, 74, 76–77, 82, 101, 108, 111, 118, 130, 183, 274
    first 56, 68, 72, 74, 84, 88, 100, 109–112, 131
    second 70, 81–82, 85, 87, 97, 103, 107–108, 110–111, 171, 191
    singer's 47–48, 51, 71, 74–77, 79, 149, 153, 218, 282
    high-amplitude 77, 89
    speaker's 74, 77, 84
    tuning 68, 107, 110
Formant amplification of harmonics, example 72
Formants, lowest 70
Fundamental frequency 38, 42, 51, 64–65, 69, 72, 76, 85, 107, 109–112, 149, 153, 159–160, 170–171

G

Gackle's phases 230
Gastric reflux 244, 257, 263, 272, 274
Gaviscon Advance 264
Gender identity and expression 238–240
Girls 30, 224–225, 227, 229–230, 232–233, 235, 238
    adolescent 231, 236
Glides 101, 114–115, 127
Glottal
    hard 50, 201
    soft 50, 201
Glottal closure
    firm 46–47, 50, 65, 69, 74, 141, 149, 164, 171–172, 174, 291
    moderate 46, 110, 141, 288
    scale 45
Glottal tension, excessive 47
Glottis 22, 24, 36, 38–40, 42, 45, 49–50, 54, 59–62, 183, 205–206, 245, 271, 290–291
Granuloma 272
Gum line 67, 93–94, 119, 123

H

Hamstrings 256
Harmonic crossovers 107, 109, 167
    destabilizing 107, 109
    preventing 72
Harmonic frequencies 45, 48, 64–65, 67–69, 72, 75–76, 82, 85, 87, 107, 117–118, 165, 167, 172
Headmix 70, 161–164, 168–169, 194, 207
Head position 12, 18, 104, 247
Head voice 65, 69, 84–86, 110, 113, 158–164, 166, 168–172, 174–175, 179–180, 183–184, 228, 230, 232–233
    accessing 164, 174, 184, 187, 233
    female 160, 170
    male 171, 184
Heels 10, 13–14, 256
Hips 16, 297
    hip/glutes stretch 256

Histamine blockers 263
Hoarseness 260–261, 263, 265, 270–271, 274
Homogeneous sound 213–214
Honey 250, 266
Hormones 223, 257, 268
HRT (Hormone replacement therapy) 3, 270
Hydration 38, 242, 257–259
Hyoid bone 39–40, 65–66, 94, 246, 249
Hypothyroidism 270

I

Ibuprofen 249, 267
Incisors 67, 70, 91, 93–94, 118–119, 130, 134, 255, 292
Inhalation 19–21, 23–26, 32–33, 35, 47, 78, 144, 156, 174, 193, 202, 253, 258, 261
    silent 33, 289
Initiation of sound 2, 30, 37, 144, 156, 245, 257
Intelligibility 4, 72, 93–94, 101–102, 112, 118, 124–125, 131
Interarytenoids 30, 45, 245
Intercostal muscles 19–20, 25–28, 33–35, 37, 49, 194, 284, 290
    external 25
    internal 25
Intonation 13, 31, 85, 93, 100, 102, 123, 138, 149, 190–197, 202, 217, 219, 285
    horizontal (melodic) 189, 197
    instability 194
    vertical 190, 197
Intonation problems 95, 104, 147, 192–195
    horizontal 189–190
    individual 190
    solving 193–194
    vertical 189
IPA (International Phonetic Alphabet) 7, 95, 127, 134, 297

J

Jaw 69–70, 72, 79–81, 90–93, 96–98, 103–104, 111–113, 116, 118–121, 123–127, 133–134, 245–248, 254, 293
    movements 97, 125–126, 141, 204, 248–249
    position 3, 66, 97–98, 100–101, 118, 120, 126, 292–293
    protrusion 170
    tension 81, 247–248
Jazz 46, 69, 118, 140, 173, 177, 194, 200, 203–204
    singers 101, 109, 189

K

Knees 10, 14, 17–18, 27–28, 256, 289
    locked 14, 253

L

Laryngeal mask airway (LMA) 271
Laryngitis 263, 275
    inflamed vocal folds risk 265
Larynx 12, 39–45, 65–66, 70–72, 78–79, 83–84, 111–113, 117, 168, 183, 186–187, 204, 245–247, 249–252
    position 3, 101, 120–121, 146, 174, 183, 292, 294
    high 78, 141, 171
    low 78, 89, 108, 117–118, 143, 185, 188
    structures, illustrations 39–43
    tension 142, 144, 180, 186, 247
    ventricles 75
Leaps in pitch 30, 185–186, 188–189, 197, 285
Legato 2, 126, 199–211
Legit
    modern 85, 113, 118, 289
    roles 163–164
Legs 10, 16–17, 28, 245, 253, 255–256, 289
Lips 55–56, 62–63, 71, 97–98, 101–103, 111–113, 116, 118–121, 123–125, 127–128, 252, 255, 277, 287–288
Loratadine (Claritin) 259
LPR (laryngopharyngeal reflux) 263–264
Lungs 20–28, 33–34, 36, 39, 66, 244, 253, 265–266, 289–290

M

Marcato 203, 210
Martellato 203, 210
Medications 257, 264, 266–267, 269, 271
    anti-inflammatory 249, 267
    cold 266
    erectile dysfunction 268
Melismas/runs 28, 199, 201–211, 282
    learning 205
    singing choral 206
    technique 204
Menopause 241, 243, 270
Menstrual cycle 239, 268
Messa di voce 155, 207, 212, 217, 287, 295
Mezzo-sopranos 113, 167, 177–178, 185
Mucus 242, 257, 259, 262, 265–266
    effects of dairy products 262–263
    excess 259, 262, 265
    persistent nasal/pharyngeal 263

Muscle memory 5, 48, 186, 189–190, 195–196, 205, 216, 237, 278, 282
Muscles
　atrophy 241, 244
　cheek 186, 252
　cricothyroid 40, 42–43, 51, 84, 135, 144, 158–160, 162–163, 166, 168, 183–184, 241
　inhalation 25, 261
　jaw 144, 247
　laryngeal 30, 48, 135, 139, 141, 143, 170, 186, 204, 224, 241, 284
　leg 253, 256
　masseter 248
　neck 12, 24–25, 254
　respiratory 32
　thyroarytenoid (TA) 42–44, 51–52, 111, 117, 135, 143, 145, 158–161, 165
Musical theatre 1–2, 8, 46–47, 50, 52, 82–83, 85, 95, 101, 118, 124, 178–179, 181, 193
　performers 46, 110, 112, 124, 142, 163–164, 274–275
　roles 178, 208
　teachers 3, 31, 120, 292
　types of shows 181–182
　voice requirements 181
　vowels 101
Music folders 13, 253
Myoelastic-aerodynamic theory 38

N

Naproxen sodium 249
Nasal
　consonants 55, 58, 67, 86, 88, 123, 126, 133, 169, 188, 293
　irrigation systems 266
　passages 58, 79, 86, 88, 90, 293
　pharynx 65, 67, 88
Nasality 67, 80, 88, 90, 104, 169, 287, 293
Neck 15, 17, 28, 35, 91, 183, 190, 245, 248, 252, 276, 283, 286, 288
　muscle tension 33
Neutral vowels 95, 105–106
　stressed vs. unstressed 106
New Voice and Emerging Voice categories 238
NSAIDs 266–267

O

Octave slides 174, 285, 294
　ascending 174
　downward 185, 188
Onset 34, 53, 60, 62, 199, 202–203, 207, 224, 253, 265–266, 284, 290–291, 295
　breathy 49, 53–54, 60, 207, 290
　coordinated 49–51, 53, 60–62, 142, 144, 155, 187, 202, 209, 224, 288, 290–291
　glottal 49–51, 53–54, 60, 141–142, 156, 199, 202–203, 208, 210, 265, 290
　hard-glottal 50–51
Oral pharynx 65–67, 79, 81, 84, 117, 273
Ornaments 138, 150, 203–204
Orthodontics 237
Otolaryngologist (ENT) 272–273
Overtones 45, 47, 64, 85

P

Palate 70, 79–80, 287
　hard 88–89, 123, 127, 129, 237
　raised soft 80, 143
Passaggio 113, 121, 164–166, 169, 171, 183, 190, 193, 254, 286–287, 293
　first 109, 113, 161, 164, 167, 169, 174, 180, 254
　second 113, 161, 167–168, 180
Performance spaces 87, 153, 221
　modern 152
Pharyngeal space 83, 90–91, 277
Pharynx 30, 63, 70, 75, 78–80, 82–86, 91, 117, 121, 144, 170, 172, 245–249, 274
　constriction 246
Phases of vocal development 229–231
Pitch 41–44, 60–61, 107–113, 131–133, 135–136, 154–155, 157–161, 163–166, 168–172, 178–181, 189–191, 193–197, 202–206, 291–295
　accented 203
　accuracy 149
　comfortable 177
　control 40, 48, 173, 191, 224, 235, 240
　high 26, 28–30, 43, 78, 80, 107–109, 111–112, 128, 170–171, 183, 185, 207, 229, 241
　low 41, 63, 72, 86, 110, 113, 158–159, 161, 171, 174–175, 180, 183–185, 187–188, 229
　matching 195, 224
　perceived 85, 102, 125
Placement 86, 89, 91, 167, 219
　"forward" 86, 88–89
　sections and voice matching 222
Polyps 3, 51–52, 209, 272
Pop/rock 139, 159, 171, 182, 184
　musicals 178, 204
Position
　head and chin 12
　highest point of tongue 96

lip 69, 98, 101, 119–120, 284, 292
tongue resting 83, 93
Postnasal drip 265
Posture/alignment 2, 9–10, 12, 14, 17, 136, 234, 253, 274, 276
   good seated 16–17
   optimal singing 10
   overeager 14–15
PPIs (proton pump inhibitors) 263–264
Pregnancy 269
Premenstrual phase 268
Pressed phonation 191, 244
Pressure, subglottal 29, 46, 183, 207
Puberty 161, 223–224, 227, 230, 236
Pulse register (vocal fry) 173

Q
Quadriceps stretching exercise 14

R
"r"
   American 129, 134
   flipped 129–130
   retroflex 129–130, 134, 298
      pre-vocal 129–130
   rolled 129–130
Rag doll 17, 289
Range 76–78, 111–113, 136–137, 149, 163–165, 167–168, 177–182, 184–188, 227–231, 238–241, 243, 278–280, 287–288, 291–292
   comfortable 178, 180, 230–231
   extension 173, 187
   increasing 2, 177, 186
   safe 178
Reflux
   gastric 262–264, 274
   laryngopharyngeal 263
Register
   head (upper) 65, 69, 84–86, 110, 113, 158–164, 166, 168–172, 174–175, 179–180, 183–184, 228, 230, 232–233
   lower (chest) 69, 77, 155, 158–159, 163–164, 166–169, 173–175, 184–185, 228, 233, 284, 287, 292, 294
   middle (mixed voice) 84, 120, 155, 158, 160, 162, 167–169, 185, 187, 207, 230–231, 233, 293
   pulse (vocal fry) 173
Registers 49, 51–52, 69–70, 109, 156–159, 162, 164–166, 170–171, 173, 175–177, 184–185, 193–194, 233, 237–238
   blending 162
   in unchanged voices 233

Register transitions 3, 55, 93, 109, 157, 165, 167–169, 173–174, 182, 224, 230, 234, 237
   female 166
   male 166, 169
   sudden in contemporary styles 165
Release of sound 2, 20, 22, 33–35, 37, 54, 62, 134, 144, 156, 194, 203, 290, 295
   coordinated 62, 291
   glottal 54
Resistance, glottal 46–47, 61
Resonance 47–48, 50–51, 63–64, 67–68, 70–71, 85–86, 88–90, 102–103, 117–120, 125–126, 158–159, 200, 247–249, 284
   balanced 104, 206
   cavity 85, 117, 159, 231
   conductive 85–86, 88, 159
   enhancing 84, 89
   improved 55, 223, 228
   nasal 67
   pharyngeal 91, 101–102, 104, 117, 265
   subglottal 165
   sympathetic 85
Resonators 10, 37, 63, 67–69, 74, 85
Respiratory muscle training 32, 242
Reverberation 3, 87
Ribs 9–10, 21, 23–25, 29, 33–34, 183, 253, 283, 287, 290
Ridge, alveolar 123, 129, 255
Riffs/melismas 28, 199–211, 282
Rock 1, 10, 46–47, 49–52, 54, 69, 74, 83–84, 118, 140, 157, 173, 177, 182

S
Scat 203–204
Schwa 95, 106, 114, 124, 297
Scoops in pitch
   intentional 125
   unintentional 30, 44, 124–125, 134
Screams 208–209, 212
Self-to-other loudness ratio, improved 220
Semi-occluded vocal tract. See SOVT
SFF (speaking fundamental frequency) 70, 225–227, 231, 240–241, 269
SFF
   age chart 227
   by vocal developmental stage 230–231
Shoulders 10, 13, 17–18, 23, 27–28, 220, 222, 245, 252–253, 255, 276, 283, 286–287, 289
   hunched 14, 253
   movement 23–24, 35
   raised 17, 23

Singer's formant 47–48, 51, 71, 74–77, 79, 149, 153, 218, 282
Sinuses 85–86, 88, 262
Smile 72, 82, 101, 104, 117, 120, 186, 292
   exterior 82
   inner 81–83, 91
   wider 82, 163, 252
Soft palate (velum) 21, 67, 79–80, 82–84, 88–91, 97, 100, 117, 123, 170, 186, 264, 273, 293
Sopranos 68, 76–77, 104, 111–113, 149, 167, 177–178, 180–182, 185, 187, 192, 217, 219–220, 233
Sore throat 263, 275
Sound level 29, 45, 59, 63–65, 68–70, 77, 87, 107, 110, 124, 135, 138, 152–153, 217
Sound waves 37–38
SOVT (Semi-occluded vocal tract) 3, 54–55, 282
SOVT exercises 5, 53, 55–59, 142–143, 169, 236, 238, 277, 283–285, 288
   benefits 55
   categories 56, 58
   continuous pressure 57, 285
   effects of 55, 59
   lip trills 56, 58–59, 62, 261, 278, 284, 288, 290
   pulsating 56–57
      massage effect 57, 284, 288
   straw phonation 5, 53, 55–59, 173–174, 183, 185, 188, 236, 238, 261, 278, 284, 286, 288
   straws 55, 57–59
   suggested order 58
   tongue trills 55–56, 58–59, 273, 284, 287–288, 290
Spacing of choral singers, 24-inch 222
Speaking fundamental frequency. *See* SFF
Sprechstimme 199, 208
Squalls 208–209
Staccato 2, 199–211, 265, 295
Stage of vocal development 53, 224–225, 227, 229
Staggered breathing 31, 148, 193, 206, 217
Sternocleidomastoids 23
Sternum 10, 17, 21–23, 26, 204, 253, 287, 289
   elevated 10, 16, 21
Straight tone 135–138, 147–149, 213
Straws 55–56, 58–59, 290
Stretch 28, 62, 92, 160, 186, 248, 254–256, 273, 279, 283–287, 292
Strohbass 173

Styles
   belt 73–74, 162
   classical legit 52, 67, 79, 93–95, 112, 114–115, 132, 162, 167, 185–186, 199
   gospel 1, 49, 101, 140, 173, 203–204, 209
   jazz 49, 84
   legit 2, 8, 47, 110, 157, 178, 182–183, 200
   pop/rock 74
Subglottal pressure 29, 46, 183, 207
Support
   muscles 33, 35, 192, 290
   of phonation 29–30, 35, 47, 56, 143, 175, 207, 253, 278
   of singers 7, 220, 238–239, 278
Surgery 51, 239–241, 271–273
   vocal fold 271–272
Suspension, of breath 19, 24–25

T

Teeth
   lower 94, 97, 119
   upper 82–83, 252
Tenors 29, 41, 68, 76–77, 165–166, 178–180, 184, 187, 191–192, 212, 219–220, 224, 227–228, 232
Tension 13–15, 17, 19, 24, 26, 40–41, 104–105, 141–142, 149, 186–187, 245, 247–248, 253–254, 276–277
   excess 12, 24, 146, 183
   extraneous 3, 12–13, 15, 146, 155, 204, 245, 253
   facial 248, 252
   glottal 49, 285
   leg 17, 253
   lip 252
   muscular 251, 253, 261
   neck/pharynx 245, 247
   reducing 2, 14, 40, 81, 84, 144, 156, 183, 245, 282, 289
   shoulder 252–253
   unproductive 13, 24
Tenuto 203, 210
Tessitura 149, 177, 179–181, 193–194, 260, 280
   high 30, 132, 180–181, 219, 241, 268, 280
Testosterone therapy 239–240
Throat 12, 21, 26, 33, 36, 40, 51, 83, 91, 116, 246, 255, 261, 263–266
Thyroarytenoids (TA) 42–44, 51–52, 111, 117, 135, 143, 145, 158–161, 165
TA-dominant production 158, 207

Timbre 4, 8, 14, 64–65, 68, 74, 93–94, 101, 126, 170, 177, 218, 223, 242
Tonal color 63, 74, 100–101, 116, 120, 145, 148, 155, 163, 292
Tongue 65–67, 69–70, 81–83, 89–94, 96–98, 100–101, 116–121, 123–124, 126–127, 129–130, 134, 249–251, 255, 291–293
   contracted 251
   elevation 95
   excessively flat 249
   fronting of the 109
   groove 251
   hump (arch) 70, 83, 96–98, 100, 103, 109, 117, 120, 291, 293
   position 3, 40, 65, 67, 70–71, 90, 94, 96–97, 100, 111, 118–119, 237, 292–293
   forward/elevated 85, 104
   higher 172
   and tension 40, 65
   relaxation 254
   tip 67, 255
Tongue tension, excessive 124
Tonsillectomy 3, 273–274
Tonsils 265, 273
Trachea 28, 40, 47, 79, 271
Transgender 238–239
   females 177, 240
   males 239
Tremolo 142, 144–145, 147, 151, 156
Tremulant 153
Tremulo 151
Trillo 150–151
Trills 35, 150, 203, 287
Triphthongs 114–115
Trumpet mouth shape 84, 109, 113, 171, 186

U

Under-singing 191
Unilateral vocal fold paralysis 173
Upper chest breathing 23–24, 26–27, 35, 247, 253
   shoulder movement 23
Upper register 110–111, 158–162, 164, 166–167, 173–174, 178, 187, 194, 212, 231, 233, 235, 293–294

V

Vibrato 2–4, 8, 85, 119, 135–155, 171, 183, 218, 221, 243, 284, 295–296
   artificial 151
   in choral singing 147–148
   consistent 25, 139, 142
   control 149
   desirable rate and extent 136
   in early music 147, 150, 152
   extent 137–138, 153, 284, 287, 289
      classical style range 137
      increasing 155
      wider 140
   inconsistent 141–142
   minimal 85, 136–141, 146, 148, 154–155, 183, 213, 284
   moderate 136–138, 146–154
   modifying 145–146, 149
      healthy 147
   narrow 143
   natural 151, 154
   noticeable 138, 140
   perception of 135–136, 147
   problems 145, 147, 245
   rate
      control of 143
      ideal 136
   rates 136–137, 142–145, 147, 282
   terminal 138, 140, 146, 154–155, 284
   widening extent 146
   wider 137–138
Vibratory cycle 40, 47, 169
Vocal change (adolescents) 224–226, 232, 234–235, 238
Vocal classification 177, 181
Vocal development, stage of 53, 224–225, 227, 229
Vocal fatigue 59, 139, 200, 260, 268, 275, 280–281, 288
Vocal fold
   abnormalities 52, 272
   closure 3, 38, 44–47, 49–51, 53, 60, 67, 69, 141–142, 168, 183, 240, 245, 291
   compression level 52
   cysts 52, 272
   edema 242
   hemorrhage 209, 267
   hydration and dehydration 257–259
   nodules 3, 52, 265, 272–273
   polyps 265, 274
   swelling 240, 274
   vibration 38–39, 47, 56, 58, 64–65, 127, 157–158, 161, 167, 169, 183
   destabilize 107
Vocal fry 49, 51, 173, 265
   onset 49
   relaxed 156, 173, 209, 212
   tense 173
   un-pitched 296
Vocal health 2–3, 51–52, 180–181, 184, 187, 236, 242, 244, 257, 261, 265, 274–275, 278–280, 289
   amateur singers 275
   professional singers 274–275

Vocal loading
    excessive 237
    point system 260
Vocal registers. *See* registers
Vocal rest 148, 264–265, 272, 278, 280
Vocal therapy 272
Vocal tract 12, 26, 34, 38–39, 59, 63–66, 68–72, 78, 82–86, 109–111, 163, 223, 245–247, 249–250
    length 3, 71
    resonances 41, 47, 68, 205
    shape 74, 79, 83
    structures, illustration 66, 249–250
Vocal tract adjustments 47, 79, 182
Voce faringea 172
Voce Umana 150, 153
Voice
    aging 241–244, 282
    breathy 173, 236, 244
    categories 177, 238
    change 3, 223–224, 226, 234–235, 242
    chest and head 65, 113
    developing 181, 214, 218, 236, 238
    lessons 6, 257, 260
    matching/placement 196, 213, 221–222
    matching strategies 222
    modal 184, 187, 229
    quivering 150
    shaking 151
    speaking 59, 164, 225, 227, 262, 288
    therapy 58, 240–241, 272–273
    transgender 177
    types 77, 163, 165–166, 177, 182, 185
    young 30, 207, 229, 233, 236
Voice change, earlier 224, 231
Voice classification 113, 167, 177
    formal 181
    standard choral four-part 178
Voice teachers 5–7, 12, 19, 145, 150, 214, 217, 238–239, 241, 253, 257, 275, 281, 287
Voice types, major 165
Vowels 50–51, 54, 60–62, 67–72, 81–83, 93–97, 100–127, 129–134, 190–193, 209–210, 215–216, 282–284, 286–289, 291–294
    back 96
    bright 82, 218
    cardinal 7–8, 95, 98–99, 284, 286
    chart 96, 111
    color 101, 119–120, 281, 292
    in contemporary styles 101
    dark 92, 100–101, 107, 116, 120, 249, 252, 292
    final 115–116, 293
    formant frequencies 102
    formation 4, 40, 70, 93, 97–98, 118, 136, 282, 284
    integrity 104, 118–119, 123, 125, 292
        preserving 107
    lax 254
    low F1 formant 113
    major 96
    modification 3, 68, 104, 107–112, 118, 121, 165, 187, 285
        excessive 112
        for females 110–111
        first-formant 113
        for males 108, 110
        second formant 113
    nasal 67
    production
        covered 213
        uniform 215, 222
    rounded 96
    shadow 131
    symbols, IPA 7, 95–96, 129, 210, 298
    tonal color of 100, 116, 119
Vowel sounds 7, 12, 54, 82, 94–95, 114, 119, 192, 201, 210
    consistent 185
    intermediate 94
    unintended 124
Vowel Spectrum 71, 96–97, 100, 107–108, 112, 118–119, 254, 284, 286, 292
Vowel-to-vowel continuity 199
Vox Humana 153–154

W
Warfarin 267–268
Warm-up
    process 281–282
    sequence 279, 282–284, 288
Warm-ups 5–6, 15, 36, 55, 58, 61, 142, 192–193, 260–261, 274, 279, 281–283, 286, 288–289
Whistle register 3, 170–171, 179
Wobble 137, 142–145, 147, 151, 155, 243

Y
Yawn 78–80, 116, 175, 248
    incipient 78

Z
Zinc 266–267

Julia Davids, D.M.A. enjoys a thriving career as a singer, conductor, and music educator. Dr. Davids is the Artistic Director of the Canadian Chamber Choir, Music Director for the North Shore Choral Society, and Director of Music Ministries at Trinity United Methodist Church. With over 25 years of experience working with singers, she is sought after as a clinician and guest conductor. Julia has degrees in music education, vocal performance, and conducting from Western University, the University of Michigan, and Northwestern University. She is Stephen J. Hendrickson Professor of Music and Chair of Choral Activities at North Park University, Chicago.

Stephen LaTour, Ph.D. is a psychologist, choral singer, and church soloist. Dr. LaTour's research has appeared in numerous psychological, management, and healthcare journals. He was a professor at Northwestern University for 17 years and president of an international research firm for more than 30 years. Memberships include the Acoustical Society of America, the research scientist honor society, Sigma Xi, and the American Psychological Association.